MW00994769

TIDAL WAVE

OSPREY
PUBLISHING

TIDAL WAVE

FROM LEYTE GULF TO TOKYO BAY

THOMAS McKELVEY CLEAVER

OSPREY PUBLISHING
Bloomsbury Publishing Plc
PO Box 883, Oxford, OX1 9PL, UK
1385 Broadway, 5th Floor, New York, NY 10018, USA
E-mail: info@ospreypublishing.com
www.ospreypublishing.com

OSPREY is a trademark of Osprey Publishing Ltd

First published in Great Britain in 2018

A catalogue record for this book is available from the British Library.

ISBN: HB 9781472825483; PB 9781472825490; eBook 9781472825476; ePDF 9781472825469; XML 9781472825506

18 19 20 21 22 10 9 8 7 6 5 4 3 2 1

Maps by bounford.com
Index by Zoe Ross
Originated by PDQ Digital Media Solutions, Bungay, UK
Printed and bound in Great Britain by CPI (Group) UK Ltd, Croydon CR0 4YY

Cover: USS *Bunker Hill* on fire following *kamikaze* hits, May 11, 1945. This view aft down the flight deck shows her crew fighting fires. (Naval History and Heritage Command)

Osprey Publishing supports the Woodland Trust, the UK's leading woodland conservation charity. Between 2014 and 2018 our donations are being spent on their Centenary Woods project in the UK.

To find out more about our authors and books visit www.ospreypublishing.com. Here you will find extracts, author interviews, details of forthcoming events and the option to sign up for our newsletter.

CONTENTS

Foreword by RADM Doniphan P. Shelton, USN (Ret)　　6

Prologue　　8

CHAPTER ONE: The Final Battle　　14

CHAPTER TWO: October 25, 1944　　30

CHAPTER THREE: The Big Blue Blanket　　45

CHAPTER FOUR: Halsey's Typhoons　　83

CHAPTER FIVE: The Forgotten Fleet　　112

CHAPTER SIX: Tokyo　　131

CHAPTER SEVEN: Iwo Jima　　144

CHAPTER EIGHT: Prelude to Okinawa　　153

CHAPTER NINE: The Fleet that Came to Stay　　169

CHAPTER TEN: The Murderous Month of May　　206

CHAPTER ELEVEN: Admiral Nimitz Writes a Letter　　227

CHAPTER TWELVE: Finale　　249

CHAPTER THIRTEEN: Gyokusen　　286

Bibliography　　*315*

Index　　*317*

FOREWORD

My friend Tom Cleaver is very good at putting a lot of detail into a very readable book – as is the case in Tidal Wave, the story of World War II from Leyte Gulf until the signing of the peace treaty aboard the USS Missouri in Tokyo Bay.

I would like to add just a few lines to his account of the *kamikaze* attack on USS *St Louis* (Cl-49) on November 27, 1944, at 1000 hours.

One of the four *kamikazes* that hit us went down the hangar spaces aft causing a number of explosions and AvGas fires. The good thing was that the fire mains were ruptured and put out the fires almost as soon as occurring. The bad thing was that the Shore Party beer was stored there – a complete loss.

As Tom points out, the *kamikaze* that hit us port side at the waterline was the most dangerous. It put us dead in the water, no power, we could not shoot. The bulk heads between No. 1 and No. 2 boiler operating spaces flexed. We were lucky that when the *kamikazes* returned in the afternoon they inexplicably left us alone.

Our damage control parties did a miraculous job in shoring up the flexing bulkheads and at 2200 hours, we got under way at 4 knots for the dry dock at Manus Island, 1,500 miles away. There we made sufficient repairs to steam back to the Long Beach, California shipyard for complete repairs, after which we returned in time for Okinawa, and our participation as part of the Third Fleet task force off Southern Japan prior to the anticipated landings on mainland Japan. Through my No. 2 turret periscope, I had a close up view of the *Franklin* when it was hit.

We were anchored in Buckner Bay, Okinawa when the first atom bomb was dropped. I breathed a sigh of relief we would not face the *kamikaze* off Kyushu.

Tidal Wave is fascinating reading. Read it and be informed.

Doniphan P. Shelton RADM USN (Ret)
Delmar, California, 2017

The Allied Counteroffensive, September 1944 to August 1945

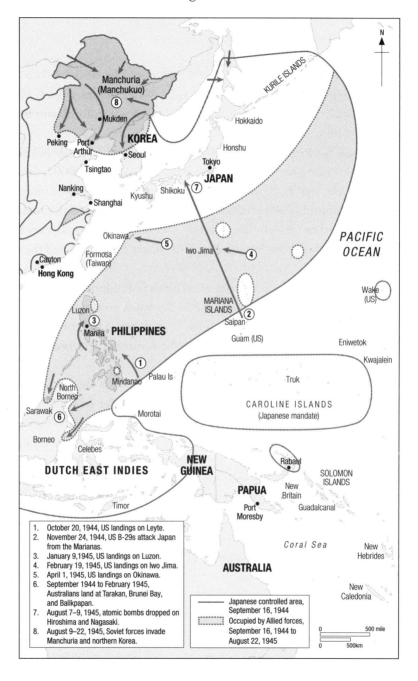

1. October 20, 1944, US landings on Leyte.
2. November 24, 1944, US B-29s attack Japan from the Marianas.
3. January 9, 1945, US landings on Luzon.
4. February 19, 1945, US landings on Iwo Jima.
5. April 1, 1945, US landings on Okinawa.
6. September 1944 to February 1945, Australians land at Tarakan, Brunei Bay, and Balikpapan.
7. August 7–9, 1945, atomic bombs dropped on Hiroshima and Nagasaki.
8. August 9–22, 1945, Soviet forces invade Manchuria and northern Korea.

———— Japanese controlled area, September 16, 1944

┄┄┄ Occupied by Allied forces, September 16, 1944 to August 22, 1945

0   500 mile

0   500km

PROLOGUE

This volume, *Tidal Wave*, tells of a much different war than that in my previous book, *Pacific Thunder*. *Tidal Wave* takes up the story at the moment the US Navy had achieved the goal for which it had planned and worked for 20 years: the destruction of the Imperial Japanese Navy, a victory that immediately rang hollow when the admirals and crews discovered they were now facing an enemy willing to see itself totally destroyed in a fight to the death. The *kamikaze* was the most terrifying phenomenon any Westerner faced, since it flew against every Western philosophical belief about the conduct of war and the sanctity of life. Men came to hate the enemy in a deep, personal way they had not before, even after taking an oath of personal vengeance on seeing the destruction wrought at Pearl Harbor. The captain of the battleship *Missouri* faced a near-mutiny for his decision to give the remains of the Japanese pilot who crashed his airplane into the ship the honorable burial accorded to an honorable enemy. The final ten months of the war saw more death and destruction than had been inflicted since the attack on Pearl Harbor, and the end of the war saw the most terrible weapon in human history unleashed on Japan, the necessity of which is debated to this day. This is the story of how a bloody war became bloodier and barely escaped turning into a cataclysmic apocalypse.

I first visited Japan 19 years after the end of the war. The war was recent enough that its reminders were still easy to find, both in Japan and the other countries I visited that had experienced the bloodiest war in human history.

I was fortunate that my sister had a pen pal in Japan. Yoshiko Tsuruta was my "astral twin," born at the same time as me, who was now a student at Tokyo University of Education (now known as the University of Tsukuba). She was eager to meet a "real" American, and I was privileged to get an insight into the country and its people that most *gaijin* (foreigners) rarely experience, since her family shared her curiosity. The Japanese are intensely private people – they could not be otherwise in a country so densely populated – and even good friends rarely visit each other's homes before they have been friends for many years. I was invited to stay with Yoshiko and her family from the first time I arrived in the country, and during the 18 months I spent in the Far East, I used up most of my leave time making other such visits. While in their home, I followed the rule "when in Rome, do as the Romans do." I lived in the Japanese manner, sleeping on a tatami mat with a wooden block for a pillow, learning to use chopsticks, and even by the end successfully managing to adapt myself to the Japanese toilet, something few Westerners ever manage. By the time I returned home, I felt I had an understanding of the country and its people that was foreign to most of my fellow sailors.

Over the course of these visits, the subject of the war came up early. On my first visit, I was taken to see the *Mikasa*, Admiral Togo's flagship at the Battle of Tsushima Strait that established Japan as a major power, there in her concrete drydock outside the Yokosuka Naval Base. The ship is a monument to Imperial Japan, and more specifically to its navy. To say I felt a bit strange visiting while wearing the uniform of the navy that had defeated that navy, a lone American among a throng of Japanese, would be an understatement. As I looked at the models of Imperial Navy warships that lined the bulkhead, I thought to myself: "... sunk at Guadalcanal... sunk at Midway... sunk at Philippine Sea... sunk at Leyte..." (I was even then a serious student of the Pacific War and had been for as long as I can remember). Afterwards, over lunch, Yoshiko asked me why we had fought the war. She proceeded to tell me the Japanese version of the history of the Pacific War. The two stories – American and Japanese – could not be more different if they had taken place on different planets.

We ended up spending the afternoon in that teahouse as I told her the American history of the war, including the history of the Japan–China war that preceded Pearl Harbor. She was shocked at what she heard, but to her credit she wanted to learn more. At her school, she eventually met Professor Saburō Ienaga, perhaps the most interesting Japanese academic historian of the war, author of *The Pacific War 1931–1945*. Professor Ienaga first wrote about the war in 1947 in a work titled *New Japanese History*, which was the first to deal with Japanese war crimes. The work was censored in 1953 by the Japanese Ministry of Education for what was called "factual errors and matters of opinion" regarding those crimes. Ienaga sued the Ministry for violation of his freedom of speech, with the result that *The Pacific War* was published in 1961 (it was only translated into English and published in the United States to little notice in the 1980s). Ienaga was later nominated for the Nobel Peace Prize in 1999 and 2001 by Noam Chomsky, among others, for his work.

Yoshiko read the book, and the war became a topic she and I discussed honestly, attempting to reconcile Japanese and American memory. She did not share that with her family or friends, since the topic was so shocking to Japanese sensibilities. To this day, unfortunately, Japan has yet to come to terms with this history in the way Germany has come to terms with Hitler and the Nazis. The current government, which has as its goal changing the postwar pacifist constitution – is even less interested in historical truth than its predecessors.

About a third of my overseas tour was spent at Okinawa, where we were based. As a budding historian, I made several visits to the south end of the island, where the major fighting had occurred. Eighteen years of monsoonal rains had yet to wash away the remains of the trenches, which were reminiscent of World War I battlefields. There was no place one could step without putting foot on some remnant of the battle; bullet casings were everywhere. I stood on what was at that time called "Hacksaw Ridge." I leaned down to pick up what I thought was a strange stone, only to be startled by the realization it was a human bone fragment. We visited Kerama Retto, "the graveyard of ships," where a senior petty officer I worked for who had been there during the war told me one could "smell the stench of death in the air" when the wind was right before seeing the island itself.

I also visited other cities in Japan, most notably Hiroshima and Nagasaki. However, the first time I realized the real scope of the destruction inflicted in the war came when we were in the port of Kobe several weeks after having first met Yoshiko and her family. A shipmate and I went walking along the Ginza (every Japanese city has one, not just Tokyo) and eventually discovered as sunset was coming that we had wandered far away and were now lost in a residential suburb. We turned the corner and confronted a sight I have never been able to forget. There was a huge empty field, covered with straggly low vegetation, out of which stuck twisted fire-blackened girders. It reminded me of a science-fiction portrayal of what things would look like following an atomic war. I was later to learn that those 1,500 acres were the last part of the city that had yet to be rebuilt from the fire raid of March 16–17, 1945, almost 18 years to the day before our discovery. When I spoke of this in a later visit with my friend, she told me her family's story of surviving the Tokyo fire raid on March 10, 1945 that had begun the B-29 firebombing campaign. The story of how her mother saved her older brother while pregnant with her by jumping into a drainage canal is still chilling to recall.

My visit to Nagasaki in 1964 changed much of my perception of Japan. When we docked, the pier was filled with young Japanese students. There were anti-US protests in Japan at the time over the renewal of the Security Treaty, and we thought that was what we were seeing. We could not have been more wrong! They were there as citizens of Nagasaki to do what the people of Nagasaki have done ever since the war: welcome foreigners and try to establish ties of friendship and brotherhood. I learned the Christian history of Nagasaki and the island of Kyushu from another young Japanese woman as she took me to visit the house where Puccini had written "Madame Butterfly" and to the Atomic Museum, where I stared into the upturned helmet of a Japanese soldier and realized the "ivory" that lined its interior was not ivory.

The story of how the people of Nagasaki responded to the bombing is little known outside of Japan. It bears telling. After the war, there was much discussion of how to prevent such a disaster happening again, led by the Christian churches. Eventually, a decision was made that the city should devote itself to the promotion of "international brotherhood" as the only way of achieving this. Many cities around the world are dedicated to this or that purpose; the overwhelming majority of the residents have no knowledge of that. The people of Nagasaki do know. If they see a stranger on the street, they will do the very un-Japanese thing of coming up to you and asking if they might help, could they perhaps buy you a cup of tea and rice cakes? I don't think there has ever been an act of truly Christian forgiveness on such a scale anywhere else. It most certainly stands in stark contrast to Hiroshima, which adopted the stance of international victim and still seeks to make an American feel guilty standing at the Ground Zero memorial.

This experience is why I chose to use this book to tell the story of the unknown bomb and the city it destroyed. It's really unsurprising when one studies the event that the Air Force gave it as little publicity at the time as it did. It's almost surprising that "Bockscar," the B-29 that carried the bomb, was preserved at the US Air Force Museum. Needless to say, the story of how Nagasaki – the most Christian, pro-Western, anti-Imperial city in Japan – was destroyed as the alternative to abandoning the bomb over the ocean, is not what one will read in that museum. It is a tale of the purest irony.

To this day, the question of the use of the bombs can stir controversy. As an American, it is not hard to be conflicted. The official explanation was that it ended the war without the loss of millions more, and this explanation is not without merit. I know personally of two men who were both important in my life whose lives were very likely saved by the bombs. One was Gunnery Sergeant James F. Eaton, later my father-in-law, who was scheduled to hit the beach on Kyushu in November 1945 in the first wave when the First Marine Division landed. The other was Chief Petty Officer L. Thomas Cleaver, my father, who had survived the sinking of his radar picket destroyer at Okinawa only to receive orders at the end of his survivor's leave back to another such ship to participate in the invasion. He was so certain he would not survive that the day he received those orders, on my first birthday, he sat down and wrote a letter to me that I only found 45 years later on his death when I went through his papers. In it, he told me who he was, why he had gone to war, and what his hopes were for his only son in the future. It was written so I would know who my unknown father was. Fortunately, I was able to know both these good men in the years after.

Marine Colonel William E. Barber, who I came to know while researching what became *The Frozen Chosen*, told me how he and the other officers of the 6th Marine Division had gone to the Kyushu beach they were scheduled to land on after they arrived for occupation duty in September 1945. The defenses were still there, and they were able to talk to the Japanese officers who would have directed the defense. At the end, it was the considered opinion of every officer from the commanding general to the most junior company commander (Barber) that they would not have overcome those defenses, and that there would have been no way to evacuate any survivors from the beach. Yes, the official explanation for the bombs carries truth.

However, there are other aspects to the war's ending. Given that in the end the Allies allowed Hirohito to remain Emperor of Japan, which was the one sticking point to the Japanese leaders when they received the Allied peace proposals, there is a case to be made that the war could have ended at least a few months earlier after the taking of Okinawa. The role of the Soviet Union, which entered the war on August 9, 90 days to the day after the end of the European war as Stalin had promised to do at Yalta, is one that is largely ignored in the United States. Yet the Japanese knew the Soviets could invade northern Japan with little opposition 90 days before the American Kyushu landings; their knowledge of what had happened in Germany in the division of the country between the Western Allies and the Soviets was a major factor in the Emperor's decision to stop the fighting before this invasion could happen. The Japanese government was debating the Soviet invasion of Manchuria that had happened at midnight, when they received word of the Nagasaki bombing. For them, Nagasaki wasn't as important as the news of the Soviet troop buildup on Sakhalin Island for an invasion of Hokkaido.

In the end, the Pacific War validated every argument made by those who believed in the potential power of naval aviation, which is the centerpiece of this story.

Thomas McKelvey Cleaver
Los Angeles, California, 2018

CHAPTER ONE

THE FINAL BATTLE

The first quarter moon hung in the western sky gleaming dimly through scattered clouds over the Pacific; the moonlight was sufficient to illuminate the many wakes of the huge formation of ships below. At 0300 hours, an observer would have heard the calls to reveille echoing across the still-dark sea throughout the darkened fleet.

In the big boxy aircraft carriers that steamed in the center of the formations, crewmen crawled out of their racks in humid bunking compartments and began pulling on their dungarees; young pilots stumbled to their feet in their cramped staterooms and threw lukewarm water on their faces to awaken fully before staggering off to the wardrooms for a quick breakfast. The fleet had sortied from Leyte Gulf in the Philippines on July 1 for what would turn out to be its final deployment of the war, and the limited supplies of fresh food taken aboard then were running out now, six weeks later. Spam sandwiches and the chipped dried beef in gravy over toast known universally as "SOS" ("shit on a shingle") were once again making their appearance on the menu. Below decks, enlisted men shuffled through chow lines.

The wail of alarms across the fleet brought crews to pre-dawn General Quarters. Crews tumbled into the gun tubs and unlimbered 20mm and 40mm antiaircraft guns in readiness as they strained their eyes into the western sky where the Pacific sunrise lit building cumulus clouds in all quarters. The fleet had not been subjected to *kamikaze* attack in several days and was just returning from a day spent out of range, while the carriers refueled their thirsty escorts. Would today be the end of that pause?

It was Wednesday, August 15, 1945, just another of many long tiring days faced by the men of the United States Third Fleet. In recent days, rumors had raced through the destroyers, cruisers, battleships and aircraft carriers of the mightiest fleet the world had ever seen that the war could end at any time. Those who passed on the rumors were quickly reminded by their salty seniors of the old navy saying, "Believe nothing that you hear, and only half of what you see."

Task Group 38.4, commanded by Rear Admiral Arthur W. Radford with his flag aboard *Yorktown* (CV-10) and composed of the fleet carriers *Shangri-La* (CV-38), *Bon Homme Richard* (CV-31), and *Wasp* (CV-18), accompanied by the light carriers *Independence* (CVL-22) and *Cowpens* (CVL-25), exemplified the fast carrier striking force in the summer of 1945. Centered around six carriers, it was numerically the strongest task group in Task Force 38. The squadrons aboard the six carriers included a total of 133 Grumman F6F-5 Hellcats, including 36 dedicated night fighters aboard "Bonnie Dick"; 137 Vought F4U Corsairs, including 36 brand new F4U-4s, aboard *Wasp*; 45 Curtiss SB2C Helldiver dive bombers, including 15 of the latest SB2C-5, aboard *Wasp*; and 80 of the newest TBM-3 Avenger torpedo bombers. Able to strike the enemy by day or night, Task Group 38.4 packed more punch than the entire prewar carrier force combined. Altogether, Task Force 38 was centered around ten fleet carriers and six light carriers in three task groups.

The British Pacific Fleet, assigned as Task Force 37, had joined Task Force 38 on July 16, augmenting the force with four fleet carriers carrying 200 additional aircraft: Supermarine Seafire IIIs, Fairey Firefly Is, Grumman Avengers and Hellcats, and Vought Corsairs. Unfortunately, three of the British carriers had been forced to retire three days before to the advanced British base at Manus

Atoll in Admiralty Islands south of the Philippines, known to the sailors of the Royal Navy as "Scapa Flow with bloody palm trees," owing to the lack of British tankers for replenishment. The carrier HMS *Indefatigable*, with her escort, the battleship HMS *King George V*, cruisers HMS *Newfoundland* and *Gambia*, and destroyers HMS *Barfleur*, *Wakeful*, *Wrangler*, *Teazer*, *Termagant* and *Tenacious*, and HMAS *Napier* and *Nizam*, remained with the Americans as Task Group 38.5. The Seafires of 24 Naval Fighter Wing, operated by 887 and 894 squadrons, had the best low-altitude performance of any fighter in the fleet and were the first line of defense against Japanese low-altitude *kamikaze* attacks.

Aboard *Yorktown*, veteran of the early days of the Central Pacific Campaign that had taken the fast carrier force from a tentative raid on Wake Island by four carriers only 22 months earlier to regular strikes against targets on Honshu and Hokkaido islands since July 10, the young pilots of VF-88, Fighting-88, made their way to the squadron ready room for the morning briefing. Air Group 88 was one of the newest in the fleet, having come aboard *Yorktown* at Leyte only in the past June, while the fleet licked its wounds and caught its breath after the battle of Okinawa, site of the worst losses since the early days in the Solomons three years before. VF-88 had taken heavy losses in the six weeks since Admiral William F. Halsey, Jr. had brought the fleet to the waters off Japan, with ten pilots now gone, including squadron leader LCDR Charles Crommelin, lost in a freak midair collision with his wingman over Hokkaido 30 days earlier – the last of four legendary brothers to die in the Pacific War. They were unsure of Lieutenant Malcolm W. Cagle, the former squadron executive officer who now led them; the combat-experienced division leaders who had joined the squadron during training in the past year doubted that Cagle, who hadn't become a naval aviator until 18 months earlier and whose flying experience had been confined to the Training Command until he was given the plum position of squadron XO, could fill Crommelin's shoes. These experienced men were "AvCads" – reservists commissioned for the duration of the war after graduating from flight school –

while Cagle was a "ringknocker," an Annapolis graduate. They knew that as a "regular" Cagle was the beneficiary of the rule, "The Navy takes care of its own." Over the next 30 years, Cagle would make a name for himself as a senior aviator in the Korean War and a carrier commander in the Vietnam War, eventually attaining the rank of vice admiral and retiring as Commander of Naval Education and Training at Pensacola, the home of naval aviation. But that was the future. Today, Lieutenant Cagle's leadership ability was in doubt. When the popular Crommelin went down and Cagle became the commander, he told the pilots that if they had any suggestions, he'd like to hear them; no one replied, since as one recalled, "We observed body language that said 'I don't want to hear it.'"

The squadron's assignment this morning wasn't that different from previous missions, but the men were electrified by Cagle's announcement that the Japanese were likely to surrender today, though the exact time was not yet known. The mission was to prevent an aerial *banzai* attack by any Japanese fliers who refused the orders of their emperor to surrender. Two divisions – eight F6F-5 Hellcats – would join up with eight other Hellcats from *Wasp*'s VF-86 and a further 16 F4U-1D Corsairs from *Shangri-La*'s VF-85 and VBF-85 to attack airfields in the vicinity of Choshi, the easternmost city of greater Tokyo. The eight Fighting-88 Hellcats were to split into two groups when they reached Tokurozama Airfield. Two pilots would stay high to receive and relay the hoped-for ceasefire message that might be broadcast at any time. The others – Lt(jg)s "Howdy" Harrison, Maury Proctor, and Ted Hansen, and ensigns Joe Sahloff, Wright Hobbs, and Gene Mandenberg – would strafe anything they found on the airfield. Launch was set at 0430 hours.

A few miles away from *Yorktown*, Task Group 38.1 was readying for battle as flight deck crews aboard the task group's two light carriers, *Belleau Wood* (CVL-24) and *San Jacinto* (CVL-30), each prepared a division of F6F-5 Hellcats for a final patrol over Japan. Aboard *San Jacinto*, four F6Fs of VF-49 were ready for takeoff.

Aboard HMS *Indefatigable*, the flight deck was abuzz with activity as men worked in the pre-dawn grayness to ready the Seafires for their first offensive operation since returning to the waters off Japan in mid-July. Three Seafire IIIs of 887 and four of 894 Squadrons were assigned to escort six Avengers of 820 Squadron and four Fireflies of 1772 Squadron for a dawn strike against the *kamikazes* at Kisarazu Airfield, 30 miles south of Tokyo. This was officially the last air strike by units of the Fleet Air Arm in World War II. Like VF-88's assignment, the mission was being flown to prevent any attempted attack on the Allied fleet as it steamed a hundred miles east of Tokyo Bay.

With their briefings completed, the pilots and aircrews of the four squadrons made their way up to the flight deck to man their aircraft. Among them was Sub-Lieutenant Fred Hockley, assigned for this mission as flight leader of the four Seafires from 894 Squadron, which would fly close escort. Son of a foreman with the Cambridge water board and heavily involved in his local church and competitive swimming before the war, Hockley had joined the Royal Naval Volunteer Reserve when the war broke out and trained as a naval fighter pilot. He was a combat veteran now, having flown the Seafire III in operations over southern France a year ago and against the Japanese since the Palembang strikes in January 1945 that marked the arrival of the British Pacific Fleet. As he slipped into the Seafire's tight cockpit and adjusted his Sutton harness, Hockley thought to himself how lucky he was to be in command of the last Fleet Air Arm fighter mission of the war – it would be a tale to tell the grandchildren he hoped someday to have.

The three 887 Squadron Seafires that would fly high cover were led by Sub-Lieutenant Victor Lowden. Born in Bangkok, where his father worked as an accountant, and educated at St John's College, Cambridge, Lowden had arrived in the Pacific and joined 887 in May while the Royal Navy was engaged in stopping *kamikazes* based in the Sakishima Islands from attacking the Allied fleet off Okinawa. Since the fleet's return from Australia the month before, he had engaged in combat over Shikoku and Honshu and attacks on shipping and shore installations near Sendai.

Takeoff for Task Force 38 on this last day of war commenced just as the sun appeared over the eastern horizon, though the sea was still dark. Throughout the fleet, pilots lifted off their carriers and climbed up into the morning light, each man hoping that the recall order might come before they arrived over the enemy coast. Nearly 200 American and British aircraft were headed for the Japanese capital.

At about 0530 hours, Hockley could just see the dark mass of the coast of Honshu ahead through the thickening clouds. At that moment, the Avenger leader passed the word that they were aborting the attack on Kisarazu Airfield owing to the poor weather and would attack their secondary target, a chemical weapons factory at Odaki. When Hockley pressed his radio switch to reply, he discovered when no one responded that his radio transmitter had malfunctioned; moments later the receiver also died. Nevertheless, he decided to press on with the mission, relying on hand signals to his wingman, Ted Garvin, who could relay his instructions via radio. He looked over at Garvin and tapped his helmet headphones, to indicate radio problems.

Leading the four Fighting-88 Hellcats inbound to Choshi, division leader "Howdy" Harrison spotted the great volcano Fujiyama, its snow-capped peak gleaming in the early morning light high above the Tokyo plain and the waters of Tokyo Bay. The seven other *Wasp* Hellcats and the 16 *Shangri-La* Corsairs were dark silhouettes in the brightening sky. High clouds were now visible in all directions.

As the Allied flyers pressed on toward their targets, Japanese radar picked up the formations and the alert was sounded at the airfields that dotted the Tokyo region.

Atsugi Airfield east of Tokyo was the main base for the Imperial Naval Air Force in the capital region and was home to the 302nd Kokutai (air group), one of the last remaining elite units of the Imperial Japanese Navy. The group had been created in March 1944 to provide defense for the capital against the expected B-29 raids. Two of the group's three *Hikotai* (squadrons) were equipped with the Mitsubishi J2M3 *Raiden* (Thunderbolt), known to the Allies by the code name "Jack." The J2M3 was optimized as a bomber interceptor and was at a disadvantage when it entered combat with Hellcats, Corsairs or P-51D Mustangs. Thus, the third squadron flew the venerable A6M5c *Zero-sen*, which was still the main air superiority fighter for the IJNAF, despite its manifest obsolescence, to protect the heavier interceptors. The pilots of the 302nd *Kokutai* thought of themselves as dedicated Samurai; there was no thought of surrender among these men who were willing if necessary to crash their airplane into one of the silver giants attacking their homeland.

Commander of the 302nd was 23-year-old Lieutenant Yukio Morioka, the youngest Japanese air group leader of the war. Originally trained as a dive-bomber pilot in 1942, Morioka had missed the great carrier battles and had taken the opportunity to become a fighter pilot in the spring of 1944 when he was assigned to the 302nd. He had been trained in flying the Zero by the group's leading ace, Ensign Sadaaki "Temei" Akamatsu, a man who was infamous in the Imperial Navy. A Navy pilot since 1932, he had seen action over China, where he quickly became an ace, and had been one of the high scorers in the early days of the Pacific War. He had a wicked reputation as an undisciplined rebel and womanizer, and had been broken in rank several times. Now, however, his wild flying skills stood him in good stead and he was the only IJNAF pilot who preferred the J2M3 *Raiden*, having once shot down three P-51s in one mission while flying one; he had shot down nine F6F Hellcats since the first American naval air strikes against Tokyo back in February. He was considered the "old master" by the other pilots of the 302nd, who listened closely to his advice to use "hit-and-run" tactics against the Americans. In eight years of combat, Akamatsu had yet to get so much as a scratch from the enemy.

The 302nd had engaged in combat with B-29s from the Marianas since their first appearance over Japan the previous November. On January 23, 1945, Morioka had nearly died, when a gunner aboard a B-29 of the 73rd Bomb Wing he was attacking shot off his left hand. It was considered a miracle that he had been able to land successfully despite shock and loss of blood. After a brief stay in the hospital, he was fitted with an iron claw with which he could control the throttle of his fighter, and returned to combat in April. As of this morning, he was the victor over four American aircraft. On August 3, he shot down the P-51D flown by 2nd Lt John J. Coneff of the 457th Fighter Squadron of the Iwo Jima-based 506th Fighter Group in a wild fight over Tokyo Bay to thwart the rescue of Captain Edward Mikes of the 458th Fighter Squadron; ten days later, on August 13, he led four Zeros that chased and shot down an American Navy PBY-5A Catalina that had just taken off after rescuing a Hellcat pilot in Tokyo Bay outside the Japanese Navy base at Yokosuka.

With the warning of the coming Allied air attack, Morioka manned his A6M5c Zero, known to the Allies as a "Zeke-52." He took off quickly with his wingmen, Ensigns Mitsuo Tsuruta, Muneaki Morimoto and Tooru Miyaki, close behind and followed by a second flight of four Zeros as they climbed into the brightening sky. Akamatsu's formation of four J2M3s trailed Morioka's Zeros as they climbed through halls of clouds.

The pilots of the 302nd *Kokutai* knew nothing of what had happened to their country in the previous nine days since a lone B-29 devastated the city of Hiroshima on August 6 with an atom bomb, followed three days later by the devastation of Nagasaki with a second atomic blast. This second bomb coincided with the launching of an offensive in Manchuria, by the previously neutral Soviet Union, that was advancing quickly through the ranks of the vaunted Kwantung Army, now a ghost of itself after its best units had been withdrawn to stand against the expected invasion of Kyushu. Since the Hiroshima attack, Japanese leaders had remained locked in intense debate about whether surrender was an option and, if it was, then what form it would take. The very thought of surrender disgusted many in the senior military leadership. Just the previous day, an attempted *coup d'état* by the Japanese Army had been discovered and crushed.

On approach to Odaki, the Fireflies and Avengers dropped to 1,000 feet over the flat plain and bored in for their rocket and bomb runs. Just at that moment, two Zekes were spotted below the bombers. Sub-Lieutenant Randall Kay, leader of the second 894 pair, called out that they were probably decoys. A moment later, Kay spotted 12 Zekes that appeared out of the clouds, flashing past the three 887 Seafires 3,000 feet above the four 894 fighters.

With his radio out, Fred Hockley didn't hear Kay's shouted warning "Break! Break!" and realized the formation was under attack only when he saw his wingman break sharply away from him to the right. Hockley was a moment too late flinging his Seafire after the others. Suddenly, his fighter was wracked by the heavy hits of 20mm shells from the Zeke he saw in his rearview mirror, locked on his tail. Holes appeared in his wing and engine cowling, followed by smoke. The Seafire was mortally injured.

Hockley managed to pull away as his attacker turned to face another Seafire. He pulled back his canopy, unfastened his Sutton harness, pushed open the cockpit side flap and baled out. Falling clear of the fight, he opened his parachute. In a matter of moments he hit the ground hard, outside the village of Higashimura. It took a moment for him to catch his breath and disentangle himself from his parachute. When he stood up, he faced a very surprised and very scared Japanese air raid warden. Fred Hockley raised his arms in surrender. Engines with their throttles pushed to the maximum screamed overhead and he glanced up at the last battle the Fleet Air Arm fought in World War II.

Victor Lowden saw the 12 Zekes flash past as they dove on the four Seafires below. Instinctively, he winged over, followed by his wingmen, Sub-Lieutenants Gerry "Spud" Murphy and W. J. "Taffy" Williams. Selecting a target, Lowden pressed the fire button on the spade grip of his control column as he closed to 800 feet behind the enemy fighter. 20mm cannon shells struck the Zeke until, when about 450 feet ahead, it fell away in flames. Clearing his tail before latching onto a second, Lowden closed in and opened fire. After the first burst, his port cannon jammed and the Seafire yawed from the recoil of the starboard gun with each shot. Stomping on the rudder and ailerons, Lowden shot down the second Zeke with three bursts from 250 yards before turning after a third enemy fighter. Lowden's wingman, "Taffy" Williams, also shot down a Zeke and now opened fire at Lowden's third opponent, which quickly went down under their combined fire. The two Seafires and the surviving Zekes twisted and turned, firing for only a brief second at one another as an enemy appeared and then disappeared in their sights. Three managed to get on Lowden's tail and he hauled his Seafire around in a maximum rate turn, firing at each in succession and damaging two before his speed decayed and gave the Zekes the performance edge just as his remaining cannon fired its last shot and he was out of ammunition. Lowden quickly nosed over into a maximum-performance dive and outran his pursuers.

The three surviving 894 pilots stuck with the Avengers as the fight developed. Hockley's wingman Ted Garvin was hit and had one cannon jam when his drop tank failed to jettison. He still managed to damage one that fell away out of the fight and that he lost sight of in the clouds. Randy Kay shot down one of two Zekes attacking the Avengers with a 60-degree deflection shot, then blew the tail off the second while his wingman, Sub-Lieutenant Don Duncan, hit two that retreated damaged from the fight and then finished off a third despite getting a cannon jam.

"Spud" Murphy found himself behind a pair and quickly dispatched one while then getting locked in a turning fight with the remaining fighter. G-force pinned him in his seat as he managed to pull the nose of his Spitfire ahead of the Zeke and put a burst of 20mm into the enemy, which struck the engine and cockpit, and caused it to plummet down. He later remembered the battle:

> The enemy approached our Avengers in fairly close starboard echelon, but flying in line astern. They peeled off smartly in fours from down sun and headed for the Avengers. One section of four appeared to be coming head-on for us, but I didn't observe their guns firing. Their original attack was well-coordinated, but they seemed to lose each other after that, and could not have kept a good lookout astern.
>
> I opened fire with my flight leader from the enemy port quarter and saw strikes on the fuselage of the enemy, which was finished off by the flight leader. I disengaged from above to attack another Zeke 500 feet below. I closed in from above and astern, obtaining hits on his belly and engine. His undercart fell down and smoke and flame

were coming from the engine, but I was closing too fast and overshot. I pulled up to re-attack number two and saw a lone Zeke at the same level doing a shallow turn to starboard. He evidently didn't see me and I held fire till I was some hundred yards away. I observed immediate strikes on his cockpit and engine, which burst into flames. He rolled on his back and plummeted in flames into a cloud.

As fast as the fight had happened, it was over.

While the Seafire pilots fought off the Zekes, the Fireflies and Avengers hit their target squarely and pulled out low as they made their escape. The six Avengers came under fire from four other enemy fighters, with another eight closing in. One Avenger was badly hit but remained in formation while his wingman's turret gunner hit one of the attackers. Suddenly, four dark blue American Hellcats dove into the fight. The British pilots were unaware of the identity markings on the Hellcats, but they were the four VF-49 Hellcats from *San Jacinto*. The arrival of the four Americans broke up the Japanese attackers, and they quickly shot down four.

Above, the four Hellcats of VF-31 maintained top cover. Division leader Lieutenant Jim Stewart saw the other Japanese fighters evade the Fighting-49 Hellcats. "Let's go!" he yelled and dove after the enemy, followed closely by his wingman and by section leader Lt(jg) Edward "Smiley" Toaspern, a five-victory ace on his second tour with the squadron. Seeing the enemy fighters split up, the two section leaders split apart, with Stewart going after one pair while Toaspern pulled in behind the second. A burst from his six .50-caliber machine guns exploded one and he then hit the other, which caught fire and fell away. In the meantime, Stewart exploded one Zeke while the other disappeared in the clouds. The other enemy fighters quickly retreated into the clouds.

The four VF-31 pilots quickly joined up with their comrades from VF-49 and continued toward the target. Thirty-five minutes later, word came from the air officer on *Belleau Wood* to abort the mission and return to base. Japan had just surrendered and the war was over.

None of the British or American pilots was checking his watch as he fought, but Sub-Lieutenant Gerry Murphy of 887 Squadron, VF-31's Lieutenant Jim Stewart or Lt(jg) Edward Toaspern was the last Allied fighter pilot to shoot down an enemy fighter before the Pacific War was officially declared over.

Just because the war had been officially declared over did not mean the fighting stopped, however.

Lieutenant Paul Herschel was leading his division of four VF-6 Hellcats home to *Hancock* (CV-19) after getting the recall order when they were jumped by seven enemy fighters. They shot down a Zeke and two Jacks without loss and continued back to their carrier without further incident.

VF-88's Hellcats weren't as fortunate. At 0645 hours, the eight Hellcats and their *Shangri-La* shipmates were over the target. "Howdy" Harrison led his six Hellcats low over Tokurozama, just as the word was passed the Japanese had surrendered. Proctor's wingman Ted Hansen recalled thinking, "Oh God, let's get our fannies out of here." The six Hellcats were hit seconds later from behind and above by 17 Japanese fighters the Americans identified as several Kawanishi N1K2-J "Georges" and Nakajima Ki. 84 "Franks" as well as several Zekes and Jacks. If there were Franks present, they must have been part of a JAAF formation that stumbled on the fight at the same time as the other attackers, since the two air forces never operated together.

Turning into the attackers, Harrison opened fire. In the opening head-to-head pass, Hansen shot down what he identified as a Frank that tried to ram him, and splashed a second. A third Frank lost its wing to Maury Proctor's fire. Losing track of Mandenberg, Harrison, and Hobbs, Hansen and Proctor joined up and soon spotted a Jack on Joe Sahloff's tail, which Proctor exploded. Clearly in trouble with his fighter trailing smoke, Sahloff turned for the coast, but was never seen again.

As Proctor turned away from the exploded Jack, he was bracketed with tracers. He made a tight right turn that gave Hansen the shot to nail the Frank on his tail. As he reversed course, Proctor saw two other enemy fighters on fire. More importantly, six others in front of him and one turning behind him were still full of fight. He managed a killing belly shot when the formation of six pulled into a climb, then quickly ducked into a cloud to evade the one behind. When he popped out moments later, the sky was empty. As he flew toward the coast, he attempted to contact the others and thought he heard Hansen. Hansen heard nothing and thought he was the sole survivor until Proctor appeared overhead five minutes after he trapped aboard *Yorktown*.

The fight over, Tokurozama went into the historical record as the war's last substantial air battle. While the six pilots claimed nine kills, it came at the high cost of four missing and finally listed as presumed dead: Harrison, Hobbs, Mandenberg, and Sahloff.

Not long after Hansen and Hobbs trapped aboard *Yorktown*, Jim Stewart's VF-31 division landed aboard *Belleau Wood*. At about the same time, Victor Lowden, who had narrowly escaped being attacked by American Corsairs on his return flight by dropping his landing gear and rocking his wings to show the prominent US-style roundels, touched down on *Indefatigable* with an overheating Merlin engine, owing to a hit in the radiator; it was the last of the British strike force to do so after the badly damaged sixth Avenger ditched near the carrier's plane guard destroyer.

While Japanese records are incomplete regarding which units were engaged where on this last day of the war, 302nd *Kokutai* commander Lieutenant Morioka claimed he shot down one of six F6F Hellcats the 302nd came across "near Atsugi," which is very close to the reported location of the VF-88 Hellcats when they were hit. It is now considered likely that the 302nd *Kokutai* fought with both the VF-88 and VF-6 Hellcats, which both reported being attacked by a mixed formation of Zekes and Jacks, a formation flown only by the 302nd, while a squadron of the 343rd *Kokutai* which was equipped with the N1K-2J *Shiden* (George) and perhaps an unidentified Japanese Army Air Force unit equipped with the Ki.84 *Hayate* (Frank) were also involved in the VF-88 battle. The Seafires from *Indefatigable* appear most likely to have engaged Zeros of the 252nd *Kokutai*, which was based at Atsugi that summer. Lt(jg) Tadahiko Honma, a pilot of the 304th Hikotai of the 252nd *Kokutai*, was shot down in his A6M5 by a Seafire on August 15, 1945. Chief Petty Officer Yoshinari of the 252nd was credited with shooting down Fred Hockley's Seafire.

At noon, while the men aboard the ships of the Third Fleet celebrated their survival, the Japanese people heard a voice almost none had ever heard before. It was the voice of Emperor Hirohito.

After pondering deeply the general trends of the world and the actual conditions obtaining in Our Empire today, We have decided to effect a settlement of the present situation by resorting to an extraordinary measure.

We have ordered Our Government to communicate to the Governments of the United States, Great Britain, China and the Soviet Union that Our Empire accepts the provisions of their Joint Declaration.

To strive for the common prosperity and happiness of all nations as well as the security and well-being of Our subjects is the solemn obligation which has been handed down by Our Imperial Ancestors and which lies close to Our heart.

Indeed, We declared war on America and Britain out of Our sincere desire to ensure Japan's self-preservation and the stabilization of East Asia, it being far from Our thought either to infringe upon the sovereignty of other nations or to embark upon territorial aggrandizement.

But now the war has lasted for nearly four years. Despite the best that has been done by everyone – the gallant fighting of the military and naval forces, the diligence and assiduity of Our servants of the State, and the devoted service of Our one hundred million people – the war situation has developed not necessarily to Japan's advantage, while the general trends of the world have all turned against her interest.

Moreover, the enemy has begun to employ a new and most cruel bomb, the power of which to do damage is, indeed, incalculable, taking the toll of many innocent lives. Should we continue to fight, not only would it result in an ultimate collapse and obliteration of the Japanese nation, but also it would lead to the total extinction of human civilization.

Such being the case, how are We to save the millions of Our subjects, or to atone Ourselves before the hallowed spirits of Our Imperial Ancestors? This is the reason why We have ordered the acceptance of the provisions of the Joint Declaration of the Powers.

The hardships and sufferings to which Our nation is to be subjected hereafter will be certainly great. We are keenly aware of the inmost feelings of all of you, Our subjects. However, it is according to the dictates of time and fate that We have resolved to pave the way for a grand peace for all the generations to come by enduring the unendurable and suffering what is unsufferable.

It was still unclear if the Japanese military would follow the order of their emperor. At the same time the emperor spoke, VF-31 launched four divisions of Hellcats – 16 fighters – to relieve the Combat Air Patrol (CAP) over the task group. At 1400 hours, radar aboard *Lexington* (CV-16), flagship of Task Group 38.1, picked up a lone bogey closing on the fleet. Admiral Halsey gave the order "Shoot it down, not with hostility but with compassion."

Ensign Clarence Moore spotted the intruder and identified it as a Judy, the American code name for the Yokosuka D4Y3 *Suisun* (Comet) dive bomber that was the most commonly used *kamikaze* attack aircraft. Ensign Moore turned in behind the Judy and set it afire with two short bursts. The Judy crashed into the ocean below, the last Japanese aircraft shot down by a US Navy fighter pilot in the Pacific War.

While all this was happening, a unit from the Imperial Japanese Army's 426th Infantry Regiment arrived in the village of Higashimura to take custody of Fred Hockley. He was taken to the regiment's nearby headquarters and placed in a jail cell. Hockley was present when the men heard the voice of their emperor, telling them to "endure the unendurable" and to surrender. A colonel came to the jail and informed him of the emperor's orders. Later that evening, the cell door opened to reveal a group of Japanese officers led by a major. Hockley was removed from the cell and marched into the nearby woods, where he was forced to kneel. On the major's order, one of the junior officers beheaded Hockley with his samurai sword. The body was hidden in a shallow grave. A few days later, fearful that his body would be found when Allied occupation troops arrived, those who had committed the murder returned and dug up Hockley's body, then burned it. It did them no good, as other soldiers who disagreed with the commission of the war crime informed Allied authorities; the major who gave the order and the junior officer who carried it out were arrested in October 1945. Following a brief trial, they were hanged as war criminals in November.

Whoever had fired the last shot of the war, the bloodiest six years of recorded human history had finally come to an end. While 80 percent of the deaths in the war had happened on the Eastern Front, fighting in the Pacific had been intense and bloody, with no quarter asked or given in a battle against an enemy that preferred death to surrender. The last ten months of the Pacific War, from the victory at Leyte Gulf to the strikes on Tokyo, had been the bloodiest of the four-and-a-half-year conflict.

CHAPTER TWO

OCTOBER 25, 1944

By 1000 hours on the morning of October 25, 1944, the United States Navy had accomplished the task for which it had been created over the previous 20 years: the defeat of the Imperial Japanese Navy, which at this moment no longer posed a credible threat. *Zuikaku*, last survivor of the six aircraft carriers that had attacked Pearl Harbor 34 months earlier, lay on the bottom 100 miles north of Cape Engaño along with the carriers *Chitose* and *Zuiho*. *Musashi*, one of the two largest battleships in the world, was sunk in the Sibuyan Sea. The battleships *Fuso* and *Yamashiro* had been destroyed in Surigao Strait. Admiral Kurita's Center Force had been stopped in a desperate battle off the island of Samar and was in retreat through San Bernardino Strait. Other than the one-way mission that would be undertaken by the battleship *Yamato* in the Okinawa campaign six months later, no other Japanese capital ship would seek combat with the US fleet for the remainder of the war. The victory that had been planned over the preceding two decades had been achieved. British historian J. F .C. Fuller, writing in *The Decisive Battles of the Western World*, described the outcome of Leyte Gulf: "The Japanese fleet had [effectively] ceased to exist, and, except by land-based aircraft, their opponents had won undisputed command of the sea."

For Japan, the defeat in the Philippines was catastrophic. The Imperial Japanese Navy had suffered its greatest ever loss of ships and men in combat. The defeat meant the inevitable loss of the Philippines. This meant in turn that Japan would be all but completely cut off from the territories in Southeast Asia that had been occupied in 1942, which provided resources vital to Japan, most particularly the oil needed for her ships and gasoline for her aircraft, not to mention foodstuffs for the Japanese population. Admiral Yonai, the Navy Minister, said when interviewed after the war that he realized the defeat at Leyte "was tantamount to the loss of the Philippines." As for the larger significance of the battle, he said, "I felt that it was the end."

Forty-seven minutes after Admiral Kurita turned his fleet back to San Bernardino Strait, the naval war in the Pacific changed irrevocably when the *Shikishima* Unit of the Imperial Japanese Naval Air Force's 201st Air Group found the carriers of Task Unit 77.4.3, known as "Taffy-3," north of Samar Island at 1047 hours. At 1053 hours, an A6M5 Zeke dived on *St. Lo* (CVE-63). The Zeke pulled up at the last moment to correct the dive and the airplane hit the center of the flight deck. The 250kg bomb penetrated the port side of the hangar deck and exploded in the midst of several aircraft being refueled and rearmed. A gasoline fire quickly erupted, followed by six secondary explosions that ended with the detonation of the torpedo and bomb magazine. Engulfed in flames, *St. Lo* sank 30 minutes later. Of a crew of 889, 113 were killed or missing; 30 survivors later died of their wounds. The 434 survivors were rescued from the water by the destroyer *Heermann* and the destroyer escorts *John C. Butler*, *Raymond*, and *Dennis*. It was a portent of the storm to come that would be seen as a battle against the *kamikaze*, named for the typhoon winds that sank the invasion fleet of Kublai Khan in 1274. Over the remaining ten months of the Pacific War, 3,860 Japanese pilots would attack Navy ships; some 733 of them would hit their targets. By June 1945, Admiral Nimitz would write a letter to the Joint Chiefs of Staff in which he stated for the record that the Navy could not support an invasion of Japan in the face of this threat.

Had it not been for the Soviet invasion of Manchuria and the use of two atomic bombs that led to the Japanese decision to surrender, the human wind of the 20th-century "divine wind" might have prevented the planned American invasion of Japan, or at least seriously delayed it while the Soviets invaded the country from the north.

"Suicide attacks" had happened throughout the war, carried out by pilots of both sides, and were individual impromptu decisions made by men who were prepared to die, generally when their airplane was so badly damaged that further survival was impossible. On December 7, 1941, Lieutenant Fusata Iida, flight leader of the 1st *Shotai* aboard the carrier *Soryu*, dived his A6M2 *Zero-sen* into the main hangar of Kaneohe Naval Air Station on Hawaii during the Pearl Harbor attack when he discovered his gas tank had been hit and he had no way of returning to the Japanese fleet. He had told his men before they left *Soryu* that if his plane was badly damaged he would crash it into a "worthy enemy target."

What differentiated events such as these from what was called "*kamikaze*" was that they were voluntary, and that such action by these pilots was not expected by their superiors. While the term "*kamikaze*" would be the word that described the ten-month battle as remembered by Americans, the formal term used by the Japanese for a unit assigned to suicide attack was *tokubetsu kogeki tai*, or "special attack unit." This was abbreviated to *tokkotai*. In the Imperial Japanese Navy, the official term for these "special attack units" was *shinpu tokubetsu kogeki tai*, "divine wind special attack unit." The Japanese only informally used the word *kamikaze* during the war, but it became widely used after the conflict owing to the wide understanding of the word in other countries.

When Allied forces assaulted Suluan Island on October 17, which began the Battle of Leyte Gulf, the Imperial Japanese Navy's First Air Fleet was based at the former American airbase of Clark Field, known to the Japanese as Mabalacat, outside Manila. At the time the unit had only 40 aircraft: 34 A6M Zeke fighters of various sub-types, three B6N *Tenzan* (Jill) torpedo bombers,

Philippines operations, October 20, 1944 to July 1945

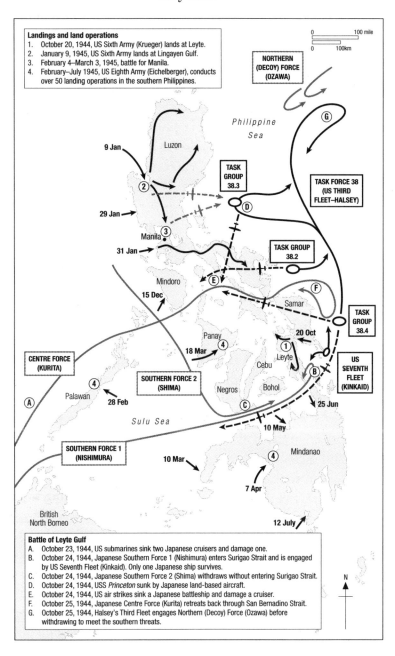

Landings and land operations
1. October 20, 1944, US Sixth Army (Krueger) lands at Leyte.
2. January 9, 1945, US Sixth Army lands at Lingayen Gulf.
3. February 4–March 3, 1945, battle for Manila.
4. February–July 1945, US Eighth Army (Eichelberger), conducts over 50 landing operations in the southern Philippines.

0   100 mile
0   100km

NORTHERN (DECOY) FORCE (OZAWA)

Philippine Sea

9 Jan   Luzon

TASK GROUP 38.3

TASK FORCE 38 (US THIRD FLEET–HALSEY)

29 Jan

Manila

31 Jan

TASK GROUP 38.2

Mindoro

15 Dec

Samar

TASK GROUP 38.4

Panay

20 Oct

18 Mar

Leyte

Cebu

CENTRE FORCE (KURITA)

SOUTHERN FORCE 2 (SHIMA)

Negros   Bohol

US SEVENTH FLEET (KINKAID)

Palawan   28 Feb

25 Jun

Sulu Sea

10 May

SOUTHERN FORCE 1 (NISHIMURA)

10 Mar

Mindanao

7 Apr

British North Borneo

12 July

Battle of Leyte Gulf
A. October 23, 1944, US submarines sink two Japanese cruisers and damage one.
B. October 24, 1944, Japanese Southern Force 1 (Nishimura) enters Surigao Strait and is engaged by US Seventh Fleet (Kinkaid). Only one Japanese ship survives.
C. October 24, 1944, Japanese Southern Force 2 (Shima) withdraws without entering Surigao Strait.
D. October 24, 1944, USS *Princeton* sunk by Japanese land-based aircraft.
E. October 24, 1944, US air strikes sink a Japanese battleship and damage a cruiser.
F. October 25, 1944, Japanese Centre Force (Kurita) retreats back through San Bernadino Strait.
G. October 25, 1944, Halsey's Third Fleet engages Northern (Decoy) Force (Ozawa) before withdrawing to meet the southern threats.

N

one G4M2 "Betty" and two P1Y1 *Ginga* (Frances) land-based bombers, and one C6N1 *Saiun* (Myrt) reconnaissance aircraft with which to hold off the American attack. The task seemed impossible. The fleet commander Vice Admiral Takejiro Ônishi met with the officers of the 201st *Kokutai* on October 19, where he announced: "I don't think there would be any other certain way to carry out the operation [to hold the Philippines], than to put a 250kg bomb on a Zero and let it crash into a US carrier, in order to disable her for a week." All of the pilots volunteered to form a unit to make such an attack.

The 201st Group's leader Commander Asaiki Tamai threw himself into organizing the new special attack force. Twenty-three outstanding student pilots he had trained volunteered for the unit, while Lieutenant Yukio Seki, commander of the 301st Chutai (Fighter Squadron), was put in command.

A 1941 graduate of the Japanese Naval Academy at Eta Jima, Seki had trained as a dive-bomber pilot in 1943 and was assigned as an instructor at Kasumigara, the "Japanese Pensacola" in January 1944; he had joined the 201st Air Group in September to take command of the 301st squadron after its previous leader was lost during Admiral Halsey's rampage through the Philippines. Before taking off on his mission, Seki made a statement that would hold true for many of those who followed in coming months: "Japan's future is bleak if it is forced to kill one of its best pilots... I am not going on this mission for the emperor or for the empire... I am going because I was ordered to."

Four sub-units, *Shikishima, Yamato, Asahi,* and *Yamazakura,* made up the Special Attack Force. The names came from a patriotic death poem written in 1764 by the classical Shinto scholar Motoori Norinaga, *Shikishima no Yamato-gokoro wo hito towaba, Asahi ni niou Yamazakura bana,* which reads:

> If someone asks about the *Yamato* spirit [Spirit of Old/True Japan] of *Shikishima* [a poetic name for Japan] – it is the flowers of *Yamazakura* [mountain cherry blossom] that are fragrant in the *Asahi* [rising sun].

One member of the 201st was not allowed to volunteer for a suicide attack. Hiroyoshi Nishizawa was the leading ace of the Imperial Japanese Naval Air Force, having fought over New Guinea and the Solomons since 1942, and personally claimed 87 victories over Allied pilots at this time. He had completed his training in 1939, graduating 16th out of a class of 71 in the most rigorous and demanding flight training program in the world at the time. A Petty Officer 1/c by the outbreak of war, Nishizawa was legendary among fighter pilots for the air show he and his fellow aces Saburo Sakai and Toshio Ota had put on over Three Mile 'Drome at Port Moresby on May 17, 1942, where they flew loops in formation directly over the Allied airfield. Flying from Rabaul, he became the top-scoring Japanese ace of the war over Guadalcanal before his unit was withdrawn with only ten pilots left in November 1942. Ordered to instruction duties, he had returned to combat only in September, when he joined the 201st. Nishizawa was ordered to lead the pilots who would escort the attackers and defend them from the Americans.

The 201st moved from Mabalacat to Cebu in the central Philippines to put themselves closer to their targets, and the *Shikishima* unit flew its first mission on October 24, 1944, with Seki leading four attackers and Nishizawa leading four escorts. The weather was bad that day with heavy clouds, and they were unable to find any targets, returning to base with only a little fuel left.

On the morning of October 25, Nishizawa led four A6M5 Zeke escorts while Seki led four old A6M2s, each carrying a 250kg bomb. The Zekes were intercepted by Hellcat defenders, and in the fight that developed, Nishizawa claimed two of the Hellcats as victories 86 and 87, his last. The escorts became separated from the attackers. One attacker dived on *Kitkun Bay* (CVE-71) and attempted to hit her bridge, but instead exploded when it hit the port catwalk and cartwheeled into the sea. Two others attacked *Fanshaw Bay* (CVE-70) but were destroyed by antiaircraft fire. The last two ran at *White Plains* (CVE-66). One was hit and shot down by antiaircraft fire, while the other, under heavy fire and trailing

smoke, aborted the attempt and instead banked toward *St. Lo*
Lieutenant Seki had found his target.

The next day, Nishizawa's Zeke was armed with a bomb and
assigned to Petty Officer 1/c Tomisaku Katsumata. Katsumata
attacked *Suwanee* (CVE-27), operating as part of "Taffy-1," outside
Leyte Gulf at 0740 hours. Other members of the attacking force had
already hit *Santee* (CVE-29), while *Suwanee*'s gunners shot down a
Zeke that made a run on *Petrof Bay* (CVE-80). *Suwanee* had entered
combat two years earlier during the North African invasion and was
a veteran of the Battle of the Atlantic before coming to the Pacific
the previous January, where she operated throughout the combat
theaters. Her experienced gunners hit a second Zeke and then hit
Katsumata's airplane as he circled to get into position for a dive. He
crashed on the flight deck and careened into a TBM-1C Avenger
that had just landed aboard. The two aircraft exploded in flames on
contact; the fire spread quickly to nine other planes. Katsumata's
bomb penetrated the flight deck and exploded in the hangar deck.
Although Katsumata failed to sink *Suwanee*, she caught fire and 85
were killed, 58 were missing and 102 wounded.

Suwannee's medical officer, Lieutenant Walter B. Burwell, wrote
a report afterwards that clearly illustrated the terrible damage that
could be inflicted by one deliberate crash:

> One of our corpsmen tending the wounded on the flight deck saw
> the plight of those isolated by fire on the forecastle. He came below
> to report that medical help was critically needed there. It seemed
> to me that we would have to try to get through to them. So he and
> I restocked our first aid bags with morphine syrettes, tourniquets,
> sulfa, Vaseline, and bandages, commandeered a fire extinguisher
> and made our way forward, dodging flames along the main deck.
> Along part of the way, we were joined by a sailor manning a
> seawater fire hose with fairly good pressure, and though the
> seawater would only scatter the gasoline fires away from us, by
> using the water and foam alternatively as we advanced, we managed
> to work our way up several decks, through passageways along the

wrecked and burning combat information center and decoding area, through officers' country, and finally out on the forecastle. Many of the crew on the forecastle and the catwalks above it had been blown over the side by the explosions. But others trapped below and aft of the forecastle area found themselves under a curtain of fire from aviation gasoline pouring down from burning planes on the flight deck above. Their only escape was to leap aflame into the sea, but some were trapped so that they were incinerated before they could leap. By the time we arrived on the forecastle, the flow of gasoline had mostly consumed itself, and flames were only erupting and flickering from combustible areas of water and oil. Nonetheless, the decks and bulkheads were still blistering hot and ammunition in the small arms locker on the deck below was popping from the heat like strings of firecrackers. With each salvo of popping, two or three more panicky crew men would leap over the side, and we found that our most urgent task was to persuade those poised on the rail not to jump by a combination of physical restraint and reassurance that fires were being controlled and that more help was on the way. Most of the remaining wounded in the forecastle area were severely burned beyond recognition and hope.

Suwannee survived and resumed air operations by 0930 hours. The CVEs of Taffy-1 fought off two more attacks, the last at 1300 hours with *Santee* being hit with minor damage. In the same attack, *Kalinin Bay* was attacked by four *kamikazes* from astern and the starboard quarter. Two attackers were shot down at close range, but the third crashed into the port side of the flight deck, damaging it badly. The fourth hit and destroyed the aft port stack, both of which attacks inflicted extensive structural damage, with five dead and 55 wounded. After being sent to Manus for temporary repairs, *Kalinin Bay* reached San Diego on November 27, where she was repaired until January 18, 1945. *Kitkun Bay* was hit by an A6M Zeke that struck the port catwalk, killing one man and wounding 16. Repairs at Pearl Harbor were completed on December 17, 1944.

Over the course of October 24–25, the Special Attack Force had launched 55 special attackers, who had damaged seven escort carriers. The attackers also hit 40 destroyers and destroyer escorts; five were sunk, 23 heavily damaged, and 12 moderately damaged.

After stopping at Kossol Roads in the Palau Islands on October 28, the escort carrier force sailed on Manus for extended upkeep on November 1.

Suwannee was sent back to the west coast for major repairs, arriving at Puget Sound Navy Yard on November 26, where her repairs were completed by January 31, 1945.

Suwannee's story and that of the other CVEs pointed to the fact that a *kamikaze* attack did not have to sink the target to be successful. A carrier that was back in the United States under repair was a carrier that was not available on the line to face the enemy. Additionally, the damage suffered by the CVEs meant that the carrier force dedicated to providing close air support over Leyte Island to the invading ground forces had been forced to depart early, with a loss of important air cover capability. Over the next several months, the fast carrier task force would be depleted by ships forced to retire damaged. Fortunately, new carriers that had been completed during 1944 were able to replace the veterans.

On October 27, the surviving pilots of the 201st *Kokutai* boarded a L2D Type 0 transport (a license-built version of the Douglas DC-3, codenamed "Tabby" by the Allies) to fly to Mabalacat on Luzon and pick up new aircraft for the unit. Over Mindoro Island, the Tabby was spotted by two F6F-5 Hellcats of VF-14 from *Wasp*. Hiroyoshi Nishizawa, Japan's greatest ace, was most likely killed by Lt(jg) Harold P. Newell, who claimed a "Helen" shot down in flames northeast of Mindoro that morning.

Combined Fleet commander Admiral Soemu Toyoda honored Nishizawa by mentioning his loss in an all-units bulletin and he was posthumously promoted to Lt(jg), which was a great honor for an enlisted man in the Japanese Navy. He was given the name *Bukai-in Kohan Giko Kyoshi*, a Zen Buddhist phrase meaning "In the ocean of the military, reflective of all distinguished pilots, an honored Buddhist person."

Even with the departure of the 201st *Kokutai*, the "divine wind" continued to blow across the Philippine Sea and soon reached gale force.

Shortly after 1200 hours on October 29, *Intrepid* (CV-11) became the first fleet carrier victim of a special attacker. A lone Zeke was spotted to starboard while the ship cruised off Luzon. Realizing from the immediate flak bursts that erupted around him that the carrier had opened fire, the pilot dived straight at the flight deck. Gun Tub 10's six 20mm cannon, manned by the ship's African-American stewards' mates, shredded the Zeke's wing with their fire, but the pilot continued and veered directly into Gun Tub 10, killing ten outright and wounding ten others.

The day was cloudy, and minutes later another Judy managed to evade the Combat Air Patrol and arrive in position over the task group. The target was "The Blue Ghost," *Lexington* (CV-16), named for the first Navy carrier lost in combat at Coral Sea. *Lexington* had been part of the fast carrier task force since the arrival of the "new navy" in the Pacific War 15 months earlier and had been Marc Mitscher's flagship when he led Task Force 58. The *kamikaze* hit the veteran carrier at the aft base of the island.

Chief Quartermaster Tom Curtis, who as a Signalman Third Class had survived the sinking of *Wasp* (CV-7) in September 1942, was working with his young crew on the signal bridge. Just before the *kamikaze* was spotted, he entered the passageway to cross to the other side of the island. "The blast of the explosion threw me against a bulkhead and knocked me out for several minutes. When I came to, I realized I had a fractured leg. The fire on the bridge I had just left was so strong I was forced to retreat to the far side of the island, where a corpsman found me and gave me a shot of morphine."

The blast quickly spread fire up the flight deck side of the structure as high as the port signal bridge, where all personnel on the exposed deck were killed. The fire caused 187 casualties, including all of Tom Curtis' young signalmen, but was out within 20 minutes through quick work by the damage-control parties and the fact the captain maneuvered the ship so that flames spread only on an empty flight deck. *Lexington* was soon ready to recover aircraft from the strike, but she had been incredibly lucky to have had an empty flight deck at the moment of the attack. Unfortunately, the damage was such she was forced to retire to Ulithi for repair the next day, taking the experienced and successful Air Group 19 with her.

Franklin (CV-13) and *Belleau Wood* (CVL-24) were in the enemy's sights on October 30. Task Group 38.4's *Enterprise* (CV-6), *Franklin, Belleau Wood* and *San Jacinto* were conducting flight operations approximately 100 miles east of Samar. Visibility was over 12 miles, the ceiling was unlimited with scattered high and low cumulus, and the wind was from the southeast at 18 knots with a light sea. At 1400 hours, *Bagley* (DD-386) moved alongside *Franklin* and began fueling. Five minutes later, the carrier launched 12 Hellcats to cover a fleet tanker force that was reported to be under air attack about 240 miles north. In the midst of the launch, a large formation of bogeys 37 miles away was picked up on radar at 1410 hours. Fueling ceased and *Bagley* cast off at 1417 hours as General Quarters sounded. The last Hellcat was off at 1420 hours. *Franklin* turned due east at 1424 hours and increased speed to 18 knots as the enemy formation appeared overhead.

Three D4Y3 Judy dive bombers angled down toward *Franklin*. The first crashed in the water to starboard, throwing up a large column of water. The second hit the flight deck in about a 20-degree glide starboard of the centerline, blowing a hole 30 by 35 feet and penetrating to the gallery deck spaces below. Wreckage of this attacker was later found in the crew's head two decks lower.

Disaster spread quickly. Thirteen aircraft on the hangar deck caught fire when their gas tanks ruptured, which set off a raging fire among the other planes in the hangar. The No. 3 bomb elevator trunk was demolished above the hangar deck; the blast flashed down the trunk and blew off the counterweighted door at the third deck level. Flames and dense smoke poured down the trunk and repair party teams were forced to evacuate. The hangar deck blast and fire killed the sailor whose duty it was to close the armored hangar deck hatch No. 1-109. Flaming gasoline poured through the hatch and started fires in a second deck living compartment. With vents still open, smoke and burning gasoline from the hangar deck fire continued down to the third deck, forcing the damage control crew to evacuate; some escaped up to the second deck while others worked their way forward along the third deck.

Hangar Deck Control turned on all hangar sprinklers and water curtains immediately after the gallery deck explosion. All those in Hangar Deck Control were forced to evacuate shortly after because of the dense smoke and heat.

Approximately ten minutes after the bomb exploded, the third deck was ripped by two additional explosions. The worst one ruptured the third deck, dishing in the overhead by nearly a foot. The second was in a compartment where a fire had been extinguished. The ship's log recorded, "The cause of these two below deck explosions is believed to have been the ignition of gasoline vapors which came down from the hangar deck through the open hatch at frame 109, through the ruptured bomb elevator trunk at frame 127, and down the auxiliary elevator ram cylinder in compartment B-324-L."

Within minutes, *Franklin* took on a three-degree starboard list. Counterflooding brought the carrier to an even keel. She then took a two-degree list to port.

> It was then realized that the initial list was caused by the tremendous volume of water from the hangar deck sprinklers, water curtains, and fire hoses that were immediately turned on after the initial blast, and which ran down to the second and third decks through the open hatch and bomb elevator trunk. The water collected on the starboard side of the ship initially and caused the increasing list.

By 1530 hours, the major fires on the flight deck were extinguished, while the hangar deck fire was extinguished by 1625 hours and the gallery deck fire by 1630 hours. By 1800 hours, all except smoldering fires were extinguished. While *Franklin* had survived, she too would be out of the war for an extended period while repairs were completed at the Hunter's Point Naval Shipyard in San Francisco. That such damage could result from a single attacker was a sobering thought for senior naval commanders.

Belleau Wood was struck by the third Judy to attack *Franklin*, which dropped a 250kg bomb that hit the water 30 feet from *Franklin* and threw up a large geyser of water on her starboard side before crash-landing on the aft end of *Belleau Wood*'s flight deck. Eleven parked aircraft were hit and caught fire, which set off ready ammunition at the gun mounts to either side of the flight deck. Before the fire could be brought under control, 92 men were dead or missing, with 97 wounded. Once the fires were out, *Belleau Wood* headed for Ulithi with *Franklin*. She would not return until January 1945. Admiral McCain's task group had been halved.

The Japanese air forces in the Philippines were so depleted that only the new form of "special attack" found any kind of success. A conventional attack with a large number of planes was likely to be wiped out before it got within range, given the low level of competence of the average Japanese pilot at this time. But a small formation did have a chance, and if only one got through and hit a major target, the effect was more devastating than any conventional attack could be. Imperial Army pilots began to emulate the Imperial Navy fliers, and soon the men aboard the fleet were forced to consider any attacking aircraft to be a *kamikaze*.

From the first day of the war, Americans had struggled to understand the Japanese willingness to commit suicide as a battle tactic. This lack of understanding only grew in the final months of the war, as bloody battles developed in the Philippines, Iwo Jima, and Okinawa. There was an inability on the part of the Allies to understand why Japan, which was obviously beaten with no hope of turning the tables on their enemies, would literally fight to the death.

Japanese culture has a different attitude toward the act of suicide than does Western culture, with suicide seen as the "honorable" conclusion to life when there is no other "honorable" recourse. The Code Bushido, which literally means "the way of the warrior", is a Japanese term for the rules of life for a samurai, loosely similar to the concept of chivalry in Europe. The "way" originates from the samurai moral values, stressing frugality, loyalty, martial arts mastery, and honor until death. The concept was born from Neo-Confucianism during Tokugawa Japan, which was a 200-year time of peace when the samurai did not engage in constant warfare as before. Bushido was also influenced by Shinto and Zen Buddhism, which allowed the violent existence of the samurai to be tempered by wisdom and serenity. The term came into common usage in Japan and the West after the 1899 publication of Inazo Nitobe's *Bushido: The Soul of Japan*, known as "Hagakure" in Japan. "Hagakure" was immensely popular among officers in the Imperial Army and Navy; its oft-quoted opening line, "I have found that the way of the warrior is to die," was unquestionably used later to inspire *kamikaze* pilots.

The samurai as a social class were abolished in the Meiji Restoration that ended the Tokugawa Shogunate. As a propaganda tool, modern Bushido was used consciously to shape and manipulate popular attitudes as part of the effort to create a unified, modern nation out of a feudal society, and to create a modern national military force made up of conscripts from all parts of society. The Imperial Rescript to the Military of 1882 proclaimed that Bushido "should be viewed as the reflection of the whole of the subjects of Japan." Warrior values were thus held as being the essence of what it meant to be Japanese itself. Thus the abolition of the samurai class did not mark the end of Bushido, but rather its spread to the whole Japanese population.

The concept underwent a great change following the Japanese military victories in China in the late 19th century and the Japanese victory over Imperial Russia in the Russo-Japan War of 1904–05 as the empire looked to expand. As the military became stronger and more independent and more deeply involved in the political direction of the country, Bushido became emperor-centered, with greater value placed on the virtues of loyalty and self-sacrifice as it became a propaganda tool used by the government and military, who modified it to suit their needs. The Bushido of "traditional" Japan was not simply a continuation of earlier traditions. It was presented as purifying, with death as a duty, which meant that the traditional concepts were virtually stood on their head. As the war turned against Japan, the spirit of Bushido was invoked to urge that everything depended on the firm and united soul of the nation. The first proposals for organized suicide attacks, which were presented in the summer of 1944, met initial resistance from those called on to die because while Bushido called for a warrior to be always aware of death, the traditional code did not view death as the sole end, but rather to die a "good death" with one's honor intact. After the defeat in the Marianas and the losses incurred with the American attacks against Okinawa and Formosa that led up to the Philippines' invasion, the attitudes changed as the desperate straits Japanese fighters found themselves in brought about acceptance of the idea that a suicidal attack against the enemy bent on destruction of Japan was a "good death."

It is not terribly difficult to look through history and find examples of warriors who, finding themselves in desperate situations, chose to die heroically rather than be killed running away. The story of the 300 Spartans at Thermopylae is well known in Western history and it is not hard to find other examples in the military traditions of all nations at any time anywhere. However, the concept of an entire national population committing itself to such a philosophy of warfare is without comparison with any other culture in any other war.

Navy ace and air combat theorist Commander John S. Thach, Jr. observed, "Every time one country gets something, another soon has it. One country gets radar, but soon all have it. One gets a new type of engine or plane, then another gets it. But the Japs have got the *kamikaze* boys, and nobody else is going to get that, because nobody else is built that way."

CHAPTER THREE

THE BIG BLUE BLANKET

November 1, 1944 was cloudy in the central Philippines, the result of the continuing monsoon season. A roar of approaching aircraft engines was heard over muddy Tacloban airstrip on Leyte. Crews on antiaircraft guns scanned the sky in apprehension, as they looked for yet another Japanese attack on the only American-held airfield on the island.

The aircraft broke out of the clouds into view, revealing the distinctive twin-boom silhouette of the Lockheed P-38 "Lightning." Men breathed a sigh of relief that Fifth Air Force had finally sent their best fighter to the Philippines to oppose the Japanese air forces. The 18 fighters roared low over the field and made a "fighter break" to the left to enter the landing pattern.

Just as the first P-38 was about to touch down on the muddy runway, a formation of Japanese Army Air Force Ki.43 "Oscar" fighters appeared over the western hills as the enemy aircraft dived on the airfield in a strafing run. It was the worst possible moment for the P-38s, which were low and slow, with flaps and landing gear extended and engines at low revs.

The lead P-38 roared to life as the pilot held the big fighter low and sucked up his gear and flaps. Followed by his wingman, the P-38 pulled up and around behind the Oscars as the enemy opened fire.

Fire flashed from the four 50-caliber machine guns and single 20mm cannon in the Lightning's nose – in a matter of moments two of the enemy fighters exploded! They hit the ground to the south side of the airfield and cartwheeled into the nearby jungle, where their fires spread as firefighters quickly arrived to battle the flames. By this time the other P-38s had broken off from the landing pattern and took off in pursuit of the fleeing Oscars.

Minutes later, the P-38s reappeared, having chased the enemy away, and resumed their landings. The first fighter on the ground braked halfway down the runway and turned off toward the parking area. The pilot shut down the two Allison engines, rolled down the side panels of his canopy and lifted the coffin lid. He pulled off his helmet and shucked his parachute as he stood in the cockpit to reveal a wiry frame with a shock of dark brown hair and a handlebar moustache. The gaudily-painted fighter bore the name "Pudgy IV" on her nose and a scoreboard with 28 Japanese rising sun flags on it. Major Thomas E. McGuire, Jr., commanding the 431st "Possum" Fighter Squadron of the elite 475th "Satan's Angels" Fighter Group glanced over at the two columns of black smoke rising from the jungle beside the field. The two Oscars he had just shot down were victories 29 and 30 for the 475th Group's leading ace. The rest of the group quickly landed behind McGuire and parked their big silver fighters between the trees as protection from another strafing attack.

Within a matter of hours, the pilots of the 431st were ordered to turn their airplanes over to the 7th Squadron of the 49th Fighter Group that had preceded them to Tacloban five days earlier and needed to make up attrition. McGuire fumed as he watched mechanics scrape off the artwork on "Pudgy IV" in preparation for the fighter to be turned over to his arch-rival in the Fifth Air Force's "ace race," Major Richard I. "Dick" Bong, who always seemed to stay two or three victories ahead of McGuire. The "Possum" pilots looked forward to getting into the thick of the fighting here and hated turning their P-38s over to their "Forty-Niner" rivals. Their spirits rose the next day when they learned they would soon be re-equipped with the P-38L, the newest and best version of the Lockheed fighter.

However, even after the 431st Squadron re-equipped a week later, it meant the land-based air defense of the American position in the Philippines was limited to 36 P-38s to face the Japanese Army and Naval air forces, which were being reinforced daily as weather allowed. Expansion of Tacloban was slowed by the heavy monsoon rains and difficult terrain. Knowing the field's importance, the Japanese made constant attacks and wreaked severe losses among the aircraft and ground installations.

One particularly successful raid destroyed 27 aircraft. Japanese pilots came up with the surprise tactic of following American formations as they returned to the field and waiting to attack until the Americans turned into the landing pattern. The 431st Squadron had been the first to experience this. Destruction of ammo dumps and fuel storage tanks by Japanese night hecklers was a regular occurrence, since there were no night fighters to oppose them. The enemy had not been so effective in blanketing an American position with such sustained and powerful air action since the bombardment of Corregidor in 1942.

There was the additional problem that the 1944 typhoon season was the most active in several years, with two typhoons sweeping near enough to Leyte in November to increase the amount of rain and bad weather. It would not be until the end of November that the Army engineers would complete the expansion of Tacloban Airfield so that the other four squadrons of the two fighter groups could fly up from Mindoro to take on the Japanese. Between October 27 and November 15, the two P-38 squadrons shot down 130 Japanese aircraft for a loss of 48 P-38s – 13 in aerial combat, 14 destroyed on the ground, one to friendly fire, and 20 operationally on the muddy field.

The liberation of the Philippines was very far indeed from a "done deal" in November 1944. In the crucible of the coming battle to take Leyte from the Japanese, General Douglas MacArthur's position was unique. His forces had swept along New Guinea so that each amphibious operation would have the full protection of his own land-based Fifth Air Force. However, by invading Leyte two months earlier than originally scheduled, MacArthur's troops were operating without the full support of his air forces, and were matched in the air by the Japanese, who fed replacements down the chain of islands from Kyushu to Okinawa to Formosa to Luzon to make up losses as quickly as possible.

This meant that Admiral Halsey's Third Fleet had to remain within range of the Philippines to provide the necessary air cover for the Leyte operation until enough airfields could be constructed to allow the rest of the Fifth Air Force to enter the battle. As of early November, there was no way of knowing how long the commitment would last. But it was clear that so long as the fleet remained off the archipelago, the ships would be vulnerable to continuing suicide attacks, which put the entire Third Fleet into greater danger from the Japanese than the Navy had experienced since the early days of the Guadalcanal campaign two years earlier.

The defeat of the Imperial Navy in the battles of Leyte Gulf meant the failure of only one part of the Japanese plan to oppose the American invasion. The effort of the Japanese Army in the air and on the ground, and Navy efforts in the air, did not diminish but rather intensified. The carriers were forced by necessity to place the dangerous threat of *kamikaze* attacks at a higher priority than providing air support to the Army forces on Leyte, which slowed the battle to force the enemy off the island.

The outcome of the battles of Leyte Gulf had no effect on the Imperial Army's plan to oppose the invasion, though the post-invasion decision to make a stand on Leyte and fight a major battle was a radical change to the Army's initial plan to defend the Philippines. The original plan had called for Luzon to be the site of the main land battle, with delaying tactics employed from the expected invasion of Mindanao until the Americans fought their way to the main northern island. Following this original plan, the 16,000 troops stationed on Leyte when the invasion came pulled back to the western side of the island, withdrawing into difficult jungle terrain suited for a defensive, delaying fight. The plan to delay the American advance was predicated on the belief this would allow the Army time to reinforce and strengthen the forces on Luzon in order to defeat them on the northern plain of Luzon.

This strategy would also buy time to strengthen defenses on Formosa and Okinawa, the logical next targets of the American offensive.

The Japanese High Command's decision to alter the earlier plan was also due to their belief in the mistakenly optimistic reports regarding American naval losses in the battle off Formosa earlier in October. Unfortunately, the truth was that claims for ships sunk were greater than the number of ships in the Third Fleet, which had suffered only damage to two cruisers. Belief that the American carrier fleet had been badly weakened led Army leaders in the Philippines to believe local land-based Japanese Army Air Force units could defeat the Americans and win air superiority over the American beachhead.

Army commanders also operated under the belief that after the Morotai invasion in the summer that had occurred simultaneously with the Marianas invasion and placed Fifth Air Force units within range of the Philippines, and the Formosa battle in early October when Halsey's Third Fleet cut off the Philippines from reinforcement by the Home Islands, that MacArthur had committed his forces without full protection or adequate preparation. This was further proof of the basic failure on the part of the Japanese leaders to understand exactly how powerful their enemy was, as had been shown in June when the secondary invasion of Halmahera had led Admiral Toyoda to assume that was the main American operation, which led to complete Japanese surprise when the Fifth Fleet arrived off Saipan a week later in full force.

There was also fear that the defense of Luzon would be more difficult if the Americans were able to build airbases on Leyte. Believing the Navy's false reports, Field Marshal Hisaichi Terauchi, commander of the Japanese Southern Army, now saw Leyte as an opportunity for a defeat of MacArthur's forces.

General Tomoyuki Yamashita, known as "The Tiger of Malaya" for having conquered Malaya and Singapore in 70 days in January and February 1942 with a force that was outnumbered by his British opponents, had been brought to the Philippines from his command in Manchuria and placed in command of the Fourteenth Army on October 10, 1944. Having seen first hand the pre-invasion large-scale carrier raids on October 17–19, he was reluctant to send more troops into Leyte to fight on an unprepared battlefield at the expense of the Luzon defenses. Unlike his superiors, Yamashita believed the American fleet was still powerful regardless of the reports of wholesale defeat at Formosa, and that the carriers could defend the American position in Leyte and defeat Japanese air operations regardless of the weakness of American land-based air forces. Terauchi ignored Yamashita's objections and ordered the immediate dispatch to reinforcements to "annihilate the enemy invading Leyte." In the face of this direct order, Yamashita gave the order that "the Japanese will fight the decisive battle of the Philippines on Leyte."

Taking full advantage of the temporary drop in American air power, a steady stream of reinforcements poured into Leyte from Luzon and the neighboring islands. Two thousand soldiers landed at Ormoc Bay on the western side of Leyte on October 26. They were followed by other convoys. Units of the Japanese 30th and 102nd Divisions based in the Visayan Islands and Mindanao landed at Ormoc during the final days of October. The veteran 1st Division, which had been pulled out of the Kwantung Army in Manchuria and sent to Luzon, was diverted to Leyte. After successfully disembarking on November 1, the division was immediately committed to the defense of the Ormoc Corridor. Units of the 26th Division arrived the next day to swell the total of Japanese troops on Leyte. Despite many damaging naval air attacks on the Leyte convoys, General Yamashita had succeeded by early November in moving at least 25,000 additional troops into western Leyte to reinforce the original defense force. Additional troops were moved at night in barges from Cebu by way of the Camotes Islands.

Following the aftermath of the battles of Leyte Gulf, Rear Admiral Frederic C. Sherman's Task Group 38.3 that included *Essex* (CV-9) and Air Group 15 – which had been in constant combat since the invasion of the Marianas in June and was exhausted – was out of bombs and torpedoes and low on provisions. Admiral Halsey ordered TG 38.3 back to Ulithi on October 28. During the transit from the Philippines, the men of Air Group 15 were elated to learn that Air Group 4, their replacement, was waiting to relieve them at Ulithi. The top-scoring naval air group of the war was finally set to go home. However, by the time the task group arrived at Ulithi, *Intrepid, Franklin* and *Belleau Wood* had all been put out of action by the *kamikazes*. Task Force 38 was short of three carriers with experienced air groups; in the face of the present threat, there was not time for a new air group to come aboard and have any time to shake things out before being committed to all-out battle. After one day at Ulithi to rearm, refuel and reprovision, *Essex, Ticonderoga* (CV-14) and *Langley* (CVL-27) headed west at flank speed to rejoin the battle. Air Group 15 diarist Aviation Radioman 3/c Ted Graham of Bombing 15 recorded that one could watch the morale drop in the gunners' ready room when the word was passed.

As the task group steamed toward the Philippines on November 2, destroyers *Claxton* (DD-571) and *Ammen* (DD-527) took *kamikaze* hits and survived, while *Abner Read* (DD-526) was sunk by a *kamikaze*. The new Japanese tactic was terrifyingly effective. Reviewing reports of previous *kamikaze* attacks, the *Essex* fighter direction officers decided that the only effective defense was to spot incoming raiders as far out as possible and position defending fighters to hit them quickly.

Commander David McCampbell, Air Group 15 commander and top Navy ace, reported to Task Group commander Admiral Sherman it was his considered opinion the most effective way to combat the threat was to hit every airfield they could as often as possible, to deny the enemy the airplanes they needed to mount their attacks.

While McCampbell presented his plan, Commander John S. Thach, Jr., Air Operations Officer on the staff of Vice Admiral John S. McCain, Sr., commander of Task Force 38 and inventor of the "Thach Weave" combat tactic that allowed Navy pilots to outfight the Zero in the early days of the war, had been considering the situation that faced Task Force 38 since the first attacks on October 25.

To Thach, the answer to the *kamikaze* threat was as obvious as it was to McCampbell.

Thach called his plan, which he presented to Admiral McCain on November 2, the "Big Blue Blanket." While defensive in effect, it required offensive operations to establish air supremacy over the enemy's airfields, well away from the precious carriers. The plan called for combat air patrols larger and operated farther afield than before, positioning a line of radar picket destroyers and destroyer escorts 50 miles from the main fleet that would spot inbound raids ahead of the fleet radar to give advance warning. It would also require improved coordination between fighter direction officers (FDO) on different carriers to allow central direction to change from ship to ship as the situation required. Thach's plan also called for increasing the size of the fighter squadrons, so that while fighters were escorted to strikes by the Avengers and Helldivers, there would be a sufficient number of fighters for offensive strikes against Japanese airfields harboring *kamikazes* and defensive air patrols over the fleet.

The recommendation was that the fighter squadrons aboard the fleet carriers be increased from 54 to 72, while the Avenger torpedo bombers were reduced to 12 aircraft per squadron from 18 and the 24 Helldivers reduced to 15; eventually Helldivers would be removed completely, since the Hellcats and Corsairs proved more capable as fighter-bombers. The light fleet carriers would see their Avengers removed completely and those air groups be entirely equipped with fighters. Thach argued this would not affect offensive strength since there was no need to plan to fight another fleet action, and that the F6F Hellcat had proven itself a better bomber than the Helldiver.

Thach's plan was logical and his argument clear. The problem was that the Navy, having anticipated after the Battle of the Philippine Sea in June that the final battle which would destroy the Imperial Navy would be fought and won that fall, had cut back on the number of men in flight training commencing in August 1944. Simply put, there were not available pilots to man the new fighters in the enlarged squadrons without stripping them from the replacement squadrons back in the United States. Obviously, flight training would have to be changed and dive and torpedo bomber pilots retrained as fighter pilots to meet the new threat, but for the moment there was a pilot shortage.

Traditionally, when the US Navy gets in trouble, when there is no alternative left, it looks to the Marine Corps for a solution. Fortunately, the Marines were in a position to make a solid contribution. Equally fortunately, Admiral McCain was one of the few "Marine-minded" Admirals in the Navy. When Thach made his suggestion that the Navy fighter squadrons aboard the fast carriers be supplemented by Marine fighter squadrons, Admiral McCain didn't need to be convinced. The decision to adopt Thach's plan Navy-wide was approved at an emergency conference in San Francisco on November 26–27, 1944 at which Vice Admiral George D. Murray, ComAirPac (Commander Air Forces, Pacific), stated that "the critical situation required the temporary employment of Marine VF squadrons on the fast carriers." Admiral Marc Mitscher, legendary commander of Task Force 58, had returned from his combat assignment to Washington at the end of October. While in San Diego, he met with Rear Admiral J. J. Clark, who suggested using Marine F4U squadrons aboard the fleet carriers, and sold Mitscher on the idea. When the results of the San Francisco conference arrived at the Pentagon, "Mitscher put the Marines aboard carriers in a day," as Marine Brigadier General Field Harris later recalled. Ten Marine squadrons were authorized for immediate carrier training and deployment aboard the fast carriers as rapidly as possible.

It was still an argument to convince naval aviators that the Corsair could operate off a flight deck, particularly a Corsair flown by a Marine pilot who was not so experienced in carrier operations as his Navy counterpart. This belief was widespread even with the record of VF(N)-101, which operated unmodified Corsairs off the fleet carriers between January and July 1944, and did so at night. *Force majeure* solved the problem. The *kamikaze* threat required many more fighters on carriers, and there were not enough Hellcats or Navy pilots available to meet the need. Five Essex-class carriers would each receive two-squadron Marine reinforcements over the next three months.

Since the late 1920s, Marine aviation squadrons had traditionally served aboard aircraft carriers, and all Marine aviators were carrier qualified. This capability had been lost in the summer of 1943, when Admiral John Towers, commander of naval air forces in the Pacific, noted in a memo dated June 25, 1943 that one-third of the naval aviators being qualified for carrier duty by the Naval Air Operational Training Command were Marines. Noting that all Marine combat squadrons were land based in the Solomons, Towers suggested that the training was wasteful and that the qualification requirement be ended. Major General Ross Rowell, Commander Marine Air Wings Pacific, agreed. On July 1, Admiral Nimitz agreed with the decision and on August 1, 1943, carrier qualification training for Marine aviators came to an end.

With the end of the Rabaul campaign in February 1943, the only job for the land-bound Marine aviators was the assignment to keep the bypassed enemy island bases in the Carolines and Marshalls knocked out. For the previous eight months, Marine Corsairs and Dauntlesses had become very proficient at turning rocks into rubble on these bypassed islands. Admiral Towers had at one time considered that Marines should be based on escort carriers to provide close air support for amphibious landings, but concluded with Rowell's lack of interest in maintaining carrier qualification for his flyers that the Corps "wasn't interested" in carriers. By the summer of 1944, the Marines were looking for employment. Chief of Naval Operations Admiral Ernest J. King had concluded that Marine aviation had grown too big for its job. In August 1944, however, Marine Corps Commandant General Alexander A. Vandegrift, the victor at Guadalcanal, achieved what had been considered previously impossible when he convinced Admiral King to agree to putting Marine air units on escort carriers to provide air support for the coming operations in the Western Pacific, which was subsequently agreed by Nimitz. In September 1944, Marine aviators suddenly found themselves training for carrier qualification again. This change would pay dividends in the Okinawa campaign.

While all these changes were under way, the forces available to the Third Fleet and the Army had to face up to the challenge in the Philippines. The monsoon, which reaches its height in the Philippines in the latter stage of the weather pattern in October–November, slowed operational progress on Leyte. Transport of supplies to forward units became difficult as roads became muddy rivers. The weather hampered radio traffic, while the physical difficulties made field telephone land lines nearly impossible to maintain, with the result that communications were constantly disrupted, making it difficult to maintain contact between units.

Far East Air Force commander General George Kenney reported that, on a visit to Tacloban, the truck transporting him and his staff from their recently-landed C-54 to the field headquarters was stuck for three hours in the mud while troops worked to free it from the oozing muck.

The nearby Bacolod air complex on Cebu became the main base for the Japanese aerial defense and "special attack" operations in the central Philippines. Halsey planned a major sweep in order to deal with the threat.

Task Group 38.3 fueled in the Philippine Sea on November 3, then set out on a high-speed run to the Philippines to strike Japanese bases on Luzon and western Leyte. As the ships headed west, the cruiser *Reno* (CL-96) took a torpedo from a Japanese submarine that flooded an engine room. She was taken under tow and retired to Ulithi.

Task Group 38.3's first strikes were flown on November 5, with a fighter sweep of 52 Hellcats from *Essex, Lexington, Langley*, and *Ticonderoga*, led by VF-15 CO LCDR Jim Rigg. Enemy aircraft were spotted on the ground at Nichols Field outside Manila. Immediately following the sweep, 88 Hellcats, Helldivers, and Avengers from the four carriers led by Air Group 15 commander Dave McCampbell attacked the field. Bombing 15 Helldivers knocked out eight aircraft and destroyed a hangar while the group's Avengers cratered the runways. The other air groups hit the field as thoroughly as they could when they flew through dense enemy flak.

McCampbell attacked several enemy fighters he spotted, in company with wingman Lt(jg) Roy Rushing. Despite having his guns jam, McCampbell shot down one Zeke with two guns and a second with only one still working. Rushing had two working weapons when he shot down his Zeke. The equipment failures demonstrated the poor mechanical state of the group's planes after nearly five months on the front line. McCampbell's victories brought his score to 32, assuring his position as the Navy's top-scoring ace.

As the first strike flew back to the fleet, McCampbell directed a second strike of 72 aircraft that attacked nearby Clark Field. Helldivers hit several hangars while the Avengers cratered the east–west runway and destroyed 12 twin-engine aircraft parked nearby. A second fighter sweep of eight Hellcats was sent out, led by VF-15's LCDR George Duncan, with two aborting because of mechanical problems. The six Hellcats scored four victories while Lt Wendell Twelves' four Hellcats assigned as escorts on the Clark Field strike ran across a formation of Zekes flown by pilots good enough to give the Navy pilots a real fight, eventually scoring six Zekes and Oscars. Nearly every pilot who returned to *Essex* reported the failure of some piece of equipment. Mechanics worked throughout the night to fix the war-weary airplanes.

Manila Harbor was the target on November 5. Ninety-eight aircraft were launched at 1130 hours to hit shipping. Lieutenant Brodhead led 12 Helldivers of Bombing 15. *Nachi*, a survivor of Kurita's Center Force, took three hits in this attack, then she was attacked by six torpedo-armed Torpedo 15 Avengers in a hammer-and-anvil attack. *Nachi's* captain managed to evade four of the six, but the cruiser was hit by the last two, which caused an enormous explosion when one hit the stern.

Among the Avengers that attacked the cruiser was the TBM-1C flown by Lieutenant Robert H. "Bob" Cosford, with his crew Aviation Machinist Mate 2/c Loyce Deen and Aviation Radioman 3/c Digby Denzell. They had been together as a crew since the squadron had formed, and had flown every mission. As he bored in on *Nachi*, Cosford felt the plane take hits. In the rear, radioman

Denzell called out to his best friend gunner Deen, with no response. When he climbed into the turret, he was met by the terrible sight of his friend's headless, bloody body. Loyce Deen had been decapitated by a 37mm shell and his body was riddled with shrapnel.

Fighter Direction Officer Wendell Mayes, who had reported aboard at Ulithi just before the Formosa strikes, remembered Cosgrove's return to the ship as "the most heart-breaking event I witnessed in the war." The badly damaged Avenger touched down and flight deck crewmen saw the wrecked rear turret. Climbing up to help, the men turned away and threw up at the sight. Just at that moment, General Quarters sounded. Mayes remembered, "We had a *kamikaze* inbound and there wasn't time to remove him from the turret. The air boss ordered that the plane be pushed to the stern. The chaplain was called, and he was buried in his plane, which was pushed over the side." Film of the event was later shown in the 1950s documentary "Victory At Sea."

The morning strike was followed by a 72-plane strike that afternoon, led by McCampbell. John Bridgers led eight Bombing 15 Helldivers to go looking for a light cruiser spotted during the previous attack but were unable to find it. Instead, they found a destroyer and attacked it unsuccessfully owing to its violent maneuvers, though it was damaged by three near misses.

While the strike force was away from the carriers, it was the turn of Task Group 38.3 to experience the hot breath of the divine wind. *Essex* picked up the incoming raid and launched an emergency Combat Air Patrol reinforcement. Again, the attackers were D4Y3 Judys, which would soon become the main JNAF suicide attack aircraft since it was a little larger than the A6M5 and fast, thus making for a difficult target, while able to carry a 500kg bomb, twice that of a Zeke.

Three bogeys were spotted inbound. The first was shot down by antiaircraft fire while VF-15's Lieutenant Crittenden dived into the sea of explosions from the fleet's antiaircraft defenses to get the second Judy, while the third attacked *Essex*, whose veteran gunners kept firing on the diving plane until it exploded 500 feet above the ship.

Wendell Mayes remembered the crew's attitude:

It was difficult at first for us to realize and accept that these attacks were not the act of some pilot whose plane was so badly shot up he couldn't get home – which had been the usual reason up till then for such an attack by anyone – and to admit that these people were determined to die, that their intention was to kill themselves and in so doing take as many of us as possible with them. It ran against everything any of us had been raised to believe as members of our Western culture, in which suicide was not seen as anything honorable other than in such extremis that one knew they would not survive in any event. I think for most of us, the Japanese were difficult to understand regardless, but this made it more so. It was terrifying to see blips appear on the radar scope and know that each of them was a man who was absolutely willing to give his life to take yours and everyone you knew and served with.

These attacks, along with the stories we heard through the fleet from the Marines of *banzai* charges on the islands, the stories of enemy pilots who had been found who preferred to kill themselves rather than be rescued and if possible to kill their rescuers, set us in the belief that the Japanese were a different species from us. We came to hate them in a way completely different from the hatred of the enemy one found aboard ship prior to this change in attacks. Before, it was more an impersonal feeling, but now it was completely personal. The result was that we aboard ship became as hard in our view of the enemy as were the Marines in any island invasion. We hated them. We cheered when we saw them blown out of the sky. The *kamikazes* were the personal enemy of every sailor from the lowest seaman to the admiral.

High winds and high seas prevented air operations on November 7, but VF-15's LCDR George Duncan led 48 Hellcats from all three carriers on a return mission to Manila at dawn on November 8 against Clark Field. Duncan strafed two G4M Betty bombers as they prepared for takeoff, and they both caught fire. He then spotted a

P1Y1 Frances as it started its takeoff run, and hit it just as it lifted off. The Frances ground looped and cartwheeled before it exploded.

The morning strike launched from the task force ran into bad weather at 0610 hours caused by a typhoon that was making its way across the East China Sea north of the Philippines. The clouds were low and the air hazy, which made target acquisition over Manila difficult. Attacking aircraft found holes in the clouds to drop through, but they were forced to make glide-bombing attacks as they were greeted by heavy antiaircraft fire from the ships in harbor.

Shortly after midday, McCampbell led 78 aircraft against Port Silanguin in southern Luzon, away from the track of the typhoon. The thin cumulus cover was still low, so the bombers were forced to glide bomb, claiming two ships definitely sunk and a possible third. A late-afternoon fighter sweep to Manila by eight Hellcats blew up newly arrived Betty bombers at Clark Field.

On November 9, TG 38.3 moved out to sea to refuel. While many celebrated Franklin Roosevelt's victory over Governor Dewey, the big news aboard *Essex* was the announcement that Admiral Nimitz had ordered Admiral Halsey to release *Bunker Hill* (CV-17) for return to the west coast, and that Air Group 15 would be aboard for the trip home; TG 38.3 would be relieved the next day and Air Group 4 would come aboard when it reached Ulithi on November 11. Before that could happen, however, other events in the Philippines took precedence. VB-15 diarist Ted Graham wrote in his diary that night that "I woke up several times with the ship shaking like hell under full power."

US intelligence had discovered the Japanese were going to make a major reinforcement effort at Ormoc Bay within the next 24 hours. No matter how tired they were, *Essex* and the rest of Task Group 38.3 headed back to the battle area.

Beginning October 27, the Japanese began reinforcing the 16,000 men on Leyte and would continue to do so with a series of convoys through the month of November and most of December. Following the landing of a division of the Kwantung Army on November 1, two subsequent smaller convoys of barges bringing troops from the Visayan Islands had been attacked and stopped over the next three days. On November 8, convoy TA-3 had departed Manila for Ormoc Bay, carrying part of a second Kwantung Army division. This was followed by convoy TA-4's departure from Manila on November 9 with the majority of the division aboard the transports. The Japanese plan was that the destroyers escorting the first convoy would be able to rendezvous with the second once the first had unloaded its troops to provide additional protection to the bigger convoy. On November 9, convoy TA-3 had been spotted and attacked by B-25 Mitchells of the 38th Bomb Group, which was based on Morotai and specialized in antishipping strikes. Late that afternoon, the B-25s, escorted by the 432nd Fighter Squadron of the 475th Group, found the convoy and sank the transports *Takacu Maru* with all hands and *Kashii Maru*. The destroyers *Kasumi, Asashimo*, and *Naganami* were able to rescue survivors from *Kashii Maru*, then caught up with the rest of the ships. A second strike by P-38s just before dark disabled the destroyer *Akishimo* and the transport *Okinawa Maru*. Convoy TA-3 slowed and then joined with TA-4 to make the run into Ormoc Bay.

At dawn on November 11, 1944, Armistice Day, the surviving troop transports, supported by five destroyers, were spotted as they rounded Apale Point, bound for Ormoc Bay. Word was flashed to Task Force 38 and the flight decks of the three carriers in TG 38.3 were abuzz with activity as aircraft were spotted for launch, since the task group was closest to the target. Similar scenes were carried out aboard the carriers of task groups 38.1 and 38.4 as 350 Hellcats, Helldivers and Avengers were brought to readiness for further strikes.

Radar spotted an inbound bogey and the Combat Air Patrol was vectored onto what was identified as a Judy. They chased it into the fleet's defensive fire, where Lt(jg) R. N. Stime set it afire. The Judy flew on as flames enveloped it before it finally hit the water near one of *Essex*'s screening destroyers.

The photo taken of this attacker on fire in its dive became one of the iconic photos of the *kamikaze* phase of the Pacific War.

Nearly 100 Hellcats, Helldivers and Avengers, the largest strike the task group had ever launched, left the carriers at 0830 hours. Led by Dave McCampbell, their goal was stopping the enemy reinforcements. The strike force spotted the convoy rounding Apale Point, in sight of its anchorage, when they arrived over Ormoc Bay two hours later. The escorting destroyers immediately began laying a smokescreen as transports increased speed and scattered.

Jim Rigg's 20 Hellcats strafed the ships while Jim Mini assigned targets to the 20 Bombing 15 Helldivers. The first division stopped the leading transport dead in the water with three hits. Seeing that, the second division diverted their attack and hit the second ship with four bombs while gutting the third with three.

Finally, the third division executed wingovers and each Helldiver followed the one ahead in a 70-degree dive on the fourth ship. The antiaircraft fire was devastating. Lt(jg) John Foote's Helldiver was hit in the bomb bay and caught fire just after "bombs away." Those behind saw him pull out of his dive and he seemed to gain altitude for a few seconds before the Helldiver nosed over and went straight in. Aviation Radioman 2/c Norm Schmidt was seen to jump from the burning bomber just before the crash, but his parachute failed to deploy. The plane exploded on impact.

The pilot of the next dive bomber in line dropped his bombs and evaded the flak as he flew wildly out of the bay.

Next in line were pilot Ensign John Avery and gunner Ted Graham. Avery's bombs were observed as hits, but the bomber took a direct hit in the engine as he started his pull-out low over the water. A wave caught the SB2C's wingtip and the plane cartwheeled between the ships and went inverted before it tucked and hit straight on in a burst of spray. Avery and Graham were likely killed instantly.

Right behind Avery and Graham, pilot Ensign Mel Livesay and gunner Aviation Radioman 2/c Chuck Swihart were hit by fierce antiaircraft fire that blew off the left wing. The SB2C went into a violent spiral and was torn apart, with only pieces hitting the water. Pilot Lt(jg) David Hall and gunner Aviation Radioman 3/c Adams, who were next in line, were also hit, but Hall stayed level and made a successful water landing very near the enemy ships. They quickly got out and into their life raft. They were rescued by an OS2U Kingfisher later in the afternoon and returned to *Essex*.

Lieutenant Barney Barnitz, two planes behind Hall, felt hits behind and below his cockpit, which struck gunner Aviation Radioman 2/c Neal Steinkemeyer in his hand and legs. The gunner's wounds and loss of blood were serious; he needed immediate attention. Barnitz headed directly for Tacloban airstrip, where he ensured his gunner was taken by ambulance to the field hospital before he took off in his damaged bomber and returned to the ship.

Right behind Barnitz, pilot Lt(jg) Bob Brice and gunner Aviation Radioman 2/c Lou Penza took hits in their left wing and fuselage, but Brice kept the Helldiver airborne and made it back to the fleet. When he found the landing gear wouldn't come down, he successfully ditched in the wake of a plane guard destroyer.

The dive-bomber attack distracted the defenders from spotting Torpedo 15's 18 bomb- and rocket-armed Avengers before they attacked the three surviving large ships, scoring hits on the second and third.

The Helldivers from *Ticonderoga* hit the two smaller transports and one of the destroyers, while the Avengers from *Ticonderoga* and *Langley* added to the destruction with rocket attacks.

By this time, many Japanese troops and sailors from the sunken transports were in the water where they were mercilessly strafed, turning the waters of the bay a foamy red.

As the survivors of Air Group 15 made their escape, escorting Hellcats spotted incoming JAAF Oscars. Lt(jg) Ralph Foltz, assigned to get post-strike photos, attacked an Oscar he spotted below at 8,000 feet. Just as the enemy fighter caught fire, Foltz came under fire from another and went at the enemy head on; at the last moment the Oscar caught fire and nosed over. Foltz's wingman, Ensign Frazelle, and Lieutenant Baynard Milton, Lt(jg) Nall, and Lt(jg) Berree also got an Oscar each, while Ensign Smith got two in spite of his cockpit heater coming on and fogging his windscreen. Two enemy fighters shot down Ensign Erickson, who managed to bale out outside Ormoc Bay, where he was later picked up by a destroyer. Aviation Radioman 3/c Pete Trombina shot down one attacking Oscar and probably destroyed another, while gunners Walt Kelly and

Roger Lemieux each damaged an Oscar, unusual scores for Helldiver rear-seaters.

Despite the losses, the mission was a success. The sunken cargo ship carried all the division's ammunition. The surviving troops who got ashore had few weapons and no ammunition or food. Convoy commander Rear Admiral Mikio Hayakawa went down with the destroyer *Shimakaze*. The price of victory, however, was the heaviest losses Bombing 15 experienced on a single mission in its tour.

Back aboard *Essex*, Dave McCampbell soon faced the greatest leadership crisis of his naval career. The three dead gunners were the most popular men in the squadron. As their loss became known, the other gunners declared that they had done enough, that they would not fly more missions. This was serious; such an act in wartime was considered mutiny in the face of the enemy and a general court martial "hanging offense." Squadron commander Mini made his way below to McCampbell, where he explained the situation. On deck, the men stood nervously in the aftermath of their action. Finally, Mini returned. He announced that McCampbell agreed with the gunners, and that they would not fly further missions, though their pilots would if necessary. Since they were no longer on flight status, they would be sent to the ship's company, which meant they would not return home with the rest of the group. No one remembered who was the first to take back his declaration, but all did and the incident was put down to fatigue. Had the group commander gone on deck, where he would have officially "witnessed" the event, he could not have resolved things as he did.

Task Group 38.3 refueled on November 12 before a final round of missions against shipping in Manila. McCampbell was again the strike leader the morning of November 13. The Helldivers sank an 8,000-ton cargo ship and two 10,000-ton cargo ships, damaging an 8,000-ton tanker and an 8,500-ton freighter. There were no losses as the planes returned to *Essex*.

The afternoon strike was led by Torpedo 15's commander LCDR V. G. Lambert. The light cruiser *Kiso* was sunk by the dive bombers, but strike leader Lieutenant Roger Noyes and gunner Aviation Radioman

1/c Paul Sheehan were lost when their bomber was hit in the wing root and engine and exploded on impact with the water. Sheehan died little more than 48 hours after his best friend, Ted Graham. Two destroyers and a 10,000-ton cargo ship were also damaged. Though he didn't know it at the time, Lambert's brother-in-law, LCDR Commander Radcliffe Denniston, skipper of Torpedo 11 aboard *Hornet* (CV-12) was the pilot leading a group of Avengers Lambert saw shot down. Japanese losses for the day were a light cruiser and six destroyers along with seven freighters, while Nichols and Clark airfields were a shambles.

All Air Group 15 aircraft had returned by 1800 hours, when radar spotted two bogeys and General Quarters sounded. Two C6N1 Myrt reconnaissance planes, two P1Y1 Frances bombers, and one Ki.44 Tojo fell to the guns of VF-15's Satan's Kittens, while five more intruders fell victim to *Hornet*'s CAP.

McCampbell led Fabled Fifteen's next-to-last strike as coordinator for 92 aircraft launched from *Essex, Ticonderoga,* and *Langley*. No definite targets were hit in the haze, while pilots realized many ships that appeared afloat were actually sitting on the bottom of the shallow harbor. Bombing 15's final losses were Lt(jg) Raymond L. Turner and Aviation Radioman 2/c Sam Dorosh, whose SB2C was hit in its dive and went straight in. One of the original members of the squadron, Turner had flown in the first mission against Marcus Island in May. John Bridgers later wrote that "Losing Ray Turner like that took the gloss off of everything that came after."

As the strike aircraft flew off, a final Oscar dove on McCampbell, who turned and hit it in the cockpit. His 34th victory confirmed him as the US Navy Ace of Aces and third-ranked American ace of the war.

The final strike was flown that afternoon and was even less consequential than the first, with nothing left in Manila Harbor to attack. With negligible defensive fire, all planes returned safely.

Admiral Sherman ordered Task Group 38.3 to head east that evening. *Essex* dropped anchor in Ulithi Harbor on November 17 and Air Group 15 departed the ship.

It was one of three naval air groups to have flown in both the Battle of the Philippine Sea and the battles of Leyte Gulf, and was the last air group from that "high tide" of the Pacific War to return home. Of the 100 pilots who had landed aboard the carrier that May morning, 45 survivors left for home six months later. Bombing 15's losses were the worst: 17 pilots and 15 gunners killed or missing in action, 25 percent of the group's total losses.

Air Group 15's record was never equaled. The dive and torpedo bombers were credited with sinking the carriers *Zuikaku* and *Chitose* and the battleship *Musashi* while damaging three battleships, one carrier, five heavy cruisers, and 19 destroyers. Every pilot in Torpedo 15 was awarded the Navy Cross for making a combat torpedo attack. Satan's Kittens of Fighting 15 shot down 318 enemy aircraft in aerial combat, including the all-time one-day record of 68.5 on June 19, 1944, and destroyed 378 on the ground. Twenty-six pilots became aces, including their commander as the Navy Ace of Aces.

Over the course of the rest of November, the Battle of Leyte ground on. While the Japanese landed reinforcements and maneuvered into position for a counterattack, MacArthur's troops continued a two-prong attack and envelopment driving through the central Leyte Valley and along the coast. Fortunately, Army engineers were able to complete a new fighter airfield at Dulag, near Tacloban, which allowed the remaining squadrons of the 49th and 475th fighter groups to move into the Philippines, but did not provide sufficient land-based force to allow the Navy to leave the area.

The Third Fleet repeatedly attacked Japanese airfields on Luzon between November 5 and 19 whenever the adverse monsoonal weather permitted.

After evading a typhoon between November 20 and 23, Task Force 38 moved into range of the central Philippines, taking position 100 miles east of Luzon on November 24, and commenced attacks against airfields on Cebu, the Visayans and Luzon. The Japanese had turned the respite into an opportunity to shuttle more aircraft down to the Philippines.

On the morning of November 25, planes from the carriers sank the heavy cruiser *Nachi* in Manila Bay, but this time the Japanese struck back with great force. Over the course of an hour at midday,

Task Force 38 suffered the strongest and most coordinated *kamikaze* attack to date. The day was cloudy, which gave the attackers the opportunity to evade the combat air patrols sent after them when radar began to pick them up at 1135 hours, and a swarm of attackers managed to get through to the fleet.

At 1250 hours, attackers appeared over Rear Admiral Gerald Bogan's Task Group 38.2, where *Hancock* was operating with *Intrepid*, *Cabot* (CVL-28) and *Independence*.

Hancock was attacked just after the crew was called to lunch. Another Judy roared toward the carrier in a dive out of the sun. The 5" 38-caliber main guns, as well as the 40mm and 20mm batteries, opened up and exploded the plane when it was approximately 300 feet above the flight deck. Parts of the enemy airplane hit amidships while the flight deck was set afire by the burning wing. Pilot Isamu Kamitake had either already dropped his bomb or failed to arm it, limiting damage. The flight deck fires were quickly extinguished without serious damage, though 15 sailors died.

After examining the remains of the airplane for intelligence, both aircraft parts and the body of pilot Kamitake were dumped unceremoniously at sea.

At 1248 hours, it was the turn of the light carrier *Cabot*. The ship's gunners managed to shoot down two attackers and set a third aflame. This plane crashed into the port side of the flight deck and destroyed or disabled several guns and a gun director. As the gunners kept up their battle with the incoming *kamikazes*, a fourth plane was hit and damaged. It crashed close aboard the port quarter and showered the flight deck with shrapnel and burning debris. Sixty-two sailors were killed or wounded, but the carrier was able to maintain her station in formation and continue flight operations while damage control parties made temporary repairs. *Cabot* was sent to Ulithi for permanent repairs, where she arrived on November 28. She rejoined the fast carrier task force on December 11.

At 1255 hours *Intrepid* took her second *kamikaze* hit within a month of the first when an A6M Zeke went into a power stall approximately 1,000 yards astern of the carrier, did a wingover from an altitude of about 500 feet and rocketed into *Intrepid*'s flight deck. The 250kg bomb it carried penetrated the deck clear to the pilot's Ready Room, which was fortunately empty, but 32 men were killed in an adjoining compartment. As the crew fought the fires, two more Zekes attacked. One was hit by antiaircraft fire and splashed into the sea 1,500 yards to starboard, but the second flew through a blizzard of tracers, power stalled, made a wing-over and dived full force onto the flight deck four minutes after the first hit at 1259 hours, an attack that was personally witnessed by Admiral Halsey from the bridge of his flagship, *New Jersey* (BB-62) steaming in formation 1,000 yards distant. This attacker crashed through the deck into the hangar, which was soon ablaze from bow to stern. Damage control managed to bring the fires under control, but their heat helped other fires throughout the ship. With the flight deck and arrester gear badly damaged, flight operations were impossible and her strike planes and CAP were taken aboard by other carriers. In company with *Cabot*, *Intrepid* made it back to Ulithi and then sailed on to Pearl Harbor. The attack cost 69 men dead and 35 seriously wounded.

Lieutenant Cecil Harris of *Intrepid*'s VF-18 shot four of the attacking Zekes out of the sky over the task force. Harris was an outstanding pilot who almost always scored multiple victories in combat. His first two fights in early October saw him score three in each. This was followed by two floatplanes on October 24 over Leyte Gulf, and a lone single Zeke on November 19. The four scored in what was his final fight brought his score to 23 in only five aerial fights. Only the damage suffered by his carrier, which forced Air Group 18 out of the battle line, prevented him from challenging Dave McCampbell as Ace of Aces.

At the same time *Intrepid* was attacked, *kamikazes* appeared out of the clouds over Task Group 38.3. *Essex* had just returned to combat with Air Group 4 aboard. The veteran air group had participated in the invasion of North Africa two years earlier, and had flown strikes against Norway from *Ranger* (CV-4) in support of Russia-bound convoys in the summer of 1943 before returning to the United States for deployment to the Pacific. Fighting 4 had traded in their FM-1

Wildcats for F6F Hellcats, while Bombing 4 had given up their SB2C-5 Dauntlesses for SB2C-4 Helldivers, with Torpedo 4 receiving new TBM-1C Avengers to replace their early Grumman TBF-1s.

At 1256 hours a Judy flown by Yoshinori Yamaguchi hit *Essex* on the port edge of her flight deck. Aircraft on deck, armed and fueled for takeoff, caught fire and caused extensive damage with 15 killed and 44 wounded. Damage control parties quickly fought the fire and 30 minutes later she was ready to resume operations. Admiral Sherman detached *Essex* to return to Ulithi for repairs. The damage was quickly repaired and the carrier returned to service with Task Force 38 in time to support the occupation of Mindoro on December 14–16 1944.

Following these devastating attacks that had almost removed an entire task group from the fleet, Third Fleet withdrew from the Philippines for a well-deserved respite at Ulithi after operating for an unprecedented 84 days throughout the Western Pacific.

The final struggle for control of Ormoc Bay did not involve the carriers, though the victory came at sea. On November 23, the Japanese attempted to send another convoy from Manila to Leyte, but it was discovered on November 24 and five of the six transports were sunk by the Mindoro-based B-25s. With the onset of more bad weather in late November, air interdiction was less effective and the Navy sent destroyers into Ormoc Bay. *Waller* (DD-466), *Pringle* (DD-477), *Renshaw* (DD-499) and *Saufley* (DD-465) under the command of Captain Robert Smith were the first to enter the bay on November 27 to shell the docks at Ormoc City. Two days after the Third Fleet retired in the face of the *kamikaze* attack, two transports left Manila, escorted by three coastal patrol vessels. The convoy was found the night of November 28 and attacked by PT boats that sank the transports and their escorts.

November 27 saw further *kamikaze* attacks against US ships patrolling Surigao Strait. Shortly after 1000 hours, a formation of cruisers and battleships were refueling from a tanker when enemy aircraft were spotted and a Combat Air Patrol was requested for protection. Fourteen enemy aircraft attacked the formation in a brief battle that saw several attackers shot down while no ships were hit. At 1130 hours there were still no defending American fighters, but a second formation of ten enemy planes arrived overhead and broke into three attack groups of four, four, and two.

The next hour would see *St Louis* (CL-49) – the first ship to get under way during the attack on Pearl Harbor and a veteran of Coral Sea and Midway where she had escorted *Yorktown* (CV-5), as well as the desperate sea battles in the Solomons during 1943 – wage a desperate struggle to survive.

Ensign Doniphan B. "Don" Shelton, who had enlisted in the Navy in 1939 and won admission to Annapolis in 1941, had joined the ship in September while she was undergoing overhaul at Mare Island after graduation from the naval academy the previous June.

All ten of this second group attacked us and the action was fast and furious. The Lou was at Air Defense, not General Quarters, which meant that I was not in Number Two turret, my GQ station, but free to help wherever needed. The wardroom was the designated collecting place for wounded, so I went between there and the Quarterdeck area as needed.

At 1138 hours, a "Val" attacker hit *St Louis* in the stern aircraft hangar where airplane and bomb exploded on impact, with fire breaking out and killing or wounding all the crews on the nearby 20mm guns. Shelton helped carry eight of the wounded to the wardroom, which was set up as an emergency treatment station.

A minute later, a second attacking Val was set afire by the ship's AA defenses. As it continued its dive on the cruiser, her captain ordered flank speed and hard right rudder. With this change, the Val overflew the ship and crashed into the water 100 yards to starboard.

By 1146 hours, there was still no sign of defending fighters. Five minutes later, two more *kamikazes* that had been set aflame by the fleet's defensive fire dived on *St Louis*. Her gunners shot down the first off the port quarter, the second just above the waterline on the port side.

Shelton remembered:

The most damaging hit, one that knocked me flat on the deck, was the *kamikaze* that dove into the ship right at the waterline between the Number One and Two boiler rooms. A twenty-foot section of armor was blown off and the area flooded. The bulkheads were flexing, all of which meant that the ship would sink if those bulkheads failed and the boilers blew up. The ship went powerless, dead in the water, and eventually drifted about four miles away from the circle.

A minute after that hit, *St Louis* was listing badly to port with smoke rising from the fires. A fifth attacker closed the ship at 1210 hours but her gunners blew it out of the sky 400 yards behind the *St Louis*. Four B6N Jills attacked at 1220 hours, but the ship was able to avoid them when a PT boat warned of their approach.

Damage-control parties managed to alleviate flooding at the waterline by 1236 hours and bring the cruiser back on an even keel by counterflooding. The major fires were out by 1315 hours. Fifteen sailors were dead and one was missing, with 21 seriously wounded and 22 minor injuries. The next day, the seriously wounded were transferred to a hospital ship. *St Louis* arrived in San Pedro Bay on November 30, where temporary repairs were made. She arrived in San Francisco at the end of December.

The final effort to chase the Japanese from Ormoc Bay saw US forces land at San Pedro Bay 27 miles north of Ormoc City on December 5. Suicide attackers sank 15 landing craft and support vessels. On December 7, the third anniversary of the beginning of the Pacific War, the 77th Infantry Division made an unopposed landing three miles south of Ormoc City at Albuera.

Despite the presence of air cover over the bay in the form of 72 P-38s of the 475th and 49th fighter groups and 46 P-47s of the 348th Fighter Group, *kamikaze* attacks resulted in the sinking of the destroyer-transport *Ward* (APD-16), which as DD-139 had fired the first American shot of the Pacific War at Pearl Harbor the morning of the Japanese attack when she attacked and sank a midget submarine attempting to enter the harbor. Hit amidships and set afire, *Ward* was sunk by gunfire from *O'Brien* (DD-725), whose commanding officer, William W. Outerbridge, had commanded *Ward* at Pearl Harbor. *Mahan* (DD-364), a veteran of the early days in the Solomons, shot down four of her attackers but took three hits by others. With *Mahan* exploding and afire from bow to stern, Commander E. G. Campbell was forced to give the order to abandon ship. *Mahan* was then sunk by torpedoes fired by *Walke* (DD-723). While the Army Air Force flyers had shot down 64 enemy aircraft over the course of the day, the results had demonstrated that, even if there was only one left, the danger was still great.

On the night of December 11, the Japanese managed to land troops in Ormoc Bay for the last time. The convoy was found by American aircraft and attacked at dawn the next day, sinking destroyers *Juzuki* and *Uzuki* and damaging destroyer *Kiri*, which nonetheless managed to escape.

The American victory at Leyte was the result of US air superiority over Ormoc Bay. Historian Irwin J. Kappes wrote, "In the end, it was the rather amorphous Battle of Ormoc Bay that finally brought Leyte and the entire Gulf area under firm Allied control."

With the retirement of the Third Fleet, air power in the Philippines reached a dangerous low. The engineers at Tacloban had managed to expand the field and put down Marston matting on the runways that allowed better operation in bad weather, and more Army Air Forces squadrons had moved up to the Philippines.

Following the victory in the Solomons and at Rabaul, the Marine air forces at Bougainville in the northern Solomons had been given the assignment of keeping bypassed Rabaul knocked out after the evacuation of Japanese air forces from the base in February 1944. The Marine flyers were thoroughly unhappy with the demands of this backwater war, since the skies over these bypassed islands were filled with as much dangerous flak as one could have found at Rabaul at the height of the air campaign, and the loss of a squadron mate was not assuaged by the thought that his death had advanced the war effort.

Major General Ralph J. Mitchell, ComNavAirNorSols (Commander of Naval Aviation in the Northern Solomons) had sought other employment for his men since assuming his position at the beginning of the summer. He had visited MacArthur, Seventh Fleet Commander Admiral Kinkaid, and Fifth Air Force Commander General Kenney to pitch them on employing his air force in whatever operation was being planned. Kenney, who would soon be named commander of Far East Air Forces, told General Mitchell the Marines would be moved to the Philippines, "if it proved necessary." By the middle of November, that necessity was obvious.

The arrival of the P-61A "Black Widow" night fighters of the 421st Night-Fighter Squadron had not led to the defeat of the Japanese night hecklers over Leyte, since the big P-61s were the size of a B-25 Mitchell medium bomber and unable to take on the agile Japanese single-seaters. In mid-November, General MacArthur wrote to Admiral Nimitz with an offer to trade his P-61s for the Marine night-fighter squadron equipped with Hellcat night fighters that was based at Peleliu. Nimitz agreed and the swap was carried out at the end of the month.

Commissioned on February 15, 1944, VMF(N)-541 "Bat Eyes" was first of eight new Marine night-fighter squadrons commissioned at MCAS Cherry Point to participate in the Central Pacific offensive. Squadron commander Major Peter D. Lambrecht had received RAF night-fighter training. The new squadrons were first equipped with F6F-3Es. That July, VMF(N)-541 received the first F6F-5Ns. The squadron arrived on Peleliu on September 24, 1944 to discover that Japanese aerial opposition was non-existent. The Marines flew night patrols that were always negative. The only aerial success occurred when Major Norman Mitchell shot down an E13A Jake floatplane over Schonian Harbor on October 31.

Lambrecht, by now promoted to lieutenant colonel, led 12 Hellcats from Peleliu the 692 miles to Tacloban on December 3. They flew their first mission the night of December 4, providing cover to Navy PT boats in Surigao Strait. A second mission that night saw 2nd Lieutenant Rod Montgomery down an Oscar just before dawn on December 5.

A week later on December 12, Captain Dave Thomsen's three-plane "dawn patrol" covering an Ormoc-bound convoy was vectored onto five groups of bogies west of Leyte that turned out to be 33 enemy aircraft. 1st Lieutenant Fletcher Miller's four Hellcats arrived just as Thomsen's trio unit knocked down five on their first pass through the enemy. Miller's division shot down six in their initial pass. Thomsen scored a second victory for a total of 12 in a ten-minute battle that turned out to be the biggest fight the "Bat's Eyes" would engage in during their Philippine assignment.

VMF(N)-541 scored four more in a 35-minute running battle during the Mindoro landings a few weeks later. The "Bat's Eyes" were unusual for an American unit since they included two enlisted naval aviation pilots, T/Sgt John Andre and T/Sgt Frank Ratchford, of whom Andre scored two J2M-3 "Jack" fighters of the four shot down. The last victories were the two scored by 2nd Lieutenant Hayes on January 3, 1945, which brought the squadron's score to 22. Returning to Peleliu on January 11, 1945, the unit was awarded the Army Distinguished Unit Citation by General MacArthur for their efforts, making the "Bat's Eyes" the only Marine squadron ever to receive the Army award.

Hours after VMF(N)-541 arrived at Tacloban, the first of 66 F4U-1D Corsairs of Marine Air Group 12 touched down, having flown 1,957 miles from Emirau in the northern Solomons via Hollandia, New Guinea, and Peleliu with navigation guidance performed by the PBJ-1s (the Marine designation for the North American B-25 Mitchell bomber) of Marine Air Group 61. The Marines were almost all veterans who averaged ten months overseas on their current tour that had seen them bombing bypassed Japanese islands in the Marshall and Caroline Islands, with many on their second tour after serving in the Solomons previously. With the arrival a week later of Marine Air Group 24's two squadrons of SBD-6 Dauntless dive bombers, General Mitchell was about to show the Army what the term "close air support" really meant.

The battle for Leyte had demonstrated far more clearly than ever before in the Pacific War the coordinated striking power of American land, air, and naval forces. While the Japanese had anticipated an invasion of the Philippines, they had not known when or where the event would come, and were particularly unprepared on Leyte. The speed with which the invasion forces were unloaded and the drive inland despite the difficult weather led to surprise and confusion on the part of the Japanese leaders tasked with opposing MacArthur's forces. Despite heroic efforts and great courage, they had been unable to stand before the overwhelming power of American combined arms.

The decision to change the plan for the defense of the Philippines compromised the Japanese plan for the defense of Luzon and resulted in piecemeal efforts to reinforce Leyte without an overall defense plan. The cost of the reinforcement attempts was enormous in terms of ships sunk. Naval air power crippled the convoys, though 45,000 troops did manage to get ashore over the course of the month of November with 10,000 tons of supplies in the face of nearly complete American air superiority, though the bulk of their material and supplies was lost.

While these reinforcements did prolong the battle on Leyte to December 15, the losses were so great that General Yamashita's staff was eventually forced to admit that an effective defense of Luzon was now impossible. The decision to fight the decisive battle in the central Philippines had come too late for adequate planning and preparation.

The Americans learned other essential lessons in the battle for Leyte. While past operations had shown what could be accomplished with the protection and support of air power, Leyte demonstrated that the lack of aerial supremacy at a crucial point in the battle could threaten the success of an operation. Leyte had shown it was vital to establish local airbases as quickly as possible. This would be particularly the case if the enemy used the *kamikaze* tactic against a supporting fleet.

These facts were even more clearly demonstrated five months later at Okinawa and ultimately affected planning for the invasion of Japan.

Once the Japanese force on Leyte was defeated, the rest of the campaign became a question of organizing and deploying the American forces.

However, there would be another month of difficulty for the Third Fleet as they faced both a determined enemy and the power of the weather in the western Pacific.

The Leyte defeat brought American air forces within range of the South China Sea and placed them in position to sever the sea lanes that connected Japan with the needed resources of her southern Empire. Without access to the resources in the Netherlands East Indies and Malaya, Japanese hopes for successfully continuing the war were drastically reduced.

The Third Fleet returned to action in early December to provide support for the invasion of Mindoro. The fleet was reorganized from four task groups to three owing to damage inflicted by the *kamikaze* attacks in November, to maintain striking power.

John Thach's "Big Blue Blanket" strategy that had been approved in early November was finally ready for roll-out.

On December 14, 186 Japanese aircraft were launched from bases on Luzon, Negros and Panay to hit the Mindoro-bound convoys. Unfortunately, the Japanese assumption that the Americans were headed for Negros or Panay rather than Mindoro meant that most of the Japanese strike aircraft, including 50 *kamikazes*, missed the convoys. Instead, they ran into Task Force 38, fresh from Ulithi. The fleet's Hellcats splashed two-thirds of the attackers while the rest fled to smaller islands.

Lieutenant R. H. Anderson of *Ticonderoga's* VF-80 – known as "Vorse's Vipers" for their squadron commander – was among the Hellcat pilots who scored against these attackers. The squadron tangled with what they reported as a mixed formation of Zekes and Oscars; this was undoubtedly a misidentification since IJNAF and JAAF units never flew together. Anderson claimed five in a fast-paced five minutes to become the 28th and final Hellcat "ace in a day" in 1944. Squadron-mate Lieutenant Richard L. "Zeke" Cormier, who had finally managed to transfer from flying Avengers on Atlantic antisubmarine patrols, started an eight-victory run when he shot down four in the same fight, while his division leader Lieutenant Patrick D. Fleming also added four to an eventual score of 19. Cormier would later win fame as the second leader of the famed Blue Angels flight demonstration team when the unit returned from the Korean War.

December 14 saw the loss of Lieutenant Alex Vraciu, one of the top Navy aces, who had first entered combat a year earlier in VF-6 as wingman to Butch O'Hare. Vraciu had transferred to VF-16 aboard *Lexington* when *Intrepid* was torpedoed in February 1944, and had flown combat through the spring and through the Marianas Turkey Shoot. He had returned in November to join VF-20 aboard *Enterprise*. Attacking Bamban Airfield on Luzon, Vraciu was finally brought down not by a Japanese fighter pilot but by anonymous antiaircraft gunners. Baling out of F6F-5 BuNo 58831, he managed to evade capture and made contact with Filipino guerillas, with whom he operated for six weeks before returning to US forces. Navy policy was that pilots who had spent time behind enemy lines were not allowed to return to combat for fear of capture. Vraciu's year of outstanding combat finally came to an end as he returned to the United States to pass on his skills to younger pilots.

Vraciu's squadron-mate, Lt(jg) Douglas Baker, a 16-victory ace, was also lost over Luzon during the same mission after shooting down an Oscar and three Zekes in his final fight.

The Big Blue Blanket held sway over the southern Philippines until December 16, engaging the enemy in the air while simultaneously covering airfields to destroy the enemy before he could strike. The Task Force 38 pilots, joined by the newly arrived Marines on Leyte, and aircraft from the CVE Support Force covering Mindoro, claimed 60 enemy aircraft shot down and over 200 destroyed on their airfields, while Mindoro was successfully invaded on December 15 with light ground losses. However, *kamikazes* made attacks against the ships involved. One formation of 20 was reduced to ten by Army Air Force fighters, and shipboard antiaircraft fire knocked down four more, but LSTs 738 and 472 were hit and damaged so badly they were finally sunk by escorting destroyers.

Between October 25, 1944 and the end of the Navy's commitment of support for operations in the Philippines in December, 421 Japanese Navy and 400 Japanese Army aircraft were dispatched on special attacks, with the majority happening in November. The IJNAF fliers claimed 105 hits on ships, while the JAAF scored 154. While only 16 ships were sunk, including two escort carriers and three destroyers, the damage to the fleet carriers had a serious negative effect on shipboard morale as well as restricting the operation of the Navy's primary offensive weapon.

Unknown to the Navy at the time, the fleet had dodged what might have been a mortal blow by the Japanese suicide attackers. Earlier in the summer of 1944, Ensign Mitsuo Ohta of the 405th *Kokutai*, working with students of the University of Tokyo's Aeronautical Research Institute, created a design for a rocket-powered, human-guided flying bomb. When he submitted the design, the Imperial Navy concluded the concept showed merit; full development of the weapon was assigned to engineers of the Yokosuka Naval Air Technical Arsenal (*Dai-Ichi Kaigun Koku Gijitsusho*). The result was the MXY7. Powered by three rocket engines and guided by a human pilot, the MXY7 was essentially a rocket-powered 2,646-pound bomb with wings. 155 Ohka Model 11s were built at Yokosuka and another 600 were assembled at the Kasumigaura Naval Air Arsenal.

The operational concept was that the Ohka would be carried within range of its target by a G4M2 Betty bomber. Once released, the pilot would fire the rocket motors and the bomb would accelerate to 600mph, too fast for interception by defending fighters and too fast to be accurately tracked by antiaircraft guns on the ships. It was believed that one hit in the hull by the Ohka would sink any ship. When this was attempted at Okinawa, however, the distance to be flown from their operating base meant the Bettys were exposed to American defenders. The losses incurred on the few missions attempted resulted in the Ohka being called the Baka (fool) by the Americans. However, had these weapons been deployed in the Philippines, where the numerous Japanese-held airfields in the central archipelago would have meant the attackers could come from many locations and directions, the result might have been different with so much better an operating environment.

Pilots were trained as part of the *Jinrai Butai* (Thunder Gods Corps) and it was planned that they would deploy to Formosa and Luzon to oppose the expected American invasion. Halsey's attack against Formosa and Okinawa in October created such havoc, however, that it delayed air transport of the 55 bombs that had been produced up to that point. The Japanese decided that the bombs would be transported by sea. Their transport would be one of the most interesting and tragic ships in the history of the Imperial Navy.

Originally, there had been three super-battleships planned: *Musashi, Yamato* and *Shinano*.

Following the loss of four fleet carriers at Midway in June 1942, the half-completed *Shinano* was redesigned to become the largest aircraft carrier built, at an all-up weight of 71,189 tons, until *Forrestal* (CVA-59). The ship was finally launched in October 1944 and commissioned on November 19. Despite not being ready to put to sea, *Shinano* was ordered to sail from Yokosuka Naval Arsenal in Tokyo Bay to Kure Naval Base in the Inland Sea on November 29 to complete fitting out, since it was feared the ship would be bombed after American B-29 bombers flew over Yokosuka. She would also take aboard the first 50 Yokosuka MXY7 Ohka-11 bombs and transport them to Luzon once her fitting out was completed. The destroyers *Isokaze, Yukikaze* and *Hamakaze* had just returned from the Battle of Leyte Gulf and were in need of rest and repair, but they were assigned to cover *Shinano*. At 1800 hours on November 28, the task group set sail for the Inland Sea, with civilian construction workers still aboard the enormous carrier.

A little more than two hours later, at 2245 hours, the submarine *Archerfish* (SS-311) picked up the Japanese ships on her radar and commenced following on a parallel course. *Shinano* detected the submarine's radar, but the requirement that the ships were to zigzag cut her forward speed sufficiently that *Archerfish* was able to keep pace. At 2248 hours, lookouts spotted the submarine at the surface. Captain Toshio Abe ordered a course change to outrun *Archerfish* and increased speed to 25 knots. At 2322 hours, *Shinano* was forced to slow to 18 knots to allow the destroyers to maintain position in the heavy sea. At 0256 hours on November 29, Abe ordered a course change to the southwest that put the carrier on course directly at the submarine.

At 0258 hours, Commander Joseph Enright ordered *Archerfish* to dive. He fired four torpedoes at the huge carrier at 0304 hours. The first hit flooded refrigerated storage compartments and an empty aviation gasoline storage tank in the stern. The explosion killed most of the engineering personnel asleep in the compartment above. The outboard engine room was flooded when the second torpedo struck the starboard outboard propeller shaft at the point where it entered the hull. The No. 3 boiler room was flooded by the explosion of the third torpedo, and all those on watch were killed. The two adjacent boiler rooms were flooded as a result of structural failures from the explosion. The starboard air compressor room and adjacent antiaircraft gun magazines were flooded by the fourth hit, which also ruptured the adjacent oil tank.

Immediately following the torpedo hits, the reports Captain Abe received led him to believe the damage manageable and he ordered the ship to maintain maximum speed. This increased the flooding, causing the carrier to list 10 degrees to starboard within minutes. Three thousand tons of water were pumped into the port bilges to counter the list, but it soon increased to 13 degrees. Realizing *Shinano* was more damaged than he first thought, Abe ordered the ship to turn toward Shiono Point. The flooding was out of control and she listed 15 degrees at 0330 hours. At 0420 hours Abe ordered the empty port outboard fuel tanks flooded. This briefly reduced the list to 12 degrees. At 0500 hours the civilian workers were ordered to be transferred to the escorts. *Shinano* was moving at 10 knots with a 13-degree list at 0530 hours; this increased to 20 degrees at 0600 hours when the starboard boiler room flooded. The valves of the port trimming tanks were raised out of the water and with lack of steam the engines shut down around 0700 hours. In an unsuccessful attempt to reduce the list, Abe ordered the engineering compartments evacuated and the three outboard port boiler rooms flooded at 0800 hours. The two destroyers *Hamakaze* and *Isokaze* were ordered to tow the huge carrier, but combined they weighed only one-fourteenth of *Shinano*'s displacement and were unable to overcome her deadweight. The first cable snapped and a second attempt was aborted. *Shinano* lost all power at 0900 hours. The list passed 20 degrees and had reached 30 degrees at 1000 hours when Abe gave the order to abandon ship. As the crew dived overboard, *Shinano* heeled over. Her flight deck touched the water and seawater flowed into the open elevator well, which sucked many seamen back in as she sank.

At 1057 hours on November 29, *Shinano* capsized and sank stern first in 13,000 feet of water. Abe was lost, along with 1,435 officers, men and civilians. The 1,800 survivors were kept on the island of Mitsuko-jima until January 1945 to keep the loss a secret.

The 50 *Okhas* that might have made the Philippines battle even more desperate now rested on the seabed.

Efforts continued to produce the Ohka and get it to the Philippines. The carrier *Unryu* had been launched in the summer of 1944 but lack of fuel and aircraft left her unable to participate in the Battle of Leyte. In December, she was ordered to transport aircraft and supplies to Luzon, including 30 *Okhas* that were loaded aboard on December 13, 1944. At 0830 hours on December 17, *Unryu* departed Kure Naval Base on her maiden voyage, escorted by the destroyers *Shigure, Hinoki,* and *Momi* under the overall command of *Unryu*'s commander, Captain Kaname. The typhoon that created such problems for the Third Fleet also roiled the waters of the Formosa Sea, and the convoy settled in at a speed of 18 knots.

At 1600 hours on December 19, *Unryu*'s convoy was 200 nautical miles southwest of Shanghai when the ships turned due south and were soon picked up on radar by *Redfish* (SS-395), which was on her second war patrol. Eleven days earlier, *Redfish* and *Sea Devil* (SS-400) had torpedoed and heavily damaged the carrier *Junyo* as she headed toward Sasebo from the Philippines, which put the carrier out of action for the rest of the war. The submarine dived at 1624 hours.

At 1627 hours, Commander L. D. McGregor spotted the masts of the convoy. *Redfish* made a submerged attack and fired a spread of six torpedos shortly after 1630 hours as *Unryu* turned into a perfect position for attack. *Unryu's* lookouts spotted the torpedoes and Captain Kaname turned to comb their wakes. The first three passed ahead. At 1635 hours, the fourth torpedo hit *Unryu* under her bridge, hitting the Control Center below the bridge, forward of No. 1 boiler room. The control room, No. 1 boiler room, and forward generator room were flooded, while the bulkhead separating No. 1 from No. 2 boiler room on the port side was damaged. The second boiler room also flooded and ignited a fire in the forward crew space. Fire also started in the lower hangar deck where the *Okhas* were stored. Power died and the carrier slowed. *Redfish* fired her four stern tubes at destroyer *Hinoki* at 1640 hours, but the destroyer evaded them, leaving the submarine temporarily unarmed. McGregor kept her near the surface while his torpedomen sweated a reload. He fired the one they managed to load at *Unryu* at 1645 hours. At 1650 hours the torpedo struck the carrier below her forward elevator. At that moment, the fire in the lower deck hangar ignited the aviation fuel, which spread to the 30 *Okhas,* which began exploding. The exploding warheads tore the ship apart and her entire bow was wrapped in flame. *Hinoki's* commander, Captain Konishi gave the order to abandon ship at 1655 hours, but she sank two minutes later, carrying 1,241 officers and men with her. *Shigure* picked up 147 and returned to Sasebo Naval Base on December 22, 1944.

While *Shigure* and *Momi* were rescuing survivors, *Hinoki* came within an ace of sinking *Redfish,* depth-charging the submarine as McGregor finally took the submarine down. *Redfish* hit bottom at only 200 feet and endured a two-hour depth-charging. Just after sunset, McGregor surfaced and ran east at top speed. The submarine had been badly damaged and was forced to return early from patrol, after which she was sent to the United States for further repair.

At the end of 1944, 80 *Okhas,* which could have caused real havoc for the Third Fleet had they been deployed in the Philippines, lay at the bottom of the ocean in the twisted wrecks of the last two

Japanese aircraft carriers to be sunk in the Pacific War. The Navy would not meet the Thunder Gods until one destroyed *Mannert L. Abele* (DD-733) at Okinawa five months later.

CHAPTER FOUR

HALSEY'S TYPHOONS

Following the three days of strikes in support of the Mindoro invasion, Admiral Halsey ordered the Third Fleet to head east into the open Pacific. They were to rendezvous with the Ulithi fueling group to refuel and transfer aircraft from the five CVEs carrying replacements to the seven fleet carriers and six light carriers of Task Force 38. That day, the aerologists received warnings of a new typhoon, codenamed "Cobra." Seas became increasingly heavy as the typhoon approached, but Halsey wanted to finish fueling because many of the destroyers were nearly out of fuel. Because they were due to take on fuel, several of the "little boys" did not take on sea water to maintain stability, since it would only have to be pumped overboard again before they could receive the precious fuel oil.

Unfortunately, Commander George F. Kosco, Halsey's meteorologist, did not have sufficient information on the typhoon and its likely track. Kosco advised Halsey early on the morning of December 17 that the storm was well to the east and would turn north.

Halsey believed it would be possible for the fleet to remain together and finish fueling. In the increasingly heavy seas, fueling operations proceeded slowly as tow lines snapped and fueling hoses parted; several collisions were narrowly avoided. Halsey had promised General MacArthur that Third Fleet would return to combat with Philippines strikes on December 19, and was reluctant to halt fueling. However, sea conditions were such that by midday, with the ships of the fleet floundering in mountainous seas and gale-force winds, the admiral concluded that further attempts were only courting disaster and ordered operations stopped.

Unfortunately, meteorologist Kosco again misread the storm's projected course as being to the northwest and recommended the fleet steam southwest. Halsey gave the order at dusk for the ships to turn to the new location. Unfortunately, Kosco was wrong, with the result that the Third Fleet was steaming directly toward the heart of an intensifying typhoon.

In spite of the warning signs of worsening conditions as the night became even darker, the fleet remained in formation. With radio antennas broken off, and the weather inhibiting what radio communication was possible, ships remained in their stations, with captains unwilling to risk their career by violating the order to maintain formation, despite the danger to their ship.

By midnight, it was obvious the fleet could not reach the new rendezvous. Admiral Halsey ordered the fleet to turn northwest. As it turned out, this put the Third Fleet even more squarely into the typhoon's path. Over the rest of the night, the wild storm only increased in power.

Aboard *Monterey* (CVL-26), Lieutenant Gerald R. Ford, a 31-year old reservist and lawyer from Grand Rapids, Michigan, recently promoted to assistant navigator after serving as gunnery officer in charge of the fantail 40mm mounts, was in the wheelhouse as Officer of the Deck on the mid watch (0000–0400 hours) in the early hours of December 18 (Ford would later become the 38th President of the United States). During these hours, the wind built to over 60 knots, with gusts recorded at 100 knots with lashing rain. The sea became increasingly wild, with waves cresting at 40 to 70 feet before cascading over the bow and crashing into the wheelhouse as they washed on down the flight deck, such that at times it was impossible to see outside. In 18 months aboard *Monterey*, Ford had never seen such a storm. As breakers crashed overhead, the men in the wheelhouse could barely hear the sounds of distress through the howling gale – the deep blasts of battleships and cruisers, and the shrill whoops of destroyers. *Monterey* was a carrier built on a cruiser hull and thus top-heavy in her design. She rolled like a destroyer in the heavy sea.

Following his relief at 0400 hours, Ford made his way below to officer's country and strapped himself into his bunk. He had only pulled the blanket over him when the klaxon call of General Quarters reverberated through the ship. When he crawled out of his bunk, Ford thought he smelled smoke wafting through the passageways. His battle station was General Quarters Officer of the Deck. He raced through a rolling companionway dimly lit by red battle lanterns to reach the skipper's ladder outside that led to the wheelhouse, and began to climb. As he hung on the ladder and reached the flight deck, a 70-foot wave broke over the ship and *Monterey* violently rolled 25 degrees to port. Ford was knocked flat on his back and slammed across the flight deck. Moments from going overboard, he managed to slow his slide and twist to his side so he could fall onto the catwalk where he grabbed hold of a stanchion. He got to his knees and started back up the ladder. This time he made it.

While Ford fought for his life, aircraft chained down on the hangar deck broke loose when the ship rolled 30 degrees port, then 30 degrees starboard. They slammed against each other as they bounced off the bulkheads. The collisions ignited full gas tanks and soon the hangar deck was a sea of flame. Because of a quirk in the ship's design, the flames were sucked into the air intakes for the lower decks and fires broke out below the hangar deck.

By the time Ford arrived in the wheelhouse, *Monterey* was ablaze from stem to stern. Orders had been received from Admiral Halsey to abandon ship, but Captain Stuart Ingersoll was determined to save his ship if he could. Ford was ordered to go below and assess the situation. Owing to smoke having been sucked into the engineering compartments, *Monterey* had gone dead in the water and wallowed in the waves. Damage control parties slipped and fell while they desperately sprayed fire hoses to quell the blaze. Ford reported to Ingersoll when he returned to the wheelhouse that there was a fighting chance of saving the ship.

Below, sailors donned breathing masks and entered the burning hangar. Firehose teams slipped and fell, thrown from side to side and sliding across the deck as the carrier rolled in the wild sea. Their first priority was to find and carry out the injured and dead.

The fight was exhausting over the next several hours, but by dawn the fire was out and the men emerged from the dark hellhole. Three men had died in the flames and 40 were injured. *Monterey* would require long-term repair at the Bremerton Navy Yard, where she arrived the first week of January 1945. She returned to the combat zone at the end of March and participated in the Okinawa campaign.

Monterey wasn't the only carrier that barely escaped loss. *Cowpens* had her hangar door torn open. The main radar, a 20mm gun sponson, the whaleboat, and jeeps, tractors, and the crane were lost overboard, while eight aircraft were destroyed in the hangar deck and one sailor was lost at sea. *Langley* suffered damage to her gun sponsons, while several aircraft were damaged in the hangar deck. *Cabot* was damaged by the storm sufficiently to need a week of repair at Ulithi. Aboard *San Jacinto*, planes on the hangar deck were slammed around and destroyed air intakes, vent ducts and sprinkling system, which caused widespread flooding. All of these incidents were due to the top-heavy design of the light carriers.

The escort carriers operating with the Ulithi refueling group also suffered damage in the typhoon. *Anzio* (CVE-57) suffered damage that required major repair before she could rejoin the fleet in time for Iwo Jima. *Nehenta Bay* (CVE-74), which was assigned as an antisubmarine escort for the fleet oilers along with *Anzio*, was damaged by high waves that swept the ship. The CVEs assigned to carry replacement aircraft for Task Force 38 were also damaged. The hangar deck crane broke loose on *Altamaha* (CVE-18) and crashed into aircraft tied down there, causing a fire that was difficult to put out owing to the fact the crane also broke the fire mains. *Cape Esperance* (CVE-88) suffered a flight deck fire that required major repair at Pearl Harbor, while *Kwajalein* (CVE-98) lost steering control when the electrical system shorted out from water. There had been 146 aircraft aboard the CVLs and CVEs, which had been lost in the storm, a heavier loss than Task Force 38 had suffered at the hands of the Japanese in the Philippines campaign.

At 0500 hours on December 18, Halsey surrendered to the inevitable and all ships were ordered to make best speed to the south. By this point, the ships of the Third Fleet were spread across 2,500 square miles of ocean. Some ships were in better condition than others. *Hancock* recorded only scattered showers in the morning, while *Wasp* found mid-morning seas that were recorded as "mountainous." At one point, she passed so close to the eye of the storm that it painted on the surface search radar screen; an image taken of the screen was probably the first time any human had seen a typhoon's cyclonic heart.

While the carriers ran into trouble, it was nothing like what the "small boys" dealt with. With 100-knot winds, 70-foot seas and torrential rain, the little ships had great difficulty, especially since there were no orders given allowing them to maneuver as sea conditions warranted for safety. (This part of the struggle against the storm was dramatized in both the novel and the motion picture of "The Caine Mutiny," where the event that leads to the "mutiny" is Captain Queeg's refusal to alter course into the wind, as he blindly follows his last orders. Its author Herman Wouk actually experienced Typhoon Cobra and was writing from memory.)

For three destroyers the event became fatal. *Spence* (DD-517), a Fletcher-class destroyer that was a veteran of Commodore Arleigh A. "31-Knot" Burke's famed DesRon-31 "Little Beavers" destroyer division in the Solomons, had pumped the saltwater ballast from her tanks on December 17 in preparation for fueling. Unable to refuel when the hoses broke repeatedly, *Spence* was drastically unstable. At first light the morning of December 18, the gallant ship was wallowing in deep troughs when she took a 72-degree roll to port. All electrical power was lost because water shorted out the system. The ship was plunged into darkness, the pumps stopped and the rudder was jammed hard right. At approximately 1045 hours, *Spence* made another deep roll to starboard, continuing on 180 degrees as she sank. Twenty-four crewmen were able to get out of the wreck before it went down. African-American Steward David Moore managed to get to a raft where he saved two others, who together survived two days in the vicious seas.

Hull (DD-350) and *Monaghan* (DD-354) were older prewar Farragut-class destroyers that had been refitted with nearly 500 tons of additional topside weight in the form of additional antiaircraft batteries, radar, and other equipment, which made them top-heavy even in normal operating conditions. Acting as escorts for the fueling group, both ships had sufficient fuel to provide stability, but their dangerous top-heaviness proved their undoing. Their inexperienced captains continued to follow orders to maintain formation, even when this meant taking the sea broadside on. By mid-morning on December 18, both were eventually rolling so violently in the troughs and leaning so far over that seawater flooded down their stacks and disabled their engines. Without power, they lost all control and were unable to turn into the wind. At the mercy of the wind and sea, both capsized and sank, with *Hull* sinking at 1100 hours and *Monaghan* at 1130, when the last of her generators gave out and the ship lost power with her rudder jammed. One survivor recalled that *Monaghan* rolled violently seven times before she broached and was carried to the crest of a wave, where she fell over and was buried in the crashing waves.

The other two destroyers that were nearly empty of fuel and unstable were *Hickox* (DD-673) and *Maddox* (DD-731), which were however both able to pump seawater into their empty fuel tanks, giving them sufficient stability to ride out the storm with only minor damage. LCDR J. H. Wesson, commander of *Hickox*, saved his ship by disobeying orders to maintain course and heaving to in order to face the storm.

By mid-afternoon, the worst had passed and the wind and sea moderated. At dusk, some ships reported seeing the sunset, and by nightfall the winds had dropped below 60 knots. At 1848 hours, Admiral Halsey ordered all ships to post additional lookouts to spot any men washed overboard. At midnight, he received the first reports of loss when *Tabberer* (DE-418) reported she had rescued ten survivors from *Hull*, including the captain. Badly shaken by the news, Halsey ordered an all-out search. It was clear that he would not fulfill his promise of air strikes on December 19. The morning of that day dawned clear and placid in the Philippine Sea, but by December 21 the remnants of Typhoon Cobra had settled over northern Luzon and all flight operations in the Philippines were canceled. The Third Fleet took course for Ulithi and repairs.

Tabberer (DE-418) put in the most heroic performance of any ship during the typhoon. A small John C. Butler-class destroyer escort, she lost her main mast and radio antennas as well as sustaining other damage. Despite this, the little ship stayed on the scene and over the next three days recovered 55 of the 93 survivors of the other destroyers who were eventually rescued. *Tabberer*'s captain picked up men found in the sea by bringing the ship to a halt 50 yards upwind of the target and letting the waves and wind carry the ship to the floater. Twenty-eight *Hull* survivors were found on December 19, with survivors from *Spence* being found the next day when *Tabberer* joined up with *Swearer* (DE-186) and *Knapp* (DD-653). On December 21, *Brown* (DD-546) found the last 12 survivors of *Hull* and the six who were the only survivors of *Monaghan*. *Tabberer*'s captain, LCDR Henry Lee Plage, was awarded the Legion of Merit for his action, while the entire crew earned the new Naval Unit Commendation, which was personally presented to them by Admiral Halsey. A total of 93 survivors of the three ships were rescued, but over 800 sailors perished.

In addition to the loss of the three destroyers and the damage to the light and escort carriers, the battleship *Iowa* (BB-61) lost one of her OS2U-3 Kingfisher seaplanes and had a propeller shaft bent. The cruisers *Baltimore* (CA-68) and *Miami* (CL-89) required major repair. Destroyer *Dewey* (DD-349) lost her steering control and radar when salt water entered the forward stack and shorted out the main electrical switchboard. Destroyers *Aylwin* (DD-355), *Buchanan* (DD-484), *Dyson* (DD-572) and *Benham* (DD-397) and destroyer escorts *Donaldson* (DE-44) and *Melvin R. Nawman* DE-416) all required major repair.

Destroyer escort *Waterman* (DE-740), fleet oiler *Nantahala* (AO-60), fleet tug *Jicarilla* (ATF-104) and ammunition ship *Shasta* (AE-33) were damaged.

Reviewing the event, Admiral Chester Nimitz wrote that the typhoon's impact "represented a more crippling blow to the Third Fleet than it might be expected to suffer in anything less than a major action."

At Ulithi, a court of inquiry was convened on December 26, chaired by three admirals, in the wardroom of the destroyer repair ship *Cascade* (AD-16). LCDR James A. Marks of *Hull*, the only surviving captain of the ships lost, was the sole "defendant." His defense of his actions was that *Hull* had not been released from station until early on December 18 and that he was following orders. He was exonerated.

The most prominent witness was Admiral Halsey, who testified that solid evidence of a typhoon had not been confirmed until 0100 hours on December 18. His commitment to resuming strikes on Luzon "was uppermost in our minds until the last minute," which is why he had continued the attempt to refuel.

On January 3, 1945, the court returned a 200-page, single-spaced report with 157 "Findings, Opinions and Recommendations." The losses of *Hull* and *Monaghan* were attributed to their inexperienced captains, older designs and top-heavy retrofits. LCDR James Andrea, captain of *Spence*, was posthumously faulted for failure to ballast his tanks and for not removing topside weight. Commander Kosco was admonished for relying too much on remote weather reports rather than the situation at hand. Task Force 38 commander Vice Admiral John S. McCain, Sr., was admonished for turning his carrier groups directly into the typhoon's track. In judging the actions of a popular fleet commander, the court's words regarding Halsey were measured if not equivocal. The carefully parsed conclusion was that Halsey's "mistakes, errors and faults," were "of judgement under stress of war operations," rather than "offenses." On January 22, Admiral Nimitz approved the court's findings. Nimitz stated for the record that Halsey's mistakes and errors stemmed from "a commendable desire to meet military commitments," and no further official action was taken. Nimitz sent his commander what has been called an "exceedingly frank" personal letter that has never been declassified. Halsey's fighting qualities had been judged essential for the road ahead.

Typhoon Cobra resulted in additional weather reporting infrastructure being created in the Navy; this organization eventually was established as the Joint Typhoon Warning Center.

While the court of inquiry sat at Ulithi, another important event took place in the great anchorage.

The F4U Corsair had been the Navy's original choice for its fleet fighter with which it would fight the coming war when the first prototype took to the air in 1940. A major requirement had been performance that would equal a land-based fighter, combined with the strong (and heavy) airframe necessary for carrier operation. Indeed, on October 1, 1940 the Corsair became the first American fighter to exceed 400 miles per hour in level flight, a speed considerably in excess of anything then flying in the Army Air Corps, powered by the brand-new Pratt and Whitney R-2800 double row radial, the first aircraft engine capable of producing 2,000 horsepower. The first tests showed that the airplane would require considerable further development before it could enter production, however. An unfortunate crash of the first and only prototype imposed additional delays.

When the Navy finally received its first production F4U-1 on July 31, 1942 and commenced carrier operation tests, it soon became obvious that getting the fighter into service would be difficult. The heavily-framed "birdcage" style canopy and the low position of the pilot's seat provided inadequate visibility over the extended nose for deck taxiing and, more importantly, for landing aboard a carrier. The airplane had a nasty stall in landing configuration, with the right wing dropping without notice at the stall, a dangerous condition for bringing an airplane on board an aircraft carrier. More seriously, the Corsair had a bad tendency to "bounce" on touchdown, which could cause the arresting hook to miss the wire with the airplane then slamming into the crash barrier, or even going out of control from the bounce to end up striking airplanes spotted forward on the flight deck. The enormous torque of the R-2800 Double Wasp engine also created operational problems for wartime-trained pilots. Navy pilots assigned to the Corsair project spoke disparagingly of the F4U as the "hog", "old hosenose" or "the bent-wing widow-maker" and eventually the sobriquet "ensign eliminator." It was no mount for the timid.

Navy fighter squadron VF-12, the first squadron to take the Corsair into operational service in January 1943, found carrier compatibility to be so difficult that they rejected the airplane altogether. VF-17 took the Corsair aboard *Bunker Hill* in the summer of 1943 and with great effort "tamed the beast." The bounce was solved by decreasing the air pressure in the oleos so the gear was not so stiff, while the wing stall problem was fixed by attaching a triangular "stall warning" strip to the inboard leading edge of the right wing. Still, there was no solving the issue of the long nose and the visibility problem. By the time Air Group 17 and *Bunker Hill* arrived in Pearl Harbor at the end of September 1943, the decision had been made to remove the Corsair from the decks of Navy carriers and give it to the Marines.

In the hands of the Marines, the Corsair chewed through Japanese air opposition in the Solomons and over Rabaul to become the airplane that more than any other contributed to the ultimate Allied victory in the South Pacific.

Fortunately, the Navy was able to drop the Corsair because there was an alternative. When the first developmental delays became apparent, the Navy requested that Grumman come up with an "interim" fighter. This "interim" fighter became the F6F Hellcat, one of the most successful aircraft designs ever. Given the same engine as the Corsair, the Hellcat was not as fast, but its handling was so docile that an average graduate of Navy flight training had no trouble getting off and on the flight deck, while the Hellcat's maneuverability and heavy armament made it more than equal to its Zero opponent so long as the American pilot kept his speed above 200mph to negate the Zero's low-speed handling. The Hellcat went on from the fall of 1943 to become the only fighter aboard the Navy light fleet carriers and fleet carriers in the Pacific.

By 1944, the British Fleet Air Arm was successfully operating the Corsair from escort carriers, without the landing gear or stall-warning fix. The F4U-1A had gone a long way to solving the visibility problem by raising the pilot's seat. The F4U-1D that appeared in the spring of 1944 and was operational with Marine squadrons in the Central Pacific by the end of the summer was not only a world-class fighter, but a fighter-bomber that could carry a heavier load than the SB2C Helldiver, and carry it farther than the designed-for-the-purpose dive bomber could fly.

Three days before the end of the year, Marine fighter squadrons VMF-124 and VMF-213, with 54 pilots, four ground officers, and 120 enlisted men, reported aboard *Essex* to join Air Group 4 on December 28, where they became the first Marine fighter squadrons aboard a fleet carrier. VMF-124 was commanded by Lt Col William A. Millington, while Major David E. Marshall led VMF-213.

Millington had led VMF-124 for the previous 18 months and was a respected aviator and popular leader; as senior officer he was in charge of both squadrons. Each pilot had made 12 carrier landings on the light carrier *Bataan* (CVL-29) and *Macassar Straits* (CVE- 91) off the West Coast, and on *Saratoga* (CV-3) off Hawaii. Besides Millington, VMF-124 had only four combat veterans, while VMF-213 had three, which included Captain Gus Thomas, the squadron's leading ace from the Solomons. The 54 Marine aviators averaged 400 hours each in the Corsair. The Corsairs replaced the SB2C-4s of Bombing 4, which gave the air group 55 F6F-5 Hellcats, 36 F4U-1D Corsairs, and 15 TBM-3 Avengers.

Both squadrons were Solomons veterans. Formed on September 7, 1942 at Camp Kearney, north of San Diego, VMF-124 received the first F4U-1s sent to a Marine squadron the next month and left San Diego on January 8, 1943. Arriving at Guadalcanal on February 12, the squadron flew its first combat mission that afternoon.

VMF-124 remained in the Solomons until September 7, 1943, during which time the unit took part in the Russells, New Georgia, and Vella Lavella operations.

VMF-213 was commissioned on July 1, 1942 at Ewa, Hawaii. Equipped with F4F-4 Wildcats, the squadron left Hawaii on February 21, 1943. Arriving at Espiritu Santo in the New Hebrides on March 1, they were re-equipped with Corsairs on March 11. Once trained on the new fighter, VMF-213 relieved VMF-124 at the Russell Islands on June 17, 1943. There, they took part in the invasions of New Georgia and Bougainville before departing for return to the United States on December 9, 1943.

The two squadrons had both reorganized and trained in southern California until they were assigned for a second tour and departed San Diego September 18, 1944 aboard *Ticonderoga*. They arrived at Pearl Harbor on September 24 and the next month became the first Marine Corsair squadrons to undergo carrier training in preparation for joining the fleet.

Lt Col Millington later recalled that, "We were made to feel much at home aboard the *Essex*, from the admiral on down. Our officers and enlisted got along fine with our Navy shipmates and we became an integral part of Air Group 4." VMF-213's Captain Thomas remembered, "There was nothing like being out of the mud, bugs, pests and filth that we had in the Solomons. Carrier duty provided good food, clean bedding, showers, and all the conveniences."

Beginning with the new year of 1945, Admiral Halsey would release a man-made "typhoon" on Japan from Saigon to Okinawa.

Task Force 38 sortied from Ulithi on December 30, 1944, bound for Formosa and the Pescadores for a series of air strikes against targets on Formosa and Luzon to furnish support to the American landings at Lingayen Gulf on January 9. Task Force 38's mission was the disruption of enemy communication facilities and destruction of their supply lines by sustained air strikes against enemy aircraft, airfields, ground installations, naval forces and shipping, a task made more difficult by poor weather throughout the northern Philippines and Formosa during this time. While en route to Formosa, *Essex's* LSO, Lieutenant "Billy" Sunday, commenced further carrier training with the Marines immediately. Lt Col Donald S. "Hoppy" Hopkins, then a first lieutenant and Colonel Millington's wingman, remembered that, "Carrier operations were very different from land-based activity. The Navy F6Fs were routinely carrying 1000-pound bombs and that presented a challenge to the Marine Corsairs." Three accidents occurred on December 30–31. Hopkins explained:

> Despite the care exercised by the Air Department in allowing all safety margin possible, three accidents occurred in two days time, all undoubtedly due to the pilots lacking familiarity with the airplane in its higher loading condition with full ammunition and full belly tanks. The first loss was 2nd Lieutenant Thomas "Tom" Campion, Jr. who tried to smartly clear his takeoff slipstream by a hard right bank at slow speed. The Corsair was very unforgiving of that maneuver and he promptly spun in, landing on his back. Tom could not be seen after the plane entered the water. The next day, 2nd Lieutenant Barney W. Bennett took a wave off and attempted a left hand turn at slow speed. He spun to the left and also landed on his back. No sign of him after the plane struck the water. Both Campion and Bennett were VMF-124 pilots.

The third crash 15 minutes later involved a VMF-213 pilot who was recovered. After a week of operation, however, all pilots became more confident in handling the airplane aboard the ship.

Task Force 38 arrived off Formosa the evening of January 2 and *Essex* commenced her launch shortly before dawn the next morning. A cold front was moving slowly across Formosa during the morning and continued southeast past the task force the following night. This caused numerous squalls and heavy overcast conditions as the carriers launched strikes throughout the day, with pilots forced to climb through the cloud deck on instruments before they finally broke out in clear skies at 10,000 feet. West of the central mountains, the cloud deck thinned, with breaks appearing. The cloud ceiling over the targets averaged 4,500 feet, which prevented steep dive-bombing.

Lt Col Millington led the first carrier-based Marine fighter squadron into action when eight VMF-124 Corsairs escorted Torpedo 4 Avengers over airfields in south central Formosa. Once the Avengers had dropped their loads, the Corsairs then strafed Kagi Airfield and destroyed ten enemy aircraft on the field. Lt Col Millington drew first blood for the Marines when he spotted two Ki.45 "Nick" twin-engine fighters near the group's rendezvous point over the western mountains. Millington reefed around tight and pulled deflection on the nearest, which lurched under a rain of fire from his six 50-caliber machine guns and headed down toward the cloud-wrapped mountains, while the other made an escape. Filthy weather over Formosa kept most Japanese aircraft on the ground and, in addition to Millington's victory, only 29 other aircraft were reported shot down by Task Force 38 fighter pilots. The Marines also strafed a train they came across and other installations. 1st Lieutenant Robert W. "Moon" Mullins became lost in the bad weather and was last heard over the radio heading out to sea. No one observed what happened to him and he was reported missing in action.

VMF-124's Captain Edmond P. Hartsock led two divisions of Corsairs that escorted Avengers on bombing attacks against other airfields, with the Marines then going down for strafing runs. Southern Formosa was covered with a solid low overcast. Returning to the carrier, 1st Lieutenant Donald R. Anderson crashed at 1220 hours after trying to climb through the 5,000-foot overcast to get a navigational fix from a destroyer. The cause was not determined but was believed to be weather-related.

The Marines realized from these losses that they were still woefully unprepared for carrier operations, and that they lacked training in navigation and instrument flying. Two days later over northern Luzon, the wretched weather continued to exact a toll.

On January 6, Corsairs from both squadrons took part in strikes against Aparri and Camalaniugen airfields in northern Luzon. With segmentsegmentHALSEY'S TYPHOONS

the bad weather, there was no airborne opposition and the Marines strafed a beached freighter, a small cargo vessel, several warehouses and other targets. VMF-213's Captain Thomas led a TARCAP (target combat air patrol) over northern Luzon the next day in exceptionally bad weather. Thomas was the only one who managed to find Aparri Airfield and strafe it after the four Corsairs became separated. First Lieutenant Daniel K. Mortag, 1st Lieutenant Robert M. Dorsett, and 2nd Lieutenant Mike Kochut were listed as missing in action; they likely fell victims to the weather conditions. Second Lieutenant William H. Cloward was forced to bale out of his Corsair on return to the ship when his fuel gave out, while 2nd Lieutenant Robert D. Green ditched nearby.

Both were picked up by *Cotton* (DD-669) and returned to *Essex* in return for the standard fee of ten gallons of ice cream for each aviator.

During their first nine days of operations, the two squadrons had lost seven pilots and 13 Corsairs, none by enemy action. Their Hawaiian carrier qualifications had been flown in clear skies with reduced fuel and no ordnance, which was poor preparation for operating a fully loaded Corsair off a carrier in near-zero conditions. Colonel Millington recalled after the war:

Certainly we felt the Corsair was superior in performance to the F6F, and it really was a good carrier plane in all respects. Our operational losses were largely due to insufficient instrument flying experience and navigational experience under fleet conditions. Also, losses on carrier takeoffs and landings can only be charged to lack of sufficient experience under actual fleet conditions.

On January 5, *Enterprise* joined Task Force 38, having just returned from Pearl Harbor with Night Air Group 90 aboard as the first fleet carrier assigned solely to night operations. The new air group was led by Commander William I. Martin, who had successfully pioneered night air attack from *Enterprise*'s deck a year earlier during the first strike on the Japanese Naval Base at Truk with Torpedo 10. VF(N)-90

97

was led by LCDR R. J. McCullough with 30 F6F-5Ns and six F5F-5Es, while VT(N)-90 was led by Lieutenant Russell F. Kippen with 27 TBM-3D radar-equipped Avenger torpedo bombers, with the majority of the pilots having previously served with Commander Martin in Torpedo 10, where they had become skilled in flying off an aircraft carrier at night.

The day after *Enterprise* arrived, 16 Hellcats were launched in darkness for a predawn strike against Clark Field, where they encountered fierce flak. When the Hellcats returned to the ship at 0900 hours, air group members who had not seen combat were amazed to see one Hellcat with its entire left horizontal stabilizer and elevator shot away by flak. Despite the damage, squadron commander McCullough brought the Hellcat aboard on his third attempt. He missed all the arresting wires and barreled into the parked aircraft ahead, where he knocked one plane overboard and smashed the tail of another. McCullough managed to get out as his Hellcat burst into flames and went over the side himself, where he was picked up by a destroyer. The burning Hellcat was pushed overboard before the fire could spread. At dusk, a flight of Hellcats was launched to strafe airfields. Lieutenant Carl S. Nielsen shot down an Oscar, a Zeke, and a Dinah to open the squadron's score. The next day weather was so bad that flight operations were canceled, but a night heckler mission of four Avengers was launched. The flight found no enemy planes or ground defense, but did find visibility so bad it was unable to determine what damage it did when it attempted to bomb airfields.

Following the strikes in support of the invasion of Luzon, Task Force 38 returned to Formosa on January 9, but the weather was still bad with a sharp cold front over the island and it was difficult to fly effective strikes. VMF-124's Captain Howard J. Finn led a strike against airfields in south central Formosa. While the Marines encountered no airborne opposition, they destroyed 18–20 aircraft found on Kaputsua Airfield, with Finn setting afire a Ki.57 "Topsy" (a transport derivative of the Ki.21 "Sally" bomber) and hitting two additional Sally bombers. The Corsairs dropped 500lb bombs through the overcast over Tochien Harbor, which resulted in one large fire.

That night, Admiral Halsey aimed the Third Fleet south, directly toward the Southeast Asian mainland. The fleet transited Bashi Channel into the South China Sea. With better weather, the Marines concentrated on flight operations training, as the Third Fleet headed toward French Indochina for the first Allied strikes on the Southeast Asian mainland in the war in an operation codenamed "Operation *Gratitude*."

Over the next two days, Third Fleet crossed the center of the South China Sea, attempting to avoid detection by staying within edges of the weather system of a growing typhoon over Mindanao. A northbound Japanese convoy of 12 ships including tankers was spotted, but Halsey declined to attack it because he wanted to surprise the Japanese forces in French Indochina, where intelligence believed the hermaphrodite battleships *Ise* and *Hyuga*, which had survived the battle off Cape Engano, were at Cam Ranh Bay.

The fleet was 65 miles east of Cam Ranh Bay at dawn on January 12. However, reconnaissance flights reported very few ships present. Admiral J. J. Clark later wrote in his memoirs that the convoy was spared to no good end since the two ancient battleships, which were of no combat value, were not found at Cam Ranh Bay. It was Admiral Clark's belief that Halsey wanted to get the two ships to finish off bad feeling about "the battle of Bull's Run."

In place of the attack on the non-existent battleships, Task Force 38 struck Indochina on a 400-mile front from Cap St Jacques at the mouth of the Mekong Delta south of Saigon, north to Cam Ranh Bay, Qui Nhon, and Tourane (known to a later generation of Americans as Da Nang). Convoy HI-86 was spotted north of Qui Nhon, and the ten merchant ships plus six escorts were attacked by *Hancock*'s and *Hornet*'s air groups. Only three escorts were left afloat, while the rest of the convoy was sunk or beached and burning. The planes thoroughly hit all targets without worry of aerial opposition.

Essex's task group was northeast of Cap St Jacques at the southern end of Task Force 38 that morning when seven Corsairs from VMF-124 and five from VMF-213, led by Lt Col Millington, were launched in strikes against Saigon. The Corsairs met no air opposition, and strafed Bien Hoa and Long Tranh airfields, a destroyer escort found in the Mekong River, and other small craft.

At 1330 hours, *Essex* launched a strike to hit airfields, shipping, and shore installations in Saigon Harbor. Famed *Time* magazine war correspondent Robert Sherrod was aboard to cover the operation and decided to make the flight with Torpedo 4 in order to write a firsthand account. The aviators, who all respected Sherrod for his previous work in the Pacific, thought he was crazy to make the mission when interviews with returning flyers would have given him what he needed. Sherrod was checked out with a life jacket and parachute and put aboard the TBM-3 flown by the experienced Lieutenant B. R. Trexler.

The strike group consisted of 14 TBM-3 Avengers of VT-4, loaded with four 500lb bombs each, led by Squadron executive officer Lieutenant L. L. Hamrick, 12 F6F-5 Hellcats of VF-4 with VF-4's Lieutenant L. M. Boykin leading the first division and Lieutenant N. P. Byrd, Jr. and Lieutenant W. W. Taylor leading the other two four-plane divisions, and eight F4U-1Ds from VMF-213 led by VMF-213's Major James M. Johnson. The Hellcats were each loaded with 1,000lb bombs as fighter-bombers. *Essex*'s force was joined by Hellcats and Avengers from *San Jacinto*'s (CVL-30) Air Group 45. The formation was forced to remain at 1,000 feet owing to a low overcast. Five miles from the coast, they climbed through the clouds to break out at 14,000 feet. On the way in, many burning ships were spotted along the coast from Cam Ranh Bay to Cap St Jacques. Reaching the harbor area east and southeast of Saigon, a light cruiser was spotted on its side in shallow water, victim of a previous attack.

The Hellcats dropped their thousand-pounders on a large cargo ship that was already afire. Lieutenant Taylor scored a direct hit, with several other damaging near-misses, and one pilot bombed a tanker nearby. Byrd's division also strafed oil storage tanks, setting two afire.

The Marines hit airfields around Saigon where they found many aircraft on the ground and destroyed ten, probably destroyed another ten and damaged ten more. Flak over one of the airfields hit the engine of the Corsair flown by 2nd Lieutenant Joseph O. Lynch, who was forced to make a wheels-up landing in a rice paddy three miles west of Trang-Bang. He was seen to leave the plane, and F6F-5s from Fighting-4 strafed the F4U-1D. Fortunately, Lynch was able to make contact with the Free French resistance and evade capture by the Japanese or the collaborationist Vichy French, who were still running the country.

Approaching Saigon from east-northeast at 8,500 feet, the Avengers pushed over into glides of 40–55 degrees at 290 knots. Leading the attack, Lieutenant Hamrick spotted an oil storage concentration across the Mekong and pulled off his attack on the ships, instead turning and releasing his bombs on the storage tanks from 1,000 feet. The explosion when the tanks were hit rose higher than his altitude. Hamrick later reported, "When I dropped my wing to go into the dive, I was past my target. I spotted a dozen oil storage tanks up to the north of us so I circled and dropped my four 500-pounders on them. What an explosion!"

Ensign Hewett and Ensign Bissell chose a cargo ship 200 yards up Arroyo L'Avalanche from the river as their target. The ship was hit amidships by one of Hewett's bombs, followed closely by one of Bissell's bombs. A ship tied up to a pier at the Saigon Navy Yard was attacked by Lt(jg) Ward and Ensign Landre, who also set fire to several buildings. Ensign Bell's bombs straddled a ship that was under way and heading downstream, while Ensign Hopkins scored two hits on a second ship under way and Lt(jg) Souza hit a third directly amidships with one 500lb bomb.

Lieutenant Trexler, with Robert Sherrod in the turret, led Ensigns Cole and Gray to attack a ship heading upstream and hit its stern, while his wingmen missed.

Lt(jg) Don Henry's bombs hung up and he requested permission to go back for a second strike. Advised not to do so, he turned away from the formation on his own and was never seen again. After the war, Robert Sherrod took an interest in Henry's fate and investigated the incident. He concluded that Henry had been shot down and joined up with six members of a PBM Mariner crew who had made a crash landing at Quong Ngai on January 26, 1945.

Somehow they found their way to the primitive Hmong village of Pletonang, in the mountains north of Saigon. There on the morning of March 12, 1945, two months to the day after Henry was shot down, they met their fate at the hands of a cruel and remorseless enemy. After accepting their surrender, the Japanese commander ordered them to kneel, tied their wrists together, shot them in turn, then kicked each backward into a shallow grave.

Hellcats flew 1,065 of Task Force 38's 1,457 combat sorties on January 12, almost three-quarters of the total sorties. Fighting 3, which had scored only eight victories since arriving in the western Pacific aboard *Yorktown* in October, scored 11 victories over Saigon, with Lieutenant John L. Schell scoring a Ki.61 Tony and an A6M3 Hamp over Tan Son Nhut Airfield.

While 14 enemy aircraft were shot down in total, 12 Hellcats succumbed to flak while strafing targets. Lt(jg) Blake Moranville, a six-victory ace from VF-11, was hit in his engine over Tan Son Nhut Airfield and belly-landed in a rice paddy. Captured quickly by the Vichy French, he became one of only two Navy aces captured by the enemy during the Pacific War. In early June 1945, after several months' captivity, he and four other pilots were taken to Hanoi just before fighting broke out between the French and Japanese forces. Moranville marched to Dien Bien Phu with a unit of the French Foreign Legion, then was flown to Kunming, China, from where he safely returned home at the end of the war.

Task Force 38 lost 16 aircraft in the Saigon attacks, with two of these coming from *Essex's* air group, for a score of 41 ships sunk throughout the region, with 31 others damaged, and 112 enemy aircraft destroyed on the ground. Operation *Gratitude* drastically reduced the ability of the Japanese to transport essentials to the Home Islands from the southern Empire. This "pinch" would be felt in Japan until 1946. Robert Sherrod's report summed up the result: "By any accounting, January 12, 1945 must be regarded as one of the great days of the US Navy."

Third Fleet turned northeast the next day, ahead of the approaching typhoon, which was now moving west across the South China Sea.

On January 14, the destroyers took on fuel from the carriers and the fleet approached Formosa from the south. The island was struck the following day. While the destruction of shipping and shore installations in and around Takao Harbor (now Kaohsiung) was not as dramatic as that achieved in Indochina, it was decisive nevertheless.

Despite bad weather, *Essex* launched Air Group 4 on a mission to hit Takao Harbor on January 15. Twelve VT-4 Avengers escorted by nine VF-4 Hellcats were led by Air Group 4's CAG, Commander George Otto Klinsmann. Flying through difficult weather, they reached Takao to find it closed in by clouds. Klinsmann then led the strike to the Pescadores Islands. When they arrived at Mako-Ko Harbor, they spotted a destroyer under way in the harbor, a destroyer escort at anchor, as well as four cargo ships and a tanker. Klinsmann assigned targets by divisions. Antiaircraft fire from shore installations and the ships was "most intense."

After assigning targets, Klinsmann led his Hellcats in a rocket and strafing attack, while sending Lieutenant Blackwell's division against ground installations at the naval base. Blackwell later reported:

Commander Klinsmann picked the destroyer as a target for his division, scoring two rocket hits himself just aft of amidships from reports of others on the flight. Lieutenant White fired his rockets at the largest of the cargo ships. Lieutenant White saw his rockets hit about 50 feet to port of the vessel. Ensign Hinricks aimed his thousand-pounder at another cargo ship but missed. A small harbor craft was strafed vigorously by a single VF without obvious effect.

The after-action report for Torpedo 4 recorded:

The low cloud cover compelled VT pilots to employ very shallow glides, greatly reducing the accuracy of the drops. Lieutenant Hamrick scored with a hit directly amidships on the tanker. Ensign Gardner placed one bomb on the stern of the same ship. Lt(jg) Ruth hit a cargo ship amidships with a 500 pounder. There were many near misses, none of which appeared to be damaging, on all four of the ships attacked. The destroyer appeared to be burning on departure, probably as a result of VF attack.

Blackwell's report continued:

> Immediately after this attack, Commander Klinsmann's plane was seen covered with oil from an AA hit probably in the oil line. This necessitated immediate return to the ship without further observing results. Lieutenant Blackwell's division, which had been attacking shore installations at Mako, was ordered to escort the TBMs. Commander Klinsmann's division, plus Ensign Olson, started back toward base. Because of the clouds the flight soon lost sight of land. Lieutenant White, Lt(jg) Maikowski, and Ensign Olson broke off from the others and flew toward Formosa to check their position against known land.

Rather than risk flying an additional 50 miles to the ship through bad weather, Klinsmann decided to ditch near two US picket destroyers. The combat report concludes:

> His wingman, at his request, went over the forced landing check off procedure and got a 'thumbs up' on each item. Both DDs [destroyers] were informed of the impending water landing and were standing by to effect the rescue. Klinsmann made a perfect water landing and was observed to abandon and clear his plane before it sank. Lt(jg) Martin, the group commander's wingman, had experienced engine trouble on the return flight and as the two DDs had the Commander in sight, and in view of the Commander's apparent good condition and position for a quick rescue by either of the DDs, the wingman departed for base upon receiving a wave of one hand from him indicating that the Commander was able to take care of himself from then on. One of the DDs reported having Commander Klinsmann in sight, successfully throwing him a life line with a life buoy ring attached, and as he was pulled alongside and about to be hoisted aboard he lost his grasp on the ring, floated clear of the bow

and sank before the DD could position itself again. The DD reported that neither Commander Klinsmann's life jacket nor life raft were inflated.

Klinsmann hadn't bothered to inflate the rubber raft, which wasn't easy to release and inflate, while inflating his Mae West too soon could be cumbersome. The most likely reason he sank as he did was that he carried extra gear. Yeoman Don Alexander stated: "I'm not talking about one or two pounds! He had a couple of extra boxes of shells in his flight-suit pockets, and extra survival equipment. If he went down over land he wanted to be able to survive. This extra weight certainly would inhibit his ability to stay afloat."

Klinsmann's loss sent great sadness through the rest of Air Group 4. Blackwell wrote:

Otto had been with us since the early days on the *Ranger*. He was a good pilot; respected by the dive bombers because he first led their 'Top Hat' squadron; supported by VT-4 because he knew how to bomb; and acknowledged by his fellow fighters in VF-4 because he readily adapted to the Hellcats and never hesitated to lead his group into the most intense action.

John Selka, Klinsmann's plane captain, stated, "He was a wonderful man, a great leader; a gentleman. He treated everyone, including enlisted men, like his own family." Don Anderson added:

I share the same feelings about George Otto Klinsmann. He was always thinking of his people, his pilots, his crewmen. I was his chief yeoman, and he was like a father figure to me. After the debriefing reports were checked by the ACI officers, I had the job of typing them and turning them over to Cdr Klinsmann. I was so busy typing reports for Otto that I rarely got ashore for R&R.

As the senior aviator in Air Group 4, Lt Col Millington assumed the position of acting commander of the air group to replace Klinsmann.

This was the only time a Marine aviator ever commanded a US Navy air group. Millington's work would be cut out for him because Halsey was still out to strike the Japanese. Third Fleet headed west that night and on January 16 launched strikes against the British colony at Hong Kong, which the Japanese had occupied since December 1941, the port of Canton, and targets on the southern Chinese island of Hainan. VF(N)-541, the Hellcat night-fighter squadron of Night Carrier Air Group 41, which had operated aboard *Independence* as the only night strike unit of the fleet since the previous July, closed their account with the Japanese when former SBD pilot Lieutenant William E. Henry shot down an Oscar for his tenth and the squadron's 46th confirmed victory.

While VF(N)-41 scored a success, VF(N)-90 experienced their worst day of the war to date. Two four-plane patrols were sent to strike the Hong Kong and Canton area at dusk. Returning at around 2100 hours, the first three landed aboard safely. The fourth Hellcat crashed the barrier and went over onto his back. Proving the strength of Grumman's fighter, the pilot was unharmed and crawled out of the wreckage on his own. The next, flown by Ensign Edwin G. Nash, flew into the water astern of the ship and exploded on contact with the water. The sixth Hellcat also hit the barrier, while the seventh made a wheels-up landing. Lt(jg) Robert F. Wright failed to return. The squadron's logbook recorded, "It was one of those frightfully unlucky days that makes a person stop and wonder if this aviation business is entirely practical after all and especially at night."

The daylight strikes inflicted extensive destruction on docks, refineries and the naval station at Hong Kong, while huge oil fires were started at Canton. Aerial opposition was negligible because of the bad weather, but VMF-124's Captain William J. Bedford managed to run into trouble on a fighter sweep over southern Hainan Island through very bad weather conditions. The flight strafed three ships and set one on fire, after which it was intercepted by nine Zekes. In the fight that ensued, 1st Lieutenant George R. Strimbeck's wingman 2nd Lieutenant John H. Westvedt slid out to starboard so they could start a "Thach weave," but Strimbeck turned away in a tight 180-degree turn that gave the Zeke a perfect no-deflection shot. Strimbeck, who had not jettisoned his belly tank and was still carrying two 250lb bombs, was hit in the belly tank and immediately burst into flames. He was seen to parachute from the burning fighter.

Over the course of the strikes on Formosa and the Chinese coast, 14 ships had been sunk and 40 more Japanese aircraft destroyed on the ground.

The next day, the fleet turned east and ran ahead of the approaching typhoon's storm. Three days were spent evading the typhoon's rising waves until on January 19 they were able to refuel successfully out of the typhoon's path in the lee of Luzon. During this time, *Essex* sent both Hellcats and Corsairs as Combat Air Patrol to deal with the bogeys that now showed up on the fleet's radar screens. Brown and Byrd from VF-4 each shot down a G3M2 Nell bomber, while the Marines were victorious over eight twin-engine bombers and scored one probable. First Lieutenant William G. McGill was credited with three victories, while 2nd Lieutenant Powhatan M. Kehoe, 1st Lieutenant George W. Stallings, Captain William J. Bedford, and 1st Lieutenant James L. Knight were credited with a Nell each and Captain Robert W. Kersey shot down a JAAF Ki.49 Helen.

Third Fleet passed through Bashi Channel back into the Formosa Sea during the evening of January 20. With better weather, Halsey struck Formosa again the next day, during which *Essex*'s Marines flew three TARCAP patrols over south central Formosa. Six F4Us led by acting CAG Lt Col Millington bombed Kobi Airfield, a railroad roundhouse and factory near Shimie, then strafed a nearby chemical factory, which they set on fire. Second Lieutenant John T. Molan was hit by defending fire and managed to get back to the task force, where he made a forced landing near *Essex* and was picked up by *Caperton* (DD-650). VMF-213's Captain Thomas led a six-plane sweep that strafed 15 planes on Tsuina Airfield and destroyed all of them. Returning to the carrier, they found the task group under enemy attack and two were forced to land on another carrier on account of low fuel. Maj William M. Crowe led eight Corsairs over the same area and attacked 16 aircraft at Tsuina, burning two.

Lieutenant Charles M. Craig, acting commander of VF-22 aboard *Cowpens*, became the first Navy "ace in a day" of 1945 when he led his division into a formation of *kamikaze* attackers off Formosa headed for the fleet and flamed five Ki.44 Tojos. The *kamikazes* made several determined missions against Task Force 38 this day.

VF(N)-41's Lieutenant Henry recalled the difficulty of fighting at night and then being a daytime spectator during daylight *kamikaze* raids when the fleet struck Formosa.

A few days out of the China Sea, the day fighters were hitting Formosa and we did CAP or standby all night until the second day, then suicide planes came out by the dozens and it was decided to put up some of us VFN to help.

I was sitting in my plane, turning up, parked in the landing area when I saw everyone get off the flight deck. I soon saw why. A Judy was heading for us from the port quarter. All I could do was sit and look. As he flew over the battleship next to us, they got him and he rolled over and crashed in our wake. They decided not to launch me.

Later that afternoon, they decided to try to put some of us up again. This time I was in the plane on the port catapult. Here came a Zeke heading for us. He had trouble pushing over to hit us, and was going to overshoot, so he flattened out and flew into the side of a CVL right next to us, *Langley*. He burst into flames but most of the plane fell into the water and the fire went out. About 30 minutes later I saw a CV on fire off our starboard bow.

The carrier was *Ticonderoga* (CV-14), which suffered 143 killed and 202 wounded.

That night, Halsey turned northeast and advanced toward Okinawa. *Enterprise* launched six TBMs led by CAG Martin and squadron commander Kippen to hit targets on the west coast of Formosa and the port of Kiaohsiung in order to deceive the enemy that the fleet had sailed north. Kippen led Lt(jg) Chester G. Koop and Ensign John P. Wood with their Avengers armed with two 500lb bombs and eight rockets each. Kippen was to attack as soon as they reached Kiaohsiung, while Martin first searched the west coast for shipping then attacked afterwards. Over Kiaohsiung, many searchlights came on, so Martin flew over the harbor as a searchlight decoy to cover the attack. Kippen radioed he was starting his attack, but that was the last ever heard from him. His target was a cargo vessel tied alongside a dock, which exploded and started fires ashore that spread quickly. Commander Martin recalled, "A few minutes later an explosion was seen near the mouth of the harbor which is believed to be Kippen's plane when it hit the water."

Martin ordered individual attacks while the Avengers circled north of the port. Lt(jg) Koop set a small-arms factory on fire, causing many other explosions. Wood set a dock afire. Immediately after, explosions were seen over the harbor and two fireballs fell into the water. All of the first division was now gone. Martin ordered Lt(jg) Jennings to attack. As he entered his dive, searchlights converged on him. As he pulled out, the lights went off as explosions erupted.

Martin and Ensign Crowley then made their attacks, setting afire wharves, dock installations, and warehouses. The three surviving Avengers departed just before dawn and returned to *Enterprise* safely. The loss of Lieutenant Kippen, one of the Torpedo 10 originals, was felt throughout the squadron so strongly that Commander Martin declared a "medical emergency." Flight surgeon LCDR Edwing G. Hurlburt passed out 2oz bottles of "medicinal brandy" to the fliers.

On February 22, Lt Col Millington led a 15-plane strike against the airfield on Ie Shima Island just northwest of Okinawa with no observed results. Again, there was no aerial opposition. On Luzon, the army noted a lack of Japanese air operations. Halsey's strikes had had their desired effect. He reported the results of the operation to Nimitz: "a 3,757-mile cruise in the South China Sea with the first carrier attacks on the China and Indo-China coast, cutting through the last sea route to Japan's southern empire."

The fleet fueled again on February 23 and set course southeast for Ulithi Atoll for much-needed rest after a strenuous month of continuous operations. During the voyage, Lt Col Millington wrote an analysis of the air group's actions since December 30. He particularly commented on the high number of operational losses for the Marines and their Corsairs and made specific recommendations to reduce these losses in the form of additional and more realistic carrier qualification training before squadrons were sent on to the fleet. He mentioned the serious weather problems and recommended increased emphasis in stateside training on instrument flying and navigation. He recommended refinements in the positioning and communications system used by the picket destroyers and suggested increased combat air patrols over the pickets to minimize ship losses to *kamikazes*. Millington also suggested that predawn launches be discontinued because of poor visibility, and also the discontinuance of mixed flights with different types of planes which had varying speed differentials: "the attendant risks and pilot strain is not compensated for."

The night of January 25, 1945, VT(N)-90's Lt(jg) Robert B. Hadley recorded in his diary:

> We've gotten back to those southern latitudes where one encounters the National Geographic beauties of tropical seas. We went out on the gun gallery just before turning in tonight and found a perfectly glorious night – one of those magic scenes with a moon so big and bright that it seemed like it was sitting on the yard arm of the ship in the next station. Fleecy clouds, made silver by moon light, puffed across the sky and the somber deathly blackness of the ship's island superstructure swayed gently across that billowy background. Fifty feet below, the inky water swept past and seemed to go down, down into an eternity of time and contemplation. The blackness of the water was broken by the white, fluorescent wash from the bow or the crest of a breaking wave. A scene of complete peace and security, despite the harsh note of grim reality supplied by the nearby mass of the 5-inch gun mount and the barrel projecting out toward the moon.

On January 26 Third Fleet entered Ulithi anchorage. Halsey and McCain left for shore leave and planning duty and Admiral Raymond

Spruance resumed command of the Fifth Fleet, while Admiral Marc Mitscher resumed command of Task Force 58.

Halsey's command had been mired in controversy over his abandonment of the amphibious force in Leyte Gulf to be present aboard his flagship and witness the destruction of the Japanese carrier fleet, and then with the near-disaster of Typhoon Cobra. However, he had redeemed himself over the last month with his brilliant display of carrier striking power across Southeast Asia, China, and the Western Pacific, which resulted in Japan being cut off from the crucial raw materials in the Southern Empire so necessary to continue the war.

Night Air Group 41 and *Independence* departed Ulithi to return to the United States, leaving *Enterprise* and Air Group 90 to make the fleet's presence known in the darkness.

During their tour of duty aboard *Essex*, the first Marine fighter squadrons to go aboard a fleet carrier had proven the Marines could meet the challenge. VMF-124 and VMF-213 were credited with ten Japanese aircraft shot down, 16 destroyed on the ground, and at least 11 ships damaged by bombs or rocket fire.

On February 10, 1945, Lt Col William Millington was relieved as commander of Air Group 4 by Commander Fred K. Upham, restoring Navy control to the air group. Later that day, *Essex* and the rest of the Fifth Fleet raised anchor at Ulithi and headed north-northwest. Their target was Tokyo. This would be the first carrier-based attack on the Japanese Home Islands since the Doolittle Raid of April 18, 1942.

Before the Fifth Fleet departed on this mission, a major change came in the operation of the now-huge fighter squadrons aboard the fleet carriers. A squadron of 73 aircraft and 110 pilots was now seen as administratively unmanageable. Commander Naval Air Forces Pacific ordered that these squadrons be broken into two 36-plane units, a fighter (VF) and a fighter-bomber (VBF) squadron. The existing squadron commanders retained command of the fighter squadron, while the executive officer formed the fighter-bomber squadron. Maintenance remained as before and both squadrons flew the same aircraft. In following months, some carriers would operate VF squadrons of F6F Hellcats and VBF squadrons of F4U Corsairs.

CHAPTER FIVE

THE FORGOTTEN FLEET

While Admiral Halsey and the Third Fleet turned away from Okinawa and set course to Ulithi on January 23 at the end of their epic mission, another fleet was headed east across the Bay of Bengal. This fleet, the Royal Navy's Far Eastern Fleet, had departed Trincomalee, Ceylon, on January 16, destination Sydney, Australia, where it would become the British Pacific Fleet and join in operations with the US Navy for the final battles of the Pacific War. The fleet with its four carriers was now 100 miles off the coast of the island of Sumatra in the Netherlands East Indies. The previous two days had been too stormy to launch the planned strike against the Pladjoe oil refineries in southern Sumatra, but this morning the sky had cleared sufficiently to allow operations.

Operation *Meridian One* was important to the Royal Navy, as it marked the beginning of British naval operations in the Pacific Theater. After *Kido Butai*, the fast carrier striking force of the Imperial Japanese Navy, had struck the Royal Navy base at Trincomalee in March and April 1942, and also sank HMS *Hermes*, the Royal Navy had been all but completely driven from the Indian Ocean. Two months earlier, the British had been forced to retreat from Singapore, their main Asian base, and continued moving west after the loss of the Andaman Islands off Malaya. By the end of April, the main surviving units of the fleet were based at Addu Atoll in the Maldives. Admiral Nagumo's successful strikes at Trincomalee, coupled with the Japanese advance on India through Burma, created a strategic situation in South Asia so dire that Prime Minister Churchill feared a successful invasion of Ceylon would allow the Japanese to link up with the German Afrika Korps then stormed through the Libyan desert in North Africa in a drive that made it appear possible the British Eighth Army would be defeated in Egypt, allowing a German advance into the Middle East.

The British forces had also been hampered by the fact that the primary area of operation for the Royal Navy was the Mediterranean and the North Atlantic; the Eastern Fleet became little more than a convoy escort force. With the Allied capture of Sicily, the primary Axis threat to the Mediterranean sea lanes was removed, which allowed the Royal Navy to begin planning a more forceful return to the Indian Ocean.

By 1944, American forces were liberating British territories in the Central Pacific and extending US influence throughout the region. This strategic situation created a political and military imperative that British presence be restored in the region and British naval forces participate more directly in the war against Japan. While many in His Majesty's Government believed British territories, such as Hong Kong, should be liberated by British forces, their position was opposed by Prime Minister Churchill on the grounds he did not wish to be seen as a visibly junior partner in what had become a primarily American war.

The prime minister's experience with the Anglophobic US Chief of Naval Operations, Admiral Ernest King, led him to believe a British presence in the Pacific would be unwelcome and that Commonwealth military force should concentrate on pushing the Japanese out of Burma and Malaya. Churchill's position was opposed by the leadership of the Royal Navy, who were supported by the Chiefs of Staff, who held the position that such a commitment to the Pacific War would strengthen British influence in the postwar period. So strongly did they hold this position that they would have considered mass resignation were it not adopted as government policy.

The British were right to be concerned. President Franklin Roosevelt was not favorable to continued European control of their Asian empires, and was of the opinion that the British, French and Dutch should be prevented from reclaiming their lost territories, with those countries placed under an American-led trusteeship through the planned United Nations while they were readied for independence. Only his death prevented this from happening.

While Admiral King was a notorious Anglophobe, he had in fact been favorably impressed by the performance of HMS *Victorious* during her tour with the US Navy in the South Pacific in 1943. In the dark days after the loss of *Hornet* at Santa Cruz in October 1942, when the US Navy had only *Enterprise* and *Saratoga* as the survivors of the prewar carrier fleet, King had gone hat in hand to the Admiralty and requested a British aircraft carrier as temporary reinforcement pending the arrival of the new-construction Essex-class carriers. *Victorious*, known by her code name "Robin," crossed the Atlantic in December 1942 and joined *Saratoga* at Noumea in March 1943 after being modified with American equipment. The two carriers operated in the Solomons between April and June, providing air support for the invasion of New Georgia. Each side had learned important lessons from the other. The Americans adopted much of the British system of fighter direction for air defense, which would be crucial in the coming Central Pacific campaign, while the British learned much about modern carrier air operations with their emphasis on the speed of the "operation cycle," knowledge that was put to use in the next year to create a British Pacific Fleet whose carriers would be capable of operating successfully in the final battles of the Pacific War.

Even considering the success of *Victorious'* South Pacific deployment, Admiral King was extremely reluctant to see the Royal Navy participate in what he considered "his" war, believing the British would require US support for their operation that he felt would be better employed in support of the fast carrier task force. When it appeared the British would proceed with their planned deployment, he insisted the proposed British Pacific Fleet be self-sufficient. King's objections were finally overruled by President Roosevelt at a meeting in which the BPF was formally offered and accepted by the president. As a sop to his naval commander, FDR agreed that the British fleet should depend on British resources, though they were provided with an advanced base at Manus Atoll in the Admiralty Islands between New Guinea and the Philippines. British sailors would come to consider Manus as "Scapa Flow with bloody palm trees."

The Royal Navy provided the majority of the fleet's ships and all the capital ships, but the BPF also included tankers and supply ships from the Royal Fleet Auxiliary (RFA), and escorts from the Royal Australian Navy, Royal Canadian Navy and Royal New Zealand Navy. Many of the naval aviators were New Zealanders and Canadians, though there were also Dutch and South African aviators aboard the ships. Port facilities in Sydney, Australia, and Wellington, New Zealand, also supported the fleet.

British naval operations in the war against Japan began when HMS *Illustrious* arrived in Ceylon in January 1944. In March 1944, the battlecruiser HMS *Renown* and battleships HMS *Howe*, HMS *Queen Elizabeth* and HMS *Valiant* joined *Illustrious* and became part of the US Navy Task Force 58.5, which comprised *Saratoga* and three destroyers that were detached from Task Force 58 after the successful invasion of Kwajalein and sent to the Indian Ocean to demonstrate US operating procedures. *Illustrious* embarked 1830 and 1833 squadrons, both operating the Corsair II (the British designation of the F4U-1A), while *Saratoga*'s fighter squadron, VF-12, the first USN squadron to equip with the Corsair a year before, was now flying F6F-3 Hellcats that they had chosen over the F4U after experiencing difficulty getting carrier-qualified in the "birdcage" F4U-1.

Several weeks of training resulted in a marked operational improvement on the part of the FAA aircrews. On April 19, Operation *Cockpit* saw the combined Anglo-American fleet strike the Japanese oil port on Sabang Island off northern Sumatra. The Japanese were completely surprised by the attack and the port facilities were heavily damaged.

VF-12 shot down three G4M Betty bombers, while the *Illustrious* Corsairs burned 12 parked aircraft.

For the Japanese, the refineries on Sumatra and Java were of supreme importance as the source of all aviation gasoline for the Imperial air forces. The captured refineries in Sumatra were beyond range of Allied aircraft in India or Australia, which allowed operation with impunity. Operation *Cockpit* marked the opening of a campaign against the refineries. Operation *Transom* followed on May 17. Again, the enemy was surprised by the strike against the refinery at Surabaya, Java, and the installation was severely damaged. With the British carriers and their fliers now "blooded," *Saratoga* departed the next day and returned to the Pacific.

The campaign against the Sumatra oil refineries was originally assigned to the newly arrived Boeing B-29 Superfortresses of the Twentieth Bomber Command, which had recently commenced operations in India and China. On the night of August 10/11, 1944, 54 B-29s of the 444th Bomb Group of the 358th (Very Heavy) Bomb Wing flew from the China Bay RAF base near Trincomalee on a night radar attack against the Pladjoe refinery at Palembang, the first since its capture in 1942. The bombers flew individually straight to Siberoet Island, off Pandang, Sumatra, then direct to Palembang. The B-29s were still new on operations and 12 of the big bombers aborted for various reasons, while 39 managed to reach the target, though only nine reached Palembang itself, where they were forced to drop 36 500lb GP bombs and 16 photo flash bombs through heavy overcast. Two hit the Pangkalan Brandan refinery, the secondary target, and one bombed the Djambi Airfield. Eight dropped mines in the Moesi River, the main shipping route for all of Palembang's gasoline and oil. At the time, the result was unobserved, but later intelligence considered the effort unsuccessful.

The 4,030-mile, 19-hour, 40-minute flight from Ceylon to Palembang and the Moesi was the longest single-stage flight made by USAAF aircraft during WWII.

The East Indies Fleet was created in August 1944 when Admiral Sir Bruce Fraser, former commander of the Home Fleet, raised his flag in the gunboat HMS *Tarantula* as Commander-in-Chief East Indies Fleet, later moving his flag to the battleship HMS *Howe*. Over the course of the summer of 1944, HMS *Victorious* joined the fleet in July, followed by HMS *Indomitable* in August and HMS *Indefatigable* in September.

Vice Admiral Sir Bernard Rawlings commanded the fleet in action, while famed Vice Admiral Sir Philip Vian commanded the carriers, which were ordered to strike the Indonesian refineries since they could attack with less warning and greater accuracy than land-based bombers.

When HMS *Victorious* arrived in July 1944, her two squadrons of Corsairs, 1834 and 1836 squadrons of 47 Naval Fighter Wing, attracted the attention of Major T. Ronald Hay, Royal Marines, who was serving as a staff officer to Admiral Somerville. Hay had joined the Royal Marines in 1935 and begun flight training with the Fleet Air Arm in the wake of the Munich Crisis in 1938. Assigned as a fighter pilot just before the outbreak of war in 1939, Hay scored two victories flying the Blackburn Skua from HMS *Glorious* off Norway in 1940, and scored a further seven victories in the Mediterranean in 1941 while flying Fairey Fulmars. He was very interested in the Corsairs operated by 1830 and 1833 squadrons, since the aircraft was such a vast improvement on what he had previously flown. As one of the only FAA graduates of the RAF's Wing Leader Course, arrangements were quickly made for Hay to assume command of 47 Fighter Wing prior to the unit entering combat against the Japanese.

Operation *Crimson* saw the British capital ships shell the port on Sabang Island on July 21 under air cover by *Illustrious* and the recently arrived *Victorious*. The fire of the 12 battleships and cruisers, directed by naval aviators trained as artillery spotters, inflicted heavy damage on the oil facility.

1830 Squadron opened their aerial score by shooting down three Ki.43 Oscars, while 1833 Squadron shot down two Oscars and a Ki.21 Sally bomber. As they retired to the fleet, the Japanese mounted an attack, and Sub-Lieutenant Ben Heffer of 1837 Squadron was launched from *Victorious*. As he later recalled:

I was directed towards the enemy at 1645 hours and sighted five enemy aircraft. There was a large storm astern of the fleet, but *Victorious* managed to vector us onto the enemy. A Japanese aircraft dived past me and I followed him down, hitting him in the port quarter with a long burst of fire. He was weaving, but flames were coming from his port wing. He disappeared into a cloud and, following him, I came out dead on his tail at a range of about 100 yards. After another long burst, the aircraft went up in a burst of fire.

Victorious and *Indomitable* struck targets in Sumatra in Operation *Banquet* on August 25.

Ronnie Hay led *Victorious'* 47 Naval Fighter Wing, which shared escort duties with the Hellcats of *Indomitable's* 1839 and 1844 squadrons of 5 Naval Fighter Wing led by LCDR T. W. Harrington. Hay's Corsairs concentrated on the airfield at Padang. He later remembered, "After the attack, the fighters roamed the area looking for the most impressive buildings. These were then machinegunned in the hope the Japanese overlords were present."

Operation *Light-B* saw *Victorious* and *Indomitable* again strike Sumatra as a diversion to the American landings at Peleliu, hitting the railway repair yard in Sigli on September 15. Poor weather provided disappointing results.

Victorious and *Indomitable* next struck Japanese facilities in the Nicobar Islands on October 17 in Operation *Millet*, with the intention of distracting the enemy from the Leyte landings.

Withdrawing over October 18 on account of the weather, the carriers returned on October 19. Discovered by the enemy at 0840 hours, the carriers came under attack at 0930 hours by 12 Oscars of the First Reserve Flying Unit. In a fierce 40-minute air battle, Canadian Corsair pilot Sub-Lieutenant Leslie Durno shot down one Oscar and shared the destruction of two others, while 1836 Squadron's Lieutenant Edmundson opened the Hellcat's Pacific score by shooting down another, though at a cost of two Corsairs and a Hellcat shot down by the other Oscars. Minutes later, Hellcats from

Indomitable found the enemy's top cover and in a short, sharp fight, South African Sub-Lieutenant Edward Wilson of 1844 Squadron shot down two Oscars. Overall, the Hellcats and Corsairs shot down seven Oscars. Major Hay, who was in the center of the fight, later remembered that:

> The Corsair was just the right aircraft for that war. It was certainly better than anything we had, and an improvement on the Hellcat. It was more robust and faster, and although the Japanese could out-turn us in combat, we could out-climb, out-dive and out-gun him. By far the most healthy improvement was its endurance, as with about five hours' worth of fuel in your tank you didn't have the agony of worrying whether or not you would make it back to the carrier.

Hay was not the only Royal Navy pilot who was impressed by American carrier aircraft. While the Royal Navy had invented carrier warfare in 1918, the service had also lost control of its ability to develop and operate aircraft designed for carrier use when the Royal Naval Air Service and the Royal Flying Corps were combined into the independent Royal Air Force in April 1918. While the US Navy retained control of naval aviation and spent the next 20 years developing aircraft specifically suited for their role aboard ship, the Royal Navy was forced to make do with "navalizing" aircraft primarily designed to be operated ashore by the RAF. The service regained control of the Fleet Air Arm only in 1938, which was not enough time to catch up with the US Navy or the Imperial Japanese Navy.

In 1939, the primary FAA shipboard fighter was the RAF Gloster Gladiator fighter biplane, equipped with a tailhook as the Sea Gladiator. The aircraft did not even display the technical advances of the Grumman F2F and F3F biplane fighters, which had entered service before the Gladiator and were in the process of being replaced. The Fleet Air Arm was at least a generation behind the US Navy or the Imperial Japanese Navy in terms of aircraft development. The first all-metal monoplane "fighter" was the Blackburn Skua, which was supposed to perform double duty as a dive bomber and had a top speed of barely 200mph at a time when its land-based opponents were nearing 400mph top speeds.

Additionally, the Fleet Air Arm was saddled with the obsolete idea that a carrier-based naval fighter required a second crewman to operate communications equipment, which meant that the Fairey Fulmar introduced into service in 1941 was powered by the same Merlin engine and carried the same eight-gun armament as the RAF's Hurricane and Spitfire, although it was 50 percent bigger and 50 percent heavier than the Hurricane with no increase in power. With a top speed of only 258mph, the Fulmar was hard pressed in combat against agile Italian fighters in the Mediterranean, and could only hope to intercept the speedy trimotor S.79 Aerosiluranti torpedo bombers if it was favorably positioned for a diving attack from sufficient altitude to build up the necessary speed. Nonetheless, until the arrival of the Sea Hurricane in sizeable numbers in 1942, the Fulmar gave a good account of itself over the Mediterranean, as well as with the Arctic convoys, opposing Ju-87 and Ju-88 dive bombers and He-111 torpedo bombers.

The Royal Navy was eventually forced to adapt first the Hurricane and then the Spitfire for carrier operation in order to field a fighter that could compete with its contemporary opponents. While the Hurricane was strong enough that it went aboard ship as the Sea Hurricane with a minimum of difficulty, the light and delicate Spitfire was really unsuited to carrier operations; indeed, the overwhelming majority of "Sea Spitfires," or Seafires as they came to be known, were lost in operational accidents aboard ship rather than as a result of enemy action. While the Hurricane was rugged enough for carrier operation, its performance by 1942 was not up to that of its opponents.

In 1940, the Fleet Air Arm was introduced to the Grumman F4F Wildcat, known to the British as the Martlet. The stubby fighter found immediate favor with FAA pilots because it could survive carrier operations while still having sufficient performance to fight its Axis opponents and would be utilized by the FAA throughout the war. The experience of a fighter that was designed for the job at hand led to early adoption of the two major US Navy fighters of the war, the F6F Hellcat and the F4U Corsair. In fact, the Royal Navy made use of the Corsair in its designed role as a carrier-based fleet fighter long before the US Navy did.

One in six Corsairs produced during World War II was delivered to the Fleet Air Arm. All told, 2,012 Vought-built F4U-1 and F4U-1A (known as the Corsair I and Corsair II respectively), Brewster-built F3A-1s (Corsair III), and Goodyear-built FG-1Ds (Corsair IV) went to the FAA between 1943 and 1945; the 430 Brewster-built F3A-1s represented half of Brewster's total production. The FAA used the Corsair in larger numbers than any other US naval aircraft operated by the service. The Corsair was a generation ahead of anything in the domestic inventory at the time of its arrival and by the end of the war, 18 Fleet Air Arm fighter squadrons were equipped with the Corsair.

The British never seemed to have the problems the US Navy did about taking the Corsair to sea. The FAA "circular approach" for a carrier landing allowed the pilot to keep the deck in sight over the long nose right up to landing, and was eventually adopted by the US Navy when Corsairs finally joined the fleet in 1945. Even the F4U-1 "birdcage" Corsair Is were regularly flown off British escort carriers during initial training in 1943 while the US Navy claimed the aircraft was incapable of operating off an Essex-class fleet carrier, and the FAA did so without the modifications to the oleo strut air pressure and the starboard wing spoiler for stall warning, though these modifications did show up with the widely-used Corsair II, the first version to go into combat. Additionally, the British Corsairs after the Corsair I had eight inches clipped from each wingtip to enable them to be stowed with wings folded aboard British fleet carriers with their smaller hangar compartments; this resulted in a higher roll rate and lessened the airplane's tendency to float on landing. The first carrier combat missions were flown by Corsairs of 1834 and 1836 squadrons of *Victorious'* 47 Naval Fighter Wing in Operation

Tungsten, the Home Fleet strikes against the German battleship *Tirpitz* in Norway in April 1944. The Far East debut of Corsair carrier combat operations came a week later when *Illustrious'* 1830 and 1833 squadrons of 15 Naval Fighter Wing attacked Sabang.

Second to the Corsair in terms of widespread first line service was the Grumman F6F Hellcat, originally named "Gannet" after a large North Atlantic seabird. Universally known to its pilots regardless as the Hellcat, the British fighters took the name officially in March 1944 when the FAA adopted the official US Navy names for their US aircraft. Beginning in May 1943, 252 F6F-3s were supplied to the Fleet Air Arm as the Gannet I under lend-lease, with an additional 930 F6F-5s delivered after August 1944 as the Hellcat II; some 100 were delivered as the Hellcat PR II, modified similarly to the F6F-5P for photo reconnaissance, while a further 80 radar-equipped F6F-5Ns were delivered as the Hellcat NF II.

800 Squadron was the first FAA unit to operate the Hellcat, taking delivery of its first aircraft in July 1943 and flying the first antishipping strikes off the Norwegian coast from the escort carrier HMS *Emperor* in December in company with 804 Squadron, the second unit to re-equip with the Hellcat. The squadrons flew escort for the first strikes against the *Tirpitz* on April 3, 1944. Over Norway on May 8, 1944, 800 and 804 squadrons came across a formation of Bf-109Gs and Fw-190As from the Luftwaffe's *Jagdgeschwader* 5. The Hellcats shot down two Bf-109s while Lt Blyth Ritchie, a Mediterreanean Sea Hurricane veteran who had previously scored 3.5 victories in 1942, bagged a Fw-190. Six days later, on May 14, Ritchie became the first FAA Hellcat pilot to "make ace" when he shot down a He-115 seaplane and shared a second with 804 squadron commander LCDR Stanley Orr. These were the only Hellcat victories scored by the FAA in the European theater.

800 and 804 squadrons participated in Operation *Dragoon*, the Allied landings in the south of France in August 1944. This turned out to be the final FAA Hellcat operation of the European Theater. The next month, the two squadrons were combined as 800 Squadron; *Emperor* and her Hellcats transited the Suez Canal and joined the Far

Eastern Fleet. During October and November, 888 Squadron joined 800 aboard *Emperor*, flying Hellcat FR II photo recon fighters, and the two squadrons flew strikes against Japanese positions along the Burmese and Malayan coasts and the Andaman Islands. FAA Hellcats had already gone to war in the Indian Ocean that August, when HMS *Indomitable* arrived with the Hellcat-equipped 1839 and 1844 squadrons of 5 Naval Fighter Wing.

The final American aircraft on the decks of the British Pacific Fleet's carriers was the Grumman TBF Avenger. The FAA had quickly seen the Avenger's value as a strike aircraft and deliveries under lend-lease began in late 1942. Initially named "Tarpon" for the large Atlantic fish, the name was changed to Avenger in January 1944. Grumman built 402 TBF-1Bs, which were actually the TBF-1 and the TBF-1C sub-types, without further differentiation as the Tarpon I; 334 Eastern Aircraft-built TBM-1Cs were taken on as the Avenger II, with 222 TBM-3s as Avenger IIIs. The FAA learned to differentiate their Avengers by production source, as they did with the Corsair, after discovering that the "same aircraft" built by different manufacturers was not really the "same aircraft." While the US Navy re-equipped its units completely with ever-newer versions of the Avenger, all the British Avengers were used throughout the war, with squadrons operating both Avenger Is and Avenger IIs simultaneously, distinguished only by their different camouflage schemes (Grumman-built Avenger Is used the correct FAA-approved camouflage colors of dark slate gray, extra-dark sea gray and sky, while the Eastern Aircraft-built Avenger IIs were painted in US "equivalent colors" of olive drab, neutral gray and sky gray, respectively).

While the American aircraft were the majority of the fleet's air arm, there were also three British designs on the fleet's flight decks.

The Fairey Barracuda was an ungainly-looking shoulder-wing monoplane used as both a dive and torpedo bomber. The Barracuda was Fairey Aviation's second attempt to create a modern replacement for the venerable Swordfish torpedo bomber that gained fame attacking the Italian fleet at Taranto in November 1940 and damaging the German battleship *Bismarck* sufficiently that the battleships of the Home Fleet could catch their German opponent and sink her in May 1941. The open-cockpit biplane Swordfish was obsolete when it entered service in 1934, but went on to be one of five British aircraft in front-line service in 1939 that were still serving in 1945 as it flew off the smallest escort carriers, in weather so appalling other aircraft were chained to their decks.

Fairey submitted the design in response to Air Ministry Specification S.24/37 for a three-seat torpedo and dive-bomber aircraft. The first prototype flew on December 7, 1940.

The aircraft used Fairey-Youngman trailing-edge flaps to come aboard at a safe speed. Lowering these large flaps to reduce speed in a dive-bombing attack disturbed the airflow over the rear of the airframe, which necessitated the strange high-set tailplane. The most important sub-type was the Barracuda Mk.II, powered by a 1,640hp Merlin 32; 1,688 rolled off production lines at Fairey, Blackburn, Boulton-Paul and Westland line between 1942 and 1945.

On April 3, 1944, 42 Barracudas took part in Operation *Tungsten*, their first combat operation. The bombers arrived over Alten Fjord, Norway, at the very moment *Tirpitz* was about to depart her anchorage for sea trials. Their dive-bombing attacks scored 24 direct hits, damaging the battleship so badly it was out of action for several months for repairs. Other attacks in the summer of 1944 were less successful. The Barracuda arrived in the Far East with 810 and 847 squadrons aboard *Illustrious*.

Victorious operated a Barracuda squadron and all three units took part in the oil strike operations that began in August 1944.

The Fairey Firefly I continued the design philosophy of the preceding Fulmar in having a dedicated navigator-radioman as a second crewman. The design was the result of FAA Specification N8/39, which called for a two-seater armed with either four 20mm cannon or eight .30-caliber machine guns using the then-new and untried Rolls-Royce Griffon, issued in July 1939 while the Fulmar prototype was still under construction. Fairey's response was a somewhat smaller, Fulmar-type aircraft with 20mm cannon and an empty weight barely less than the Fulmar's loaded weight. Specification N5/40 was written around the mock-up after it was inspected and approved on June 6, 1940. The first Firefly I flew on December 22, 1941. The aircraft used the Fairey-patented area-increasing Youngman flaps, which gave the necessary maneuverability in air combat and lowered the heavy aircraft's landing speed for carrier operation. The first production aircraft was delivered on March 4, 1943, which was a very respectable timetable for wartime aircraft development. Every other British-designed carrier aircraft ordered in the same timeframe ran into development difficulties and none flew before the end of the war. The Firefly was thus the only British-designed modern high- performance carrier aircraft to operate off British carriers in the war it was designed for.

Unfortunately, the Firefly lacked the performance to operate in its designed role of fleet defense fighter, even with the 1,735 horsepower of the Griffon IIB. The greatest fault in the design lay with the choice of placing the radiator in a large cowling directly beneath the engine, resulting in a high-drag configuration, and the requirement for a second crew member, which added weight. With a top speed of only 319mph and a climb rate under 2,000 fpm, though it had a useful range of 774 miles on internal fuel, the Firefly I was used as a strike and tactical reconnaissance aircraft, a mission for which it was more than capable. A Firefly I tested at the US Navy test center at NAS Patuxent River in 1944 more than held its own in air combat maneuvering against the F6F Hellcat; those flaps worked.

1770 Squadron was first to be formed on the Firefly in October 1943, followed in February 1944 by 1771 Squadron. 1770 went aboard HMS *Indefatigable* and gave the type its baptism of fire in Operation *Mascot*, the failed attack against *Tirpitz* on July 17, 1944. That November, *Indefatigable* and 1770 Squadron, led by Major Vernon "Cheese" Cheesman, joined the British Pacific Fleet.

Indefatigable's 24 Naval Fighter Wing operated the legendary Supermarine Seafire. The navalized Spitfire first joined the Royal Navy in late 1942 and entered combat in the summer of 1943, providing the primary air defense for the Allied fleet at Salerno that September. The Mk I and Mk II sub-types were minimal conversions of land-based Spitfires equipped with an A-frame arrestor hook under the rear fuselage and catapult spools. Without folding wings, these Seafires could not be struck below on a carrier; all maintenance at sea took place on the open flight deck.

The F. Mk III was the first fully-navalized Seafire, first flown in November 1943. Cunliffe-Owen, the company responsible for modifying the Seafire I and Seafire II, developed a folding wing for the Seafire III, which allowed below deck stowage. The L. Mk III, powered by the Merlin 55M engine with a cropped impeller to give maximum performance below 5,000 feet, quickly replaced the original F. Mk III. At low altitude, the Seafire III outperformed the A6M5 Zero when tested against each other. The aircraft had a superior low-altitude climb rate and acceleration to either the Hellcat or Corsair, which made it the best low-altitude short-range fleet interceptor available in the Pacific. 887 and 894 squadrons, the most-experienced Seafire units in the Royal Navy, went to the Pacific aboard HMS *Indefatigable*.

The Royal Navy's carriers had been developed for a different kind of war than had those of the US Navy. The British ships were designed for operation in the Atlantic and Mediterranean, where they did not need the range and sea-keeping ability of the American carriers. Since their opponents would be land-based aircraft that were expected to outperform the defending carrier fighters, the ships were designed with an armored flight deck, and with much more armor throughout the ship than was the case with the Essex-class ships. The result for the British was that their hangars did not open on the sides as with the *Essex* carriers, which meant that aircraft could not be run up on the hangar deck to speed up the launch of multiple strikes. A British naval air group numbered only some 45–50 aircraft, as opposed to the 90-aircraft force on an Essex-class carrier. The Americans initially derided the British carriers with their heavy armor and reduced capacity, but when the *kamikazes* became the primary threat, the ability of a British carrier to shrug off a hit that would have heavily damaged if not sunk outright an American carrier rightly impressed the Americans, who adopted this feature in their postwar carrier designs.

On January 1, 1945, the BPF carriers left Trincomalee to undertake their last strike from the old base, Operation *Lentil*. HMS *Indomitable*, *Victorious* and *Indefatigable*, escorted by the cruisers HMS *Suffolk*, HMS *Ceylon*, HMS *Argonaut* and HMS *Black Prince*, launched an attack on January 4, 1945 against the former Royal Dutch Shell refinery at Pangkalan Brandan in northern Sumatra. Ninety-two Avengers and Fireflies, escorted by Hellcats of *Indomitable*'s 1839 and 1844 squadrons and Corsairs from *Victorious*' 1834 and 1836 squadrons, targeted the installation.

Sixteen fighters sent ahead as a "Ramrod" attacked the airfields at Medan and Tanjong Poera. 1834 Squadron's Leslie Durno spotted a Ki.46 Dinah twin-engine reconnaissance plane with wheels and flaps down for landing at Medan Airfield. Durno and his wingman attacked the Dinah and damaged it, then Durno turned in astern of the enemy plane and fired a five-second burst that staggered the Dinah before it blew up at the edge of the runway. Minutes later, he spotted a Ki.21 Sally bomber, which he set afire with an eight-second burst. This victory made Durno both the first FAA Corsair ace and the first FAA pilot to score five Japanese victories.

The strike force was launched 90 minutes after the fighter sweep, with 32 Avengers and 12 rocket-firing Fireflies escorted by 12 1836 Squadron Corsairs to bomb the refinery. Several Oscars attacked the strike force at 0850 hours. Sub-Lieutenant D. J. Sheppard, RCNVR, of 1836 Squadron, Number 3 in Wing Leader Ronnie Hay's flight, was able to latch onto an Oscar in the swirling dogfight and shoot it down. He later reported, "The Jap's cockpit seemed to glow as I hit him with a long burst, and I could see the bullets striking the engine and cockpit. He leveled out at 300 feet and then went into a climbing right turn. I fired again and the pilot baled out as the aircraft rolled over and went into the sea." Ten minutes later he spotted a second Oscar and closed in before opening fire. The Oscar blew up under the weight of his fire. Sheppard had scored two in his first combat.

The strike force inflicted heavy damage on the refinery and oil storage tanks, while a small tanker was set on fire and two locomotives were hit. Two aircraft were lost to antiaircraft fire, but the crews were rescued.

Following the fleet's return to Trincomalee, the British Pacific Fleet weighed anchor and headed east-southeast into the Indian Ocean on January 16 on the first leg of its transfer to the Pacific theater of operations. The slow and awkward Barracudas were gone from the strike squadrons, replaced with Grumman Avengers. Admiral Vian's Task Force 63 planned a final strike against the Indonesian oil refineries during their passage to Australia, called Operation *Meridian One*. The targets were the Palembang refineries at Pladjoe and Songei Gerong. Bad weather over the Indian Ocean delayed the strike from January 22 to 24.

Illustrious, Victorious, Indomitable and *Indefatigable* began launching their strike aircraft at 0600 hours on January 24, 1945: 43 Avengers and 12 Fireflies, escorted by 48 Hellcats, Corsairs and Seafires, headed for the Pladjoe refinery while 24 Corsairs were assigned to sweep the airfields at Lembak and Tanglangbetoetoe. *Victorious'* Major Ronnie Hay was assigned as the strike coordinator leading a top cover of 12 Corsairs. 12 Fireflies of 1770 Squadron were assigned as close escort for the Avengers, led by Major Cheesman, each armed with eight 60lb rockets for flak suppression. Eight Corsairs from 1830 Squadron formed the middle cover, while eight Corsairs from 1833 brought up the rear.

Japanese radar picked up the strike force over Sumatra. Lieutenant Hideyaki Onayama led twelve Ki.44 Tojos from the 87th *Sentai* (regiment) to intercept the strike force some 20 miles west of the refinery. Hay scored his first Pacific victory when he spotted a Tojo approaching from out of the sun. The Tojo flashed past and Hay dived after it. "After a five-minute chase I caught up with him at nought feet and 250 knots. I gave him a two-second burst which hit his engine and he crashed but did not burn." Hay climbed back to altitude to coordinate the strike, and ran across another Tojo and shot it down. Sub-Lieutenant Sheppard also shot down a Tojo. More Oscars joined in the fight, while Japanese antiaircraft batteries below opened fire as the attackers neared the target.

Just before the first Tojos struck, Major Cheesman's engine began running rough and he was forced to pass leadership of the 1770 Squadron Fireflies to Lieutenant Dennis Levitt and return to *Indefatigable*. Moments later, the Fireflies came under attack by Oscars of the 26th *Sentai*. They turned into the enemy fighters and Levitt shot down the first enemy aircraft to fall to the Firefly, while Sub-Lieutenant Phil Stott shared a second with his wingman, Sub-Lieutenant Redding.

Hellcat pilot Sub-Lieutenant Edward Taylor shot down a Tojo during the fight. When added to his previous victories in the Mediterranean, he became the only South African Navy ace. Minutes later, he shared the destruction of a Ki.45 Nick twin-engine fighter from the 21st *Sentai* with his wingman.

The fierceness of the air battle is shown by claims for 14 Japanese aircraft shot down and six probable kills. The Corsairs that struck the airfield destroyed 34 enemy aircraft and damaged a further 25 on the ground. Despite the presence of protective barrage balloons that forced the Avengers to drop their bombs from 3,000 feet, the refinery was successfully hit. Fleet air losses were heavier than previous raids: seven aircraft were shot down over the target and 25 aircraft – many damaged from antiaircraft fire – were lost in crash landings back aboard the carriers. The attack cut output at the refinery by 50 percent for three months, with most of the refined oil in the storage tanks destroyed by fire.

The fleet rendezvoused with the tankers again over January 26–27. Owing to poor weather and inexperience, the tankers suffered damage as ships being refueled failed to keep station and hoses parted, greatly delaying the operation.

On January 29, the carriers returned for Operation *Meridian Two*, a strike against the refinery at Songei Gerong, Sumatra. Poor weather gave low visibility and the strike force launch was delayed for 25 minutes by a rain squall. Once again, Ronnie Hay acted as strike coordinator.

Defensive aerial opposition was strong; pilots claimed 30 shot down with another 38 destroyed on the ground, for the loss of 16

British aircraft. Just after the Avengers made their bombing runs, Hay was attacked by a Tojo he quickly downed, then an Oscar that tried to latch onto his tail as the Tojo fell burning.

Hay's element leader, Don Sheppard, also claimed two in this fight to become the second Corsair ace and the only one to score all his victories in the F4U.

The fleet came under attack from the "Shichisi Mitate" Special Attack Corps. Major Hitoyuki Kato led seven Ki.21 Sally and Ki.48 Lily bombers in low-level suicide attacks. New Zealander Sub-Lieutenant Keith McLennan, who manned the alert Hellcat of 1844 Squadron aboard *Indomitable*, was launched to intercept the *kamikazes*. Within minutes of retracting his landing gear, McLennan was in the middle of the enemy bombers and shot down two in quick succession, then shared a third with Seafire pilot Sub-Lieutenant Elson of 894 Squadron. With a total of 3.5 victories, McLennan was the most successful New Zealand Navy pilot of the war.

Meridian Two stopped all production at the Songei Gerong Refinery for two months, and, over the rest of the war, production was never more than a quarter of pre-attack levels. For the loss of 25 aircraft in the three January operations, production of aviation gasoline on Sumatra was cut to 35 percent of its pre-attack level. The shortage would have a dramatic effect on the Burma campaign in the final six months of war. These strikes, coming as they did in coordination with Halsey's South China Sea strikes, meant Japan was now almost completely cut off from petroleum supplies, the control of which were the major reason why Japan had gone to war in 1941.

The British Pacific Fleet arrived in Sydney, Australia, in mid-February and began preparations to join the US Navy in the coming invasion of Okinawa.

CHAPTER SIX

TOKYO

The ships of the Fifth Fleet stood out of the anchorage at Ulithi Atoll on the afternoon of February 10, 1945, course north-northwest. The next morning, it was announced throughout the fleet that the target was Tokyo, capital of the Japanese Empire, 1,500 miles distant. The first carrier strike against Japan proper since the Doolittle raid of April 18, 1942 was regarded with some apprehension by the men of Task Force 58, since this would be the first combat mission for half the air groups.

After spending a day training with Marine assault forces at Tinian on February 12, the fleet refueled on February 14, and, as the ships continued steaming north-northwest, crews broke out sweaters, peacoats and heavy work jackets that hadn't been worn since they had left the United States. With snow showers and squalls in all quadrants that prevented detection by Japanese patrols, the fleet began its run-in to the launch point 125 miles southeast of Tokyo at 1900 hours on February 15. That night, the squadron diarist of VT(N)-90 aboard *Enterprise* recorded:

> It's amazing how clear the atmosphere is this evening – a result, in part of our northerly position. It seems as though the ship is in the exact center of an immense disk of deep blue-gray. The horizon, clear

around the compass, is a sharp circle contrasting the deep blue of the cloudless sky. It seems hard to believe that this scene of serenity can be the overture to death and destruction.

It had been a thousand days since *Enterprise* and *Hornet* and their 16-ship task force had dared to cruise these waters as they closed to 800 miles from Honshu to launch the Doolittle Raid. This time, 116 ships were headed to a launch point only 60 miles from the imperial capital.

Among the carriers of Task Force 58 was *Bunker Hill*, which had returned to the western Pacific only at the beginning of February after undergoing repairs at the naval shipyard in Bremerton, Washington. Stopping at Pearl Harbor, she picked up Air Group 84, which included the Corsairs of VMF-221, commanded by Major Edwin S. Roberts, Jr., and VMF-451, commanded by Major Henry A. Ellis, Jr. What was most remarkable about Air Group 84 was that VF-84 was the first US Navy carrier-based fighter squadron to enter combat mounted in the Corsair, making the air group the first all-Corsair unit in the fleet. *Bunker Hill* had first come to the Pacific in September 1943 with VF-17 aboard, the first Navy Corsair squadron to qualify for carrier deployment.

VF-17 had been ordered off the ship upon arrival in Pearl Harbor and the squadron had gone on to fame as the "Jolly Rogers" in the final Solomons battles that saw the major Japanese base at Rabaul cut off and left to wither on the vine. The dark blue F4U-1Ds of VF-84 were direct descendants of VF-17's F4U-1As. Squadron leader LCDR Roger Hedrick had flown with VF-17 as executive officer, and four other veterans of the earlier squadron now held senior positions in VF-84. Hedrick had not been able to appropriate the pirate's flag marking and VF-84 was quickly known after their formation in May 1944 as "The Wolf Gang." The 71 F4U-1Ds of the three fighter squadrons were flown as one unit, with Navy and Marine pilots flying whichever aircraft they were assigned for a mission, regardless of "ownership." Fifteen SB2C-4 Helldivers of VB-84 and a similar number of TBM-3 Avengers of VT-84 rounded out the air group.

Among the Marines in Air Group 84 was Captain James Swett in VMF-221, a Medal of Honor winner at Guadalcanal, where he had shot down seven attacking Val dive bombers during the final major Japanese strike against the island in April 1943. Veteran ace Major Archie Donahue, who had served in VMF-112 in the Solomons, was executive officer of VMF-451.

New Marine squadrons were also aboard the brand-new *Bennington* (CV-20) with VMF-112 led by Major Herman Hansen, Jr. and VMF-123 commanded by Major Everett V. Alward, while *Wasp* had VMF-216 commanded by Major George E. Dooley and VMF-217 led by Major Jack R. Amend, Jr. in addition to Air Group 4's Marines aboard *Essex*. Altogether, 180 Corsairs were now embarked on the fast carriers, a remarkable turnaround from only two months earlier. Major Hansen, at 25 a veteran of the Guadalcanal campaign two and a half years earlier, remembered his first sight of the Fifth Fleet from the air when he flew a combat air patrol over the *Bennington* task group: "There had never been such a collection of combat ships and there never will be again. The fleet spanned the ocean from horizon to horizon."

Shortly before departure from Ulithi, Admiral Marc Mitscher and his staff had come aboard to make *Bunker Hill* the flagship of Task Force 58. The carrier operated as part of Task Group 58.3, which also included *Essex*, flagship of TG 58.3 commander Rear Admiral Frederick C. Sherman, and light carrier *Cowpens*, battleships *South Dakota* (BB-56) and *New Jersey* (BB-62), the new battlecruiser *Alaska* (CB-1), heavy cruisers *Indianapolis* (CA-35) and *Boston* (CA-69), accompanied by light cruisers *Pasadena* (CL-65), *Wilkes-Barre* (CL-103) and *Astoria* (CL-90), escorted by 14 destroyers.

The fleet's strike force was centered in Task Groups 58.1, 58.2, 58.3 and 58.4, composed of nine Essex-class fleet carriers and five light carriers. Task Group 58.5 operated *Enterprise* and *Saratoga* with air groups dedicated to night operations. The now-elderly *Saratoga* had been assigned as a training carrier when she returned to Pearl Harbor in September 1944 after a refit following her cruise with the British fleet, during which she trained aviators in night operations.

Hurriedly sent west on January 29, 1945 to reinforce *Enterprise* for night operations in the coming strikes against Japan, she operated 56 F6F-5Ns of VF(N)-53 and 17 TBM-3Ds of VT(N)-53.

At 0400 on February 16, two hours before the rest of Task Force 58 launched their strikes, *Enterprise* launched an "RCM" mission, something brand new in naval warfare. RCM stood for Radar Counter-Measure. The single, specially modified TBM-3D Avenger was equipped to confuse Japanese radar installations in order to disrupt the enemy's ability to locate and intercept the incoming strikes.

By 0635 hours, Task Force 58 was 60 miles off the coast of Honshu. *Bennington* launched a division of Corsairs from VMF-112 that found a Betty 30 miles off the coast, which was shot down by Major David Andre and his wingman. Major Hansen led eight Corsairs escorting Avengers and Helldivers on the first strike, which managed to find their way through the horrid weather with thousand-foot ceilings and snow showers to hit Oshima, Mobara and Katori airfields, where they left 20 aircraft burning on the ground, while other Wolfpack Corsairs escorted strikes that hit Konoike and Hokoda airfields outside Tokyo, where the Corsairs strafed and rocketed aircraft in their revetments. First Lieutenant James Hamilton's F4U-1D took a hit in the belly, but he managed to head back out to sea where he ditched near a lifeguard destroyer and was picked up.

VMF-123 participated in a sweep southwest of Tokyo that resulted in the Corsairs running across five Zekes, one of which was shot down by squadron commander Alward. The *Essex* Corsairs were the first American aircraft to fly over the Imperial Palace when they escorted TBMs, but the *Essex* Marines found no enemy aircraft airborne on this mission. In the afternoon, 11 Corsairs from both squadrons ran across a formation of Zekes near Tokyo, engaging in a fight that saw Gus Thomas shoot down two of them to run his score to 18.5, while a third Zeke and a Val were also shot down in the fight and the flight burned 17 more on the ground at Tenryu Airfield.

Bunker Hill's Corsairs claimed eight victories – five by VF-84, two by VMF-221 and a single by VMF-451. *Wasp*'s Corsairs had a difficult initiation in air combat. A division of VMF-217 led by squadron commander Major Jack Amend escorted Helldivers and Avengers to Hammatsu Airfield, where 60 enemy aircraft were observed on the ground; the Marines burned six. At the rendezvous point, Amend was attacked by a Zeke that hit him badly enough that he had to bale out, while his wingman 1st Lieutenant Vernon Salisbury shot down the Zeke. Two other Corsairs failed to return to the ship. Over the course of the day, Corsairs shot down 17 enemy aircraft while the nine squadrons lost ten aircraft and eight pilots.

In late 1944, the Navy had implemented an organizational change for fighter units that saw the veteran VF-9 divided in half, with half the experienced pilots going to form the nucleus of a rebuilt VF-12, now led by Coral Sea veteran LCDR Noel A. M. Gaylor. The Navy had decided to form five-man fighter teams that could be "grown" from the ground up, trained as a unit, and sent to any new squadron with a minimum of adjustment and indoctrination. The five-man team was composed of a division leader, a second section leader, and three wingmen, who alternated turns to put four aircraft in the air. While the idea seemed good in theory, it created problems in practice. By this time, there were many Naval Academy graduates with high flight time as instructors who believed they were ready for combat assignments. Thus, many of the five-man teams were organized around an Academy graduate who had rank and seniority, but no combat experience, with a combat-experienced Aviation Cadet (AvCad) assigned as the section leader, with three "nugget" ensigns fresh out of flight school filling out the division. Morale suffered. In the squadron, the Academy men – the "ringknockers" as they were known to the rest – tended to gravitate to one another, while the experienced pilots who resented being led by someone they felt they had to "nursemaid" stayed together, and the youngsters kept to themselves. The "team" concept suffered, but it came at a time when the fast carrier force was undergoing previously undreamed-of expansion, and would not be changed for the remainder of the war.

One AvCad had proven so outstanding during his previous tour that he became a division leader in his old unit, VF-9. Lieutenant

Gene Valencia, with seven victories during the previous deployment, was given a division while the squadron was training at NAS Pasco, Washington. Valencia managed to find three enthusiastic "Jaygees" (junior grade lieutenants) for his division: Joseph Roquemore, who became his wingman, second section leader James B. French, and Clinton L. Smith as French's wingman. The pilots worked relentlessly under Valencia's intense leadership to become a true fighting team. Jim French later recalled, "We were at Pasco for six months, and most pilots flew about 70 or 80 hours a month. But Gene had us flying 100 hours a month."

Since this was more than was authorized, Valencia had to find access to more fuel. While stories abounded about "misappropriation," French stated: "Actually, we sort of traded for it. We slipped the service crews a few bottles from our booze ration, and they filled up our airplanes for us." Unfortunately, while on the way to Hawaii, Roquemore died of pneumonia. Valencia came across a young Jaygee in VBF-9, Harris E. Mitchell, a 21-year-old Texan, who fitted right in during training in Hawaii. Intent on building an elite team, Valencia wanted to put purple lightning bolts on their Hellcats, but regulations prohibited that. In the end, each pilot had a distinctive flying helmet. Valencia did everything he could to foster a group identity. When flight operations were finished for the day and other pilots drifted to the officer's club, Valencia's foursome sipped champagne or mint juleps from frosted glasses. While Gene Valencia never endeared himself to his superiors throughout his naval career, his pilots knew they would be ready the day they entered combat. That day came when they went aboard *Lexington*, which had just returned from stateside repair following the November *kamikaze* hit in the Philippines. Fighting-9 was on its third combat tour of the war, following action in North Africa in November 1942, and the stunning sweep at the outset of the Central Pacific campaign from October 1943 to March 1944 that had seen it return from the deployment as the top-scoring Navy fighter unit of the war to that date. It was now third-ranked behind VF-15 and VF-2, which had taken advantage of the opportunities presented at the Marianas

Turkey Shoot and Halsey's rampage through the Philippines to become the first and second top-scoring squadrons.

During the first strike on February 16, six-victory ace and squadron commander LCDR Herbert N. Houck led his formation through rain and snow squalls and came across what was identified as a mixed formation of Zekes and Ki.27 Nates; the Hellcats shot down 12 of the enemy aircraft.

Other VF-9 veterans were also airborne for these strikes. Lieutenant Hamilton McWhorter, who had flown with Fighting-9 in North Africa and during the squadron's first Pacific tour the year before, during which he became both the first Hellcat ace in December 1943 over the Gilberts and the first Hellcat double ace during the Truk strikes in February 1944, had been transferred to VF-12 after the squadron returned to the United States. Chick Smith, Reuben Denoff, John Franks and Hal Vita also found themselves transferred to VF-12, and participated in the squadron's second WestPac deployment after their tour aboard *Saratoga* the year before. Today, McWhorter was about to demonstrate the value of the newest piece of gear in the Hellcat, the lead-computing gyro gunsight. "The F6F-5, which we had in VF-12, had the gyro-controlled lead-computing sight. That thing was a beauty. If you could put the pipper on the enemy, you were going to hit him. It was so much superior to gut instinct and luck, which was what I'd used for deflection shooting before." Inbound to Tokyo, McWhorter found a Zeke and attacked the enemy fighter. "I was in an almost 90-degree overhead pass on him. I put the pipper on his nose and watched incendiary strikes all over his engine and cockpit. I hosed him like that for about 2 or 3 seconds, and he flamed." All of the VF-9 pilots who came over to VF-12 with McWhorter during this final tour became aces, with Hal Vita being the only Navy ace of the war to have a Vichy French Curtiss Hawk 75 in his scoreboard. "I'm sure that the use of the lead-computing sight had a lot to do with it," McWhorter recalled. "It just took out a lot of the guesswork."

Hancock's Hellcats of VF-80 were the most successful scorers over Tokyo. Air Group 80 was led by LCDR Alexander O. Vorse, one of the true veterans of the Pacific War. He had first entered combat three years earlier as a member of VF-3 aboard the old *Lexington*, where he learned air combat from John Thach and practiced it with Butch O'Hare, before participating in the Battle of the Coral Sea where he first scored, followed by duty aboard *Saratoga* at Eastern Solomons and *Enterprise* at Santa Cruz.

The "Vipers" ran across several enemy formations during the morning sweep and claimed 24; five-victory ace and squadron CO LCDR L. W. Keith doubled his total in the fight, while CAG Vorse led another sweep that claimed 13 in a fight that saw Vorse down four to bring his wartime score to 11.5. In other missions that day, the squadron ran across more aerial opposition. Lieutenant A. L. Anderson managed to shoot down two Oscars, a Tony, a Zeke, and a Tojo in one fight to become an "ace in a day," while Lt W. C. Edwards, Jr. added two Nates, two Zekes and an Oscar to an existing score of 2.5 to become the same.

Five of the VF-80 pilots ran across more Zekes and Oscars between Imba and Mobara airfields at approximately 1200 hours. Lieutenant Pat Fleming shot down five Zekes to become the squadron's third "ace in a day," while section leader Lieutenant Zeke Cormier shot down three more. A final sweep later that afternoon saw three pilots claim four more victories, which brought the day's total to 71 confirmed and 15 probables. It was a record that would remain unsurpassed by any other American fighter squadron, made possible by the fact all those scoring belonged for VF-80, since the air group didn't divide their Hellcats into VF and VBF squadrons.

VF-9 put up a second strike in the afternoon, entering a 200-foot ceiling that did not break open until they reached 20,000 feet, to strike Emba Airfield 40 miles north of Tokyo. Valencia's division remained on top as high cover while the other three divisions hit the airfield. Spotting an enemy fighter in his rearview mirror, Valencia left wingman Mitchell behind momentarily while he pressed an attack on what turned out to be a Tojo. The enemy fighter remained just out of gun range, so he fired four rockets, which fell short. Mitchell caught up to his leader, opening fire on the Tojo; when it caught fire, the enemy pilot baled out. The division hunted enemy planes in the air and on the ground over the next hour, during which Valencia scored two while French and Smith emerged with three shared victories.

The Fighting-Nine pilots were saddened to return to *Lexington* and discover they had lost their CAG. Commander Phil Torrey, who had led VF-9 into their initial combat and scored the first Hellcat victory ever over Wake Island in October 1943, was last spotted making a pass on a Tojo before disappearing in the aerial confusion. Fighting-Nine CO Herb Houck was "flighted up" to CAG, while Lieutenant John S. Kitchen assumed command of VF-9.

San Jacinto's VF-45 scored 28 during the day, second to VF-80, with squadron CO Commander Gordon Schecter becoming yet another "ace in a day" over two missions, while Ensign R. R. Kidwell also scored five in two missions.

Air Group 4's first strike wasn't launched until 1407 hours. Major Marshall of VMF-213 led eight Hellcats, 11 Corsairs and 13 Avengers, along with four Hellcats and 9 Avengers from *Cowpens*, with the Ota Aircraft Assembly plant in Tokyo as their target. Unfortunately, their late launch meant a change in target. The fliers attacked Mawatari Airfield, inflicting considerable damage to the hangars and other installations. Captain W. J. Bedford and Captain M. L. Parks led their two divisions in strafing the field following their bomb runs. The Corsairs hit ten twin-engine aircraft they identified as Bettys, setting four on fire, while the Avengers lit up the hangars on the south end of the airfield. Several other sweeps were launched through the afternoon and by the end of the day the two Marine squadrons had claimed five enemy aircraft shot down, with 15 claimed by Fighting-4's Hellcats.

With the weather closing in during the late afternoon, two divisions of VF(N)-90's F6F-5N Hellcats were launched from *Enterprise* on a "zipper" mission to hit the Japanese airfield at Yokosuka in order to prevent any Japanese attempts to attack the fleet. Ninety minutes after these Hellcats left the ship, the specially-modified electronic warfare TBM-3D was launched with a Hellcat escort to orbit over Tokyo Bay and jam Japanese radar. The mission also succeeded in identifying 23 separate enemy radar installations, valuable information when the fleet returned to these waters. VT(N)-90 launched 11 TBM-3D radar-equipped Avengers at 0130 hours on February 17 to search for enemy surface units and shipping trying to slip out of the Inland Sea. The search was unsuccessful since there were no ships to find, so the planes attacked airfields on Nii Shima and Hachijo Jima, south of Tokyo Bay. Six more Avengers were launched at 0300 hours to heckle targets south of Tokyo with the intention of deceiving the Japanese by generating misleading radio traffic about future American plans.

The weather was so cold on February 17 that pilots flew in long underwear, and rainwater froze in gun breeches at high altitude where the outside air temperature at 25,000 feet was 55 below zero. With the worsening weather, strikes were canceled before the full schedule was completed. Several formations were able to break through to Tokyo, however, where the weather was somewhat better.

Three air groups joined together to fly the biggest strike of the attack, a bombing mission against three Japanese aircraft factories in Tokyo. Twenty-two F6Fs, 7 F4Us, and 13 TBMs came from Air Group 4, with Air Group 84 sending 12 F4Us, 15 SB2Cs, and 15 TBMs, while Air Group 46 launched 8 F6Fs and 9 TBMs.

VMF-124's Captain W. J. Thomas led the seven Corsairs that escorted 13 Torpedo-4 TBM-3s to strike the Nakajima Tama Aircraft Engine Plant on the northwestern edge of Tokyo. The Marines encountered 24 Tonys, Oscars, and Tojos, just after they crossed the coast south of Tokyo, that harassed the formation through their approach, bombing run and post-strike rendezvous southwest of the city.

Thomas and his division were at 17,000 feet and had just crossed the shoreline when four Zekes came at the Corsairs and slow-rolled as they flashed past, trying to draw the escorts away from their charges. Five Oscars were spotted above that followed the attackers into the target area, where they were joined by two more. Four of the Oscars followed the Avengers when they entered their bombing runs, but couldn't get through defending escorts. Section leader 1st Lieutenant Dahl found his guns were frozen when he attempted to counter an Oscar on his tail by turning into the enemy and opening fire. The maneuver put the Oscar on the tail of his wingman, Lieutenant Goetz. Dahl turned toward the Oscar and managed to open fire successfully. The Oscar flicked away and the two Marines rejoined and went after it. When the Oscar turned to attack them, Goetz fired a burst that hit its engine and set the enemy fighter on fire. Dahl witnessed the enemy's crash.

While Dahl and Goetz were involved with their Oscar, four others attacked Thomas and his wingman, Lieutenant Reynolds. In the ensuing fight, Reynolds flamed one while Thomas hit another that dived away with its engine smoking. When another Oscar turned in on Reynolds' tail, Thomas opened fire and set it aflame before it fell away.

Thomas's flight was credited with definitely shooting down two Oscars while two others were credited as damaged after they were seen smoking and burning, though there was no witness to the final outcome. None of the *Essex* bombers was lost despite heavy antiaircraft fire, and the target was successfully bombed.

VF-4's Lieutenant D. E. "Diz" Laird shot down three, which, combined with his two Luftwaffe kills scored during *Ranger*'s Norway strikes in Operation *Leader* during the summer of 1943, made him the only Navy ace of the war with victories against both Germany and Japan. (Hollis Hills, who scored five as a US Navy pilot in 1944, scored one FW-190 shot down while a member of the RCAF.)

In addition to the main Tokyo strike, *Essex* launched several fighter sweeps. Captain Hartsock's VMF-124 Corsairs attacked Teteyama Airfield at 0708 hours while Major Marshall's sweep attacked coastal shipping, during which 2nd Lieutenant R. D. Greer destroyed a Judy he found. Over the course of these missions, the *Essex* Marines were credited with seven victories and the Red Rippers of Fighting-4 claimed eight.

The other two air groups were equally successful in finding and hitting their targets despite the bad weather. Air Group 84's Navy and Marine Corsairs ran into aerial opposition that saw the Navy fliers equal their previous day's score of five while the Marines shot down an additional 11.

In another strike, Major Alward of VMF-123 bagged a Tojo and then attacked a train with rockets, which exploded so spectacularly he had mud still caked on his windscreen when he recovered aboard *Bennington*.

VF-80's Pat Fleming led three divisions on a sweep southwest of Katori Airfield, where the Hellcats ran across Nates, Oscars, Zekes and Tojos. Fleming scored an additional four on top of the previous day's five that took his wartime total to 19 and made him the fourth-ranked Navy ace, while the others claimed a further eight. The Vipers had scored a stunning total of 83 over the two days of strikes. Overall, the fleet's Hellcat fighter squadrons were responsible for 68 victories, with an additional 13 by *Yorktown*'s Hellcat fighter-bombers of VBF-3 in addition to their previous day's total of 23.

When the fleet turned away to the south shortly after noon as the weather became worse, total claims for the two days of strikes were 340 in the air and 200 more wrecked on airfields. Sixty fleet aircraft had been lost to enemy action and a further 30 to operational causes owing to the bad weather and heavy seas. Several ships were also sunk in Tokyo Bay, including the 10,600-ton *Yamashiro Maru*. Over 1,000 American planes participated in the strikes. Losses were unexpectedly high, largely owing to the large number of inexperienced fliers on their first combat missions.

On the evening of February 24, Task Force 58 returned to strike Tokyo a second time following a week spent supporting the invasion of Iwo Jima, when the fleet closed to 175 miles southeast of Tokyo. The next morning, 174 B-29s of the XXI Bomber Command destroyed approximately 643 acres of the snow-covered city, dropping 453.7 tons of incendiaries and some fragmentation bombs. Tokyo was spared the intended fire when high winds at altitude spread the incendiaries, preventing a good concentration.

The next morning, *Essex* launched a fighter sweep led by Lt Col Millington at 0727 hours in atrocious weather. Shortly after they made landfall, the Corsairs ran into Japanese opposition and several dogfights took place. Captain Finn and 2nd Lieutenant Donald A. Carlson joined in damaging another Oscar, while three other Oscars were hit but not confirmed by others in the flight. The Marines strafed Kumagaya and Matsuyama airfields, where Carlson was forced down because of a hit in his gas tank. He made a hard landing in a plowed field and radioed to those above, "Good luck to you guys. Say howdy to my wife. I'll be seeing you at Mike's." He made good on the promise six months later when he arrived in Hawaii "alive and as well as a man could expect who had lost his teeth during frequent beatings, had been starved and put in solitary confinement for 40 days." The fight was Air Group 4's final confrontation with the enemy.

At the same time that Air Group 4 experienced its final combat, Roger Hedrick led 16 VF-84 Corsairs on a sweep to Katori Airfield, where they ran into eight Ki.84 *Hayate* fighters, known to the Americans as "Frank." Hedrick, a 9-victory ace with VF-17 in the Solomons, quickly disposed of two Franks, flying through the fireball when the second exploded right in front of him. Lieutenant Willis Laney's division ran across a group of Zekes and he flamed two. Hedrick then made his final score of the war when he set a Zeke on fire that crashed on the beach below. Having destroyed nine, VF-84 then expended their rockets on targets of opportunity. In all, the fighters of Task Force 58 claimed 160 Japanese planes destroyed, of which only 37 were taken on the wing.

High seas and bad weather prevented further strikes against Tokyo, and Admiral Mitscher ordered the carriers out of the Tokyo area the next day. Scheduled strikes against Nagoya, Kobe, and Osaka were canceled when high seas prevented the fleet from reaching a favorable launching position. On February 27 the fleet refueled southwest of Iwo Jima and took replacement aircraft from the supporting CVEs.

CHAPTER SEVEN

IWO JIMA

With Japanese air power in the Home Islands sufficiently checkmated, Fifth Fleet turned toward Iwo Jima on February 18. The amphibious forces were set to invade the next day. The island was important because of its location, halfway between the Marianas and Japan, and only 600 miles from Tokyo. By the end of May, three airfields would nearly cover the island, providing safe haven for B-29s shot up over Japan that could not make the full 1,200-mile flight back to the Marianas, while long-range P-51 Mustangs based there would provide escorts for the bombers on their raids over the Home Islands.

As the Fifth Fleet headed toward Iwo Jima, the amphibious forces had already arrived off the island on February 16 to begin "softening up" what one Marine later described as "a bad-smelling pork chop, burned black, five miles long and two-and-a-half miles wide." On the first day, one of the strangest events of the entire invasion happened at 1413 hours, when an OS2U-3 Kingfisher floatplane from *Pensacola* (CA-24) flown by Lt(jg) D. W. Gandy USNR reported he had a Zeke on his tail. A moment later he called that he was going after the enemy fighter, and then shortly exulted, "I got him, I got him!" Gandy was over Mount Suribachi at 1,500 feet when his radioman called that a Zeke was on their tail. The enemy fighter fired a short burst as it dove past while Gandy zigzagged, then made a tight right climbing turn that put him 500 feet right in front of the Kingfisher. Gandy opened up with his single .30-caliber machine gun and hit the enemy fighter's cockpit, engine and wing root. He continued firing as the Zeke smoked, burst into flames and crashed on the side of the volcano.

VMF-124's Lt Col Millington led a flight of 24 F4Us and 24 F6Fs that were launched at 0642 hours on D-Day, February 19, 1945, to support the invasion. The fighters strafed the flanks of the landing beaches and the high ground beyond, dropping napalm and firing rockets, then strafed the beaches just ahead of the first landing craft.

Bad weather prevented another strike on D-Day, and would hamper air support throughout the campaign.

One of the most unique squadrons taking part in the invasion was VOC-1, which operated 28 FM-2 Wildcats aboard *Wake Island* (CVE-65), in the highly-specialized role of naval gunfire direction. Originally commissioned in December 1943 as VOF-1 (Observation-Fighter Squadron) in answer to the experience of ship-based observation units during the invasions of North Africa and Sicily where it was found that the Curtiss SOC-3 Seagull simply couldn't survive in hostile airspace, the squadron had been the third after VF-12 and VF-17 to receive the F4U-1 Corsair, which allowed the gunfire spotters to defend themselves. The pilots had been specially trained as artillery spotters at the US Army Artillery School at Fort Sill, Oklahoma.

Despite the fact they had "cured" their Corsairs of all the problems associated with the F4U's use aboard carriers, the Corsairs were taken away and the squadron was mounted on F6F-5 Hellcats when they went aboard *Tulagi* (CVE-72) to participate in Operation *Dragoon*, the invasion of Southern France.

While spotting gunfire for the invasion on August 20, 1944, Ensign Alfred R. Wood saw and shot down two Luftwaffe He-111H bombers over Lyon, France, one shared with Lt Rene E. Poucel, while division leader LCDR John H. Sandor and Ensign David Robinson shot down a third Heinkel bomber. The next day, Lt(jg) Edward Olszewski shot down two Ju-52s over the Rhone River, while his wingman, Ensign Richard V. Yentzer, shot down a third Ju-52. With two other German aircraft shot down by the Hellcats of VF-74, these were the only US Navy Hellcat victories in Europe. The squadron had been responsible for the destruction of 825 trucks and other vehicles, with another 334 damaged by the naval gunfire they spotted.

After transferring from the Hellcat to the Wildcat, the squadron went aboard *Wake Island* in Hawaii in November 1944 and participated in the invasion of Luzon in January 1945, where pilots were credited with 11 more aerial victories. During the Iwo Jima invasion, squadron pilots flew two and even three missions a day between February 16 and March 10 for a total of 2,375 flying hours calling gunfire for battleships, cruisers and destroyers. Owing to the bad weather throughout the invasion, there were many days where VOC-1's Wildcats were the only American aircraft over the island.

While the rest of Task Force 58's aircraft were forced by the weather to remain aboard their ships, *Enterprise* launched six Hellcats at 1630 to provide dusk CAP over the island. While this mission proved uneventful, their replacements launched two hours later proved the worth of night fighters when they were vectored on eight interceptions. Shortly before 1930 hours Lieutenant James Wood made radar contact with an enemy Ki.49 Helen, a twin-engine heavy bomber, and splashed it after a 30-minute pursuit.

Task Group 58.5, *Enterprise*, *Saratoga*, and their escorts was dissolved on February 21. *Saratoga* joined Rear Admiral Calvin Durgin's Task Group 52.2, the escort carrier force operating northeast of Iwo Jima that provided direct air support for the Marines, where she would fly night patrols over Iwo Jima and nearby Chichi Jima. *Enterprise* joined Task Group 58.2, where she operated with *Lexington* and *Hancock*.

Venerable *Saratoga* was now "Queen of the Jeeps" (escort carriers were known as "jeep" carriers), but her reign was short lived. Her radar picked up a large bogey, estimated at 20 to 25 aircraft, 75 miles distant, just before 1630 hours that same day. At first, the bogey was identified as friendly owing to the fact other combat air patrols and antisubmarine patrols were returning to the task force. Twenty minutes later, however, the six *Saratoga* fighters that were sent to investigate positively identified the enemy formation and quickly downed two Zekes. Nine minutes after that, six Judy dive bombers popped out of the low cloud cover and attacked the old carrier. Despite deadly antiaircraft fire, the Judys hit *Saratoga* with three bombs in three minutes and two suicide attackers damaged her when they glanced off her starboard side. Two more suicide hits wrecked the forward flight deck, and large fires were set off in the hangar deck that damage control parties fought for 90 minutes before bringing them under control at 1842 hours. At 1846 hours, five more suicide attackers were spotted. Four were shot down by *Saratoga's* defending gunners, but one dropped a bomb that exploded over the flight deck just before the Judy hit and bounced over the side. *Saratoga* began recovering planes an hour later, but her war was over. With 192 wounded and 123 killed or missing, *Saratoga* was spared further attack, but the Japanese sent raids throughout the night to hit the invasion fleet.

While the *kamikazes* went after *Saratoga*, *Bismarck Sea* (CVE-95) was attacked at 1845 hours when she was hit by a Judy on her starboard side near the rear of the flight deck under the 40mm gun tub. The *kamikaze* crashed through the hangar deck into the magazines below. Two minutes later, another attacker was spotted in the last light of day as it dived out of the cloudy sky and hit the aft elevator shaft. This Judy exploded on impact, which destroyed the fire-fighting saltwater distribution system, preventing further damage control as the fires spread. At 1910 hours, the "abandon ship" order was given. *Bismarck Sea* burned fiercely for three more hours before she rolled over and sank, taking 318 of her crew with her. The little CVE was the last US Navy aircraft carrier sunk during World War II. Over the next 12 hours, three destroyers and three destroyer escorts managed to rescue 605 officers and men from her crew of 923. Despite darkness, heavy seas and continuing air attacks, 378 men including her captain were pulled from the water by the crew of *Edmonds* (DE-406). Thirty of *Edmonds'* crew went into the water to rescue wounded.

Lunga Point (CVE-94), *Keokuk* (AKN-4) and *LST-477* also came under attack, but all three escaped with relatively light damage.

The badly damaged *Saratoga* returned to the United States, where the Navy decided that owing to her extensive damage and age, she would become exclusively a training carrier. Repairs included removing the aft elevator and turning the hangar deck into classrooms. She returned to Pearl Harbor on June 1, 1945 and continued training aviators throughout the summer. Following the surrender, she took part in Operation *Magic Carpet*, returning 29,204 veterans to the United States, the largest number of any ship participating. She was finally taken out of service in December 1945. Over a 17-year career, during which she was instrumental in developing naval aviation's operational capability and the tactics that would lead to victory in World War II, *Saratoga* set a record of 98,549 landings and received eight battle stars for her World War II service. In the summer of 1946, she was sunk in Test Baker of the Operation *Crossroads* atomic bomb tests at Bikini Atoll.

While *Saratoga* fought for her life, all VF(N)-90 fighters aboard *Enterprise* were manned at 1700 hours, but it was not until 1748 hours that the first night CAP was launched. The two Hellcats operated with other F6F-5Ns from the *Essex* and *Randolph* (CV-15) night-fighter detachments. They were vectored on several intercepts until an hour after sundown, but the enemy managed to evade each interception.

Enterprise launched eight VT(N)-90 Avengers on a search for eight missing *Saratoga* planes led by commanding officer Lieutenant C. B. Collins. The planes experienced poor visibility as they flew under a low ceiling while they searched out to 150 miles due south of Iwo Jima before returning to a rendezvous point five miles east of the island. Four Avengers piloted by Collins, Lt(jg) Gordon Hinrichs, Lt(jg) Ernie Lawton and Lt(jg) Joe Jewell were the first to arrive. When they emerged from the overcast at 400 feet, they discovered they were immediately astern of *Tennessee* (BB-43). They turned hard left, which put them abeam of *Idaho* (BB-42), with other ships of the invasion fleet nearby. The *kamikaze* attacks had the ships' gunners alert and on edge. An LST was first to open fire, followed by every ship that could bring her guns to bear.

Lawton and Jewell managed to climb back into the clouds, but Collins and Hinrichs dove for the water, which put them at masthead height between two lines of ships that included *Idaho* and *Tennessee*, as well as the battleships *Nevada, Texas* and *Arkansas* and the cruisers *Chester, Pensacola, Salt Lake City* and *Tuscaloosa*. All of them fired at the "enemy" aircraft and the curtain of antiaircraft was "continuous, heavy, and accurate."

Hinrichs ditched his shot-up Avenger, but was then nearly run down by a sub-chaser with its crew lined up at the rail with pistols and Thompson submachine guns. Hinrichs "cussed them out in considerable detail and length" before they identified him and his crew as American. When the three were brought aboard, Hinrichs told one deckhand that "if he was as handy with a line as he was with those goddamn guns, they'd have been aboard five minutes earlier." While Hinrichs and his crew were rescued, Collins and his crew were never found; he was the second VT(N)-90 commander lost in as many months.

The Marines on Iwo Jima took Mount Suribachi on February 23 and raised the American Flag. Task Force 58 set course to the north, leaving *Enterprise* to provide night air cover until the island was declared secure on March 9. The venerable carrier, the only survivor of the prewar fleet carriers, was about to add a new record to her already-illustrious tally.

Enterprise's original assignment was provision of dusk and night CAP. Now she was assigned additional responsibilities as the sole large carrier on station. *Kamikazes* were staging through airfields in the northern Bonins and the "Big E" was given the job of suppressing the airfields. She was also assigned responsibility to provide daytime CAP for the escort carriers. This required her to operate aircraft 24 hours a day. Between February 23 and March 2, *Enterprise* had a minimum of two and a maximum of 22 planes in the air at any given time. No other carrier in World War II accomplished such an operation.

Unlike the day carriers, which launched an entire deck-load for a single strike, *Enterprise* launched no more than four to eight aircraft at a time, but there was continuous flight deck activity owing to the

24-hour operation cycle. Operations began at 0630 hours, when the first four-plane CAP was launched, with further CAP launches every three hours till dusk. Six to 12 Hellcats were launched at 1645 hours for dusk patrol over Iwo. Between 1815 and 0415 hours, these patrols were relieved every two hours by launching two Hellcats. At 1530 hours, the final day fleet CAP mission was launched. The fleet CAP was relieved at 1815 hours by the first night CAP, which was relieved at three-hour intervals until 0315 hours. The Airedales never received more than a 30-minute break from launching or landing aircraft.

Avengers flew search missions and antisubmarine patrols during the day, as well as target-towing missions for fleet antiaircraft practice. Depending on good weather, at sunset two Hellcats and four Avengers would be launched for airfield suppression over Chichi Jima. Four single-aircraft night heckler missions were flown starting at 1815 hours, with either a Hellcat or Avenger sent to bomb the Chichi Jima Airfield in an effort to slow the enemy's efforts to repair the damage caused by the dusk strike, with the last mission launched at 0145 hours. On March 6, predawn strikes were added to target Susaki Airfield, the Futami seaplane base, and any shipping discovered in the vicinity of Chichi Jima.

While these operations took their greatest toll on the pilots and flight deck crews, the whole crew had to adapt to the new procedures and routines to support these operations. Day and night shifts were created in the air department divisions, so flight operations had only half the number of men usually at work. This meant there were only three crews of plane handlers to spot planes on deck during the day and four at night, rather than the normal seven, which doubled the workload for each crew. Flight deck operations were changed to involve the least aircraft possible. The deck park was forward of amidships, leaving the after deck free for landings, while aircraft were launched from the two catapults, which reduced the amount of deck required. Hangar deck operations were also changed to require only half the usual number of handler crews.

With only three landing signal officers aboard, the LSOs often worked 13-hour shifts, more than twice what was considered reasonable. There was only one qualified catapult officer; he worked 18-hour shifts, since he was required to be present for all catapult launches. Despite the exhaustion from the near-continuous flight activity, only three serious accidents happened. A Hellcat proved once again the fighter's legendary toughness, plowing into the rear of the *Enteprise's* island on February 27 with the pilot escaping injury, though the plane was a write-off. Two accidents on March 1 and 5 involved Hellcats going into the barriers when they lost their tail hooks on touchdown.

The flight deck went quiet for 45 minutes in the late afternoon of March 2 owing to a thick warm front that brought heavy rain and zero visibility after 174 hours of continuous operations. *Enterprise* had launched 406 flights, an average of 50 every 24-hour period. During this time, Night Air Group-90 expended tens of thousands of rounds of .50-caliber ammunition, 261 100-pound bombs, 154 3½-inch rockets, and 94 5-inch rockets. *Enterprise* had proven that it was possible to conduct the kind of all- weather operations that became standard over the next 60 years. Continuous small-scale heckler operations were shown to be an effective, less-expensive alternative to periodic, large-scale heavy bombing raids for neutralizing enemy airfields.When the front passed, operations resumed at their former pace.

The next day, six Avengers struck Chichi Jima in a daylight strike and torpedoed a small freighter in Higashi harbor on the outlying island of Haha Jima. Over the next five days, *Enterprise* maintained the same grueling operating schedule, with only a few interruptions owing to continuing poor weather.

The purpose of the invasion was realized on March 4, when the first damaged B-29 made an emergency landing on the recently repaired Airfield Number 1. Two days later, the first P-51D Mustangs of the VII Air Force's 21st Fighter Group arrived on the island. Their presence relieved *Enterprise* of her responsibility for air defense of the island, though she continued to mount night heckler raids and predawn strikes against Chichi Jima's airfield for three more days. By March 9, all of the 21st Fighter Group's Mustangs were present on Iwo Jima and *Enterprise* could be relieved. The last plane from the last strike against Chichi Jima trapped aboard at 2120 hours on March 9. At 2121 hours, *Enterprise* set course due south, putting Iwo Jima behind her at 20 nautical miles per hour.

During her two weeks of duty at Iwo Jima, *Enterprise* was never attacked and her aircraft destroyed or damaged only three enemy planes and eight freighters and barges. While the long hours the crew put in had not translated into tangible results for the effort, Captain Grover B. Hall's action report for February 10–22 accurately stated: "One does not employ a night watchman and determine his worth in terms of the number of bandits he kills. His value is determined by the number of bandits which his presence discourages from approaching."

The invasion of Iwo Jima was originally planned to last two weeks, but the island was not declared secure until March 16, 1945. The battle cost the United States 4,554 Marines and 363 Navy men killed. Of the 21,000 Japanese defenders, fewer than 3,000 survived.

CHAPTER EIGHT

PRELUDE TO OKINAWA

Following the second Tokyo strike, Task Force 58 arrived 75 miles southeast of Okinawa on March 1. The next month of operations would see the fast carriers strike this island, which was the final invasion target ahead of the invasion of the Home Islands, as well as making further strikes against Kyushu to cut off the defenders of Okinawa from support.

Essex launched her major morning strike at 0715 hours, led by new CAG Commander Upham at the head of 16 Avengers from Torpedo-4, 15 Hellcats from Fighting-4 and 16 Marine Corsairs led by Major Fay V. Domke and Captain Edmond P. Hartsock; their target was Naha Airfield on the west coast of the island. Over the target, Corsairs strafed antiaircraft positions to silence the defenses, followed by the Navy Hellcats. The Avengers made their glide-bombing attacks while the fighters returned for repeated strafing runs.

Essex sent a second strike against Naha with VMF-213's Major Marshall leading 16 Corsairs, eight Hellcats and 15 Avengers. This attack was hindered by adverse cloud conditions. VF-4's Lt(jg) Doug Cahoon was hit by flak; his Hellcat exploded on impact. The tail of the Avenger flown by Lt(jg) Scott Vogt was blown off by flak just as he dropped his bombs. As the bomber crashed on the airfield, one parachute was seen to open.

Air Group 4 pulled off from the attack and trapped back aboard to complete the last combat mission of their deployment successfully.

The Fifth Fleet retired to Ulithi at the conclusion of the Okinawa strikes, arriving at the fleet anchorage on March 4. While at Ulithi, Air Group 4 departed *Essex* and the ship welcomed Air Group 84, the last air group to serve aboard during the war. The Marines of VMF-124 and VMF-213 had shot down 23 enemy aircraft and destroyed 64 on the ground in two months of operation. *Essex*'s new fighter-bomber squadron, VBF-84, inherited the Marine Corsairs. The two Marine Corsair squadrons aboard *Wasp* also departed, with VBF-86 assuming title to their Corsairs.

Thirty-two of 54 pilots in VBF-84 were former SB2C pilots put out of a job when VB-84 and its Helldivers was disbanded at the end of 1944.

Intrepid returned to the western Pacific after repair for the damage suffered the previous November carrying Air Group 10, the only other naval air group besides Air Group 9 to fly three tours, and the only one to fly all three tours in the Pacific. Fighting-Ten had first flown F4F Wildcats off *Enterprise* and at Guadalcanal in the fall of 1942, when they were led by the legendary Jimmy Flatley. They had transferred to Hellcats on return from Guadalcanal and returned to *Enterprise* in time to participate in the fast carrier offensive that concluded with the Marianas Turkey Shoot. Now flying the F4U-1D Corsair, they were the only Navy squadron to fly Wildcats, Hellcats and Corsairs in combat. VBF-10 was the first fighter-bomber unit to take the new 11.75-inch "tiny Tim" rocket into combat. The pilots of both squadrons were also the first to utilize G-suits since VF-8 had pioneered that equipment a year previously.

Air Group 5 also returned for a second tour, now aboard *Franklin* (CV-13). VF-5, VMF-214 and VMF-452 all flew Corsairs. *Hancock*'s new VBF-6 was also equipped with Corsairs. In all, there were now seven Navy and six Marine squadrons flying the Corsair, a remarkable turnaround in less than four months.

The fleet now prepared for participation in the looming invasion of Okinawa, set for the end of the month. Admiral Mitscher warned his captains that they could expect the largest and most sustained *kamikaze* attacks experienced so far, since intelligence believed the Japanese had at least 1,000 planes in Kyushu for use in such attacks. The fleet's first mission would be to neutralize that threat as much as possible with a series of air strikes on Kyushu, the southernmost of the Home Islands.

Mitscher's warning was prophetic. As he and his commanders met aboard *Bunker Hill*, Vice Admiral Matome Ugaki, now commander of the Fifth Air Fleet, bid farewell to the volunteer flight crews who were preparing to depart on a long-distance, one-way mission to attack the American fleet anchorage at Ulithi, 800 miles southeast. Ugaki, formerly chief of staff to the legendary Admiral Isoroku Yamamoto and later commander of the Center Force battleships at Leyte Gulf, had come to see the deployment of Operation *Tan*, a preemptive strike against Mitscher's fast carriers.

Twenty-four P1Y1 Frances attack bombers were launched that morning. Bad weather and mechanical problems along the way reduced their number to a handful, but one Frances swept into the lagoon just after sunset. The pilot spotted *Randolph*, which was loading ammunition under spotlights. The call to General Quarters came just before the bomber crashed into her flight deck aft, destroying 14 aircraft and setting her ablaze. Three hours later the fires were out, but *Randolph* would not be part of Task Force 58 when the fleet sortied three days later.

Unbeknown to American intelligence, there were more than *kamikazes* waiting for them on Kyushu. The Imperial Japanese Navy Air Force was ready to deploy its newest and best fighter, flown by a unit that had among its members the best pilots the service had left. The 343rd Naval Air Group had been organized only weeks earlier by Captain Minoru Genda, perhaps Japan's most outstanding naval aviator and one of the best Japanese naval officers of the war; he had been chosen by Admiral Yamamoto to plan the Pearl Harbor attack. With his reputation, Genda had been able to get nearly every surviving IJNAF ace assigned to the unit, including Saburo Sakai. Because of these pilots, the unit was known as "the Squadron of

Experts." They were the only unit to be completely equipped with the Kawasaki N1K2-J *Shiden-Kai*, a new development of the fighter American naval aviators had first met over Guam during the invasion of the Marianas and named "George."

The N1K1-J *Shiden* the Americans fought over the Marianas was a land-based development of the most powerful Japanese floatplane fighter ever designed, the N1K1 *Kyofu*. By the time that airplane had reached production status, the nature of the war had changed so much that there was no use for it. The N1K1-J had a very similar airframe to the earlier fighter, with long stalky landing gear owing to the position of the wing.

Finally introduced into combat in the summer of 1944 following a prolonged gestation, the *Shiden* quickly proved itself an outstanding fighter, remaining a potent adversary to the end of the war. However, it had several shortcomings, the primary problem being the unreliability of the Homare 21 engine, Additionally, the wheel brakes were so poor that pilots often landed on the grass next to a paved runway in order to reduce the landing roll without brakes. While American Navy pilots had encountered only a few N1K1 fighters in the Marianas and the Philippines, the opinion among those who had run into it was that when there was a competent pilot in the cockpit, the George was a dangerous adversary.

The effort to put right the shortcomings of the original design led to the N1K2-J *Shiden-Kai* (Kai: first modification), with a nearly completely redesigned airframe. The wing position was changed from mid to low, and all 20mm cannon were housed within the wing rather than the underwing fairing, as was the outer weapon of the earlier design. Effort was also put into simplifying the airframe for ease of production; the N1J-2-J had only 43,000 parts compared with 66,000 for the N1K1-J. While the Homare 21 engine was modified, it proved no more reliable in the N1K2-J, however, and continued to create problems for pilots and maintenance crews. Excellent results were found when the prototype N1K2-J first flew on December 31, 1943. While full-scale production was set to begin in the summer of 1944, the prototypes experienced prolonged development troubles that required changes, which inexorably slowed production. Further delays came in delivery of engines, landing gear assemblies, aluminum extrusions and steel forgings as a result of the B-29 strategic bombing campaign, which came into its own in November 1944. Only 60 N1K2-Js were produced in 1944, with only 294 in 1945 by the end of the war. The "Squadron of Experts" were mounted in an airplane that equaled their enemies', but like their German counterparts flying the Me-262 in the JV-44 "Squadron of Experts," they would be "too little, too late."

While Task Force 58 headed toward Japan, Hamilton McWhorter experienced the most terrifying minutes of his career as a fighter pilot.

With the *Randolph* having taken a *kamikaze* hit, while she was undergoing repairs, the squadron went ashore and was stationed at the Marine airbase on Falalop Island. We were sent out on a strike mission on Yap Island about 90 miles to the west. There was no aerial opposition, but the flak was still very intense. Just as I was recovering from a strafing run on a heavy antiaircraft gun position, I took a huge hit. I looked out and the right wing was on fire – the flames were going back past the tail! I unstrapped and opened the canopy to bale out, because I was sure the wing was going to come off immediately. Fortunately, common sense overcame the panic of the moment and I stayed with the airplane long enough to get out over the ocean, and then the fire burned itself out. I stayed unstrapped and kept the cockpit canopy open all the way back to Falalop, for fear the wing would still come off. When I got back and they checked the airplane, it turned out a flak round had hit in the right wing gunbay and set the gun charging hydraulic fluid on fire, popping all the ammo. On the terror scale of 1–10, that was about a 25.

The Fifth Fleet began its run-in to Kyushu the night of March 17. A scouting line of 12 destroyers positioned 30 miles ahead of the fleet split into two radar patrol groups to provide early warning of incoming attacks at dawn on March 18, one 30 miles west and the other 30 miles north of the launch point. Each group was covered by a CAP of eight fighters under the control of fighter direction officers aboard the destroyers. When an attack was spotted, the CAP was reinforced to 16 fighters. The first bogey appeared on the radar screens at 2145 hours on March 17; from that point the fleet was continually shadowed, though *Enterprise* night fighters shot down two. The destroyers also attacked two submarine contacts.

Task Force 58 was 100 miles east of the southern tip of Kyushu at 0545 hours on March 18 when the first fighter sweep was launched, composed of 32 Hellcats and Corsairs from each of the four task groups. The sweep was followed 45 minutes later by 60 Avengers and Helldivers escorted by 40 fighters from the four groups.

The Japanese were forewarned of the impending American attack and relocated many aircraft away from coastal airfields. In response, the afternoon strike targets were changed to locations further inland that were originally listed for attack on March 19. The afternoon missions made claims of 102 enemy aircraft shot down and 275 destroyed or damaged on the ground.

The Jolly Rogers of VF-17 had returned to combat when they came aboard *Hornet* at the end of January, mounted for this tour in the F6F-5 Hellcat, rather than the Corsairs they had flown the year before. Squadron commander LCDR Marshall U. Beebe, who had narrowly escaped death as commander of composite squadron VC-39 aboard the ill-fated CVE *Liscombe Bay* when the carrier was sunk during the Gilberts campaign, led the squadron on a sweep of Kanoya Airfield with his wingman, Lieutenant Robert C. Coats. The squadron repeatedly ran across Japanese fighter formations in the airfield vicinity, claiming a total of 32 victories. Beebe and Coats both returned to the carrier with "ace in a day" claims of five each.

Essex's VBF-83 was the most successful Corsair squadron on March 18. In fighting over Tomioka Airfield, the Corsairs bagged 17 Zekes and a Judy, with a further nine probables. Major Hansen led four divisions of VMF-112 who ran into 20 Zekes as they headed toward Kanoya East Airfield at 19,000 feet. Five enemy fighters were shot down in the Marines' first pass, with four more in the second. The Corsairs returned to *Bennington* to find none had been damaged in the fight.

Enemy attacks on the fleet were slight in terms of the number of aircraft involved, but the attacks were carried out in an aggressive and determined manner. With cloudy skies, single enemy aircraft used the cover to dodge the combat air patrols and make attacks on the fleet. While many such attackers were shot down, *Yorktown* and *Enterprise* were hit by bombs, while the recently-returned *Intrepid* experienced a near miss by a twin-engine plane shot down by gunfire. *Yorktown*'s damage was minor and the bomb that hit *Enterprise* failed to explode; thus all carriers continued flight operations. The problem was that little, if any, warning was being provided by radars; at times the first indication a ship was under attack was visual sighting by the close screen, with the picket destroyers providing invaluable warning with their visual sightings. The task group combat air patrols shot down a total of 12 aircraft, while shipboard antiaircraft fire got 21.

A photo reconnaissance mission flown by an F6F-5P from *Bunker Hill* found a large number of major Imperial Navy ships in Inland Sea harbors. Admiral Mitscher decided to attack the ships at Kure Naval Base and Kobe Harbor on March 19, while fighter sweeps flown against airfields on Shikoku and western Honshu would precede and follow the strikes to defend the fleet against attack.

A search flown by VT9N)-90 Avengers over the night of March 18–19 reported the possibility of a battleship and carrier leaving the Kure Channel, but a subsequent predawn search failed to find any ships. The first fighter sweep was launched at 0525 hours, followed an hour later by the strikes. They were about to run into an unexpected enemy.

Major Tom Mobley led 16 VMF-123 Corsairs on a dawn sweep of Kure and Hiroshima. Hearing pilots of VBF-10 calling for help, Mobley started to turn his formation when they were hit by 30 N1K2-J *Shiden-Kai* fighters flown by Genda's "Squadron of Experts." Two F4Us were shot out of the formation immediately. These Japanese pilots were vastly different from the sorry lot the

Bennington Corsairs had clobbered the day before, flying two and four-plane units, using disciplined tactics and shooting accurately. The unfortunate Marines had just run into the best Japanese Navy pilots left. Outnumbered two to one, the Marines fought for their lives. Mobley shot down one enemy fighter, then took 20mm hits from a well-flown *Shiden-Kai* and had to pull out of the fight. He turned over command to Captain William A. Cantrel, a Solomons veteran who had shot at one Zeke over "The Slot" and missed. In two minutes over the Inland Sea, he shot down two Shidens. With his Corsair damaged and wounded in his foot, Cantrel organized a withdrawal. Eight of the Corsairs were badly shot up. During a 30-minute running fight, the aggressive Japanese hunted down cripples. Cantrel managed to hit two as he protected his charges. Finally out at sea and away from the Japanese, one Corsair gave out and the pilot parachuted near a picket destroyer. Back aboard *Bennington*, three of the surviving Corsairs were so badly damaged they were immediately pushed overboard. The Marines had lost six F4Us and two pilots, while they claimed nine shot down. Cantrel was awarded the Navy Cross for his leadership.

Among the 343rd pilots encountered by the Marines was Lieutenant Naoshi Kanno, who was the top-scoring Naval Academy graduate of the Pacific War. Based at Yap, Kanno first saw combat over the Marianas in June 1944, flying the N1K1-J *Shiden* with the original 343rd Air Group, and was credited with 30 victories that summer. While at Yap, he used the head-on attack to shoot down several Seventh Air Force B-24 Liberators. When Genda reorganized the 343rd, Kanno was named commander of the 301st *Hikotai*, which was the unit that initially took on the VMF-123 Corsairs during the battle of March 19. Kanno was one of the 13 unit members shot down when he was hit by a VBF-10 Corsair that came to the Marines' rescue, though he was able to parachute safely. Kanno was credited with 13 more victories before he was killed attacking B-24s over Yaku Island on August 1,1945.

Under his command, the 301st had the highest casualties of any 343rd squadron, though it was also the top-scoring squadron.

The top naval leadership of the Pacific War (from left to right): Admiral Raymond A. Spruance, Commander of Fifth Fleet; Admiral Ernest J. King, Chief of Naval Operations and Commander in Chief of the US Fleet; Admiral Chester W. Nimitz, Commander in Chief of the Pacific Fleet and Pacific Ocean Areas; and Brigadier General Sanderford Jarman, US Army. (Naval History and Heritage Command)

Task Force 58 commander Vice Admiral Marc Mitscher, with US Navy Ace of Aces David McCampbell. (US Navy National Museum of Naval Aviation)

TF-38 commander Vice Admiral John S. McCain and Third Fleet commander Admiral William F. "Bull" Halsey confer aboard Third Fleet flagship USS *New Jersey.* (Naval History and Heritage Command)

Future 38th President of the United States Lieutenant Gerald R. Ford, navigator aboard USS *Monterey* (CVL-26). (Gerald R. Ford Library)

F4U-1D Corsairs of VMF-113 in 1945. With the F4U-1D, the Corsair reached its full potential both as a potent air-to-air fighter and a deadly ground attack fighter-bomber. (US Navy National Museum of Naval Aviation)

Battleship USS *Indiana* (BB-58) underway at sea in 1944, probably in late January while the ship was en route to the Marshall Islands to support the Kwajalein invasion. (Naval History and Heritage Command)

USS *Meredith* (DD-726) at sea, April 16, 1944. She is painted in Camouflage Measure 32, Design 3D. (Naval History and Heritage Command)

USS *Enterprise* (CV-6) hit by a *kamikaze* piloted by Lieutenant Shunsuke Tomiyasu off Okinawa, May 1945. The hit put the legendary carrier out of the war. (Naval History and Heritage Command)

USS *Belleau Wood* (CVL-24) burning aft, after she was hit by a *kamikaze* while operating off the Philippines on October 30, 1944. Flight deck crewmen are moving undamaged TBM torpedo planes away from the flames as others fight the fires. USS *Franklin* (CV-13), also hit during this *kamikaze* attack, is aflame in the distance. (Getty Images)

USS *North Carolina* (BB-55) in heavy seas during Typhoon Cobra. (Naval History and Heritage Command)

Halsey's typhoon destroyer: an unidentified destroyer fights heavy seas during Typhoon Cobra. (Naval History and Heritage Command)

SB2C-4s of VB-3 operating from USS *Yorktown* (CV-10) over Iwo Jima, February 1945. (Naval History and Heritage Command)

A hole in the flight deck of USS *Randolph* (CV-15) resulting from a *kamikaze* hit on March 11, 1945. The Americans were not expecting the long-range *kamikaze* attack by IJNAF Frances bombers against the Ulithi anchorage. (Naval History and Heritage Command)

Sailors scramble with hoses to extinguish fire aboard USS *Franklin* (CV-13), as water pours from the open doors of the ship following an attack by an IJNAF Judy dive-bomber while the ship was off the coast of Kyushu on March 19, 1945. View from the USS *Santa Fe* (CL-60). (Getty Images)

Firefighters aboard the aircraft carrier USS *Hancock* (CV-19) hose down damage caused by a Japanese *kamikaze* attack on April 7, 1945. Hancock was damaged sufficiently to send her back to Ulithi for repairs that lasted until June and removed Air Group Six from further combat. (Getty Images)

Japanese super-battleship *Yamato* underway during trials, October 30, 1941. Armed with nine 18-inch cannon, she was the largest battleship in the world. (Naval History and Heritage Command)

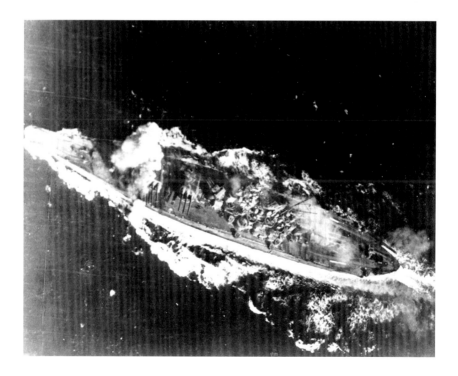

Yamato hit by a bomb, April 7, 1945. (Naval History and Heritage Command)

USS *Bunker Hill* (CV-17) burns after taking a *kamikaze* hit off Okinawa, May 1945. (Naval History and Heritage Command)

Crewmen aboard USS *Enterprise* fight fires after a *kamikaze* strike off Okinawa in May 1945. (Naval History and Heritage Command)

F6F-5 Hellcats of VF-83 and F4U-1D Corsairs of VBF-83. The record 79-day deployment of USS *Essex* during the Okinawa campaign saw the ship steam 33,865 nautical miles, endure 357 raids (183 day and 174 night), while her gunners claimed destruction of 11 Japanese aircraft. Air Group 83 shot down 220 enemy aircraft, including 69 in one day. (US Navy National Museum of Naval Aviation)

Grumman delivered the 10,000th F6F Hellcat in May 1945, 21 months after commencing production. This was one of the secrets of American victory in World War II. (Naval History and Heritage Command)

Seafire IIIs aboard HMS *Implacable*, August 1945. (Australian War Memorial)

The Japanese surrender aboard USS *Missouri* (BB-63), September 2, 1945. (Naval History and Heritage Command)

The 343rd had received early warning of the approach of the American formations when the US planes were spotted by a C6N Myrt that managed to get the word back before it was shot down. All three squadrons took off from Kanoya Airfield. The Shidens of the 407th *Hikotai* were the first to encounter Americans when they came across VBF-17 Hellcats. Three aircraft were lost on both sides in the initial attack; one Hellcat and two Shidens were shot down by enemy ground fire, two fighters collided in mid-air, and one Hellcat later crashed while trying to land back aboard *Hornet*. In the end, the 407th *Hikotai* lost six fighters while shooting down eight VBF-17 Hellcats.

The Japanese had originally mistaken the VMF-123 Corsairs for Hellcats. Of the nine victories claimed by the Marines, not one was actually shot down. Kanno's *Hikotai* then ran across the VBF-10 Corsairs. Two F4Us were separated and shot down, while the Americans claimed four N1K2s before they managed to escape. Hellcats of Fighting-9 shot down two Shidens when they attempted to land low on fuel. In the fighting, the 343rd Air Group claimed 52 victories, while the Americans claimed 63. Actual losses were 15 Shidens and 13 pilots, the Myrt with its three-man crew, and nine other fighters from other units. American losses were heavy: 14 fighters were shot down and seven pilots lost, in addition to 11 other aircraft shot down by the heavy flak over Kure. The difference was that the Americans would make good their losses in a week, while the 343rd did not regain full strength for six crucial weeks.

Avengers and Helldivers from Task Groups 58.3 and 58.1 concentrated on the warships at Kure, while those from Task Group 58.4 went after the ships that had been spotted at Kobe, and Task Group 58.2's bombers concentrated on targets and installations in the Kure Naval Air Depot area. These attacks were only moderately successful, primarily owing to the extremely heavy and accurate AA fire encountered, with one group alone losing 13 aircraft over Kure. At Kure, slight damage was inflicted on the battleship *Yamato*, several hits were scored on the hermaphrodite battleship aircraft carrier *Ise*, while slight damage was inflicted on two aircraft carriers. Heavy cruiser *Tone*, which had last been encountered at the battle off Samar in October 1944, was set afire. The light cruiser *Oyodo* was severely damaged and last seen burning badly. At Kobe, what was identified as an escort carrier was hit by three 500lb bombs, and a submarine was slightly damaged.

Just after dawn on March 19, Task Group 58.2 was steaming 20 miles north of the other task groups, 50 miles off the coast of Kyushu, closer than any other unit of the fleet. Both carriers in the group had launched strikes shortly before dawn, with *Franklin* launching a fighter sweep to Kobe, followed 30 minutes later by a strike force of Avengers escorted by Corsairs to hit the ships in the harbor. Thirty-one Corsairs and Avengers, fully fueled and armed, were warming up on the flight deck for the next launch. The crew had been called to General Quarters 12 times in six hours over the preceding night and were already exhausted. The alert status was downgraded to Condition III by Captain Leslie E. Gehres, whose strict discipline and autocracy was disliked by many crewmen. This allowed the crew freedom to leave their GQ station to eat or sleep, while all gun crews remained at their stations. There was building cumulus in all quadrants, with 7/10 cloud layer at 2,500 feet.

At the ship's most vulnerable moment, a D4Y Judy dive bomber suddenly popped out of the clouds directly overhead. It made a low-level run, dropping what were later identified as two 250kg bombs. The first hit the centerline of the flight deck and exploded after penetrating to the hangar deck. Sixteen of the aircraft in the hangar were fully fueled while five were partially fueled. They went up like bombs when the fire spread. Soon their guns began going off as the fire touched their ammunition. The hangar deck was devastated by the explosion of gasoline vapor. The fire spread through open hatches that allowed it to spread to the second and third decks, while the aircraft explosions shredded the flight deck overhead. It quickly spread to the Combat Information Center and Air Plot, which were knocked out. There were only two survivors of the near-instantaneous destruction.

The hangar deck explosions knocked the aircraft on the flight deck together, which caused further fires and explosions. One of the

12 "Tiny Tim" 11.75-inch air-to-surface rockets that were ignited, launched and struck a glancing blow to the island before it hit other aircraft. *Franklin*'s executive officer, Commander Joe Taylor, remembered that, "Each time one went off, the firefighting crews forward would instinctively hit the deck. I wish there was some way to record the name of every one of these men. Their heroism was the greatest thing I have ever seen."

The second bomb hit aft, tearing through two decks before it exploded. Unfortunately, though the forward aviation gasoline system had been secured, aviation gas was still flowing in the aft lines. This explosion fanned the below-decks fires, triggering ammunition, bombs and rockets. Power throughout the ship was lost within minutes. The captain's order to flood the magazines could not be carried out because the water mains had been destroyed in the explosions and fires. All shipboard communications were lost. The carrier drifted helplessly within sight of Kyushu as she took on a 13-degree starboard list.

Just before TG 58.2 commander Rear Admiral Ralph Davison left *Franklin* by breeches buoy to transfer his flag to *Miller* (DD-535), he suggested to Captain Gehres that he order the ship abandoned. Thinking of the many men still alive below decks whose escape was prevented by the fire, Gehres refused. Many had already been wounded or killed within minutes of the explosion, while others were blown overboard or forced to jump because of the fires. Surgeon LCDR George W. Fox, MD, was killed while tending the wounded and was awarded a posthumous Navy Cross. On hearing Gehres' announcement that he was going to fight the fire, 106 officers and 604 enlisted men volunteered to stay and fight the fires with him.

Moments after the first attack, another Judy dived on *Wasp*. The defending gunners shot it down, though its bomb fell free and penetrated the flight deck before it exploded between the second and third decks. Fortunately, damage-control parties were able to put out the fire quickly and, within an hour, *Wasp* was able to resume flight operations, despite her top speed being reduced to 28 knots when a boiler room flooded and lost power.

Task Force 58 was attacked throughout the day as the enemy sent both conventional and *kamikaze* attacks against the fleet. *Intrepid* crewman Ray Stone later wrote in his diary that "the Japanese response to our raids was intense and fanatical."

Shortly after 0800 hours, lookouts on *Intrepid* spotted a large twin-engine bomber low over the water and headed for the ship. 40mm battery commander Lieutenant William Lindenberger ordered his guns to open fire when the attacker was 6,000 yards distant and headed right at him. He described what happened next in his diary:

> Our 5in [guns] let him have it, but he kept coming. My 40mm plus 2 two others got the range on him and set him afire at about 3000 yds. He kept coming. At 2000 yds, I saw my tracers going into him consistently, he was burning from wing tip to wingtip but he kept coming. I thought he was going to crash into us at my gun but just before he hit his right wing dipped and he paralleled the ship at 100 to 150 fleet. There was an explosion – water started raining down on us and then a thick smoke appeared. My gunner was as steady as a watchmaker during the run but afterward he shook like a leaf.

The attacker had been deflected at the last moment by the carrier's massed antiaircraft fire. Burning debris spewed over the starboard side of the ship, damaging aircraft and starting fires on the hangar deck when it hit the water and exploded. A stray 5-inch round from *Atlanta* (CL-104) killed one and wounded 44 others when it hit *Intrepid* by mistake. The ship was fortunate that overall damage was minor with light casualties, but a shock was sent through the crew by the event that came so soon after their return to combat.

One of the heroes of the fight to save *Franklin* was LCDR Joseph T. O'Callahan, S.J., the ship's Catholic chaplain. Before the war, Callahan was a Jesuit professor of mathematics and physics at Trinity College. He had reported aboard only 17 days earlier. Despite being wounded in one of the explosions, Chaplain Callahan moved through the carnage on the flight deck and administered last rites; a photograph of him engaged in this work is considered one of the iconic photos of the Pacific War. Once he was through with his religious work, he organized and directed firefighting and rescue parties. As if that were not enough, he led men below to the magazines where they retrieved hot shells and bombs that threatened to explode, bringing them to the flight deck where they were thrown overboard.

Engineering officer Lt(jg) Donald A. Gary was another of the men whose efforts were crucial in the fight. A former enlisted machinist's mate commissioned a year previously, Gary discovered 300 men who were trapped in a blackened mess compartment filled with smoke. With no obvious way out, the men were increasingly panic-stricken from the incessant explosions. Lieutenant Gary took command and promised them they would escape. He left and groped his way through the dark, debris-filled corridors, ultimately discovering an escape route. Returning three times to the mess compartment despite menacing flames, flooding water and the possibility of additional explosions, he led men out in groups until the last was safe. That task completed, he organized fire-fighting parties to battle the hangar deck fires. He then managed to enter Fireroom No. 3, where he was able to raise steam in one boiler and restore partial power.

Chaplain O'Callahan became the only man in World War II publicly to refuse the award of the Navy Cross, on the grounds he had done only what was expected. He was awarded the Medal of Honor in February 1946 after the personal intervention of President Harry Truman, the only Navy chaplain so honored during the war. His citation reads:

For conspicuous gallantry and intrepidity at the risk of his life above and beyond the call of duty while serving as chaplain on board the USS *Franklin* when that vessel was fiercely attacked by enemy Japanese aircraft during offensive operations near Kobe, Japan, on March 19, 1945. A valiant and forceful leader, calmly braving the perilous barriers of flame and twisted metal to aid his men and his ship, Lt Comdr O'Callahan groped his way through smoke-filled corridors to the open flight deck and into the midst of violently exploding bombs, shells, rockets, and other armament. With the ship rocked by incessant explosions, with debris and fragments raining down and fires raging in ever-increasing fury, he ministered to the wounded and dying, comforting and encouraging men of all faiths; he organized and led firefighting crews into the blazing inferno on the flight deck; he directed the jettisoning of live ammunition and the flooding of the magazine; he manned a hose to cool hot, armed bombs rolling dangerously on the listing deck, continuing his efforts, despite searing, suffocating smoke which forced men to fall back gasping and imperiled others who replaced them. Serving with courage, fortitude, and deep spiritual strength, Lt Cmdr O'Callahan inspired the gallant officers and men of the *Franklin* to fight heroically and with profound faith in the face of almost certain death and to return their stricken ship to port.

Donald A. Gary was also awarded the Medal of Honor in the same ceremony with Chaplain O'Callahan. The guided missile frigate *Gary* (FFG-51) was named in his honor in 1983.

Men jumped into the sea to get away from the fires and the light cruiser *Santa Fe* moved in close to rescue them, then approached *Franklin* to take off wounded and nonessential personnel. As the cruiser came alongside to fight the fires, *Franklin* rolled toward her, battering her superstructure with the carrier's imposing flight deck overhang. As the carrier went dead in the water, Captain Harold C. Fritz kept *Santa Fe* close alongside. Wave action clapped the two together, with the rending sound of gun sponsons crushing and antennas snapping. Aboard the destroyer *Hunt* (DD-674) 1,000 yards off *Franklin's* beam, a signalman monitoring the carrier with his 40-power telescope was witness to a hangar deck explosion so violent it shattered parked planes and sent their engines flying through the hangar. A large group of sailors near the bow were forced back by the flames and fell off the bow "like a huge herd of cattle being shoved over a cliff," the sailor later reported.

Survivors climbed across radio antennas from the carrier to *Santa Fe* and slid down lines from the flight deck to the cruiser's forecastle.

Commander Thomas H. Morton, gunnery officer of the battleship *North Carolina* (BB-55) was a witness to the ship's desperate fight for survival as the battleship maintained formation behind the burning carrier. "The Franklin was a huge mass of explosions, flames, and a tremendous column of smoke. There must have been hundreds of her crew in the water. Some had jumped, some had been blown over, and some were badly injured."

With the fires aboard *Franklin* finally brought under control in the late afternoon, *Pittsburgh* (CA-72) moved in and a towline was rigged. *Franklin's* rudder was jammed hard to starboard, which limited the towing speed to five knots. The task group moved protectively around the stricken carrier, while the other task groups launched fighter sweeps against airfields on Kyushu to disorganize any attack as the fleet withdrew slowly south. That evening an attack by eight aircraft was intercepted 80 miles out by VF(N)-90 Hellcats from *Enterprise* and five aircraft were shot down.

Franklin and Task Group 58.2 were 40 miles to the north of Task Force 58 at dawn on March 20, 160 miles from the nearest enemy base. Japanese snoopers finally made their appearance at 1630 hours when 15 enemy aircraft came in low and very fast as they went after the ships, splitting up for individual attacks. *Wasp's* fighters shot down seven, while seven others were shot down by shipboard gunfire.

Two Judys attacked *Enterprise* about 1730 hours in separate attacks. The near misses caused no serious damage. Moments after the second near miss, however, two 5-inch shells fired by another ship in the formation slammed into the 40mm gun tubs forward of the bridge, killing seven and wounding 30. Spreading fires set off 20mm and 40mm shells and threatened the fueled and armed planes on the hangar deck, where eight were destroyed. Damage-control parties fought the fire for 20 minutes, at which point she came under attack a third time with another near miss off the port quarter; 15 minutes later the fires were out for good.

By the end of the day, *Franklin's* repair parties had managed to un-jam the rudder and work up speed to 15 knots under her own power. More snoopers appeared at sunset, however. The night fighters were unable to intercept them owing to the snoopers engaging in radical maneuvers and use of window to jam radars. At about 2300 hours, an unsuccessful eight-plane torpedo attack was made on Task Groups 58.3 and 58.1, while shadowing aircraft continued to report the fleet's position during the night.

The next day, a large bogey was detected by radar at 1400 hours, 100 miles northwest of the fleet. Reinforcements were quickly launched and 150 fighters were soon airborne over the fleet. Thirty-two Bettys and 16 Zekes were intercepted by 24 fighters from Task Group 58.1, 50 miles distant. All were shot down for the loss of two American planes. Task Force 58 had dodged a dangerous attack; the Bettys were each carrying a small plane under their fuselage. This was the combat debut of the Thunder Corps.

Franklin was able to proceed under her own power to Pearl Harbor, where she was cleaned up and repaired sufficiently to permit her to sail under her own power through the Panama Canal and on to New York City in an epic journey of 12,000 miles. She entered the Brooklyn Navy Yard on April 28. After the end of the war, *Franklin* was opened to the public for Navy Day celebrations so that civilians could see first hand what the Navy had faced in the last nine and a half months of war. Film footage of *Franklin*'s ordeal was later woven into the 1949 feature film *Task Force*, with Gary Cooper in the role of Captain Gehrens.

In addition to the 807 dead, there were 487 wounded. *Franklin* had suffered the greatest loss of life on any Navy ship in the war after *Arizona* at Pearl Harbor. She survived the most severe damage experienced by any US Navy fleet carrier that did not sink. *Wasp* had suffered an additional 200 casualties from the attack that damaged her.

For the first time in its year-long existence, Task Force 58 had fared poorly in a sea battle. As the fleet shielded the cripples, Admiral Spruance withdrew from Japanese home waters. The invasion of Okinawa was now less than ten days away and Admiral Mitscher sensed the task force faced an intense fight.

Task Force 58 arrived off Okinawa on March 23, 1945. The final great battle of the Pacific War was about to begin.

CHAPTER NINE

THE FLEET THAT CAME
TO STAY

By the spring of 1945, the Allied advance that had begun 32 months before at Guadalcanal was now aimed directly at the Japanese home islands. Okinawa, only 350 miles south of Kyushu, was seen by Allied planners as the logical end to the island-hopping campaign. It would be a springboard for the final assault on Japan itself, with airfields located only two hours away from the initial invasion target, Kyushu. The Japanese could read maps with equal facility and the strategic importance of Okinawa was not lost on the high command, which declared Okinawa "the focal point of the decisive battle for the defense of the Homeland" in March 1945.

The Okinawa campaign is better remembered as a slow struggle of attrition ashore that took on aspects of World War I trench warfare by the end, with over 12,500 Americans missing or dead and 82,000 wounded, with an additional 26,000 cases of "combat fatigue" serious enough for sufferers to be removed from their units. Enemy dead included 77,166 Japanese soldiers, and 42,000 to 150,000 civilians were killed, committed suicide or went missing, a significant proportion of the 300,000 estimated prewar local population.

At sea, however, Okinawa is the single bloodiest battle in US Navy history. By the time the island was declared secure after an 82-day-long struggle that lasted from April 1 until June 22, 1945, the Navy suffered 4,900 men killed or drowned and 4,800 wounded. Thirty-six ships were sunk and another 368 damaged: 122 destroyers, 19 aircraft carriers, 10 battleships, 12 cruisers and 69 auxiliary ships were hit as the Japanese flew 1,465 *kamikaze* aircraft in large-scale attacks from Kyushu, 185 individual sorties from Kyushu, and 250 individual sorties from Formosa between April 6 and June 22. Of the 145 ships sunk or damaged heavily enough to be out of action for 30 days or more, four were lost to mines, five to suicide small craft, three to coastal batteries, and 133 to Japanese air attacks. Additionally, 768 aircraft were lost in combat or operational accidents.

The losses and protracted length of the campaign led Admiral Nimitz to relieve the principal naval commanders early so they could rest and recuperate from the stress of command in conditions of the Okinawa battle. Thus, while Navy began the campaign as the Fifth Fleet under Admiral Spruance, it ended as the Third Fleet commanded by Admiral Halsey.

The result of the battle for Okinawa led to a complete change in US plans to defeat Japan and bring about surrender.

On March 23, 1945, Allied forces arrived off the Ryukyu Islands. Task Force 58, composed of 88 ships, including 11 fleet carriers, six light carriers, seven battleships and 18 cruisers, took position east of Okinawa in preparation for pre-invasion strikes. Radar picket destroyers were assigned in three-ship groups at four locations north of Okinawa to provide early warning of air raids coming from Kyushu.

Over the next week, American and British aircraft attacked airfields as far away as Formosa and Kyushu in an attempt to destroy the *kamikaze* aircraft before they could be put to use. American intelligence badly underestimated the enemy air forces on Formosa, estimating there were only 89 planes on the island; in fact, the Japanese had approximately 700 there.

The Japanese response to the American arrival was not as strong as expected. Suicide attackers that came from Okinawa and airfields in the surrounding islands made their first appearance on March 26, when the radar picket destroyer *Kimberly* (DD-521) was struck by a Val dive bomber, setting the after deckhouse afire. The next day a *kamikaze* hit *Nevada* (BB-36), which suffered casualties and damage when the aircraft exploded overhead when hit by antiaircraft fire and showered the ship with burning debris. Another splashed close to *Tennessee* (BB-43), while a third holed *Biloxi* (CL-80).

O'Brien (DD-725), which had survived a direct hit by German artillery off Cherbourg during the Normandy invasion and a suicide attack during the invasion of Lingayen Gulf in January, was not so lucky this day. The ship came under attack from several aircraft and her gunners shot down one, but the second, another Val dive bomber, crashed into her port side amidships, with its 550lb bomb detonating high-explosive rounds in the ship's forward magazine. The blast demolished most of the forward superstructure, including the radio shack and Combat Information Center. With 50 crewmen killed and extensive damage, *O'Brien* was out of the war. It was a harbinger of the terrible events that would happen over the next 85 days.

In response to requests from the Navy, B-24s from MacArthur's Fifth Air Force in the Philippines bombed airfields on Formosa. Unfortunately, the Japanese had dispersed aircraft away from the airfields, so the strength of the *kamikazes* there was not depleted. Task Force 57, the British Pacific Fleet commanded by Vice Admiral Sir Bernard Rawlings and composed of four fleet carriers, two battleships, five cruisers and 14 destroyers, was positioned west of Okinawa near the Sakishima Islands with the task of blocking air attacks from Formosa.

Despite his protests against using the Marianas-based B-29s for "tactical" missions, General Curtis LeMay sent the Superfortresses to attack *kamikaze* airfields on Kyushu; here again the Japanese had successfully dispersed their aircraft. More importantly, the B-29s of the 313th Bomb Wing based on Tinian began minelaying operations. Shiminoseki Strait between Kyushu and Honshu was the first target. The mines included pressure mines, magnetic mines and acoustic mines, a combination that made it impossible for the Japanese to sweep for them.

On the morning of March 31, Spruance's flagship, *Indianapolis* (CA-35) was hit while she stood by in her fire-support sector off Hagushi beach. Other ships were seen under attack when an Oscar burst out of the clouds, executed a wingover and dived on her starboard quarter. The 20mm guns opened fire, but there was not time for the larger weapons to track the incoming enemy. Tracers smashed into the plane and it seemed to falter as though the pilot had lost control, but it plunged on to hit the port side of the main deck aft, while its bomb separated before impact and smashed through the deck into the crew's mess below, where it ripped through a table at which several sailors were seated for breakfast. The bomb continued through the crew living quarters and through a fuel tank before it burst through the hull and exploded underwater. Oil combined with seawater and gasoline shot back through the hole like a geyser through the hole on the main deck. An OS2U-3 Kingfisher was thrown from its catapult car to land upside down on the hangar deck. *Indianapolis* settled by the stern and listed to port, but damage control crews were able to localize and then control the flooding. Within 20 minutes, the ship got under way and crossed 30 miles of open sea to Kerama Retto. With nine dead and 20 wounded, and with severe damage, *Indianapolis* needed the attention of the full repair yard there.

Spruance remained aboard the next day as the landings went ahead on schedule and a salvage ship attended to the flagship. When the salvage crew lost the port propeller trying to retrieve it for repair, the admiral was forced to transfer to the old battleship *New Mexico* (BB-40).

Vice Admiral Richmond K. Turner, now Commander, Amphibious Forces, Pacific, headed the Joint Expeditionary Force, Task Force 51. This was composed of 179 attack transports, attack cargo ships, 187 LST transports and landing craft to put 182,000 men from six divisions of the Tenth Army ashore at Hagushi: the 7th, 27th, 77th, and 96th, as well as the 1st and 6th Marine Divisions. April 1, 1945 was known as "L-Day" rather than the traditional "D-Day." Many noted that the date was not only Easter Sunday but also April Fool's Day, and wondered what the Japanese had in store. Beginning at 0830 hours, 16,000 soldiers and marines were put ashore on the Hagushi beaches, meeting no opposition. By nightfall over 60,000 troops were ashore.

Task Force 52, the Amphibious Support Force under Rear Admiral William H. P. Blandy, counted ten older American battleships, including several of the Pearl Harbor survivors *Tennessee*, *Maryland*, and *West Virginia*, in addition to nine heavy and light cruisers, 23 destroyers and destroyer escorts, and 117 rocket gunboats for fire support; they would fire a combined 3,800 tons of high explosive at the island in the first 24 hours of the invasion.

Task Group 52.1, the Carrier Support Force, was composed of 18 escort carriers with 450 aircraft for close-air support of the ground forces. Of particular interest were the four CVEs that carried Corsairs and Avengers of the squadrons from Marine Air Groups 31 and 33, the final product of the decision made in November 1944 to bring Marine close-air support to future invasions.

VOC-1, the artillery spotters, were also present, still aboard *Wake Island*. The pilots had had little opportunity to catch a break after their stint at Iwo Jima, which they had departed on March 11. L-Day saw the Wildcats and Avengers busy spotting for the naval gunfire barrage that preceded the landings. The pilots kept to a busy schedule for the next three days until *Wake Island* came into the sights of the *kamikazes* on April 3. Just at sunset, two Zekes came out of the clouds, heading straight for the ship. One barely undershot and crashed into the sea "about an arm's length from the port bow." The other had better aim and hit the little carrier just below the waterline, causing a fire that was quickly extinguished, but the damage was sufficient to send the ship to Kerama Retto, where the damage specialists determined she would need repair at Guam.

The pilots hoped they had earned a ticket home, but their skills as artillery spotters were too valuable. Thirty minutes before *Wake Island* got under way on April 5 to head southeast to Guam, the pilots of VOC-1 were ordered to *Marcus Island* (CVE-77), where they traded places with the pilots of VC-87. Commander Bringle's pilots started operations anew at dawn on April 6. They were joined in their work by LCDR R. M. Allison's newly arrived VOC-2 aboard *Fanshaw Bay* (CVE-70). In addition to artillery spotting, the pilots flew local and target combat air patrol, as well as flying ground-support missions for the troops ashore. The operations were intense, as they had been at Iwo Jima, with pilots logging two or three missions a day throughout the month of April.

Fortunately, the massive flotillas of troop-laden transports were so well protected by Turner's air and surface forces that no Japanese bombers or *kamikazes* were able to disrupt the most vulnerable part of the main assault, since their recognition skills were so poor that they tended to attack the first ship they ran across, regardless.

Most importantly, a major opportunity to kill large numbers of invading troops before they got ashore was lost when those aircraft that did attack failed to go after the transports. Captain Elliott B. Strauss, captain of the attack transport *Charles Carroll* (APA-28), recalled, "The Japanese were foolish not to go after the transports, rather than the destroyer screen, because if they had actually sunk a couple of transports it would have interfered with the invasion force much more."

Admiral Ugaki's *kamikazes* fared better on L+1, when attack transport *Henrico* (APA-45) was damaged slightly by a *kamikaze* while under way for a subsidiary landing with the Army's 77th Division.

Over the course of the first five days following "L-Day," the Marines found little resistance, and secured Yontan Airfield then pushed across the island to the deserted fishing village of Ishikawa 20 days ahead of schedule, while the Army turned south and found increasing opposition by the second day. By the fifth day they could see Shuri Castle, which was the center of the planned resistance to the invasion. The *New Yorker*'s John Lardner described the action: "So far, the Okinawa invasion was like a fierce, bold rush by cops hunting gunmen, into a house that suddenly turned out to be only haunted."

Operational accidents took their toll among the fleet. On the night of April 2/3, *Franks* (DD-554) had a glancing collision with *New Jersey* (BB-62), during which the destroyer's captain was mortally injured when the battleship's anchor sliced off the port side of the *Franks'* bridge. Quartermaster First Class Michael Bak Jr. remembered, "when I got to the bridge, my God, half the port side of the bridge was sliced away. It was just like a knife going through at a 45-degree angle."

Following the collision, *Franks* was one of the first damaged ships to enter Kerama Retto. The cluster of mountainous islands, located 15 miles west of Okinawa, had been taken on March 28 for use as a fleet anchorage and a forward base for Martin PBM Mariner flying boats, which would patrol the Ryukyus. The Americans were surprised to discover 250 suicide attack boats that were hidden in caves and grottoes throughout the islands. During the course of the Okinawa campaign, many other ships would follow *Franks* into the protected waters of Kerama Retto, where their dead would be removed for burial at sea and the wounded transferred to hospital ships while emergency repairs were made to allow the ships to cross the Pacific to the US west coast for repairs. The waterway would come to be known as "The Bone Yard."

On Kyushu, the Japanese Army and Navy had over 1,500 aircraft assigned for "special attack" missions against the invasion force. Admiral Ugaki planned mass *kamikaze* missions of over 300 aircraft to swamp the defenses. During the first few days following the landings, Japanese aerial opposition was light. After only one *kamikaze* attack against the battleship *West Virginia* on April 1, the enemy reaction in the air began in earnest on April 6 when 400 aircraft were launched from Kyushu to strike the fleet. There would be three more heavy air attacks through the month.

April 6 was the day the Battle for Okinawa truly began in earnest. The weather over the East China Sea that afternoon was clear with a few high, scattered clouds. *Bush* (DD-529) plowed through the waves at RP1, the northernmost radar picket location. At 1330 hours, radar operator Ed Cregut in *Bush's* Combat Information Center spotted a huge, fast-moving blip 90 miles northwest. Cregut notified the watch officer and the air plot began tracking it. After several minutes, it was confirmed that it was not a cloud – the bogey was traveling at 145 knots, straight at the ship. "My God," the watch officer murmured, "there must be hundreds." Over the next 15 minutes, three more large formations popped up on the radar screens.

Aboard *San Jacinto* (CVL-30), Lieutenant Jim Cain and seven other pilots of VF-45 listened as Lieutenant Bill Plauche, Air Group 45's air intelligence officer, informed them that intercepted Japanese radio messages indicated that the enemy was planning to send large formations of *kamikazes* against the ships of the invasion fleet. Things were about to change from the relative quiet of the past five days, and the eight Fighting-45 pilots would be on the front line, assigned as combat air patrol for two different groups of radar picket destroyers that would be immediate targets for the incoming suicide attackers. They would relieve the combat air patrols over the RP1 and RP2 positions.

At 1345 hours, *San Jacinto* turned into the wind as the word went out over the public address, "Pilots! Man your planes!" The first two of the eight dark blue Hellcats were launched at 1400 hours. At 1430 hours, the Hellcats were released by *San Jacinto*'s Combat Information Center – "Rocket Base" – and directed to "look alive, be alert, and kick Axis."

At the same time that "Rocket Three" left *San Jacinto*, 50 enemy aircraft were spotted over *Bush*. The four Hellcats orbiting over the destroyer called "Tally-Ho" as they dove to attack. Within a matter of minutes, the Hellcats had splashed six, while *Bush*'s main batteries claimed two. Suddenly, lookouts called another bogey, low. It quickly resolved itself as a Jill, less than four miles away at an altitude of 100 feet and closing fast. The 5-inch and 40mm guns locked on the onrushing Jill with accurate fire, knocking off pieces of the wing and setting the aircraft afire, but it still kept coming. *Bush* swung to the right in an attempt to dodge the incoming enemy, but the pilot matched the turn and struck the destroyer on the starboard main deck at 1515 hours. Almost simultaneously, the Jill's torpedo exploded, ripping out plating from the forward fireroom back to the forward engine room. In the fireroom, men struggled to get topside but escaping steam killed all but one, who finally made it to the main deck.

Lieutenant Cain sent the second division to its control destroyer, which was south and west of Okinawa.

> I checked in with my destroyer control ship – callsign "Silver Fox" – which was about 40 miles north of the island. On the way to our station, my section leader, Lieutenant (jg) Danny Paul, tally-hoed a bogey at 2 o'clock down. I picked up the bogey, which I estimated to be seven or eight miles away and heading south at approximately 7,000 feet. My division was at 10,000 feet.
>
> I rolled into my run at full military power and the other three Hellcats followed in a loose trail formation. I charged my guns and fired a short test burst. The chase was on. As we neared it, we identified the single bogey as a Val dive bomber. I closed rapidly, but it seemed to take forever. I fired a one-second burst from dead astern, but my tracers fell considerably short. Finally, two or three minutes later, I closed to maximum range – approximately 1,100 yards – and fired another short burst. It was still short of the target. I bore on in until the Val covered a good part of my gunsight, and then I fired another two-second burst. The Val was hit hard. It rolled upside down in flames the full length of the fuselage, and the pilot baled out. His chute opened and he floated down to the water. Someone suggested that a few rounds into the chute might be appropriate, but I replied, "Hell no!" and we rejoined to proceed to our assigned station.

Cain's Hellcats met a "hot" reception from *Colhoun* (DD-801), the radar picket they were assigned to protect, when several 5-inch shells burst nearby as they took up their assigned patrol at 10,000 feet. Within a matter of minutes, the fighters were vectored after an incoming bogey.

> We flew about 30 miles to the north, in the direction of Kyushu, and tally-hoed the bogey at a distance of about seven miles. It was a

single Tony. It made a weak firing pass at my division from ahead and toward the right. In my opinion, he never came within firing range before he dived for the deck, still heading south, toward Okinawa. I was one of the most experienced pilots in our squadron. I had approximately 2,500 hours of flight time and was a former aerial combat instructor. I knew that a smart leader would never – *never!* – follow a single in a dive.

Good sense, good logic, and good strategy be damned; I followed the Tony down with all six 50s blazing from dead astern. Though our guns were bore-sighted at 500 yards, I began firing from about 1,000 yards, extreme range. Our speeds were about equal. I could not close and he could not get away. I followed him all the way to Okinawa and then we played follow-the-leader as he jinked below mountaintops and over valleys and hills in the northern part of the island. This went on for 15 minutes or more. My gun camera registered several hits but no fire. He was listed as a probable. Since I could not close on the Tony, I finally broke off and started my climb back to relocate the three aircraft of my division, which I had lost track of in the melee.

Cain was about 60 miles south of RP2 and had radio contact with the rest of the division.

I requested a position and was told that they had rejoined and were south of base at 8,000 feet. I executed a rapid climb and soon saw three fighters at what I took to be between 7,000 and 8,000 feet. I advised that I had them in sight and would rejoin in the number-four slot and then resume the lead. I circled 180 degrees to the left and was coming up behind them from below. I closed from below at a very rapid rate and was about to reduce throttle when, to my amazement, I saw that the three single-engine aircraft I was joining had meatballs on their fuselages. They were Zekes!

Cain's guns were still charged. He pulled behind the enemy fighters at approximately 300 yards.

I was dead astern and my gunsight covered all three of them. I never really attempted to aim. As I closed to 200 yards, all six .50s were blazing away. The port wingman blew up, and then the leader. The starboard wingman blew up about ten seconds later. I never stopped firing until I passed through the wreckage. I do not believe the pilots ever saw me since they took no evasive action. It all happened within 30 seconds. By then, all my guns had burned out and the rounds were tumbling within 100 yards. There was a lot of fire and smoke. As I penetrated the burning wreckage, I remembered to say a short prayer: 'Good Lord, please don't let me hit one of their engines or a large portion of any of the exploding aircraft.' My Hellcat did sustain some damage from flying debris, but there was no major damage.

With his fight over, Cain rejoined his unit. At that moment, *Colhoun* received *Bush*'s distress call. The destroyer picked up speed and headed toward RP1 with Cain's Hellcats leading the way. Several other bogeys were intercepted and Cain's wingman, Ensign Henry Nida, used up his ammunition shooting down a Jill and an Oscar, then the two of them attempted to cut the tail off a Judy. "I had a slight collision with the Judy, but I could not shoot him down because my guns were gone. The Judy's tail gunner must have fired his machine gun at me as there were three holes found later in my port wing." Section leader Lt(jg) Danny Paul and his wingman, Ensign Norm Bishop, each shot down two Zekes. "Rocket Three" was forced to break off their CAP owing to lack of ammunition and head back to *San Jacinto*.

Colhoun reached RP1 at 1610 hours to find *Bush* dead in the water. Twelve to 15 *kamikaze* attackers circled the wounded destroyer. Commander G. R. Wilson, *Colhoun*'s captain, signaled *LCS-64* to maneuver alongside Bush and take off wounded, while he positioned his ship to fight off the coming attacks.

At the same time, many other Japanese flights of the first *Kikusui* ("Floating Chrysanthemums" or mass attack) broke through the American aerial defenses north of Okinawa. Two converted destroyer-minesweepers, *Emmons* (DD-457/DMS-22) and *Rodman* (DD-456/DMS-21) were attacked off the island's north coast. One *kamikaze* hit *Rodman* and its bomb exploded at the base of the forward superstructure, killing 16 and wounding another 20. *Emmons* splashed another 12 over the next hour while Marine Corsairs shot down a further 20, but four attackers still hit *Emmons*, severing her stern and demolishing the forward gun mounts and bridge.

At 1700 hours, a sixth attacker zeroed in on *Bush*, which was transferring casualties to *LCS-64*. A seventh *kamikaze* was spotted inbound as *LCS-64* hurriedly cast off and *Bush* opened up with her 40mm antiaircraft guns. *Colhoun* was also under attack; she shot down a Zeke that crashed between the two destroyers, then took on a Val off the starboard bow and a Zeke on the starboard quarter. The Val was hit with the first 5-inch salvo and crashed 50 yards off the ship's starboard beam. The Zeke was hit and set afire, but continued in. It hit port amidships moments later and destroyed the port 40mm mount before it slid across the boat deck and hit the stern stack with a glancing blow that sent it back into the starboard 40mm mount. The crews of both mounts were killed in the inferno. The Zeke's bomb penetrated the engineering spaces and exploded, killing the after engine room crew and cutting the main steam line to the forward engine room. Ten minutes after the attack began, *Colhoun* still had steering and propulsion and power to operate the main guns, but the ship was in bad shape.

At 1717 hours, two Vals and a Zeke made runs on *Bush* and *Colhoun*. Colhoun exploded one Val while combined fire from *Colhoun*, *Bush* and *LCS-64* destroyed the second, but the Zeke hit *Colhoun* and penetrated to the forward fireroom, where it exploded. Four more *kamikazes* appeared overhead, stalking the ships. *Colhoun* now had no power and her guns could be only manually controlled and fired. Three *kamikazes* made flanking runs from ahead, but the gunners managed to down one. The other two came on. The first hit the after stack and swung around to take out the Number Three gun mount, with its belly tank separating and spreading flame over the after deckhouse before the Zeke bounced over the side and exploded, ripping a hole below the ship's waterline. The second attacker was hit by fire from *LCS-64* and *Bush* and crashed between the ships.

By 1800 hours, *Bush's* bow began to settle. *Colhoun* was dead in the water. *LCS-64* had departed 20 minutes before with the wounded. At 1830, a heavy ocean swell smacked the destroyer and *Bush* caved in amidships and sank within minutes with the survivors cutting loose rafts and going into the water.

Aboard *Colhoun*, men heard aircraft overhead and the two airplanes were identified as Hellcats. The fighter direction officer still had his radio and managed to establish radio contact with the planes.

VF-17's Lt(jg) Willis "Bill" Hardy in F6F-5 BuNo 72748 "White 33," with his wingman Lt(jg) H. G. "Crash" Morgan, heard the distress call. The two were returning to *Hornet* and had limited fuel, but they turned back and found the badly wounded burning destroyer on the dark sea below. They soon ran across several D4Y Judy dive bombers. Hardy turned into them and quickly shot down three, his first kills in his first combat. *Colhoun's* fighter director officer came back on the air and warned of two others inbound. Hardy consulted his gas gauge and tried to beg off. "It sure would be appreciated," was the reply. "We're afire amidships and they're stalking us. When the sun goes down they're going to clobber us. Come fifteen degrees right and you'll be on their tails." Despite low fuel and the gathering darkness, Hardy and Morgan followed the vector.

Moments later, Hardy spotted a Judy and turned in for a beam shot. Surprisingly, the Judy had a rear gunner, who opened fire just as Hardy did. He was forced to dive away but quickly pulled back up and saw the Judy was on fire just as it nosed over and left a fiery track into the dark ocean below. "Okay," the fighter director officer called, "if you head south now on the way back to your ship, you'll run right into the other one." A moment later Hardy found the Judy in the last light of day. He had to pump the gun charger with his foot to fire single shots; one hit the Judy's gas tank and the plane exploded. Bill Hardy was an ace in his first air combat, which lasted a grueling 70 minutes. The two Hellcats picked up a phosphorescent trail and managed to land aboard *Hornet* in the dying twilight with nearly-empty gas tanks.

At 1845 hours, *Cassin Young* (DD-793) arrived at RP1 with *LCS-84* and *87*. *Colhoun* was sinking slowly. At 1915 hours, *LCS-87* came alongside to take off the wounded. By 2045 the wounded and the other surviving crew were aboard *LCS-87*, which cast off as *Cassin Young* stood by to sink *Colhoun* with gunfire. The gallant destroyer disappeared beneath the dark water at 2105 hours after taking five rounds in her hull.

LCS-64 returned to RP1 during this process and commenced searching for the survivors from *Bush*. Shortly before midnight she found the ship's whaleboat and took aboard the survivors. By 0300 hours on April 7, 150 survivors had been found by *LCS-64*, joined by *LCS-84*. Many of those rescued would die before dawn, however.

In all, the battles over the radar picket stations saw nine destroyers hit off Okinawa, with three sunk and the other six badly damaged; three would later be scrapped as unrepairable. This was in addition to ten other ships sunk, including two ammunition ships and an LST sunk off Kerama Retto. Crew losses included 367 dead and 480 wounded, many badly burned – heavier casualties than had been suffered ashore that day. The Japanese had launched 700 aircraft, half of them *kamikazes*, and lost over 350 attackers to defending aircraft and ships' antiaircraft fire over the course of ten identified major raids during the afternoon. Radio Tokyo claimed 60 ships sunk and 61 crippled. April 6, 1945 was the fourth-heaviest day of aerial fighting in the Pacific War, with the fighter squadrons aboard the carriers responsible for 257 of the Japanese losses.

The top scorers this day were Commander J. J. Southerland II's VF-83 aboard *Essex*, which scored 56 in six combats. Southerland, who had dueled with Saburo Sakai over Guadalcanal on August 7, 1942, shot down two Ki-61 Tony fighters. During one fighter-bomber mission to Kyushu, 15 Hellcats of VF-83 and 12 Corsairs of VBF-83 ran across several formations of southbound Japanese; the Hellcat pilots shot down 26 while the Corsairs added an additional six. Lt(jg) Hugh N. Batten and his wingman, Lt(jg) Sam J. Brocato, flying a special combat air patrol near Yoro Shima, sighted nine bomb-laden Zekes headed toward the fleet. Batten took advantage of the eight-tenths cloud cover and haze to approach undetected from the enemy's rear. The two Hellcats remained together through violent aerobatics and in ten minutes had shot down eight of the nine, all confirmed by gun camera film.

For *Belleau Wood*'s VF-30, April 6 was remembered as "Turkey Shoot Number Two." Fourteen F6F-5 Hellcats led by Lieutenant R. F. Gillespie were launched at 1430 hours to provide air cover over the northern part of Okinawa. Minutes after arriving on station at 1530 hours, several small enemy formations were spotted. In a two-hour running gunfight, the *Belleau Wood* pilots fought over 60 Vals, Zekes, Tojos and Oscars, flown by pilots the Americans later reported as inexperienced, unaggressive and poor marksmen. All 14 Americans scored, and in the end they chalked up 26 Vals, 14 Zekes, five Tojos and two Oscars. Three pilots became "aces in a day," when Ensign Carl G. Foster scored six, followed by Ensign Kenneth J. Dahm's five-and-a-half and Ensign Johnnie G. Miller's five. Ensign Michelle Mazzocco scored three singles and three shared for a total of 4.5, while three other ensigns scored four each. Back aboard ship, the total of 47.5 resulted in Captain W. G. Tomlinson querying task group commander Rear Admiral Jocko Clark, "Does this exceed bag limits?" Clark replied, "Negative. This is open season."

In addition to Bill Hardy's five, VF-17 knocked down a further 20, while VBF-17 scored 21.

Airplanes were not the only forces the Japanese committed to "special attack," however. The battle would also see the final appearance of what was left of the Imperial Navy's surface force in combat. The once-formidable Combined Fleet had been reduced to a few still-operational warships at Kure Naval Base and Hiroshima on the Inland Sea.

In a March briefing to the emperor regarding the Army plans for the defense of Okinawa, the emperor had asked, "Where is the Navy? Have they no ships?" Feeling pressured by the emperor's statement, the naval high command developed Operation *Ten-Go* over the course of the month under the direction of Admiral

Toyoda, commander-in-chief of the Combined Fleet, as the navy's contribution to the defense of the island. Japanese planners had considered four likely scenarios for the battle. The first, Operation *Heaven One* (*Ten-ichi-go*), would become the final Japanese naval operation of the Pacific War, known in Japanese history as the Battle of the East China Sea.

Operation *Ten-ichi-go* was essentially a special attack mission, using the remaining large warships, which included the battleship *Yamato*. She was still the world's largest battleship, mounting nine 18-inch naval rifles. The plan called for the battleship and her escorts to fight their way through the American fleet to Okinawa, where they were to then beach themselves between Higashi and Yomitan and fight on as shore batteries until they were destroyed. After their destruction, the surviving crew would continue to fight with the army.

Since there was no available air cover, the ships would be nearly helpless when the Americans spotted them and launched concentrated attacks. On March 29, the small fleet left Kure for Tokuyama, off Mitajiri, Japan, to position themselves for the attack.

Vice Admiral Seiichi Ito, commander of the *Ten-Go* force, stated his belief to Toyoda's face that the plan was futile and wasteful. Nevertheless, he had completed the plan for the operation as ordered. However, when it came to ordering his ships to take part in the attack, he refused to do so. He was not the only commander to respond negatively to the proposed operation. Captain Atsushi Oi, commander of the convoy escort forces, was very critical of the idea when he learned fuel for the attackers was to be diverted from his ships. Informed by Admiral Toyoda that the goal of the operation was "preservation of the tradition and the glory of Navy," Oi shouted, "This war is of our nation and why should the honor of our surface fleet be more respected? Who cares about their glory? Damn fools!" The navy faced a crisis of command.

Vice Admiral Ryunosuke Kusaka flew to Tokuyama on April 5 to convince Admiral Ito and the others to accept the plan. Only Ito knew about the complete plan. After Admiral Kusaka finally informed the other captains what was expected, they unanimously joined Ito, rejecting it as a complete waste of lives and valuable resources. Admiral Kusaka told them that the operation would support the *kamikaze* attacks planned by the Army since the force would divert defending American aircraft. He then concluded by saying that the emperor expected the navy to make its best effort to support the defense of Okinawa.

The commanders finally accepted the plan on hearing that the emperor expected them to fight. When crews were informed of the mission, they were told any could stay behind if desired. No one took up the offer, though 80 who were new, sick, or infirm, were ordered to leave. At midnight, the fleet began fueling.

Yamato, light cruiser *Yahagi* and eight destroyers departed Tokuyama at 1600 hours on April 6. The fleet was sighted by the submarines *Threadfin* (SS-410) and *Hackleback* (SS-295) as the ships steamed through the Bungo Suido Strait between Shikoku and Honshu. Neither submarine was able to attack, but they reported their position to Fifth Fleet and continued shadowing the Japanese.

That night, flight crews aboard the carriers of Task Force 58 got the word that the *Yamato* might be coming. Crews sweated on the *Bunker Hill*'s hangar deck to load the VT-84 Avengers with aerial torpedoes for the first time since training. The squadron's pilots had had plenty of opportunity during their stateside training to learn the use of the torpedoes, since they had been based next to the Pacific Fleet Test Unit at NAS North Island, and had volunteered to try out the torpedo modifications that were being devised to make the Mark XIV finally an effective weapon. Squadron pilots like Lt(jg) Art Turnbull had dropped over 500 torpedoes during the test runs.

Yamato and her escorts passed the Osumi Peninsula at dawn on April 7. They turned southwest, hoping to convince the submarines they knew were shadowing them that they were headed for Sasebo. An hour later, the fleet turned south and headed toward Okinawa at 20 knots. The ships assumed a defensive formation, with *Yahagi* leading *Yamato* while the eight destroyers deployed in a ring surrounding the battleship and cruiser. When the destroyer *Asashino* developed engine trouble, she was ordered to return. Captain Tameichi Hara called *Yahagi*'s crew to the bow and informed them of their mission.

> Our mission appears suicidal and it is, but suicide is not the objective. The objective is victory. Once this ship is crippled or sunk, do not hesitate to save yourselves for the next fight. We can commit suicide at any time. But we are going on this mission not to commit suicide but to win, and turn the tide of war.

American PBM Mariner flying boats spotted the fleet an hour after dawn and shadowed them. Admiral Ito ordered a turn to the west at 1000 hours, trying to deceive the shadowers that he was withdrawing. By 1130 hours it was clear the Americans had not taken the bait and he ordered the ships to turn south and resumed the voyage to Okinawa.

Shortly after 0900 hours, Admiral Spruance was given the first definite sighting reports that the enemy fleet was indeed headed to Okinawa. He quickly ordered Admiral Deyo to establish Task Force 54, with *Massachusetts* (BB-59), *Indiana* (BB-58), *New Jersey* (BB-62), *South Dakota* (BB-60), *Wisconsin* (BB-63), and *Missouri* (BB-64), the new battlecruiser *Alaska* (CB-1), five additional heavy cruisers and 21 destroyers to engage *Yamato*.

Admiral Mitscher had the same information. He commenced launching 400 strike aircraft from Task Group 58.1 (*Hornet, Bennington, Belleau Wood,* and *San Jacinto*) and Task Group 58.3 (*Essex, Bunker Hill, Hancock* and *Bataan*) at 1000 hours. The weather report was grim: there was a cloud ceiling between 2,000 and 3,000 feet that was unlikely to change.

Spruance had instructed Mitscher to allow the Japanese to come south and face the guns of Task Force 54, but Mitscher believed aircraft were the better weapon. Once his planes were off, he told chief of staff Arleigh Burke to inform Spruance that he intended to attack Yamato. "Will you take them or shall I?" Soon after, Spruance replied: "You take them."

The strike force first spotted *Yamato* at 1200 hours. The discovery that there was no air cover allowed the Helldivers and Avengers to circle the enemy just out of range of defensive fire and methodically set up attacks.

The Japanese spotted the Americans at 1220 hours. Ito ordered the ships to stop zigzagging and increase speed to 24 knots. As they passed through a heavy squall that momentarily provided protection for the 100 aircraft they had identified, the ships opened formation. They were out of the squall at 1232 hours; two minutes later, *Yamato* opened fire with her secondary armament, firing "Common Type 3" antiaircraft shells, known to the Japanese as *Sanshiki* ("beehive") rounds. At the same time, the rest of the fleet opened fire as they took evasive action. The Avengers made their attacks from the port side in order to increase the likelihood that *Yamato* would capsize.

Four bomb-carrying Avengers first attacked *Yahagi*, but missed. Hellcats strafed the ship as more Avengers came in and dropped bombs that either missed or had little effect, while others circled and took up torpedo attack positions. A torpedo hit *Yahagi* in her engine room at 1246 hours, which killed the engineering room crew when the boilers exploded and brought the cruiser to a halt. Subsequent attacks resulted in the ship being hit by six additional torpedoes and 12 bombs. Destroyer *Isokaze* tried to come to *Yahagi's* aid but she was attacked and heavily damaged; she sank 30 minutes later. At 1405 hours, *Yahagi* capsized and sank. During the attacks, the destroyers *Hamakaze* and *Suzutsuki* were heavily damaged and turned back, with *Hamakaze* later sinking.

Yamato was able to maneuver during the first attack and evade most of the bombs and torpedoes aimed at her. However, she was hit by a torpedo and two armor-piercing bombs, one of which started a fire aft of the bridge. Her speed was not affected and at 1300 hours she changed course and continued south.

VT-84's 14 Avengers broke out of the clouds and spotted the battleship five miles away at 1240 hours. When squadron leader Commander Chandler Swanson ordered the break, the formation split in half; eight, led by Swanson, attacked on the port bow, while the other six aimed to hit *Yamato* port amidships. Defensive fire hit one Avenger, which exploded. *Yamato* was hit by the first torpedo at 1245 hours, followed by two additional tin fish and two bombs dropped by Helldivers that caused extensive damage to the superstructure and knocked out power to the gun directors. The defending gun crews were thus forced to aim and fire their weapons individually, greatly reducing their effectiveness. By 1335 hours, *Yamato*'s speed had dropped to 18 knots.

Between 1337 and 1344 hours, five more torpedoes struck the battleship and she took on a list that put her in imminent danger of capsizing. Despite the destruction of the central damage-control station, a desperate attempt to prevent capsizing was made at 1333 hours when both starboard engine and boiler rooms were counter-flooded, drowning several hundred men since they received no notice to escape. Loss of the engines and the incoming water caused *Yamato* to slow to 10 knots.

Just at that same moment, the 110 aircraft of the final attack wave arrived overhead. Twenty TBM-3s from *Bennington* attacked from 60 degrees to port as *Yamato* started a sharp evasive turn to meet them, but she was hit on the port side amidships by three torpedoes that jammed her auxiliary rudder hard to port.

Yahagi's Captain Hara counted 13 bombs and seven torpedoes that had hit his ship by 1345 hours. She now listed 30 degrees to port as waves washed over her main deck. With two of the eight escorting destroyers already gone, three of the remaining six were dead in the water and on fire. Escort force commander Rear Admiral Keiso Komura turned to Hara and announced, "Let's go" at 1405 hours. Removing their shoes, the two jumped overboard just as *Yahagi* went down. Hara was caught in the resulting suction and was taken down with her for several minutes before he broke free and returned to the surface to see *Yamato* still afloat but swarmed by enemy aircraft.

The battleship had been hit by 11 torpedoes and now moved more slowly, which allowed the other Avengers to concentrate on hitting her rudder and stern. When Admiral Ito was informed at 1402 hours that the ship could no longer steer and was sinking, he ordered the crew to abandon ship. The great battleship came to a dead stop at 1405 hours as she began to capsize. At that point, Admiral Ito shook hands with the others and entered his cabin. Captain Aruga and the ship's other senior officers also refused to leave, though he ordered Ensign Mitsuru Yoshida to abandon ship when he attempted to join them.

Yamato capsized at 1420 hours and began to sink. The fire the bombs had ignited reached the magazine at 1423 hours. *Yamato* suddenly blew up with an explosion so large and loud it was reportedly heard and seen in Kagoshima, 120 miles away. A mushroom-shaped cloud rose to 20,000 feet.

Ensign Yoshida had been pulled under by the sinking ship; he was blasted to the surface and later reported that the explosion knocked down several planes circling the sinking leviathan.

Later, the destroyer *Asashimo* was bombed and sunk when she was spotted attempting to return to port. The destroyer *Kasumi* had to be scuttled after she was also crippled by air attacks. *Suzutsuki's* bow was blown off, but she returned to Sasebo by steaming in reverse. *Fuyutsuki, Yukikaze,* and *Hatsushimo* were able to rescue 269 *Yamato* survivors from a crew of approximately 2,750 in addition to 555 survivors from *Yahagi's* crew of 1,000 and an additional 800 survivors from *Isokaze, Hamakaze,* and *Kasumi,* who were taken to Sasebo where they were placed on an island to prevent word of the disaster spreading.

Task Force 58 lost 10 aircraft shot down and 12 aircrew. The planes still overhead were ordered to halt attacks on the destroyers temporarily while they rescued survivors.

During the aerial battle against the Second Fleet, the JAAF launched a *kamikaze* attack from Kyushu with 115 aircraft attacking US ships throughout the day. The carrier *Hancock* was damaged sufficiently to send her back to Ulithi for repairs that lasted until June and removed Air Group 6 from further combat. The battleship *Maryland* (BB-46) also received a minor hit. *Bennett* (DD-473), which had replaced *Bush* and *Colhoun* at RP1, took two *kamikazes* and was forced to retire to Kerama Retto's "Bone Yard." Japanese losses were 100 aircraft, with Hellcats accounting for 32.

During the day, four Corsair squadrons from Marine Air Group 31 arrived at Yontan Airfield after being transported to the battlefield aboard CVEs. VMF-311's F4U-1Cs – which differed from other Corsairs by being armed with four 20mm cannon each – were launched from *Sitkoh Bay* (CVE-86) in the middle of a *kamikaze* attack. Four Corsairs caught up with a Lily bomber and hit the twin-engine attacker hard with their cannons, but the pilot continued toward the carrier, closing to 100 yards from the ship before the right wing folded up and the burning bomber hit the water 50 yards from the little carrier. The pilots of VMF-311, 224 and 441 had been used to the milk runs of the Marshalls; they learned quickly that the stakes were much higher at Okinawa.

With the arrival of the Marines to supplement the carrier-based fighters, two task groups were kept on the line east of Okinawa, while the other two refueled farther east. The fighter squadrons maintained a 24-plane CAP over the task groups, with 12 aircraft for each radar picket destroyer. With this indefinite flight schedule, pilot fatigue became a factor in maintaining operations. The CVE force of 14 escort carriers assigned to provide air support for the troops ashore saw similar operational schedules, with FM-2 Wildcat pilots flying two or three missions a day as combat air patrol or close air support.

On April 11, the bad weather finally lifted and Admiral Ugaki ordered *Kikusui No. 2* into action. Fortunately, Corsairs of Marine Air Group 33's VMF-312, 322 and 323 had landed at Yontan that morning, bringing the strength of the island-based Marine defenders to 100 F4U-1D, F4U-1C and FG-1D Corsairs as reinforcement for the squadrons aboard the fast carriers and the offshore CVEs.

Enterprise had joined TG 58.3 four days earlier to provide night air defense and attack capability, following repairs at Ulithi to deal with damage suffered on March 18 and 20 during the Kyushu strikes. At 1345 hours on April 11, two large bogeys were spotted closing on the task group from the north. *Enterprise* opened fire on two attacking Zekes at 1408 hours and shot the first down about 1,500 yards off the starboard quarter. The second Zeke dived on the port quarter, where it struck two 40mm mounts and skittered across the deck to fall in the sea, while the bomb it carried detonated under the ship. The detonation lifted *Enterprise* bodily and whipped her so violently that the foremast struts supporting the SK radar broke and snapped off about six feet of the starboard yardarm. Damage repair crews attempted unsuccessfully to install a temporary support for the radar antenna.

Further damage occurred in the engineering spaces, with the result that the foundations of Nos. 3 and 4 main generators, Nos. 3 and 4 main engines and Nos. 3 and 4 shaft spring bearings were forced inward and upward. Both generators broke loose from their foundations at the after ends of the turbines when the supporting pedestals broke away from the cast iron exhaust casings of which they were a part, which left the ends of the turbines with no support. The No. 4 generator that was carrying the load aft under split plant operation tripped out. Electricians attempted to carry the load on No. 3 generator, but after two hours running, the vibration became so excessive that it was secured, leaving the ship dependent on Nos. 1 and 2 main generators and the emergency diesel generators. In addition, the No. 4 propeller shaft was bent slightly, while the supports for No. 3 shaft were broken. This caused intense vibration when the ship attempted to turn. Fuel tanks were also damaged and *Enterprise* trailed a fuel slick.

A bomb-carrying *Judy* tried to attack at 1500 hours but missed; hit by defending fire, it struck the water 50 feet off the starboard bow and exploded. Water spray washed over the pilothouse and part of the plane's wing was hurled onto the flight deck. The explosion also resulted in additional shock damage and slight structural damage in six tanks and voids. A Hellcat positioned on the starboard catapult caught fire from the explosion. As the fire spread to the deck, firefighting was hampered owing to shock failure of the forward fire pump. The F6F-5N was catapulted into the sea while the small fire left behind was quickly extinguished.

Enterprise gunners shot down five more attackers through the afternoon, but it was clear that the damage the carrier had suffered required her to return to Ulithi for repair. She departed the morning of April 12 and would be out of combat for the next five weeks.

While *Enterprise* was under attack, one of the most famous *kamikaze* attacks of the war occurred when 16 *kamikazes* were spotted inbound. One Zeke took aim at the battleship *Missouri* (BB-64). It came in low off the stern and was hit repeatedly by antiaircraft fire. As the pilot struggled to pull up, the *Zeke's* left wing caught the side of the battleship at the last instant, swinging the airplane hard against the hull and sending a wave of fiery debris onto the deck at 1443 hours. The remains of the pilot, Setsuo Ishino, were found among the wreckage after the fire was brought under control. When *Missouri's* captain, William Callaghan, ordered a military burial with honors for the pilot, he faced a near-mutiny from the crew, who were angry that he would recognize the pilot as a worthy enemy deserving of a military burial at sea when the crew wanted the body dumped overboard and disposed of with the garbage. Callaghan had to explain his decision to his crew, who reluctantly accepted the order. The next day, a Marine honor guard fired a salute and the body was buried at sea.

On April 12, the *Tokkotai* resumed their attacks. Among 129 aircraft that took off from bases on Kyushu at midday were nine G4M Betty bombers that left Kanoya Airbase each carrying an Ohka rocket-powered bomb. The Thunder Corps was about finally to enter combat. Over the East China Sea, the Bettys were intercepted by American fighters and five were shot down, but the surviving four escaped into the clouds and continued toward Okinawa.

At 1445 hours, lookouts in the Bettys spotted American ships. *Okha* pilot Ensign Saburo Dohi climbed down into the cockpit of his flying bomb. The first attempt to drop him was unsuccessful, but when the manual release was tripped, the Ohka fell free. Dohi fired the three rockets and was soon arrowing toward the American ships at nearly 600mph.

Mannert L. Abele (DD-733) had been crashed by a Zeke 45 minutes earlier, which demolished an engine room, broke her keel and snapped both propeller shafts, leaving the destroyer dead in the water. Most of the crew were standing by topside to abandon ship when seaman Jim Morris spotted what looked like a flying torpedo speeding low over the water toward the ship. There was no time to shout a warning before Saburo Dohi's *Okha* struck below the No. 1 stack and split the destroyer in two with the explosion of the 2,000lb warhead. *Mannert L. Aberle* went down in minutes, taking 80 men with her.

Minutes later, *Stanly* (DD-478) approached RP1. Suddenly, lookouts spotted something small and fast skimming the water and headed directly at them. The *Okha* penetrated the destroyer's thin skin at the bow with such force that it passed completely through the ship before exploding in the water 100 yards off the port side. *Stanly* was holed but still operational. As the ship evaded more air attacks, a second "mystery bullet" swept in. At the last minute, the Ohka "camelbacked" over the forward gun mounts and bounced out of control into the sea, where it quickly sank before exploding.

Bogeys arrived soon and for ten minutes the waters of "*kamikaze gulch*" – as the ocean between Hagushi and Kerama Retto was now known – became what sailor James Fahey later recalled as "suicide at its best" as a pageant of destruction played out, with the last planes of *Kikusui No. 2* hitting three destroyers and the battleship *Tennessee* while Navy Corsairs from VBF-83 chased attackers through a canopy of antiaircraft fire the desperate sailors put up over their ships.

For those aboard the targeted ships, being stationed above decks meant that at least one had some idea what was going on during these attacks, seeing the enemy shot down or a ship hit. For those below decks, from the men in the engineering spaces to the pilots in their ready rooms, an air attack was far more distressing. When a carrier's 5-inch battery opened up, enemy aircraft were approaching the task group, but the target was unknown. When the 40mm batteries opened up, it meant the enemy was within 4,000 yards, but might be aiming at another ship. If the 20mm commenced firing shortly after, it was certain that one was aboard the intended victim. At that point, there was nothing to do but wait and pray for survival.

April 12 was the top-scoring day for the Marines aboard the fast carriers. By this point, the carriers had been at sea for 60 days and the Marines had settled in to their role aboard ship. Major "Hap"

Hanson, CO of VMF-112, celebrated his 25th birthday by shooting down three *kamikazes* to make ace and win the Navy Cross, after spotting 30 inbound attackers over Anami O Shima at 9,000 feet. First Lieutenant Bert Hanson shot down an Oscar and a Zero and 1st Lieutenant John M. Callahan shot down three Oscars in five minutes. Altogether, the *Bennington* Marines shot down 26 enemy aircraft. Major Archie Donahue of *Bunker Hill*'s VMF-451 shot down one *kamikaze* over Izena Shima to bring his score to 14, while lieutenants Raymond H. Swalley, John E. Peterson, and John R. Webb shot down two each out of a total of 25 shot down by *Bunker Hill*'s Marine Corsairs.

The Navy Corsairs were also busy. Fighting-84 claimed 8 shot down while VBF-83 claimed seven. *Intrepid*'s Fighting-Ten launched 12 Corsairs, whose pilots spotted 66 inbound enemy aircraft and engaged 27. In an extended combat, all 12 pilots scored victories, while two were lost, one of which collided with a Wildcat. Eight Marines who had served with VMF-216 and 217 aboard *Wasp* and were assigned to a pilot pool on a CVE heard that the "Evil I" needed replacements and had volunteered to come aboard despite the fact the carrier had no Marine squadrons. Four of these pilots scored nine of Fighting-Ten's victories while overall the *Intrepid* Corsairs scored 26 victories in this fight.

At Yontan, the muddy field complicated operations. The field was crowded because the Army engineers were under orders to construct bomber airfields rather than fighter fields. Still, VMF-312 managed to get into the fighting and scored eight in their first combat. It eventually took the direct intervention of Admiral Spruance to get the airfield construction priorities changed.

At dawn the next day, Friday April 13, 1945, the teletypes in the radio rooms of the ships off Okinawa clattered with ALNAV 69. It began: "I have the sad duty of announcing to the naval service the death of Franklin Delano Roosevelt, the President of the United States, which occurred on April 12 ..."

Within minutes, the duty radiomen who decoded the message passed the word on the hundreds of ships. By the time commanding officers made the official announcements to their men, it was old news among the crews. For the overwhelming majority of sailors and marines in the Fifth Fleet and the amphibious force, and the soldiers and marines ashore, Franklin Roosevelt was the only president they had ever known. Shock and loss spread throughout the fleet as many wondered who Harry Truman was. But in a matter of an hour, general quarters klaxons sounded as bogeys appeared on the radar screens inbound from the north.

Bad weather limited operations on April 13, but *Kikusui No. 3* made its appearance on April 14. The rain of attackers continued for two days.

Fighting-Ten fought one of the great battles in the combat history of the F4U Corsair on April 16. *Intrepid* launched three divisions at 0645 hours for CAP over northern Okinawa, each with a different orbit point. Marine 1st Lieutenant George A. Krum, who had scored two on April 12, kept his division as high cover, while VF-10 CO LCDR W. E. Clarke maintained station over a radar picket point; after 30 minutes he was vectored northwest. The Corsairs were attacked by Zekes and Tonys, but still managed to bag five Zekes and two Tonys, including four downed by Lt(jg) C. D. Farmer.

Returning to the rendezvous point, Clarke heard a distress call from radar picket *Laffey* (DD-724). Racing to the scene, he found a big fight involving Hellcats, Corsairs and Wildcats over the ship. Spotting a milling formation of Vals and Nates, Clarke led his pilots in low and burned two Vals. He and his wingman next spotted a Betty low over the water, pursued by Hellcats. Diving on the enemy bomber, Clarke hit it solidly and saw it crash into the sea. When several crewmen emerged, the two Corsairs strafed them before heading home with a division score of nine.

The third VF-10 division, led by Lt(jg) Phil Kirkwood, was vectored toward a large bogey at about the same time Clarke spotted his first bogey. Splitting into sections, Kirkwood and wingman Ensign Horace W. Heath went below the clouds, while ensigns Norwald Quiel and Alfred Lerch went in on top. In the ensuing fight three Vals and a Nate went down. Heading back to the orbit point, Kirkwood and

Quiel heard the same distress call from *Laffey* that their commander did, and headed to help. Being closer, they arrived before Clarke, and ran into 20 *kamikazes* approaching the ship, which had already taken one hit. The two dived into the formation and fought off the attackers for an hour, later describing the fight as "a question of trying to get the Japs before they attacked the DD in groups." Kirkwood, who had flown Hellcats off *Intrepid* in 1944 and scored four, had added two more in this tour. In this running fight, he doubled his score, shooting down two Vals and four Nates, while Quiel shot down four Nates. The action was so furious, neither noticed the other American fighters that joined in the battle over *Laffey*.

In the meantime, ensigns Heath and Lerch returned to the orbit point, where they spotted 30 Nates inbound. The two broke up the formation and chased the obsolete fixed-gear fighters down to the water below, where the Nates milled around in confusion while each American shot down five. Three managed to break away and head toward Okinawa but were chased and shot down by Lerch, who ended the fight with a score of seven shot down, a feat equaled by only four other American pilots in one mission.

Over the course of four hours, Kirkwood's four Corsairs had shot down 20 *kamikazes*. Combined with Clarke's division score, Fighting-Ten had scored 29 confirmed for two F4Us slightly damaged by debris striking them.

Jubilation was short lived. VF-10 shot down 13 more enemy aircraft on a late-morning mission over Kyushu, for the loss of one plane and pilot, but at 1330 hours five *kamikazes* dived on *Intrepid* just as the carrier had turned into the wind to launch 12 Corsairs for CAP. Four of the attackers were shot down by the ship's gunners while the launch continued, but the fifth hit the flight deck aft. Twenty aircraft were destroyed, while ten sailors were killed and 100 injured. *Intrepid* burned for an hour before firefighters brought the fires under control. The hole in the deck was covered with steel plates and her airborne "chicks" came home to roost. Damage was severe enough that *Intrepid* had to retire to the United States for the third time. By the time she was ready to return, the war was over.

The land-based Marines also saw plenty of action against the *kamikazes*. Corsairs from VMF-311, 312, 323 and 441 fought *kamikazes* over the pickets, with the 12 planes of Major Bob White's three divisions of VMF-441 shooting down 17 of the total 36 Marine claims when they sailed into a formation of 25 Bettys, Vals and Zekes intent on sinking *Laffey*. Second Lieutenant William Eldridge shot down four, while 2nd Lieutenant Selva McGinty and Captain Floyd Kirkpatrick scored three each in the battle over *Laffey*. Corsairs of VMF-311 arrived to help, which led to one of the two losses by 441 when one of the 441 Corsairs had its tail chopped off in a collision with a 311 Corsair.

On her own, *Laffey* fought one of the epic battles of the radar picket line. The battle began at 0744 hours when radar picked up a single bogey that turned out to be a Val snooper that was driven off by 5-inch gunfire. At 0829 hours, radar picked up a swarm of incoming bogeys. Lookouts soon spotted over 50 Vals, Judys, Kates and Oscars, which were the formation that the Corsairs of VF-10 and VMF-311 would fight it out with.

Four Vals broke off from the formation and split into two two-plane formations, with two Vals on the starboard bow and the other two angling astern. The two forward 5-inch mounts opened fire and splashed the two Vals ahead, but the two astern commenced their attack. Flying low, one Val caught its landing gear in the water and nosed in. Converging gunfire from Laffey's 20mm and 40mm guns and 40mms aboard *LCS-51* destroyed the fourth.

Two Judys came in low and straight on the starboard beam. The starboard amidships 40mm mount shot down the first and the destroyer turned to unmask the forward 5-inch guns, which hit the second Judy, but not before its bomb dropped and exploded close aboard, showering the weather decks with shrapnel and injuring two sailors in the 40mm mount.

The seventh and eighth *kamikazes*, a Val to port and a Judy to starboard, bored in. *Laffey*'s gunners knocked down both. As the Val closed in from dead astern, it clipped the after deckhouse and drenched the ship's stern with aviation gasoline before crashing alongside, touching off fires that were quickly doused. By 0842 hours, *Laffey* had downed eight for eight.

The ninth attacker, another Val, was the first to crash into the destroyer, smashing a 20mm gun tub atop the after deckhouse and killing three. The deckhouse again caught fire, throwing off black smoke that concealed the tenth attacker, a Val approaching from dead astern. The airplane hit the main deck aft, spilling fire across the ship.

At 0847 hours, stern 5-inch mount gun captain Gunner's Mate 1/c Lawrence "Ski" Delewski spotted a Val off the starboard quarter that was so low and so close that only the 20mm gunners on the stern had time to shoot. Their rounds broke off pieces of the wing and fuselage, but momentum carried the Val into the fantail where it skidded past the 20mm mount and struck Delewski's mount. Six sailors inside were killed when the engine wedged in the gunhouse. The impact slewed the gunhouse to starboard, wrenched the port gun skyward and peeled back the gunhouse top deck. Delewski flew clear and landed 15 feet forward of the remains of his guns.

Laffey's stern was now engulfed in fire. Running at flank speed only fanned the flames, so Captain Becton was forced to slow, but still managed to maneuver to dodge another oncoming Val on the starboard quarter. The plane's bomb came loose, however, and the resulting explosion jammed the ship's rudders to port, locking *Laffey* into a 26-degree port turn.

Four FM-2 Wildcats from *Shamrock Bay* (CVE-84) arrived and shot down six attackers before running out of ammunition. At about this time, the Fighting-Ten Corsairs arrived overhead, but the sailors on *Laffey* were too busy to notice them. Even as the fighters went after the attackers, two more planes and another bomb struck the destroyer. When Lt(jg) Carl Reiman, leader of the Wildcats, who had shot down a Val and two Kates while defending *Laffey*, returned to *Shamrock Bay*, he reported that *Laffey* was a goner.

Laffey had now lost power to her main batteries forward, reducing her defense to four 20mm guns. Conditions were so bad that the captain contemplated abandoning ship. With 30 *kamikazes* still overhead, the two Fighting-Ten Corsairs were joined by Clarke's four, and shortly thereafter the 12 from VMF-311. One Marine flew so low chasing an inbound Val that he sheared off a radar antenna and sustained such damage he was forced to bale out.

At 0934 hours, *Bryant* (DD-665) arrived. Maneuvering at flank speed, her gunners splashed several *kamikazes* before one crashed the base of her forward superstructure, knocking out the CIC and radio room, killing 34 and wounding 30 more. *Bryant* managed to limp to Kerama Retto on her own.

At 0947 hours, as the Corsairs continued their battle, Val number 21 dived on *Laffey* and dropped a bomb that wiped out the port 20mm gun mount, killing the crew. Minutes later, the 22nd attacker in 80 minutes was destroyed in its dive by 40mm fire from *LCS-51*. The sky was finally clear of attackers as the Corsairs winged away. The crew set about firefighting in an attempt to save their ship. By 1100 hours, *Laffey* was down by the stern when *LCS-51* came alongside to assist in firefighting and to take off wounded. *LCS-51* took *Laffey* in tow and, by the next day, "The ship that would not die," as *Laffey* came to be known, entered Kerama Retto's Bone Yard. She had survived the most determined *kamikaze* attacks of the war, hit by four bombs and six *kamikazes* that wounded 72 crewmen and killed 31. Four other radar picket destroyers had taken hits and casualties from the 165 *kamikazes* launched that day, though fortunately none was so seriously damaged.

Temporary repairs were rushed and *Laffey* departed three days later for Saipan, arriving on April 27. On May 1 she got under way for the Todd Shipyard at Tacoma, Washington, via Eniwetok and Hawaii, arriving in Tacoma on May 24, where she eased alongside Pier 48, six weeks after her ordeal in the East China Sea. The Navy delayed sending *Laffey* into the shipyard until nearly 93,000 civilians could visit the destroyer and see for themselves the results of the *kamikaze* attacks at Okinawa and the bravery of her crew. Her repairs were completed the week of the formal surrender in September. After serving in the Korean War and throughout the Cold War, *Laffey* was the last Sumner-class destroyer to be decommissioned on

March 9, 1975. She was designated a National Historic Landmark in 1986 in recognition of her fight at Okinawa and is today moored in Charleston, South Carolina, alongside *Yorktown* (CV-10).

While *Laffey* fought her epic battle, *Pringle* (DD-477) and *Hobson* (DD-464/DMS-26) were under siege at RP14. When the first attackers swarmed in, *Pringle* shot down a Zeke. Three low-flying Vals took aim at the destroyer and were spotted heading toward the ship at a range of 10,000 yards. One Val went in when its wing was clipped by 5-inch fire while the other two circled. Then one turned toward the ship, twisting and turning as it was surrounded by antiaircraft fire while *Pringle* went to flank speed to outmaneuver the incoming attacker. The plane was obscured by smoke, until it appeared suddenly and crashed at the base of the forward stack. The impact and huge explosion that quickly followed snapped the ship's keel. Broken in half, *Pringle* sank five minutes later, taking 65 of her crew down with her.

LCS-34 and *LCS-121* approached to rescue survivors. Other *kamikazes* were still around, and *LCS-34* expended so much 20mm and 40mm ammunition in fighting them off that the gun crews were struggling through knee-deep drifts of expended shell casings and men had to be called from below decks to clear the upper deck so the gun crews could continue to mount a defense. *LCS-34* eventually pulled 87 men from the water, while *121* rescued another 28.

Even when a ship managed to survive and make it to Kerama Retto, the horror was not over for the survivors. Men had to work their way through the damage to find the remains of their shipmates, most of them horribly mutilated and burned, some beyond recognition even by dental records. The effort was so agonizing that Electrician's Mate 2/c Henry Seeba, one of the survivors aboard *Bowers* (DE-637), which had been hit by *kamikazes* south of Ie Shima on April 16, later wrote that he was convinced it would have been better to have switched places with the crew of another wrecked ship and let them handle *Bowers'* dead while he and the other *Bowers* survivors dealt with theirs. One of the men Seeba identified was a sailor who had bunked near him. He was able to identify the remains only by the smell of the Aqua Velva aftershave the man always wore, since the body was in two parts – the legs and hips were still in the trainer's seat of the Number Two mount's 3-inch gun, while his torso lay face down on the deck. Water tender Frank Martinez identified the ship's chief radioman by his wedding ring.

On April 18, shock ran through every American afloat and ashore when it was learned that Ernie Pyle, "The GI's war correspondent," who had chronicled the lives of American soldiers in and out of battle from North Africa to the Liberation of Paris, had been killed on Ie Shima island, just northwest of Okinawa. Pyle had been awarded the 1944 Pulitzer Prize for his "everyman" perspective in his war reporting and was beloved by all the men who had met him. After relocating to the Pacific, where he bucked the Navy's prohibition on using the names of sailors in reporting and received a special dispensation for him alone, he went aboard the light carrier *Cabot* during the first Tokyo strike. He said the crew had an "easy life," compared to the infantry in Europe, and had written an unflattering report of shipboard life.

Pyle had then joined the Okinawa invasion force and came ashore on Ie Shima with the 305th Infantry Regiment of the 77th "Liberty Patch" Division on April 17. Shortly before, the 45-year old correspondent had confided to his friend, *Time* magazine's Robert Sherrod, that "I'm getting too old to stay in combat with these kids." By the next day, enemy opposition had apparently been neutralized. In an effort to get to the front to talk to the troops, he was traveling with the 305th's commander, Lt Col Joseph B. Coolidge, to the new command post when they encountered enemy machine-gun fire and took cover in a nearby ditch. Coolidge later reported, "A little later Pyle and I raised up to look around. Another burst hit the road over our heads. I looked at Ernie and saw he had been hit." He had been hit by a bullet that entered his left temple just under his helmet and was killed instantly.

Ernie Pyle was buried with his helmet on, between an infantry private and a combat engineer. The 305th Regiment erected a monument, which still stands at the site of his death on the island, inscribed, "At this spot the 77th Infantry Division lost a buddy.

TIDAL WAVE

Ernie Pyle, 18 April 1945." Eleanor Roosevelt, who had frequently quoted his dispatches in her newspaper column, "My Day," paid tribute to him in her column the next day: "I shall never forget how much I enjoyed meeting him here in the White House last year, and how much I admired this frail and modest man who could endure hardships because he loved his job and our men." President Truman wrote, "No man in this war has so well told the story of the American fighting man as American fighting men wanted it told. He deserves the gratitude of all his countrymen."

Rear Admiral J. J. "Jocko" Clark, who had become a close friend of Pyle in the 1930s when he was aviation editor for Scripps-Howard and had taken him flying many times while Clark commanded NAS Anacostia in Washington, later wrote that learning of his friend's death was "one of the hardest personal losses I experienced in the war."

The psychological stress sailors experienced as they fought to shoot down *kamikazes* grew worse as the campaign went on. Ship's surgeons were forced to deal with something that had never before been seen on ships: "combat fatigue," similar to that experienced by soldiers and marines ashore. The fleet was relentlessly assaulted by *kamikazes* and conventional attackers. In daylight, sailors crewing 40mm guns aboard radar picket destroyers were able to see the faces of the enemy pilots in the last split seconds before the planes struck the ship and exploded. Frequently, there were night attacks on moonlit nights. 19-year-old Signalman 1/c Nicholas Floros, an antiaircraft gunner on an LSM, recalled *kamikazes* looking like ghostly apparitions, "like a giant bat gliding in." Admiral Spruance, who survived both his flagships sustaining damage from *kamikazes* during the campaign, described the night raiders as "witches on broomsticks."

Task Force 57, the British Pacific Fleet, arrived on March 26 and took station west of Okinawa to block *kamikaze* attacks from the Sakishima Gunto islands and Formosa. The four British fleet carriers, with their armored flight decks, were better able to absorb a *kamikaze* hit with only slight damage that might put an American carrier out of action. During their tour of duty, all four of the carriers would be hit before the fleet withdrew to reprovision on April 20. By the end of the

202

Okinawa campaign, the five British carriers that participated had been hit by eight *kamikazes*, which resulted in only 20 deaths, a testament to the value of their armored flight decks.

Beginning with their arrival, the Hellcats and Corsairs flew escort missions for bombing attacks by Avengers and Fireflies against airfields throughout the islands, while *Indefatigable*'s two Seafire III squadrons provided fleet CAP.

On April 1, the first fighter "Ramrods" (i.e. fighter sweeps) had just been launched when an inbound raid appeared on radar at 0700 hours. Sub-Lieutenant Richard Reynolds of 894 Squadron, who had shared in the destruction of two German flying boats in the Arctic in August 1944, led the CAP overhead. Just before 0730 hours, a Zeke machinegunned the battleship HMS *King George V*, then took aim at *Indefatigable*. Reynolds dove through the shipboard antiaircraft fire and pounced on the Zeke. He scored hits on the weaving attacker and set it afire just before he had to break off when the *kamikaze* hit *Indefatigable* and started a fire. Forty minutes later, the damage was under control and the carrier resumed flight operations. Twenty minutes after the first attack, Reynolds was vectored onto a Zeke that had just divebombed the antiaircraft cruiser HMS *Ulster Queen*. He knocked this attacker down with two short bursts of 20mm cannon fire, then latched onto a third Zeke that turned into him, but Reynolds knocked it down with two bursts of cannon fire. With these three and his two Atlantic victories, Sub-Lieutenant Reynolds became the only Seafire ace of the war.

LCDR Tommy Harrington, commander of 5 Naval Fighter Wing, scored his final victory of the war shortly after Reynolds' battle. "He was flying out of range and I carefully fired a good long blast over his port wing. He then very kindly obliged by executing a rather difficult turn to port, which enabled me to close and shoot this unhappy amateur down." The Oscar was another *kamikaze*.

The British didn't have everything their way. 1834 Squadron lost their CO while South African ace Edward Wilson had his engine shot up over Ishigaki and was forced to ditch. Fortunately, he was picked up by *Victorious*' ASR Supermarine Walrus.

Two days later, Canadian Sub-Lieutenant Bill Atkinson of 1844 Squadron attacked a Betty and damaged it. On April 6, he shared a Judy with Edward Wilson, bringing his score to seven and making him the leading FAA Hellcat ace.

At Spruance's request, Task Force 57 hit Formosa on April 12. Ronnie Hay was once again the strike coordinator when *Victorious'* Avengers bombed Matsuyama Airfield. That morning, Lieutenant Bill Thomson and Sub-Lieutenant Phil Stott of *Indefatigable's* 1770 Squadron spotted five JAAF Ki-51 Sonia dive bombers while they were escorting a US Navy PBM Mariner on patrol. The two Firefly pilots immediately attacked, scoring two each with the fifth Sonia as a probable. In the process, Stott's two victories made him the only Firefly ace of the war. Thomson later wrote in his logbook:

CAP over rescue Mariner (US). Sighted five Sonias 12 miles northwest of southwest point Kumi island at 1,000 feet. Claimed and attacked from 2,000 feet on port quarter. Shot down port stern aircraft in flames, then chased his wingman, who evaded me for a while – finally closed, and at 50 yards he exploded in red flames. Resumed patrol. No. 2 got two more. I claim two Sonias certain.

April 12 was also the best day for the Hellcat in FAA service, with pilots scoring a total of six victories. Sub-Lieutenant Bill Foster started the day's claims when he claimed an Oscar and a Tony at 0630 hours, while his wingman Bill Atkinson claimed a Tony probable and an Oscar destroyed.

At about the same time, Sub-Lieutenant J. H. Kernagan of the Seafire-equipped 887 Squadron attacked a mixed formation of incoming enemy fighters that broke and evaded. Chasing after, he fired two long bursts at a Zeke that caught fire and went into the ocean as he turned away and damaged a Tony with the last of his ammunition.

The fleet returned to Sakishima Gunto on April 14. The next day Bill Atkinson shot down a C6N Myrt reconnaissance plane. HMS *Formidable* had arrived and replaced *Illustrious* on April 16, but 1842 Squadron lost their CO, LCDR "Judy" Garland, when his Corsair was hit over Ishigaki. Bill Foster also shot down a shadowing Myrt. When he shot down another on April 20, he became an ace. Later that day, Task Force 57 retired to Leyte Gulf to replenish and refit.

The FM-2 Wildcat might have been superseded by the Hellcat and Corsair on the fast carriers, but the stubby little fighters still had a lot of "go" in them. On April 28, VOC-1 CO Bush Bringle and his wingman were vectored onto two *kamikaze* Vals whose pilots were wearing ceremonial robes and "looking scared to death." The two Wildcats quickly gave them a final ceremony sooner than they had planned, as the *kamikazes* flew straight and level with the Americans flying formation as they performed the execution.

The eighteen CVEs of the Carrier Support Force were not limited to flying close air support for the troops ashore on Okinawa. Throughout the month of April, they also participated in the neutralization or occupation of outlying islands in the Ryukyu chain. The airfields on these islands might have been small, but they were defended with intense and accurate antiaircraft fire.

On one strafing mission, Bringle was hit in his engine on his second pass, with the Cyclone stopped cold. As he prepared for a water landing, the engine unexpectedly restarted when he was 50 feet over the water, showing 1,200 rpm and 35 inches in the instruments. It wasn't much power but he took it happily, even though the R-1820 had no throttle or prop control. Following his wingman at 1,000 feet and 170 knots, he made it back to *Marcus Island* and trapped with a fast flat approach despite having no flaps and no throttle control, which forced him to blip the magnetos for power adjustments to get a "Roger pass" from the LSO and catch the third wire. Shortly after, *Marcus Island* returned to Ulithi to replenish and replace aircraft and provide a rest for the busy pilots.

CHAPTER TEN

THE MURDEROUS
MONTH OF MAY

If anyone had any doubts prior to L-Day, the events of the past 30 days clearly demonstrated that the battle for Okinawa was the biggest fight of the Pacific War to date. Ashore, soldiers and marines fought a grinding struggle in the south of the island against a well-organized defense willing to fight to the last man, with conditions made worse by increasing rain as the monsoon season approached. At sea, the Navy was engaged in a life-or-death struggle against an enemy equally determined to sacrifice everything if necessary. Those aboard the radar picket destroyers wondered why it was that the Japanese had centered their attacks on these relatively low-value ships, rather than continue to the main fleet where they could target the crucial carriers. Whether it was due to an actual strategy to knock out the early warning system, or just the inexperience of the attackers, the destroyers and their accompanying LCIs and LSMs at the picket locations were the front line of the naval battle at Okinawa.

Aboard the destroyers, men were reading a mimeographed handout, *Calling All Destroyers*, which compressed the fundamental lessons of *kamikaze* warfare, originally created by the destroyer *Wadsworth* (DD-516), now distributed with the imprimatur of the Pacific Fleet Cruiser and Destroyer Command.

Calling All Destroyers began:

"So long 'Frisco" must be the saddest words in the book these days when the bucktoothed Banzai Boys are waiting out here to mess up that new paint job. But remember this ... the Japs have sent out hundreds of these guys with their one-way ticket, but only a relative few have gotten hits. What's happened to the rest? Well, the same old ground rules still apply.

For lookouts, the ground rules were: "Watch the clouds. Watch the low haze over the water. Watch the 20 degrees to either side of the sun. Radar doesn't always pick them up, so if a plane suddenly pops in on you, be able to tell in a split second whether it's a *Zeke* or an F6F." For the fighter direction teams: "Let the CAP take care of them. It's easier on the nerves and the planes are built for it. Get out the bearing, course, speed and angles in a hurry." For gunners:

The more shrapnel you give him to come through, the less chance he has of making it. Fire early and save your ship. Keep shooting until his prop brushes your whiskers. In the last thousand yards, he still has a lot of smart flying to do to hit you. Work on the pilot. Aim for the cockpit with the 20s and 40s. A dead Jap can't fly a plane, and instead of making those last-minute corrections on his stick, he'll flop in the drink out of control.

On May 1, Admiral Ugaki ordered the launch of *Kikusui No. 5.* Weather intervened, and the main attacks did not come for two days. However, May 4 would be memorable indeed as the beginning of the worst fight over the radar pickets yet.

At RP10, *Aaron Ward* (DD-773) and *Little* (DD-803) were accompanied by the LCSs and an LCM. Incoming attackers were spotted by radar shortly after 1800 hours and at 1822 hours klaxons echoed across the water as the little fleet went to General Quarters when the *kamikazes* drew within a few miles. *Aaron Ward's* gunners scored first, shooting down a Zeke close to starboard and a second farther out to port. The third Zeke came out of the lowering sun and dropped a bomb off the stern, cutting off steering and power to the No. 3 twin 5-inch mount.

Action spread to the rest of the ships. *Little* waged a hopeless battle with 24 *kamikazes* overhead. Her gunners shot down two, but a third crashed the port side at 1843 hours, followed by two more within a minute of each other, while a third hit the torpedo mount in a vertical dive minutes later. Within seven minutes, *Little*'s keel snapped and the ship was a goner. She sank at 1855 hours.

Overhead, four Hellcats appeared in answer to the call for help from *Ward*'s FDO. Gene Valencia's elite VF-9 division hit the 38 attackers at 15,000 feet. Valencia's wingman Harris Mitchell later remembered the epic battle. "I discovered the true meaning of anxiety as we closed that huge gaggle, but when I looked over at Gene his expression was that of a young child who had just spotted his favorite toy under the Christmas tree." Valencia exploded the leader of four Zekes and the other three dropped their bombs and dove away. The two Hellcat sections took turns attacking while the other stayed high to provide cover. Mitchell shot two Zekes off Valencia's tail while he picked off a fourth on the tail of Clinton "Smitty" Smith. Over the course of two hours, the foursome shot down 11, claimed three probables and one damaged in a fight that went from 15,000 feet to sea level. The four Hellcats were so short of fuel they had to land at Yontan before returning to *Yorktown*. Harris Mitchell had to be towed off the runway when his engine quit, out of gas.

Below, *Aaron Ward* was in bad trouble with steering gone, fires raging and ready ammunition stores exploding. The ship collided with two LCSs attempting to close and assist in firefighting and evacuation of wounded. *LSM-195* took a *kamikaze* that ignited the onboard rockets, shut down pumps and cut water pressure; unable to fight the fires, the crew went over the side leaving the burning vessel adrift in the gathering darkness before it exploded and sank at 1920 hours. *LCS-83*'s gunners shot down an attacker aimed at *LCS-25*, then splashed an attacker headed for their ship that crashed mere feet from the bow. *LCS-14*, followed by *LCS-83*, finally made it alongside *Aaron Ward* and removed the wounded, fought fires, and pumped flooded spaces. In the meantime, *LCS-25* combed the sea for survivors of the sunken ships. After a two-hour fight to stem the fires, *Aaron Ward* was taken under tow for the Bone Yard, where she arrived around midnight.

As *Aaron Ward* was taken under tow, *Macomb* (DD-458/DMS-23) at RP9 was struck by a *kamikaze* that blew up when it hit the after gun mount and hurled dead and wounded into the sea. With *Macomb*'s seven dead at RP9, the casualty toll for May 3 was just short of 250 dead and wounded.

The next day was worse.

At 0430 hours, VF-9's four-Hellcat night-fighter detachment was vectored onto bogeys that turned out to be four Betty bombers. Ensign John Orth shot down three of them to bring his score to six as a night-fighter pilot.

The battle began over RP12 at 0630 hours when *Luce* (DD-522) took a hit that knocked out her radar and guns, followed minutes later by a *kamikaze* that crashed amidships and blew up torpedoes and ready ammunition in the 40mm mounts. *Luce* sank in a matter of minutes.

Next it was the turn of *Shea* (DD-750/DMS-30). En route to radar picket duty 20 miles northeast of Zampa Misaki, she encountered two *kamikazes*, shooting one down for certain with her 5-inch battery and the other probable before arriving on station at 0600 hours. Receiving reports of raids inbound, *Shea* sounded General Quarters. Minutes later a smoky haze from the Hagushi beaches enveloped the ship, reducing visibility to 5,000 yards. Ninety minutes later she was in the clear, and at 0854 a lone Betty was spotted six miles away. The FDO vectored the CAP to the bomber and the Hellcats shot it down at 0858 hours. An Ohka was spotted a minute later, closing at better than 450 knots on the starboard beam. Moments later, the rocket-propelled bomb crashed into the starboard side of her bridge, where it entered the sonar room and traversed the chart house passageway and hatch before exploding just to port when it hit the water. The hit caused a fire to break out on the mess deck, inside the CIC, the chart house, the division commander's stateroom, and the No. 2 5-inch mount upper handling room. Internal communication was lost throughout the ship. All power was lost to mounts No. 1 and 2, while the forward 20mm guns were damaged. The main gun director was jammed and the gyro and computer were inoperable. Casualties were one officer and 34 men killed and 91 others wounded. *Shea* listed to port 5 degrees. While the damage-control parties fought the fires, the destroyer limped to the Hagushi anchorage, searching for medical assistance. After she arrived at 1052 hours, the most seriously wounded were transferred to *Crescent City* (APA-21) while the 35 dead were taken ashore for burial on Okinawa. *Shea* then headed to Kerama Retto. After holding a memorial service for the dead on May 11, she departed for Ulithi on May 15 and ultimately returned to the United States for repairs.

Starting at 0715 hours, *Morrison* (DD-560) and *Ingraham* (DD-694) fought off what seemed an unending procession of *kamikaze* raids. *Ingraham* shot down four attackers before a fifth crashed just above the waterline on the port side, with its bomb exploding in the generator room and knocking out power. *Ingraham* was left with one operable gun; 36 sailors were wounded and 15 killed. Unable to offer any defense, *Ingraham* was forced to leave station and head for Kerama Retto.

At the same time, *Morrison* was attacked by a Zeke that broke through heavy flak and dropped a bomb off the starboard beam that exploded harmlessly. A Val and another Zeke followed with unsuccessful suicide runs, as they were shot down by the 40mm gunners with both crashing alongside. At 0825 hours a Zeke flew through intense antiaircraft fire and crashed into the forward stack and the bridge, inflicting heavy casualties and knocking out most electrical equipment.

Lookouts then spotted a formation of seven twin-float biplanes low over the water on the horizon, identifying them as Alfs. The airplanes were so slow they couldn't be followed by the gun director, while their fabric construction made them nearly invulnerable to proximity-fused shells. One came in through 20mm and 40mm fire and crashed into the handling rooms of the forward 5-inch mounts, setting off fires. One of the attackers alighted on the water as the others continued to attack unsuccessfully, with *Morrison* shooting down three more. The fourth Alf then lifted off and under cover of smoke flew into the destroyer, hitting her No. 4 5-inch mount and igniting another fire. *Morrison* listed sharply to starboard. With the internal communications circuits knocked out, it was impossible to transit the order to abandon ship to all compartments. At 0838 hours, the fires set off two explosions in the 5-inch mount handling rooms. *Morrison's* bow lifted into the air and two minutes later she sank so fast that 152 men below decks went down with her.

Overhead of the destroyers, Hellcats of VF-9 shot down 29 attackers through the course of the day, while VF-83's Hellcats splashed 24 near Izena Shima, including six by Ensign Myron M. Truax – four Type 93 trainers, a Val and an Oscar. VBF-12 and VF-46 shot down 20 between them to bring the Hellcat score for the day to 73, while Corsairs from *Bunker Hill*, *Essex*, and the newly-arrived *Shangri-La* knocked down 30 more.

Casualties on May 4 came to 1,000 dead and wounded, with the loss of two destroyers and two LSMs and another destroyer so severely damaged she was put out of action for the rest of the war.

The Royal Navy's Task Force 57 returned to Okinawa on May 4 and resumed attacks on nearly-empty airfields in Sakishima Gunto. Seafire pilots Sub-Lieutenant Reynolds and his wingman, Sub-Lieutenant Randall Kay, shot down a Hamp, which was Reynolds' final success of the war.

Just after 1130 hours, a wave of suicide attackers bore down on the British carriers. One *kamikaze* made a steep dive at *Formidable* and was engaged by the carrier's antiaircraft guns. Although it was hit and crashed into the sea nearby, its bomb came loose as it roared over the flight deck and detonated on the flight deck, producing a crater 9 feet long, 2 feet wide and 2 feet deep. A long steel bomb splinter speared through the hangar deck and the main boiler room, rupturing a steam line before it came to rest in an aviation fuel tank near the aircraft park. Eight sailors were killed and 47 wounded when a major fire broke out that destroyed one Corsair and ten Avengers. The fires were brought under control over the course of several hours, after which the crater in the deck was repaired with concrete and steel plate. By 1700 hours, the ship was able to resume flight operations.

At 1700 hours on May 9, *kamikazes* struck from Formosa. Both *Formidable* and *Victorious* were hit with aircraft on deck preparing for takeoff, while the battleship HMS *Howe* also took a hit. The two carriers lost 47 Corsairs between them in the resulting fires, but once again their armored decks protected them and both were ready to resume operations in a few hours. This proved to be the final *kamikaze* strike against the Royal Navy at Okinawa. A US Navy liaison officer aboard *Indefatigable* reported: "When a *kamikaze* hits a US carrier it means six months of repair at Pearl. When a *kamikaze* hits a Limey carrier it's just a case of 'Sweepers, man your brooms.'" Postwar analysis showed several carriers, including *Formidable*, had suffered more structural damage than had been originally apparent, which led to the ships being scrapped as beyond economic repair.

On May 25, Task Force 57 flew its final strikes of the Okinawa campaign, then retired to Australia to refit its battered ships and replenish aircraft. The British Pacific Fleet had spent 62 days at sea during the campaign, while the fighters had shot down 42 Japanese aircraft and destroyed many more during airfield strikes.

May 10 saw one of the more unusual aerial fights in the Pacific War, one that showed just how tough the Corsair was. Four F4U-1D Corsairs of VMF-312 on a dawn CAP over Ie Shima spotted the contrails of a twin-engine Ki-45 Nick recon plane at 25,000 feet. As the Corsairs climbed, so did the Nick, which had obviously spotted them too. Two of the Corsairs abandoned the chase when they topped out at 36,000 feet, but Captain Kenneth Reusser and 1st Lieutenant Robert Klingman continued the chase. Both fired off most of their ammunition to lighten their fighters and closed in on the Nick at 38,000 feet. Reusser expended the last of his ammo and damaged the port engine, while the rear gunner returned fire and hit the Corsair, forcing Reusser to break off. Klingman pulled within

50 feet of the Nick and opened fire, but nothing happened. His guns were frozen in the sub-zero stratosphere. Careful not to stall out, Klingman approached the Nick and began chewing up the airplane with his propeller, taking pieces off the rudder and destroying the rear cockpit. Positioning himself again to the rear, he approached and chewed off what was left of the rudder. Uncertain now that he could return to Okinawa 150 miles to the south and with his fighter vibrating badly from damage to the prop, Klingman executed a third buzz-saw attack and took off the Nick's right stabilizer. The Nick fell off into a spin it did not recover from and shed its wings at 15,000 feet before it hit the ocean 5 miles below.

Klingman held his altitude and turned back for Okinawa. Twenty miles north of the island he ran out of fuel and glided the rest of the way to Yontan, where he executed a dead-stick landing. The tips of his propeller were gone, and the Corsair's airframe was punctured and dented from debris and bullet holes.

Southern Japan was covered with low clouds the morning of May 11. Despite the likelihood of rain, *Kikusui No. 6* was ordered to strike the Americans. At 0640 hours, the first Zeke of the 306th Showa Special Attack Squadron of the 721st Naval Air Group lifted off the runway at Kanoya Airfield on southern Kyushu. This Zeke was followed by five more, with the last one departing at 0653 hours. Each Zeke carried a 250kg bomb. The small formation joined up and stayed low, as far away from the clouds as possible, as they headed east in search of the American aircraft carriers that had been spotted the previous day southeast of Kyushu. Squadron leader Lt(jg) Seizo Yasunori was determined to find the American carriers. As the formation crossed the coastline and headed out to sea, one of the Zekes suffered engine trouble. As the inexperienced pilot attempted to turn back, he stalled his airplane, then entered a spin from which he didn't recover before the Zeke struck the sea below. The five survivors headed on. Ensign Kiyoshi Ogawa, a Waseda University graduate who had been drafted the previous summer following his graduation, put all his attention into following his leader. Ensign Ogawa had graduated from flying school only the previous February;

flying a Zeke with fewer than 150 total flying hours was difficult, but he was determined to do his duty as a subject of the emperor when the moment came.

Task Force 58 had been fortunate since *Kikusui No. 3* had claimed *Intrepid*. *Kikusui No. 4* on April 16 had hit the radar pickets hard, as had *Kikusui No. 5* at the beginning of the month, but the suicide attackers had missed the fast carriers.

Lieutenant Yasunori spotted the dark silhouettes of American Navy fighters in the distance, and led his flight into the clouds, where they managed to evade the defenders. Other *Tokko* formations were not so fortunate when the Americans found the inexperienced pilots and shot them into the sea. Ensign Ogawa was concerned about the clouds, since he had no skill at flying blind; neither did any of the others, but Yasunori was successful in evading interception. The five Zekes headed on.

Eight VF-84 Corsair pilots were on CAP over Kikai when they spotted and jumped 30 *kamikazes*, shooting down 11. VF-17 veteran Lieutenant John M. Smith was the top scorer with two Nates and a Zeke to finish his wartime score at ten. The Corsairs turned to head back to *Bunker Hill*.

The morning sky over Task Force 58 was covered with a six-tenths cloud cover. *Bunker Hill*, flagship for task force commander Admiral Marc Mitscher, had just finished her re-spot to begin landing eight VMF-451 Corsairs of the CAP, with Smith's two VF-84 divisions inbound. Major Archie Donahue was in the groove with a "roger pass" from the LSO and caught the three wire. *Enterprise*, which had returned from repairs at Ulithi only two days before, steamed in formation several thousand yards distant.

Radar operators in *Bunker Hill*'s CIC strained to get returns in the stormy skies, but their work was made more difficult by the many small rain squalls in all quarters, which reduced the ability of the ship's radar to spot inbound attackers.

Lieutenant Yasunori led his formation between several large clouds, then broke into clear skies. There before him were the American carriers and their escorts, wakes white against the blue sea. He spotted two big aircraft carriers near each other and led his Zekes in to attack. Suddenly, dark puffs of antiaircraft explosions surrounded the formation, and one plane fell away on fire. Ensign Ogawa closed up on his leader and followed him into his dive.

At about 0745 hours, the men aboard *Bunker Hill* were suddenly aware they were under attack when Yasunori opened up with his machine guns and strafed the deck as Archie Donahue taxied up the flight deck after the Airedales had freed his hook. Donahue pulled to the side, shut down and exited his Corsair quickly. The ship had a matter of seconds to mount a defense once the enemy aircraft appeared out of the clouds. The crewmen manning the 20mm antiaircraft guns that lined the deck edge opened up, spraying tracers skyward. Yasunori was hit, but still he came on. The Zeke caught fire, but still he held his dive. When he realized his plane was out of control and he might not crash the carrier, he pulled his bomb release.

Yasunori's 550lb bomb struck *Bunker Hill* near the Number Three elevator and penetrated the flight deck, exiting the port side at gallery deck level before exploding in the ocean. Yasunori's Zeke struck the deck a moment later, destroying several aircraft and causing a large fire as the wreckage of his burning Zeke careened through several other aircraft before it went over the side into the water.

Ensign Owada had also been set on fire by defending AA when he dropped his bomb 30 seconds later. It struck forward of the island on the flight deck and penetrated into the spaces below. Owada's Zeke then hit the forward part of the island and exploded, starting a second fire. An instant later, Owada's bomb exploded in Air Group 84's ready rooms at the gallery level above the hangar deck, killing many. On the flight deck above, the fire sent backdrafts of flame into the island's narrow passageways and up the access ladders.

As fire began to spread from the wrecked ready rooms to the hangar deck, the firefighters sprayed water and foam on the airplanes on the deck to keep them from exploding.

Captain Gene A. Seitz ordered *Bunker Hill* into a hard turn to port in an attempt to clear some of the worst of the burning fuel and debris. Below, the fires spread and the carrier fell out of formation.

Wilkes-Barre (CL-103) closed on the burning carrier as her crew broke out fire hoses and turned them on *Bunker Hill*. The light cruiser came close enough that men trapped on the catwalks could jump to her main deck as other crewmen went into the sea to get away from the fires. *Cushing* (DD-729) came alongside and began fishing survivors from the sea as her damage-control teams added their firefighting to the defense of the carrier.

Fires raged for hours below decks as men struggled through the toxic air to find the wounded and lead them up to fresh air while fighting the fires. Above, the pilots of VMF-221 who had been patrolling as CAP were directed to land aboard *Enterprise*.

In the engineering compartments, Chief Engineer Commander Joseph Carmichael managed to keep his team together despite 99 of the 500 men there having been killed and wounded, and was able to keep the boilers and engines operating, which saved the ship.

The worst of the fire was contained by 1530 hours. The cost of the attack was staggering: 396 dead and 264 wounded. For the survivors of Air Group 84, the worst was to come the next day, when they had to enter the ruined ready rooms to locate, tag and remove the bodies of their flying mates. Many had died of smoke inhalation and their bodies were piled in gangways or jammed into the ready room hatchways. Sadly, Chief Engineer Carmichael discovered that while the fire was being fought, someone had taken an acetylene welding torch and cut through the safety deposit boxes in the ship's post office and had then stolen the money they contained. The thief was never caught.

Ensign Owada was identified that same morning, when salvage diver Robert Shock volunteered to go into the bowels of the ship, where the remains of the Zeke had finally settled. The wreck was half submerged when Schock found it and came face to face with the dead pilot. He searched the body and found papers he removed that later turned out to be photographs and a letter. Schock also removed the pilot's blood-soaked name tag and a smashed watch embedded in his chest, as well as the buckle from his parachute harness. The diver hid these and brought them home after the war. In 2001, Schock's son found the items following his father's death, and these were later returned to Ogawa's niece and grandniece in a ceremony in San Francisco.

Admiral Mitscher was forced to relinquish command; he and his staff were transferred by breeches buoy to *English* (DD-696) for transport to *Enterprise*, where he broke his flag and resumed command. Thirteen of his staff had died in the fires in *Bunker Hill's* island.

While *Bunker Hill* fought for her life off Kyushu, the radar picket destroyers north of Okinawa again came in for attack. The attackers appeared over RP15 at 0750 hours. At 0755, radar operators aboard *Hugh W. Hadley* (DD774), command ship at RP15, were tracking 150 bogeys. The three accompanying LCSs went to General Quarters as their crews manned the 40mm mounts. *Hadley's* FDO separated the bogeys into four raids and vectored a 12-plane CAP of Corsairs and Hellcats to intercept the attackers. By the time the fliers called "Tally-Ho!" *Hadley* and *Robley D. Evans* (DD-552) were under attack by multiple *kamikazes*. During the next 100 minutes, *Hadley* shot down 12 while *Evans* shot down 15. *Evans* was hit four times, which exploded two boilers and flooded all engineering spaces and left her dead in the water. *Hadley* took an Ohka, a Zeke and a bomb that flooded her engineering spaces, while exploding ammunition threatened to sink her. Her captain, LCDR Baron Mullaney, kept 50 men aboard to fight fires and ordered the rest to abandon ship. *LCS-83* and *LSM-193* began rescuing men in the water, while *LCS-84* came alongside *Hadley* to assist in firefighting. *LCS-82* came alongside *Evans* and rigged pumps to control flooding, while her damage control party cut a hole in the destroyer's forecastle to free a dozen sailors trapped below who were badly burned. Both destroyers were towed to Kerama Retto. *Evans* suffered 30 dead and 30 wounded, while *Hadley* lost 100 killed and wounded.

Gene Valencia's Circus fought their last battle on May 11. Vectored with divisions led by Lieutenant Marvin Franger and Lieutenant Bert Eckard into a formation of 55 *kamikazes* over the northern Ryukyus, Valencia's team fought 18 Zekes and Franks in two groups and shot down nine without loss, though Valencia pressed one attack so close that his radio was jarred loose by the exploding Frank. Valencia's Circus had scored 43 victories during the deployment, one-third of the Fighting-Nine total, including 34 in their three combats in May.

Bert Eckhard and his wingman Ensign John Kaelin tangled with 30 Zekes for 20 minutes, during which Eckhard shot down five to bring his score to seven, becoming the 42nd and last Hellcat "ace in a day" in the Pacific War. Marv Franger's division saw only one, a Frank that Franger shot down to become the only Navy pilot of the war to have scored on three deployments. He began by shooting down a Vichy French Armée de l'Air Curtiss Hawk-75 during the invasion of North Africa in November 1942, followed by five more during *Essex*'s 1943–44 tour, and the three he scored on the third deployment in 1945. His score included six different Axis aircraft types: Hawk 75A-3, Kate, Zeke, Nate, Jake and Tony.

Fighting-Nine ended their deployment in June, following the return of Task Force 38 to Ulithi. During this third tour, the squadron claimed 128.75 aerial victories and 47 on the ground. During two tours in the Pacific, the squadron had claimed 250.75 victories, plus six scored over North Africa, to become the second-ranked Navy fighter squadron after VF-15. Twenty pilots had become aces during these tours, putting the unit in third place behind VF-2 with 27 aces and VF-15 with 26. At war's end, Gene Valencia's score of 23 tied him with Lieutenant Cecil Harris of VF-18 for second top-scoring ace behind Ace of Aces Commander David McCampbell's 34.

May 11, 1945 was the Fifth Fleet's third-worst day of the Okinawa campaign. That night, Air Group 90 went to work on the Kyushu *kamikaze* airfields. The Avengers attacked unwary military airfields and other facilities that left lights on. The next night, the Japanese were prepared with radar-directed searchlights. Some pilots had their night vision ruined, but the searchlights were defeated when the pilots dropped "window," aluminum foil strips cut to the radar wavelengths. During the second night, Hellcat night fighters patrolled Kagoshima Bay and Kanoya Airfield, where they scored eight victories in the early predawn hours. Lieutenant Owen Young nearly became the first "ace in a night" when he shot down three Jakes and a Tony, then shared a Pete with Lt(jg) Charles Latrobe. Lieutenants John Kenyon and K. D. Smoth also scored singles for Fighting-90's best night of their tour. In the early morning of May 13, Charles Henderson probably shot down a George and scored a Rufe, an amazing feat for an Avenger pilot.

May 12 saw the war's first Hellcat ace score his final victory when Lieutenant Hamilton "Mac" McWhorter's CAP division received a vector from *Randolph*'s fighter direction officer. "We were orbiting at 12,000 feet when my division was given a vector to intercept a high bogey. We applied full power and started climbing. As we were passing through 20,000 feet, I spotted a single airplane about two miles ahead at about 24,000, just making a bit of a contrail." The crew of the Mitsubishi C6N Saiun (Myrt) probably didn't even know they'd been spotted. The speedy reconnaissance plane – fast enough to outrun almost all Allied interceptors – was flying at high cruising speed, headed toward the American fleet off Kyushu. "I came right up behind it and about one hundred feet below when I opened fire. It never made a move, but the engine went up and then his fuel tank flamed. I was so close when he blew up that I had engine oil all over my canopy. The Myrt went straight in as a fireball all the way down."

That evening, Admiral Spruance's flagship, the battleship *New Mexico*, was attacked by two *kamikazes* while she was anchored at her berth in the Kerama Retto anchorage. The attack came just after sunset as the rising new moon silhouetted the ships. Shortly after 1900 hours, Admiral Spruance took a walk on deck with his physician, Cdr Morton D. Willicutts, who commented on the beauty of the night and the "Indian springtime" weather. "Good *kamikaze* weather," the admiral replied. At that moment, the ship's klaxon went off. Two *kamikazes* were several thousand yards distant, headed toward the flagship with two Corsairs in vain pursuit. As the first dived on the battleship, it was near-missed by a 5-inch shell and lifted just enough that it passed over the ship from port to starboard and plunged into the water alongside. The gunners were unable to follow the second through the smoke as it made a wide circuit and bored in from starboard. Volleys from other ships hit *New Mexico*'s superstructure, killing six as the 20mm gunners fired in vain. The second *kamikaze* struck amidships; its bomb came loose and exploded in the "Jap trap" cluster of 20mm guns as the plane plowed into the aft stack, tearing open a 30-foot hole. The ready ammunition in the "Jap trap" caught fire, and flames rushed through the hole and up the stack, causing a "blowtorch" Venturi effect that probably saved the ship as the fire was pulled away from the rest of the ammunition.

Dr Willcutts excused himself to join the ship's surgeons and treat the wounded. Spruance disappeared into the smoke with a final word that he was heading for the bridge. When he couldn't be found, flag lieutenant Cy Huie went searching for his commander. He found the four-star admiral manning a fire hose with the crew, fighting the fire amidships.

Through swift action by the damage-control parties, the fires were out in 30 minutes. By midnight, 54 badly injured sailors had been evacuated to the hospital ship, while the 51 dead were gathered through the night for identification in the morning. Many were so badly burned they could be identified only by dental records. A further 55 injured men were treated on board. *New Mexico*'s crew effected repairs and the battleship remained on the line to provide fire support for the fighting ashore until she finally departed Okinawa on May 28.

Back at Ulithi, an important milestone in the history of the Grumman Hellcat played out when *Ticonderoga* brought aboard the aircraft of newly arrived Air Group 87 as she steamed outside the atoll. VBF-87's CO, Commander Porter W. Maxwell, landed his Hellcat. When he climbed out, Grumman tech rep Ralph Clark was on hand to give Maxwell a check for $500.00 for the squadron welfare fund. Maxwell's Hellcat was the 10,000th Hellcat delivered by Grumman since production had begun two and a half years earlier. While this Hellcat had been moving down the production line at Bethpage, a bucket hanging from its tail, the workers had dropped in their spare change as a contribution to the squadron that would receive the fighter and signed their names on the airframe. The names were later covered by the glossy blue paint job, but "10,000th Hellcat" was written in white on the cowling. It was a remarkable achievement of industrial production. Monthly Hellcat production by Grumman had peaked at 600 in March 1945 when this Hellcat was produced, and was at this time holding steady at 400 per month. Air Group 87 would put the Hellcat to good use when they joined Task Force 58 on May 17 and entered combat.

Enterprise went to General Quarters at 0400 hours on May 14. At 0530 hours, the sun rose over the East China Sea to reveal good flying weather with a 15-knot southerly wind driving scattered cumulus with bases at 3,000 feet. Hellcats of VF(N)-90 were inbound, having downed three more bandits since 0100 hours to give the squadron a dozen victories in three nights.

Some Japanese airfields were beyond the range of Air Group 90, but the *Enterprise's* radar registered them as they climbed out of their hidden airfields on Kyushu and headed toward the fleet. Formations and singles flew different altitudes and courses in an attempt to confuse American radar.

Enterprise's Hellcats had just entered the pattern to land when radar picked up a *kamikaze* gaggle inbound. The FDO assigned several pilots to take up defensive positions to the northwest, despite their low fuel status. The bogey resolved itself as 26 inbound attackers. Other task force Hellcats were vectored toward them and, over 20 minutes of aerial combat, 16 were shot down. Six more became victims of the task group's antiaircraft gunners. Three of the four survivors turned away. One Zeke, flown by the strike leader, 22-year-old Lt(jg) Shunsuke Tomiyasu, kept on, ducking in and out of clouds. Tomiyasu was a member of the same air group that had struck *Bunker Hill* three days earlier.

At 0623 hours, radar found 20 more bandits 20 miles out and closing. Tomiyasu's Zeke was lost in the clutter. At 0653 hours, he popped out of the clouds directly over the task force and initiated a run from the fleet's starboard side. Antiaircraft fire from alert gunners drove him back into the clouds. For several minutes he popped in and out of the clouds as he assessed the situation. He was now two miles from *Enterprise* on the same course when he reversed for a minute before turning directly toward the veteran carrier, sole survivor of the prewar fleet.

Tomiyasu was spotted when he popped out of the clouds at 1,500 feet. *Enterprise* turned hard to port to present her stern to the attacker, unmasking her guns on both sides of the flight deck. The sky was laced with tracers and black puffs of antiaircraft surrounded the green Zeke as Tomiyasu dived, heedless of the defenses, heading straight in as every gunner on the ship took aim and cut loose. At 0657 hours, he entered a 30-degree dive. Realizing he would overshoot to starboard, he snap-rolled left to inverted and pulled back on the stick in the first quarter of a split-S.

At that moment, Flag Air Operations Officer Jimmy Flatley stepped out of the flag bridge. He saw the *Zeke* coming in and threw himself back inside, yelling "hit the deck!"

Men aboard the escorting ships saw Tomiyasu perform an inverted 45-degree dive into *Enterprise*'s flight deck, hitting the ship just aft of the forward elevator. Men throughout the ship felt the tremor that went through the hull when the Zeke and its 550lb bomb exploded. The explosion was so powerful that it lofted a large section of the 15-ton elevator 400 feet into the air, while the rest flipped over and fell upside down into the elevator well. The instant was caught by a photographer aboard the nearby battleship *Washington*. The pilot's staterooms were obliterated while the flight deck was bulged upward nearly five feet. Twenty-five aircraft were destroyed and fires raged. Hangar deck officer Lt(jg) Charles B. Wilkinson barely missed death owing to the good fortune that he was standing behind a girder when the Zeke exploded in the hangar; had he been three feet nearer the elevator, he figured he would have been killed. Had that happened, no one would ever have known legendary Oklahoma University football coach "Bud" Wilkinson.

The hit was worse than that which *Enterprise* had taken at Santa Cruz. There was a serious fire in the forward hangar bay, threatening ammunition lockers, while the aviation fuel system was ruined, with lines severed and tanks leaking avgas. Seawater streamed in through breaches in the hull and three 6-inch water mains were broken. Any of one these would have been serious; combined, the threat was catastrophic.

Enterprise's crew responded. Men picked up 5-inch shells and powder bags and passed them hand to hand till they were thrown overboard. Firefighting teams fought the fire. Through their combined efforts, the worst of the fires was out in 17 minutes, with the last out two hours later. Power was lost to the forward gun mounts, but the rest responded and dispatched two more attackers during the battle to save the venerable carrier.

Enterprise lost 14 dead and 60 wounded, 30 seriously, a fraction of *Bunker Hill's* losses. Three of the dead had been aboard since the Doolittle Raid in 1942.

Lieutenant Tomiyasu's body was found the next day. Ship's surgeons sutured the wounds and the body was sewn into a mattress cover, then buried at sea with military honors. His name was incorrectly recorded as "Tomi Zai," but later researchers discovered his real name and his personal effects and some parts of his airplane were returned to his family in 2003.

In five months of action, Night Air Group 90 had lost 32 pilots and aircrew. Eighty-five Hellcats and Avengers were written off to all causes, 31 of which had been destroyed on deck by the two *kamikaze* attacks.

On May 15, Admiral Mitscher and his staff transferred to *Randolph*, their third flagship in five days. A dark joke circulated through the fleet that their commander was now a "Jonah," a shipboard source of bad luck. The next day, *Enterprise* set course first for Ulithi, then on to Pearl Harbor and the west coast for repairs. She was still under repair at the end of the war. *Enterprise*, the only prewar carrier to survive the Pacific War, the ship that had single-handedly held the line in the South Pacific after the Battle of Santa Cruz, was the last carrier to be hit by a *kamikaze*. Her war, from Pearl Harbor to Okinawa by way of Midway, Guadalcanal, Truk, the Marianas, Leyte and Iwo Jima, was finally over.

Marcus Island and VOC-1 returned to Okinawa on May 21, where the artillery spotters concentrated on spotting destroyer gunfire on the southern peninsula around Shuri Castle, site of the bloodiest fighting. The pilots were in such demand that when *Marcus Island* withdrew out to sea to refuel and replenish, two divisions were sent to operate from Yontan, where the rain and mud that was ever-present did little to improve their morale. When the ship finally departed on June 21 after organized resistance on the island had collapsed, the big guns of the Navy stopped firing for the first time in 82 days. VOC-1 had logged more combat hours per pilot than any other Navy squadron. Out of 26,000 flying hours – an average of 800 flying hours per pilot – accumulated since the unit was commissioned in December 1943, 12,664 were recorded as combat, with the majority in the Philippines, Iwo Jima and Okinawa. The squadron had scored 20 victories and was tied for third place among CVE squadrons with VC-84, a remarkable achievement for a unit devoted to artillery spotting. Eight pilots, one-fourth of the authorized strength, had been killed in combat or operational accidents.

Shortly after midnight on May 25, 1945, 165 *kamikazes* lifted off from their airfields on Kyushu for *Kikusui No. 7*, timed to support the 32nd Army's withdrawal from Shuri Castle to the final defense line on Okinawa. Among them were 12 Betty bombers, each carrying an Ohka of the Thunder Corps. Torrential rain between Kyushu and Okinawa intervened, and the attackers were forced to turn back since their pilots could not fly in such weather. Only nine of the Bettys regained their base.

At 0025 hours, a lone *kamikaze* found destroyer escort *O'Neill* (DE-188) south of the Higushi beaches and crashed into the ship at deck level forward of the bridge. Fortunately, there was no fire. A few hours later, *Stormes* (DD-780) at RP15 was hit, as well as the minesweeper *Spectacle* (AM-305) and destroyer transport *Bates* (DE-68/APD-47). Each hit caused heavy casualties, and *Bates* was sunk.

The next four days were the final mass act of the *kamikaze* war off Okinawa. That night, the Japanese struck Yontan Airfield with five Ki.21 Sally bombers loaded with commandos. Four were shot down, while the fifth crashlanded on the runway and ten commandos emerged from the wreckage. Before being killed, the grenade-wielding suicide attackers managed to destroy several airplanes and an aviation gas storage tank.

On May 25, the Marine Corsair squadrons of the Tactical Air Force on Okinawa had their most successful day when they scored 39 *kamikazes* shot down. The combined Tactical Air Force, including P-47Ns of the USAAF 318th Fighter Group based on Ie Shima, had their biggest day, with 165 attackers shot down. Still, two ships were sunk and nine others damaged.

At 0730 hours, four Corsairs of VMF-312 intercepted 20 inbound attackers, who were so inexperienced they flew straight and level while the Marines methodically shot down 12 of their number. An hour later, two other VMF-312 divisions intercepted a larger formation and shot down 16 for the loss of one Corsair. Captain Herbert J. Valentine shot down 3.5 Vals and two Zekes to become the last Corsair "ace in a day," while his wingman Lieutenant William Farrell shot down 4.5 enemy aircraft, including a Val and three Tojos.

On May 26, *Braine* (DD-630) and *Anthony* (DD-515) were attacked at RP5. *Braine* took two crashes at the No. 2 mount and the stern stack, and fires broke out. The ship lost steering control and power, and men began abandoning her. There were sharks in the water, and at least one dead sailor was retrieved by LCS-82 with an arm and leg bitten off. *Braine* survived to be towed to the Bone Yard.

That day, Admiral Spruance handed over command to Admiral Halsey on the orders of Admiral Nimitz, who was concerned that both Spruance and Mitscher were exhausted from the campaign, and the Fifth Fleet became the Third Fleet.

The next day, monsoonal rains brought the *kamikaze* attacks to an end. On Okinawa, the rain turned an already-miserable battlefield into something reminiscent of the flooded fields of Flanders in World War I. On May 29, Marine Major General Pedro del Valle, commander of the 1st Marine Division, ordered Captain Julian D. Dusenbury of Able Company, 1/5 Marines, to capture Shuri Castle. Despite serious casualties, the Marines were successful. Seizure of the castle, which had been the center of Japanese resistance, represented both a strategic and psychological blow to the enemy. The castle had been bombarded by the battleship *Mississippi* (BB-41) for three days before the Marine assault, which forced the Japanese to withdraw to the south. Captain Dusenbury received the Navy Cross for his leadership. Shuri was outside the Marines' assigned zone on the front line and only a last-minute intervention by the commander of the 77th Infantry Division stopped an American air strike and artillery bombardment of the position after it had fallen.

Following the fall of Shuri Castle, the Japanese organized a skillful night retreat, aided by the monsoonal storms and despite being harassed by artillery fire. Nearly 30,000 men took position in the last defense line on the Kiyan Peninsula, where the greatest slaughter of the battle occurred, including the deaths of thousands of civilians. On June 4 the 6th Marine Division made an amphibious assault on the peninsula. Four thousand Japanese sailors, including their commander Admiral Minoru Ota, committed suicide inside the tunnels of the underground naval headquarters on June 13. By June 17, the last of General Ushijima's shattered army had been pushed into a small pocket at the far southern end of the island. On June 18, Tenth Army commander Lt General Simon Bolivar Buckner, Jr. was killed by enemy artillery fire as he watched the progress of his troops. He was replaced by Major General Roy Geiger, a World War I Marine aviator commanding the Marines' III Amphibious Corps, who became the only Marine to command a numbered army of the US Army in combat until he was relieved by General Joseph "Vinegar Joe" Stilwell.

The last organized resistance came to an end on June 21, though some Japanese continued hiding. Generals Ushijima and Cho committed *seppuku* in their headquarters on Hill 89 in the closing hours. The bloodiest battle of the Pacific War came to an end. The American experience of the battle would lead to a complete change of plans of how to finish the war.

"The fleet that came to stay" was battered but victorious. Everyone knew the final act was still ahead of them.

CHAPTER ELEVEN

ADMIRAL NIMITZ WRITES
A LETTER

Following the success of the Marianas invasion, which established bases from which the B-29 Superfortress bombers could strike the Home Islands of Japan, the American political and military leadership had come to a consensus about the need to plan and prepare for an invasion, though some ranking civilian officials believed there was a good chance such an operation would not have to be carried out, despite the fact that the declared policy of the United States throughout the war had been the unconditional surrender of the Axis powers. The Joint Chiefs of Staff approved a report by the Joint Planning Staff (JPS) in early July 1944, declaring that the undermining of Japanese ability and will to resist by sea and air blockades to cut the country off from its sources of raw material in China and Southeast Asia following intensive aerial bombardment and destruction of Japanese air and naval strength would lead to unconditional surrender. The report pointedly stated that when these objectives were achieved, it would ultimately be necessary to invade and seize objectives in Japan itself. Following the successful invasion of the Marianas, the final step in the Central Pacific campaign was the invasion of Okinawa, which would allow the US to establish a base for the invasion of the home island of

Kyushu. That invasion in turn would allow establishment of bases for a decisive ground invasion of the Tokyo Plain.

President Roosevelt and Prime Minister Churchill stated at the second Quebec Conference in September 1944 that Allied military objectives in the Pacific Theater were "invading and seizing objectives in the heart of Japan," after "establishing [a] sea and air blockade, conducting intensive air bombardment, and destroying Japanese air and naval strength."

Army Chief of Staff General George C. Marshall and the service planning staffs who agreed with his view of the war saw the JCS/JPS report and Quebec statement as a commitment to plan, prepare, and carry out the Home Islands invasion they believed would be necessary to bring about the end of the war on the Allied terms of "unconditional surrender." The top US military leadership did not see the issue of invasion versus blockade and bombardment as an "either/or" choice, but perceived that the plan combined the two strategic concepts.

For Admiral King and USAAF General "Hap" Arnold, the Quebec Declaration was seen as a solid commitment to both the continuation and intensification of the campaign of aerial attack and naval blockade. Both were committed to an invasion of Kyushu – should it prove necessary – to gain bases to launch an even greater air and sea campaign against the heart of Japan, and thus produce a surrender without the necessity of mounting the ultimate ground invasion of the Tokyo Plain.

At the Yalta Conference in February 1945, agreement was reached with Marshal Stalin that the Soviet armed forces would enter the war against Japan with an invasion of Manchuria, 90 days after the surrender of Nazi Germany. Russian participation was seen as crucial in keeping the large Japanese Kwantung Army from being transferred to the Home Islands to mount a defense to an Anglo-American invasion.

In fact, the Quebec Statement and the JCS/JPS report were not seen as final by all of the top leadership. The debate on how to obtain a Japanese surrender continued unofficially through the rest of 1944 and the first months of 1945. While Admiral King remained publicly committed to the invasion of the Japanese homeland, nevertheless he was personally a strong advocate of operations by the Navy and Marine Corps following the seizure of Okinawa and before the invasion of Kyushu, such as taking the other islands of the Ryukyus and coastal areas of Japanese-occupied China between Formosa and Japan. It has been argued he advocated these operations to gain time for the bomb-and-blockade campaign to bring about surrender without an invasion.

In late February 1945, General Arnold learned of the proposal by 2Ist Bomber Command commander General Curtis E. LeMay that the B-29 bombing campaign be changed from daylight precision attacks at high altitude to nighttime low-level area attacks with the objective of burning out Japanese cities. In fact, the daylight strategic campaign had proven to be unsuccessful, owing to the discovery of the jet stream, the high-altitude high-speed winds that circulated over Japan at the operational altitudes of the B-29s, and largely prevented accurate bombing of the kind employed by the Eighth Air Force against Germany. The six major missions 21st Bomber Command had mounted between January 23 and February 19 had not been successful. This failure contrasted with the success of an incendiary raid flown on February 4 against the city of Kobe, which had caused significant damage to the city and the factories there.

A series of precision-bombing attacks on aircraft factories was mounted by 21st Bomber Command between February 19 and March 3. The goal was to tie down Japanese air defense units and prevent their participation in the Iwo Jima invasion. The jet stream's high winds and cloud cover prevented success and the attacks produced little damage. An incendiary raid against Tokyo on February 25 by 172 B-29s burned and damaged approximately one square mile of the urban area, demonstrating the success of the Kobe mission.

With this success, LeMay decided to adopt firebombing as the main strategy for the B-29s. Additionally, he decided to have the bombers attack at night from an altitude of 4,000–6,000 feet. In his after-action report for Mission 40 (the firebombing of Tokyo),

LeMay laid out the reasons for the change of tactics:

1) Better weather conditions – at lower altitudes, the bombers experienced winds of 25–35 knots as opposed to winds of 120–150 knots experienced at altitudes of 25,000–35,000 feet, and cloud conditions were better at lower altitudes;

2) Better use of radar equipment, since scope definition was better at lower altitudes;

3) Greater bomb loads, since missions would not involve a climb to altitude and formation flight, which led to lower fuel consumption and greater bomb loads, with the additional loss of weight for the bombers resulting from the removal of defensive armament;

4) Improved maintenance, since low-level flight would not put the strain on the delicate R-3350 engines;

5) Greater bombing accuracy, since the bombers would not be operating in high winds that could disperse the bombs beyond their targets before they struck the ground. LeMay also cited less stress on crews, and the fact that such a change would be a complete surprise to the enemy, which would lead to even less effectiveness of his already-inadequate defenses against the B-29s.

The 73rd, 313th and 314th Bomb Wings provided the attacking force. Tokyo, with a 1940 population of seven million, was one of the three largest cities in the world and was seen as not only the political capital of the empire of Japan, but also the heart of its industrial and commercial life, the site of a majority of the Japanese war industries, as well as a vital transportation and communications center, the terminus of 70 percent of Japanese railroads in the empire.

Mission 40 was flown against Tokyo the night of March 9/10. Codenamed Operation *Meetinghouse*, it was the first full-scale fire raid. Three hundred and forty-six B-29s left the Marianas the afternoon of March 9, with the first of the force arriving over the city at 0200 hours Guam time on March 10. Two hundred and seventy-nine B-29s dropped 1,665 tons of M-69 incendiaries from altitudes of 7-8,000 feet over the following three hours. A massive firestorm overwhelmed the civil defenses and destroyed seven percent of the Tokyo urban area, 16 square miles. *Meetinghouse* was the most devastating air raid of World War II. Captain Tom Bell, a pilot of one of the lead crews which dropped special incendiary munitions that provided "pathfinder lights" to those following, remembered 30 years later that the smell of burning flesh penetrated his B-29 flying nearly a mile above the conflagration.

Japanese authorities estimated 83,793 people were killed and another 40,918 injured, while just over 1,000,000 lost their homes. After the war, the United States Strategic Bombing Survey estimated casualties at 80,000–100,000. War production was substantially damaged while the defenses were weak; only 14 B-29s were lost to enemy action or mechanical faults, with 42 damaged by antiaircraft fire. The Japanese government ordered evacuation in the weeks following the attack of all schoolchildren between seven and 12 years of age from the main cities; by early April, 87 percent had been moved to the countryside.

21st Bomber Command followed Operation *Meetinghouse* with further such raids. On March 11/12, 310 B-29s bombed Nagoya. The resulting fires spread wider than at Tokyo but caused less damage; 2.05 square miles of the urban center were burned out, with no American losses. On March 13/14, 8.1 square miles of Osaka were burned down by 274 Superfortresses for a loss of two. On the night of March 16/17, 331 B-29s bombed Osaka's "twin city" of Kobe. As had happened at Tokyo, winds created a firestorm and half the city was destroyed, with ruins from the raid still visible 18 years later. 8,000 civilians died while 650,000 were made homeless. The night of March 18/19 saw Nagoya attacked a second time, with a further 2.95 square miles of the city destroyed. The crew of the one B-29 lost were rescued after they ditched at sea. With this attack, 21st Bomber Command had exhausted its supply of M-69 incendiaries. The loss of only five B-29s out of 251 in an unsuccessful night precision attack on the

Mitsubishi aircraft engine factory in Tokyo the night of March 23/24 demonstrated the success of the fire raids. During the March missions, propaganda leaflets were dropped calling on the civilian population to overthrow their government or be further bombarded.

With the first campaign having demonstrated the success of the new tactic, the Joint Target Group (JTG) created a plan for a two-stage campaign against 22 Japanese cities. The plan also recommended that daylight precision attacks on important industrial facilities continue in coordination with the area raids. LeMay and some members of Arnold's headquarters staff believed carrying out this campaign would be enough to force a Japanese surrender.

The success of the raids demonstrated to the Japanese public that the armed forces could not protect the nation. In addition to extensive physical damage, there was increased absenteeism afterwards, since civilians were afraid to leave their homes.

While it is true that the Japanese were not able to mount an effective defense against the B-29 fire raids, there were individual successes by Japanese pilots. Chief among these were pilots of the 244th *Sentai*, which had been assigned to the defense of Tokyo following the Doolittle Raid on April 18, 1942. The unit saw little action until November 1944, when the B-29s in the Marianas were finally able to target Tokyo. Equipped with the Kawasaki Ki-61 Hien, known as the Tony to Allied flyers, and its later radial-engined development, the Ki-100, several pilots of the 244th became known as "B-29 killers," and some of them scored victories at night over the bombers, despite lack of specialized night-fighting equipment. They operated in a manner similar to the German *Wilde-Sau* night fighters, flying single-seat aircraft and depending for visual location of the enemy on the light of the fires set by the bombers.

Chief among these was the leading ace of the 244th, Captain Nagao Shirai, leader of the 3rd *Chutai*. By the end of the war, Captain Shirai was credited with the destruction of 11 B-29s, five of them at night.

During the Tokyo raid the night of March 9/10, Sergeant Nobushi Negishi shot down two B-29s that were illuminated by searchlights on his first mission as a fighter pilot. Negishi flew a twin-engined Ki-45 Toryu, codenamed Nick by the Allies, specially modified as the "Dragon Slayer" by the 53rd *Sentai* with two upward-firing 20mm cannon similar to the *Schragemusik* installations used by Luftwaffe night fighters.

During the Osaka raid on March 13/14, Captain Chuichi Ichikawa, a veteran of New Guinea now flying a new Ki.100 with the 244th *Sentai*, damaged one B-29 and destroyed two others. He took down the second by ramming it then parachuting out, badly injured. Warrant Officer Tadao Sumi of the 56th *Sentai* shot down four B-29s and damaged a further three before he was forced to bale out of his Tony when he ran out of fuel.

When the B-29s hit the Mitsubishi aircraft factory in Tokyo the night of March 23/24, 2nd Lieutenant Sadamitsu Kimura of the 4th *Sentai* set the highest score of any Japanese pilot in a single night when he shot down five B-29s and damaged two more over the course of three missions that night, flying a Ki-45 Nick.

Captain Yoshio Yoshida of the 70th *Sentai* was credited with the destruction of six B-29s during night raids between March 10 and May 25 to become the top-scoring "B-29 killer" of his unit, flying a Nakajima Ki-84 *Hayate*, known to the Allies as "Frank."

Tom Bell recalled that the skies over the Japanese cities were "almost as bright as day" during the fire raids. "I was surprised the Japanese didn't manage to shoot down more of us, since they didn't have the problem of climbing to 30,000 feet to get us. We didn't have any defense but the tail guns, which meant spotting them wasn't easy."

Following the successful American invasion of the Marianas, Prime Minister General Hideki Tojo, the architect of the Pacific War, was relieved of his position as prime minister owing to not-so-discreet pressure by Emperor Hirohito. This did not signal a lessening of influence in the government by the Army and Navy. In fact, the Army and Navy ministers, as well as the operational leaders of the Army and Navy, increased both their power and influence in the government. This continued despite the defeat of both Army and Navy in the Philippines and was enhanced by the adoption of the *kamikaze* strategy, with the government actively supporting the *kamikazes* and promoting the idea that the young men of the country become suicide attackers out of loyalty to the emperor.

The Supreme War Direction Council, known as the Big Six, was now led by Prime Minister Kantaro Suzuki, who accepted the office on April 7 after the resignation of Prime Minister Kuniaki Koiso and would oversee the government until the end of the war. A former naval officer, who had seen action at the Battle of Tsushima Strait commanding a destroyer squadron that attacked the Russian fleet, Suzuki had been Vice Navy Minister during World War I and was appointed commander of the Combined Fleet in 1924. He had served as Chief of the Imperial Japanese Navy General Staff from April 15, 1925 to January 22, 1929, after which he served as Privy Counsellor and Grand Chamberlain to the emperor from 1929 to 1936. He had narrowly escaped assassination during the February 26 Incident in 1936; the would-be assassin's bullet remained in his body for the rest of his life and was revealed only when he was cremated. Admiral Suzuki was opposed to war with the United States before and throughout the conflict.

Suzuki had to deal with Navy Minister Admiral Mitsumasa Yonai, Army Minister General Korechika Anami, Army General Staff Chief General Yoshijiro Umezu, and Combined Fleet commander Admiral Soemu Toyoda, who were all dedicated to carrying on the fight to the bitter end.

Suzuki's only ally in opposition to continuing the war was Foreign Minister Shigenori Togo, who had created the Soviet-Japanese Neutrality Pact in April 1941. Fully opposed to a war he believed could not be won, Togo had worked closely with Mamoru Shigemitsu in a last-ditch unsuccessful attempt to bring about face-to-face negotiations between Prime Minister Fumimaro Konoe and President Franklin Roosevelt. After he was appointed Foreign Minister in October 1941, he signed the declaration of war, accepting personal responsibility for the failure of diplomacy. Following his resignation in 1942, he lived in retirement until Suzuki asked him to return to the Foreign Ministry. Two men dedicated to finding a way to end the war, and four men dedicated to fighting to the last ditch and potential national suicide, embodied the choice that faced the country.

Following the invasion of Okinawa, American leaders were under growing pressure to finalize the next step in the Pacific strategy. With Stalin's Yalta commitment to enter the war, the Joint Chiefs formally directed General Douglas MacArthur, Commander-in-Chief of US Army Forces in the Pacific, and Admiral Chester Nimitz, Commander-in-Chief of the Pacific Fleet and the Pacific Ocean Area, to draw up plans to invade Kyushu on April 3.

Even with this decision, Admiral William Leahy, Chief of Staff to President Roosevelt and *ex officio* Joint Chiefs chairman, and CNO Admiral King were still both reluctant to consider such an invasion unavoidable. They could not directly oppose invasion, but they supported the seizure of intermediate objectives on the Chinese coast. Following the death of Franklin Roosevelt on April 12, new President Truman, who had never been told anything regarding the conduct of the war while he was vice-president, agreed to General Marshall's plan, since he was the man he knew and respected the most. The Joint Chiefs agreed to issue instructions to invade Kyushu before the end of 1945 in their meeting at the end of April.

The Japanese were increasingly aware of the probable events, particularly after the Soviet Union formally notified them at the end of March that there would be no renewal of the Soviet-Japanese Neutrality Pact in April. Allied intelligence intercepted communications that showed the Japanese were expecting an invasion. One such message was intercepted in March from the German naval attaché in Japan, which described a Japanese report concerning their preparations for such an invasion. They expected an assault on Okinawa "shortly" and anticipated an Allied attack on the Tokyo Plain.

It was obvious to anyone who could read a map that Kyushu was the next objective. The Japanese could easily identify the six beaches on the island sufficient in size to allow a large-scale invasion.

American intelligence learned in early April through intercepted messages that the Japanese were mining harbors and coastal areas of Kyushu and were evacuating civilians from the "areas of coastal defense."

What American intelligence did not know was that the Japanese Army intended to bring the strongest units still left in the Kwantung Army to Kyushu to strengthen the defenses, though messages detailing what appeared to be the transfer of 30,000–60,000 troops were intercepted. By mid-April, intercepts confirmed that units of a division previously located in Manchuria were already on Kyushu. Other messages reported units moving from the Kurils to the Home Islands. By the end of April, MacArthur's intelligence staff concluded: "It is apparent [that the Japanese] now consider invasion certain if not imminent," citing information regarding troop movements and unit dispositions that demonstrated they were preparing for a full-scale defense of their homeland. Two weeks later, intelligence chief Major General Charles Willoughby informed MacArthur that he estimated there were 246,000 Japanese troops on Kyushu, including 128,000 in ground force units, and that four additional divisions expected to be in place by November 1 would add approximately 100,000 reinforcements.

Admiral Spruance arrived at Guam on May 31, where he met with Admiral Nimitz. The two men had grown close during Spruance's tour in Nimitz's headquarters in the year between Midway and his assumption of command of what became the Fifth Fleet in the summer of 1943, and Nimitz was glad to have Spruance directing the plans for the coming invasion, now scheduled for November, when he would return to command the invasion fleet. Spruance had supported the invasion of Okinawa only as a base to enforce a blockade of Japan, and had been adamantly opposed to the idea of an invasion of the Home Islands before the Okinawa invasion. He was now even more strongly opposed as the result of his recent experience. His first-hand account of the battle against the *kamikazes*, reinforced by others on his staff, made stark for Nimitz the stakes that faced the Navy.

Six days after Spruance arrived on Guam, the Big Six met in Tokyo. For the first time, the question of ending the war was formally raised. Navy Minister Anami and Army Minister Umezu argued so passionately for an "honorable national death" that their argument carried the day, with Prime Minister Suzuki agreeing with them. The meeting issued a final policy statement declaring that the people of Japan must pursue the war to the bitter end. Two days later, on June 8, they recited their decision to Emperor Hirohito, who formally committed the country to a decisive battle on home soil, a national *gyokusai* (the word means "to die gallantly as a jewel shatters"), fighting to the last, giving and accepting no quarter.

While US signals intelligence never broke the Japanese Navy code after the series of changes made in June and July 1942 that had reduced intelligence on naval movements to "traffic analysis," which provided limited warning of the gathering of naval forces, the Japanese Army code had been broken in the spring of 1943 and had provided good intelligence since. Between May 1 and June 15, intercepted Japanese Army messages disclosed the movement of one division from Hokkaido and one from Korea to Kyushu. Additional intercepts revealed the existence of an Army-level headquarters in southern Kyushu, with another in the north. Since Japanese organizational practice subordinated three combat divisions under an Army headquarters (roughly similar to a US corps), analysts saw these headquarters as confirmation of their estimates that the Japanese defenses comprised six divisions evenly divided between northern and southern Kyushu.

The intercepts also revealed the Japanese Army Air Force was preparing to use as many as 2,000 outdated aircraft and trainers in *kamikaze* missions. Analysts predicted there could be even more *kamikazes* available after the discovery the Japanese were constructing concealed airfields and underground hangars on Kyushu.

A reference in a decoded Army message to the progress report by a Japanese naval base commander revealed the construction of suicide boats, and the existence of a base for piloted suicide torpedoes – *kaiten* – in southeastern Kyushu.

Additional intercepts revealed the assignment of naval ground support personnel to duties and missions, including operation of antiaircraft sites around key bridges and roads, and static defense of depots and bases, which were normally performed by soldiers. The movement of a unit specially trained to oppose amphibious assaults from the Kuril Islands to southern Kyushu was discovered at the end of the month.

Two days before President Truman met on June 18 with his senior military advisers to discuss planning for an invasion, the estimate of Japanese military forces on Kyushu by the War Department was increased to 300,000.

The meeting was attended by General Marshall, Admiral Leahy, Secretary of War Henry Stimson, Secretary of the Navy James Forrestal, Assistant Secretary of War John J. McCloy and Admiral King, with Lt General Ira Eaker representing General Arnold. Using casualty figures from earlier Pacific operations, General Marshall concluded, "There is reason to believe that the first 30 days in Kyushu should not exceed the price we have paid for Luzon."

Admiral Leahy countered that a Kyushu invasion would more likely resemble the 35 percent casualty rate experienced on Okinawa, and suggested that applying a similar percentage to the Kyushu invasion would result in a more realistic casualty estimate. Leahy then directly queried Marshall about what that number would be, but he merely replied that total US personnel would be 766,700, a number the Joint Planning Staff had removed from the Joint War Plans Committee draft of June 15. General McFarland, who took detailed notes of the meeting, did not record that anyone calculated what would be 35 percent of this number.

Had they done so, they would have been confronted with the fact that 268,345 casualties was only 96,000 fewer than the eventual total of US casualties in the Pacific War. In comparison, the combined casualty figure for the Philippines, Iwo Jima and Okinawa was 133,000. The figures for 48 days of conflict after D-Day in Normandy were 63,360. For the Battle of the Bulge, the US Army's bloodiest battle in its history, they were 59,000.

Citing the long-standing planning estimate, Marshall stated there would be 350,000 Japanese military personnel on Kyushu by November. Previous experience of amphibious invasions, including Normandy, demonstrated the attackers needed to outnumber the defenders by a factor of 3:1; even with the low estimate of defenders, the US force would be too small to achieve success.

The discussion then focused on the capability of American air and naval forces to cut off Kyushu and prevent Japanese reinforcement. Marshall cited the Joint Planners' estimate that movement of Japanese shipping had already been reduced and it would be cut to a trickle if not choked off completely by November 1. Marshall's statement that "our sea action and air power will have cut Japanese reinforcement capabilities from the mainland to negligible proportions" was opposed by Admiral Leahy, supported by Admiral King.

President Truman's questions and comments show that he remained uneasy about US casualties. At one point he asked if there might be a racial connotation to the Japanese, with an American invasion uniting them to fight to the end. Citing the Japanese government's June 8 statement, Secretary Stimson stated there was every indication this would be the case. At the conclusion, Truman said that while he agreed the circumstances rendered this the best plan available, he "had hoped there was a possibility of preventing an Okinawa from one end of Japan to the other."

What the other participants in the meeting of June 18 did not know was that Admiral King had a letter from Admiral Nimitz in which he recommended that the invasion of Kyushu be canceled.

Nimitz's reasons were simple: Operation *Olympic* had been planned on the assumption that Kyushu would be defended by roughly 200,000 troops. A 3:1 superiority was a rule of thumb for a successful operation with minimal casualties, which meant the invasion would field approximately 780,000 troops. Nimitz, unlike MacArthur, was a discerning consumer of intelligence and he was aware that intelligence had picked up signs Kyushu was being heavily reinforced. By mid-June 1945, Nimitz's intelligence analysts believed Kyushu was already defended by 600,000 Japanese troops, meaning there was already a rough parity between attackers. While this did not mean failure of the invasion, it did mean American casualties would be very heavy. As a result, the Pacific commander recommended that the invasion be canceled in favor of Operation *Coronet*, the invasion of Honshu, in 1946, while the blockade and strategic bombing campaign continued.

Nimitz also stated that, as a result of the Navy's experience at Okinawa, the requirement that the fleet remain within striking range of Japan throughout the Kyushu invasion, in the face of what was now seen as a major increase in forces dedicated to *kamikaze* attacks, was untenable. For Nimitz, the Navy could no longer support the invasion.

Admiral King kept Nimitz's letter to himself at the time, awaiting the opportunity to present it when Washington became aware of the intelligence Nimitz cited and would thus believe him. The month of July would demonstrate Nimitz's prescience.

In later postwar accounts of this meeting, John J. McCloy was shown to have first raised the possibility of ending the war by guaranteeing the preservation of the position of the emperor, though as a constitutional monarch rather than the deity he was held to be. McCloy went further and proposed that, if United States' willingness to preserve the emperor failed to persuade the Japanese government, then the United States should disclose to the Japanese the secret of the atomic bomb, with a firm declaration of American willingness to use it against Japan, to secure unconditional surrender.

President Truman departed for the Potsdam Conference on July 7. At the time of his departure, only three divisions had been confirmed present on Kyushu as of the meeting of June 18. But by the time he reached Potsdam on July 15, a fourth division on Kyushu was confirmed and intelligence had discovered two newly created divisions. On July 17 the president received the report that the Manhattan Project, the largest scientific-industrial development project in history to that time, had successfully tested a plutonium implosion atomic bomb in New Mexico. He then asked Marshall what the expected casualties in carrying the planned invasions through to the Tokyo Plain in 1946 would be. Eight years later in a 1953 letter to an historian, Truman said that Marshall told him it would cost "at a minimum one quarter of a million casualties and might cost as much as a million." The number was shocking, since it was more than double the total casualties killed and wounded suffered by the United States in all theaters of the war.

Intelligence continued to reveal the Japanese were preparing for extensive deployment of suicide weapons and tactics. The most recent report was that 940 aircraft had been deployed to 18 concealed bases on Kyushu in the first two weeks of July. The Imperial Japanese Navy Air Force had been completely turned over to the suicide mission.

These force buildups were within the original projections. However, they had been achieved much earlier than expected. The estimated manpower level had now increased to 375,000, which was 25,000 higher than Marshall's June 18 forecast for November 1. When a fifth and sixth division were discovered on Kyushu, it was determined they had been there since the first week of May. This meant that, at the time of the June 18 meeting, the number of divisions stationed on Kyushu was at the level estimated for an invasion date four months in the future. The sudden discovery of three entirely new divisions on Kyushu, reported in the July 21 daily intelligence summary caused consternation. The discovery of yet another on July 23 brought the confirmed total to ten combat divisions; this nearly equaled the planned invasion force. On the same day, an intercept provided evidence that an 11th division was moving from Honshu to Kyushu. Radio traffic analysis next disclosed the existence of a third Army headquarters that had likely been there since it moved to Kyushu from Formosa in June. The presence of an 11th division on the island was confirmed on August 2; total Japanese forces on the island were now estimated at 534,000, and two other divisions were believed to be en route.

Maj Gen Charles A. Willoughby circulated a report on July 29 that now demonstrated a palpable sense of alarm over the implications of these figures:

The rate and probable continuity of Japanese reinforcements into the Kyushu area are changing that tactical and strategic situation sharply. At least six additional major units have been picked up in June/July; it is obvious that they are coming in from adjacent areas over lines of communication that have apparently not been seriously affected by air strikes.

There is a strong likelihood that additional major units will enter the area before target date; we are engaged in a race against time by which the ratio of attack effort *vis-a-vis* defense capacity is perilously balanced.

Unless the use of these [Japanese land and sea] routes [to Kyushu] is restricted by air and/or naval action ... enemy forces in southern Kyushu may be still further augmented until our planned local superiority is overcome, and the Japanese will enjoy complete freedom of action in organizing the area and in completing their preparations for defense ... this threatening development, if not checked, may grow to a point where we attack on a ratio of one to one, which is not the recipe for victory.

The Willoughby report shocked the planners in Washington. A Joint War Plans Committee memorandum to the Joint Planning Staff on August 4, which contained the increased numbers of defenders presented in the August 2 report, recommended: "The possible effects on OLYMPIC operations of this buildup and concentration" of Japanese forces should prompt US field commanders "to review their estimates of the situation ... and prepare plans for operations against ... alternate objectives." While cautiously worded, the message was clear: the increased size and scope of the opposing forces and the defensive preparations on Kyushu required a fundamental re-examination of the invasion plans.

On August 5, the official estimate of the size of the Japanese defensive force was raised to 600,000; the buildup was primarily in southern Kyushu, where the landings would occur. A later confirmation of the signals evidence brought the total number of divisions on Kyushu to 14. In fact, Japanese documents obtained after the war showed that, at the time American military intelligence was estimating 600,000 troops on Kyushu, there were in reality 900,000 soldiers on the island to repel the invasion.

At this time, Admiral King delivered Admiral Nimitz's letter to General Marshall. The military leaders of the United States were now forced to confront the fact that an invasion was most likely impossible.

The major problem facing the United States was the American policy of "unconditional surrender" which had been imposed on both Italy and Germany in their surrenders. Americans familiar with Japan, such as former ambassador Joseph L. Grew, were certain the Japanese would never accept a surrender that involved the decapitation of the country's government through removal of the emperor. On July 2, Secretary of War Stimson wrote a letter to President Truman after conferring with as many experts as he could find on the subject. Stimson was no "dove" on the war. He had been among the strongest initial supporters of an invasion. As one of the few senior American leaders to have visited Japan, Stimson knew personally the geography of the two proposed invasions, and thereby understood their difficulty. In his memorandum, he informed the president that the terrain to be attacked would favor the defense, and that American military strength would be sapped in continuous battles with determined enemy forces in small units where the defenders could inflict serious casualties on the attackers before they were overcome. He stated his belief that owing to the terrain and also the national character of Japan, which would lead to "last ditch" resistance, such a campaign would be far more difficult than the final campaign in Germany.

Stimson then pointed out that now Japan had no allies, that her cities lay open to bombing, and that her armed forces were unable to threaten American forces outside of Japan itself following an invasion. In such a situation, he recommended that the blockade and the bombing campaign be maintained, while an "olive branch" be extended to the Japanese in the form of a call to the Japanese people to surrender, with the guarantee by the Allies that they had no intention of destroying the country, and a decision to allow Japan to rebuild as a modern industrial state once the militarists had been removed from power. Stimson's proposal pointedly did not reference the emperor and included a statement that the Allies should state a willingness to accept a government under a constitutional monarchy "composed of the present dynasty."

Stimson's memorandum to the president was preceded by one written to President Truman by former Ambassador Grew, dated June 13, 1945. Grew, who had extensive knowledge of Japanese politics and culture resulting from his extended service in the country that informed his stance toward unconditional surrender, believed it was essential that the United States declare that it intended to preserve the institution of the emperor. In his memorandum, he argued that "failure on our part to clarify our intentions" regarding the status of the emperor "will insure prolongation of the war and cost a large number of human lives."

On July 7, Ambassador Grew engaged in a heated debate with Undersecretary of State Dean Acheson about the terms of a Japanese surrender as it would be presented in the coming Potsdam Declaration. Acheson and Archibald MacLeish, Assistant Director of the Office of War Information, argued that the emperor had been used by the militarists to control the Japanese people, and that as a result Hirohito was as guilty as the militarists in promoting the war, and that the institution of emperor would always be vulnerable to such use in the future. Acheson asked why, if the emperor was as unimportant in the war-making capability of the government as Grew maintained, the retention of the emperor was so important to the Japanese militarists, as they had made plain in recent pronouncements.

On July 15, General Marshall added his thoughts in a memorandum on ending the Japanese war that suggested "face-saving actions" for the Japanese. Marshall pointed out that, outside of "using gas attacks and a campaign of starvation," it was impossible for the United States to declare that it would defeat the Japanese people. Marshall suggested that any declaration be founded on previous Allied statements, such as the Cairo Declaration, in order to maintain support of the Allies. Surprisingly, as a man who had held the position that Japan must be militarily defeated, he was open to the idea that the imperial system could be maintained after the war.

The position of McCloy, Stimson and Grew regarding modification of the terms of "unconditional surrender" to allow the Japanese to retain their emperor in some changed political form was not unopposed. One of McCloy's aides, Colonel Fahey, argued passionately against such a position regarding the emperor, on the grounds it would separate the United States from China and the Soviet Union on the topic. Former Secretary of State Cordell L. Hull let it be known just prior to the commencement of the Potsdam Conference that he favored saying nothing about the postwar nature of any Japanese government until the bombing campaign against the cities had reached its height and the Japanese people were fully aware of the future that awaited them if they supported continued resistance.

The United States government was well aware of Japanese efforts to find a way to end the war, primarily through the intervention of the Soviet Union, since the Americans had broken the Japanese diplomatic code prior to the outbreak of the war in 1940.

On July 12, 1945 a cable from Japanese Foreign Minister Shigenori Togo to Ambassador Naotake Sato in Moscow concerning the Emperor's decision to seek Soviet help in ending the war and proposing a peace agreement to be brokered by the USSR was intercepted. The Japanese did not know of the Soviet commitment to declare war on Japan, planning for which was already under way at the time Ambassador Sato was directed to see if he could obtain Soviet support and assistance in such an effort to end the war. The Japanese government would fruitlessly pursue this option for the rest of the month.

On July 13, Brig Gen John Woedkerling prepared a memorandum for General Marshall regarding the Japanese peace proposal, pointing out that the proposal seemed to demonstrate that the emperor had personally intervened in favor of peace against the militarists and that possibly conservative elements opposed to the war and the militarists had triumphed in getting imperial support. He also pointed out that the proposal could be seen as an attempt by the Japanese government to stave off defeat by making an attractive peace proposal that would appeal to war-weariness in the United States; he stated his belief that the latter point appeared to be the primary motivating force behind the move, and pointed out that Ambassador Grew agreed with this analysis.

On July 17, another intercept of a cable from Togo to Sato revealed that the foreign minister had rejected the call for unconditional surrender and that the emperor was not "asking the Russian's mediation in anything like unconditional surrender" stating that "if, however, they insist unrelentingly upon unconditional surrender, the Japanese are unanimous in their resolve to wage a thoroughgoing war."

In the summer of 1944, Navy Minister Yonai had ordered Rear Admiral Sokichi Takagi to undertake a secret mission to discover a way to end the war. After finding himself among a cabal of civil servants, academics and defense officials, the admiral decided that it would ultimately be necessary for the emperor to "impose his decision on the military and the government."

Admiral Takagi wrote in the detailed diary he kept regarding a meeting held on July 20 between the prime minister, the navy minister, the chief of the general staff and the foreign minister, in which Togo read a cable from the Russians stating that the Japanese proposal was too unclear regarding the nature of the proposal to have Prince Konoe sent as a special envoy. The foreign minister also read a report from Ambassador Sato stating that there appeared to be little possibility of obtaining Russian support for the Japanese peace proposal. There was agreement among those present that the Soviet Union should be informed that the message was the emperor's formal proposal to end the war through the offices of Premier Stalin, which the emperor formally committed himself to personally, and that the purpose of Prince Konoe's visit was to conduct direct talks with Stalin regarding the proposal. There was additional discussion regarding the meeting between the Japanese naval attaché in Switzerland with officials of the Office of Special Services, in which he had been told directly that the United States would agree to retaining the emperor. The meeting broke up following the agreement to send the letter directly to Stalin requesting peace mediation.

Ambassador Sato sent a message to Foreign Minister Togo shortly after this exchange, arguing passionately that the government should consider unconditional surrender with the sole condition that the "national structure" – the position of the emperor – would be maintained. He argued that Japan had entered a war it could never win, and that it was the responsibility of those who led the nation not to wreck it. Togo responded to Sato that the Japanese people would resist to the utmost any unconditional surrender.

American signals intelligence regularly decoded all Japanese diplomatic communications, and the highest levels of the US government were aware of the Japanese attempt to negotiate a peace settlement through the offices of the Soviet Union. It was determined in Washington that no change could be made to the demand for unconditional surrender, since there had been no negotiations with either Italy or Germany regarding their surrenders and the maintenance of any existing government system.

For the United States and its allies, the problem was to find a way to force a government publicly committed to national suicide rather than surrender, whose armed forces had demonstrated time and again throughout the war their willingness to fight to the death, taking as many of their enemies with them as possible, to do the unthinkable and surrender without their national territory being invaded and subjugated, which had been necessary to obtain the surrender of Germany earlier that year.

This problem was exacerbated by the experience at Potsdam.

By July, two months after the German surrender, the Red Army was in effective control of the Baltic states, Poland, Czechoslovakia, Hungary, Bulgaria and Romania; fearing a Stalinist takeover, refugees continued to flee to the areas under control of the western Allies. A pro-Soviet government had been established in Poland that effectively shut out the "London Poles." Stalin insisted that Soviet control of Eastern Europe was necessary as a defensive measure against possible future attacks from western Europe, and claimed that the Soviet actions in Eastern Europe were legitimate since the region was naturally a part of the sphere of Soviet influence. The United States was largely in no position to oppose these moves, since the Americans still believed they would require the participation of the Red Army in the final stage of the defeat of Japan.

With signals intelligence now revealing to the Americans that the Japanese Army had stripped the best units from the Kwantung Army in Manchuria, there was a growing body of belief that the Soviets would quickly overwhelm the region without any significant losses. It was seen as likely that the Red Army might be in a position as early as September to mount an invasion of the Japanese Home Islands from the north through Hokkaido, which could come well before the planned American invasion of Kyushu in November. This could result in the Soviets having a significant share of the postwar occupation of Japan.

The naval blockade had isolated Japan from its overseas territory, while the aerial campaign was systematically destroying the ability of the Japanese to resist further. With the possibility of major Soviet action against Japan proper happening sooner than originally expected, events were now pushing toward a need to find some way to end the war as rapidly as possible.

CHAPTER TWELVE

FINALE

Admiral Halsey arrived at Okinawa on May 26, 1945 to relieve Admiral Spruance as fleet commander, and the Fifth Fleet was once again the Third Fleet. Admiral John S. McCain Sr. replaced Admiral Mitscher as commander of the fast carriers and Task Force 58 was now Task Force 38. This command structure would remain to the end of the war.

The Okinawa campaign was so stressful that pilot fatigue became a factor, and the Navy was forced to reduce the normal six-month squadron tour to four months. Second and third-tour pilots now questioned the necessity of chasing a lone enemy plane inland as they weighed risk against benefit. Many agreed with the feelings shared by a double ace after the war: "I wasn't score-happy, and I knew that one more kill wasn't going to end the war any sooner."

LCDR William "Bill" Leonard, a fighter pilot veteran of Coral Sea, Midway and Guadalcanal who served on Admiral McCain's staff, summed up the struggle against the *kamikazes*:

Instead of the classic formations making their brave approach, we would have singles coming in on us from all directions, from all altitudes. It would have been much more hairy save for the fact that many of the *kamikaze* boys were pitifully short on flight experience and got lost or fouled up. The few that did get through were bad enough.

By early June, the monsoon was in full swing throughout northern Asia, which reduced flight operations on both sides. The bad weather delayed the launch of *Kikusui No. 9* until June 3, and even then the weather was sufficiently bad that only 50 *kamikazes* were able to fly south to Okinawa, most without escorts. No hits were scored by *kamikazes* until June 6, when eight suicide attackers found the destroyer minesweepers *J. William Ditter* (DD-751/DM-31) and *Harry F. Bauer* (DD-738/DM-26) on patrol southeast of Nakagusuku Wan. Both ships were veterans of the picket ship campaign and had each been damaged by *kamikazes* in different actions in April, being repaired at Kerama Retto and returned to service in May. Over the course of a 30-minute battle with the attackers, the two ships were able to shoot down five of the attackers between them. *Ditter* was hit by the sixth attacker, which glanced off her rear stack before opening a long strip of plating on the port side, which flooded the after fire room and forward engine room. The seventh attacker crashed into the ship's port side near the main deck. *Ditter* lost all power, with many casualties caused by the fires. With expert damage control, she was kept afloat through the rest of the day and night until the next morning when the tug *Ute* arrived to tow her to Kerama Retto.

The eighth attacker crashed close aboard *Bauer*, tearing a 12-foot gash in her starboard side with two compartments flooded. What was thought to be an unexploded bomb was discovered in the forward fire room. It was identified as the attacker's engine by a bomb disposal expert dispatched from Kerama Retto. Despite being damaged herself, *Bauer* escorted the crippled *Ditter* to Kerama Retto.

On June 10, *William D. Porter* (DD-579) faced the divine wind. Owing to an unfortunate series of accidents that happened in November 1943 when the destroyer was one of the escorts for *Iowa* (BB-61) during a voyage to Casablanca, Morocco, to take President Roosevelt to the Cairo Conference, the ship was notorious throughout the Navy. Backing astern as she departed Norfolk on November 12,

1943, the ship's anchor tore the railing and lifeboat mounts off a nearby docked destroyer. When she joined the presidential task force on November 13, a depth charge fell from deck into the rough sea and exploded. This caused *Iowa* and the other escorts to take evasive action owing to the belief they were being attacked by a U-boat.

Porter next experienced the failure of No. 3 boiler, causing her to fall out of position until No. 4 boiler was brought online. Next day, President Roosevelt requested that *Iowa* perform an antiaircraft drill. Several balloons were released as targets, most of which were shot by *Iowa*'s gunners but a few drifted toward *Porter*, which shot them down, a breach of naval etiquette. The escorts then made a simulated torpedo attack on *Iowa* that went awry when *Porter* accidentally launched a torpedo that headed toward *Iowa*. Since the ship was required to maintain radio silence, the battleship was warned by a signal lamp. The first message gave an incorrect direction for the torpedo; the second mistakenly informed *Iowa* that *Porter* was backing, rather than warning a torpedo was headed at the battleship. In desperation, a radio message was finally sent warning of the incoming torpedo. *Iowa* turned hard and avoided the weapon, which detonated 3,000 yards astern in her wake.

The Navy's embarrassment was heightened by the knowledge that President Roosevelt had observed everything.

Porter's crew was placed under arrest, and the destroyer was ordered to Bermuda for an official inquiry. Chief Torpedoman Lawton Dawson was sentenced to hard labor in a subsequent court martial for failing to remove the torpedo's primer, which allowed it to fire at *Iowa*; he was pardoned by President Roosevelt on the grounds the incident had been an accident.

Porter had joined the Pacific Fleet that December and served in the Aleutians, where she participated in raids against the Kuril Islands in northern Japan. She then transferred to the western Pacific and took part in the Philippines operations before joining the Fifth Fleet for the Okinawa operation, where she successfully operated as a radar picket ship during May and avoided *kamikazes* until her luck ran out at RP15.

A Val dive bomber that had evaded radar detection dived out of the clouds, straight at the ship, at 0815 hours. *Porter* evaded the attacker and took it under fire, though it continued and struck a glancing blow to the radar mast before hitting the water nearby. *Porter* continued her evasive maneuvers, ending up directly over the crash as the Val's bomb exploded immediately beneath her. She was lifted out of the water by the explosion, with the after half of the hull torn up by the explosion. She lost all power as several fires broke out and the ship began flooding. The battle to save her lasted three hours as her crew fought to put out the fires and repair the damage to keep her afloat. Two LCSs came alongside to fight the fires and the flooding. There was more damage when several jettisoned depth charges exploded. Finally the captain ordered "Abandon ship," and sailors were evacuated by *LCS-122*. At 1119 hours, *William D. Porter* heeled over to starboard and sank by the stern. Miraculously, there were no fatal injuries.

The next day, *LCS-122* took a direct hit to her conning tower after evading another *kamikaze*. The crash and explosion killed 11 and wounded 29, including her captain. Despite heroic efforts to fight the fire, *LCS-122* had to be abandoned 20 minutes later. This was the last *kamikaze* attack for a week.

Admiral Halsey had taken the Third Fleet north of Okinawa to strike Kyushu in an attempt to destroy as many *kamikazes* as possible as well as damage the airfields from which they operated. The first strikes were flown on June 2–3, before a typhoon hit the Third Fleet early on the morning of June 5. This was a repeat of "Halsey's Typhoon" of the previous December. Again, the event was the result of bad weather forecasting and Halsey's misjudging the course of the typhoon. Again, the event involved the ships' replenishing, as had been the case in December.

On the morning of June 4, Task Group 38.1 assumed Fueling Disposition 5 Fox to commence replenishment at 0550 hours, and fueling started shortly thereafter. Task Group 30.8, the oilers and escort carriers bearing replacement aircraft, closed on TG 38.1 to commence fueling. By 0815 hours, the sea was heavy and task group commander Admiral J. J. Clark ordered the ships to return from fueling and secure for heavy weather upon receipt of information that a tropical storm was approaching from the south. At 0945 hours, Halsey ordered all task groups to secure for heavy weather. Throughout the day, the fleet ran before the storm as Halsey attempted to get firm information on the storm's location and estimated course in order to evade the worst of it.

At 1630 hours, the weather was reported better, and both TG 38.1 and 30.8 requested permission to resume fueling, which was granted at 1700 hours. At 1735 hours, information was received that there were two storm centers moving northward, one bearing 215 degrees, distance 270 miles, and the other 285 degrees, distance 175 miles. At 1745 hours the carriers were instructed to secure aircraft for heavy weather. Fueling was complete at 1930 hours, and the task groups separated but remained in company per orders, both on a heading of 110 degrees, east-southeast. Writing of the typhoon in his autobiography, *Carrier Admiral*, Admiral Clark recalled, "About the same time we got a weather report from radio Guam reporting two storm centers to the west and southwest of us. Our course of 110 degrees was taking us well to the eastward, so I felt satisfied that we were certain to avoid this storm."

Shortly after, Admiral McCain took over the tactical command of all the task groups in Task Force 38. Clark continued: "We continued eastward, with the storm still generally to the southwest." At 2230 hours, Halsey messaged McCain, suggesting the fleet change course to 150 degrees, to which McCain replied, "analysis of present weather indicates best solution is increasing speed to the east." At 0050 hours on June 5, Halsey sent a second message: "Do not approve going east, which will only keep us in front of the storm area. I recommend a course of 300 degrees until weather improves, then west." He then ordered the fleet to change course to 300 degrees without waiting for McCain's reply. Clark recalled, "We were already well clear to eastward of the storm, and if we had continued to the east, the storm would have passed well astern, but now Halsey was taking us right back into the track of the storm. Because Halsey was quite as well aware of the situation as I, there was nothing for me to do but carry out orders."

During the early morning hours of June 5, Task Group 38.1 passed through the center of an intense although small typhoon officially known as Typhoon Connie, but later known in the navy by the apt name "Typhoon Viper."

When *Hornet*'s Captain Austin K. Doyle retired to his sea cabin the evening of June 4, the ship was on a course away from the storm track. At 0130 hours on June 5, Doyle was informed by the officer of the deck that a fleet course change to 300 degrees had been ordered, which put the ship heading back into harm's way.

At 0240, radar located the storm centers 60 and 63 miles west-southwest respectively. Clark recalled, "The typhoon was powerful, with dark seas and dark, almost black, skies merging as one, accompanied by a deafening roar of wind." Doyle was finally able to confer with task group commander Clark and exchange messages with Task Force 38 commander McCain, which finally resulted in permission to change course to due north, but it was too late. At 0336 hours, two destroyers in *Hornet*'s screen reported severe damage. By 0400 hours the wind was increasing in intensity. By 0500 hours, the barometer read 28.98 inches and wind gusts were as much as 90 knots. The light carriers reported they were rolling heavily. The destroyer *Maddox* reported she had just rolled 60 degrees.

Clark described what then happened: "At 0420, I signaled McCain: 'I can get clear of the storm by heading 120 degrees. Please advise.' McCain replied that they had nothing on their scope to indicate the storm center. I replied 'We very definitely have. We have had one for one and a half hours.'" Clark then intercepted a message from McCain to Halsey requesting his advice, to which Halsey replied "Posit," which means "keep your relative position with respect to the guide." Clark wrote, "This same order necessarily applied to me also and was tantamount to a directive for me to continue the prescribed course and speed. To record the path of the storm, I had ordered continuous photographs made of the radar screen, which clearly showed its exact path. By that time there was no doubt about it, we were in the heart of the storm."

Doyle ordered *Hornet* to head into the wind on a course of 270 degrees. He later recalled that he "placed the seas about two points on the starboard bow and kept the position by alternately backing my engines." *Hornet* continued to plow through the angry sea. Admiral Clark ordered the task group to maneuver independently to avoid collisions at 0535 hours. *Hornet*'s OOD later wrote in the log that "Heavy continuous rain fell and mountainous pyramidal seas were encountered with waves 50–60 feet from crest to trough. The highest winds reached were observed at 0545 with a steady wind of 110 knots and gusts to 120 knots." A Marine orderly later remembered, "Never have I seen waves so high. Our great big ship was no more than a peanut shell in that big storm."

At 0630 hours, *Pittsburgh* (CA-72) reported her bow had broken off with a clean vertical break at Frame 26. Damage control was able to establish a watertight boundary at Frame 33. The cruiser was still able to proceed under her own power by backing down and holding her stern into the wind. At 0636 hours, all the ships of the task group were ordered to stop engines and lie to at the captain's discretion, and maneuver independently to keep the best possible position into the sea. At 0639 hours, Admiral Clark ordered *Baltimore* (CA-68) to stay with *Pittsburgh* as her broken bow was now reported to be floating down on the port side of the ship.

At 0615 hours, as the carrier plowed through heavy seas, the forward section of *Hornet*'s flight deck collapsed back from the edge to Frame 4, a distance of 24 feet, while the heavy seas demolished a 40mm gun mount.

At 0648 hours, *Belleau Wood* reported a man overboard. At 0704 hours, Admiral Clark informed the Task Group that "we are now in center of storm and expect heavy weather and high wind later. All ships make minimum speed, keeping into the sea". At 0715 hours, the battleship *Indiana* (BB-58) reported she had lost rudder control. The huge ship drifted out of control until the rudder was repaired at 0730 hours.

By 0745, the task group had passed out of the danger zone and the winds fell to ten knots as the sea subsided. At 0917 hours, *Pittsburgh* reported she was riding comfortably. *Baltimore* had managed to capture the broken bow. By 1530, the heavily-damaged cruiser and her damaged bow were under tow by the fleet tug *Munsee* (ATF-106), escorted by two destroyer escorts from TG 30.8, on her way to Guam for emergency repairs before returning to Pearl Harbor. *Pittsburgh* was out of the war.

Hornet was not the only carrier to sustain flight-deck damage in the storm. *Bennington* also suffered a collapsed forward flight deck. The damage these two fleet carriers sustained would lead to postwar modification of the *Essex*-class carriers to enclose the open bow in what was known as a "hurricane bow" to prevent such events in the future.

There were no flight operations by Task Force 38 on June 5 as the fleet maneuvered to evade the typhoon. On the morning of June 6, Captain Doyle ordered *Hornet* to commence launching aircraft to search for several LSTs that had been lost in the storm. A Corsair was launched and spun in on takeoff. It was quickly determined that shifting air currents created by the collapsed flight deck section had caused the mishap. Doyle ordered the carrier into reverse. Backing down at a speed of 18 knots, she launched 24 fighters. Over the rest of the day holes were cut in the overhanging section of the flight deck to improve airflow, and *Hornet* was able to launch aircraft over the bow on June 7, as did *Bennington*.

In addition to the damage to the two carriers, Task Group 38.1 lost 25 aircraft as a result of the storm, while 23 other ships had suffered damage that ranged from the loss of whale boats to significant structural damage, such as that suffered by the light cruiser *Duluth* (CL-87) to her bow, which reduced her top speed to 15 knots. One sailor had been washed overboard from *Belleau Wood*, while ten others were injured.

The CVE force, Task Group 30.8, was also hit by the full force of the storm. The task group suffered damage, most notably to its escort carriers, which lost numerous aircraft overboard. The forward flight deck of *Salamaua* (CVE 96) was devastated, while one man was lost overboard and four seriously injured.

On June 8, Task Force 38 flew strikes against *kamikaze* bases on Kyushu, but little aerial opposition was encountered. In the three days of strikes, the fleet's fighters "only" claimed 77 for losses of 14 to heavy antiaircraft fire. That day saw the last combat missions by Marine Corsairs from the fast carriers when Major Hap Hansen led VMF-112 and 123 off *Bennington* to strike airfields on Kyushu. Hansen was glad to see the last of Kagoshima Bay, the best-defended place he'd found in the war. "It was a major jumping-off place for *kamikazes* to Okinawa. How I hated that place!"

Task Force 38 arrived in Leyte Gulf for replenishment on June 14 and stayed for two weeks, during which time *Bennington's* Marines departed the ship to return to the United States. In nearly four months of constant combat, the Wolfpack and the Eight Balls had flown 2,500 sorties from *Bennington*. They had destroyed 231 enemy aircraft, including 82 in the air. They had fired 4,000 rockets, dropped 100 tons of bombs and shot off a million rounds of .50-caliber ammunition in fighter-bomber strikes. Between them, the two squadrons had lost 18 pilots, one-third of their original complement. Forty-eight Corsairs had been lost, 31 to enemy action.

The ten Marine Corsair squadrons that had operated aboard the fast carriers since January had collectively shot down 201 enemy aircraft for a loss of 80 Corsairs and 46 pilots to all causes. Hap Hansen recalled after the war that of the ten carriers the Marines had served on, every one of them except the *Bennington* had been hit by the *kamikazes* by the end of the Okinawa campaign.

The Marine squadrons of the Tactical Air Force on Okinawa shot down a total of 436 enemy aircraft between their arrival ten days after the invasion and the end of the campaign 72 days later. VMF-323 led the scoring with 124.5, followed by VMF-311 with 71, VMF-312 with 59.5, and VMF-224 with 55.

While at Leyte, Air Group 12 was knocked out of the war when two USAAF P-38s buzzed the fleet and one misjudged his height. The airplane struck *Randolph's* flight deck in a hit many remembered as worse than any *kamikaze*. Eleven men were killed, 14 were injured, and nine planes were destroyed. Fortunately, most of the flight crews were ashore on leave, where they commented on the strange plume of smoke on the horizon. VBF-12's commander LCDR "Rube" Denoff returned to the carrier to find one of the Allison engines of the Army fighter smouldering in his bunk. With no other carrier available, the group returned home aboard *Randolph*, their war over.

For *Hornet*, the strikes against Kyushu in May marked the end of her participation in the Pacific War. The damage to the flight deck was sufficient that she was ordered back to the United States for repair. The war was over before she was ready to return to the western Pacific. *Bennington's* damage was not as severe, and the carrier was repaired at Ulithi in time to rejoin Task Force 38 when the fleet sailed for the final campaign of the war.

The Navy had to deal with the issue of Admiral Halsey running into trouble with a second typhoon in which two fast carriers had been badly damaged, one sufficiently to remove it from the fleet at what was seen as the most crucial moment, with the Navy preparing strikes against Japan that would lead up to the invasion, as well as significant damage to a battleship and numerous other ships. While the fleet was at Leyte, a court of inquiry was convened. Admiral Clark, as the on-scene commander, was also a defendant at the proceeding. He wrote later:

Knowing that a Court of Inquiry was certain to follow, I set my staff to work preparing a chronological record of the events relating to the storm ... I transferred on 6 June by breeches buoy to call on Admiral McCain in the *Shangri-La*. His personal loyalty to Halsey made him noncommittal when I said that if he released me I could have avoided the eye of the storm, but he did say as I was leaving, "I am sorry you had to get *your* ships damaged." This nettled me because, I reflected, only a day or so before, when these ships were dropping bombs on Japanese islands, they were *his* ships. He certainly took credit for their performance in his press releases, but when they got damaged, they were no longer *his* ships, they became *my* ships.

Next, I paid my respects to Admiral Halsey on board *Missouri*. There was very little conversation. He knew and I knew who was to blame for my ships turning back into the typhoon.

Clark was well aware that he was being set up by his commanders to take the fall for what had happened to Task Group 38.1, and prepared accordingly. When called to testify, Clark had detailed answers to all questions regarding decisions made and when, and what the results had been.

> My legal counsel during the inquiry was my flag secretary, Herman Rosenblatt, a lawyer in civilian life. When Admiral Halsey took the stand, Herman questioned him in detail, establishing the blame squarely on his shoulders. Herman's attitude in court worried me; after the session with Halsey on the stand, I took Herman aside to caution him: "Herman, you can't talk to a four-star admiral like that."
>
> He replied, "Admiral, that's the only way I know to prove your innocence. If you think this is embarrassing, just say the word and I'll pull out. But I can tell you your throat is going to be cut from ear to ear unless I can hang the blame on the one man who is responsible. And that is Admiral Halsey." As I highly respected Herman's opinion, I let him handle my defense in his own way. He established the fact that Halsey alone had made the decision to turn northeastward. He did not even call his aerologist.

The court of inquiry recommended that admirals Halsey and McCain be assigned to other duties. Secretary of the Navy James V. Forrestal supported the decision and tried to retire Halsey.

Nimitz refused Forrestal's demand, citing Halsey's service throughout the war and stating he could not lose such an experienced leader at such a time, citing the fact that damages and losses from Typhoon Connie were much less than those suffered in Typhoon Cobra, where the court of inquiry had not found Halsey at fault for more than inability to know the facts of the typhoon, which Nimitz believed was the same situation here. The issue went back and forth, and was finally decided on the basis of the potential impact on morale that the heroic Admiral Halsey, well loved by his men, was not to be retired from the service. Admiral McCain was also retained, though he relinquished command of Task Force 38 two months later, immediately upon conclusion of the war.

Clark remembered Nimitz's personal reaction to the typhoon when Clark stopped through Guam on his way to the States. "He questioned me at length regarding the typhoon and expressed his sympathy to me for the damage to my ships, but expressed his great displeasure with Halsey and to a lesser degree McCain. He minced no words in charging Halsey with stupidity in both typhoons, especially the latter, where Halsey had good weather information."

In reviewing the event in later years, Clark wrote: "Keeping all this in mind, I must say that since my midshipman days I have always entertained a high admiration and deep affection for Admiral Halsey. Unstintingly and unhesitatingly, I accord him full credit for his tremendous contribution to victory. I subscribe completely to the Navy's custom of honoring rather than belittling its heroes, and I concur that exposing Halsey's faults publicly in the summer of 1945 would have served no useful purpose."

The departure of the Marine Corsair squadrons from the fast carriers did not signal the end of Marines flying off aircraft carriers. The program to create Marine air wings to operate from escort carriers for support of the troops ashore in an invasion had proceeded after the decision had been made in the fall of 1944 to create such a force.

Block Island (CVE-106), named for one of the first CVEs, CVE-21, which had been sunk by U-549 off the Canary Islands a year earlier on May 29, 1944, arrived with VMF-511's eight F4U-1Ds, eight F5F-5Ns and two F6F-5Ps. VMTB-233's 12 TBM-3 Avengers flew their first combat mission with takeoff at 0635 hours on May 10, a strike by four TBMs that attacked positions around Shuri Castle. A second mission was flown with eight TBMs, four F4Us and four F6Fs to strike the *kamikaze* bases at Hirara and Nobara airfields on Miyako Jima in the Sakishima Islands, where they took their first loss when a TBM flown by 2nd Lieutenant Douglas M. Herrin and crewed by Sergeant Joseph L. Butehorn and Staff Sergeant Edward T. Gunning was shot down during a rocket-firing pass over Nobara.

A second TBM was hit by flak and had to ditch alongside the destroyer *Butler*, which picked up the crew. The Marines flew through the rest of the month without further losses until May 27, when VMF-511's commander, Major Robert C. Maze, was lost when his Corsair was shot down during a rocket attack against Ishigaki Shima. Two days later the Ishigaki flak claimed a TBM flown by 2nd Lieutenant Jack Marconi and crewed by staff sergeants Joe Surovy and Ben Canaan when its left wing was blown off during a low-level bombing run.

Block Island was accompanied by her sister ship, *Gilbert Islands* (CVE-107), which embarked VMF-512 and VMTB-143, and arrived at Okinawa on May 21. The air group flew 42 missions for close support of forces attacking the port of Naha on Okinawa during the last week of May.

The Third Fleet sailed from Leyte Gulf on July 1, 1945, headed back to Japan. The ships would not see port again before the end of the war.

While the Third Fleet was dealing with the *kamikazes* of Kyushu and surviving Typhoon Caroline, Operation *Barney* – one of the most dramatic actions of the Pacific Fleet Submarine Force – took place.

The real submarine offensive in the Pacific did not truly happen until the submarine force successfully cured the unreliable Mark 14 torpedo, the operational vagary of which reduced the effectiveness of the fleet by nearly 80 percent. Over the first two years of the war, the submarines were forced to develop an entirely different operational doctrine, since the prewar concept of the submarines acting as auxiliaries of the fleet was discarded with the outbreak of war when the submarine force was directed to "execute unrestricted submarine warfare against the Empire of Japan" on the second day of the conflict. The torpedo problem was an ineffective exploder, which deformed under impact and led to a dud; the Bureau of Ordnance had never really tested the torpedo before the war and had resisted all reports of failure until Admiral Charles Lockwood, Commander of the Pacific Fleet Submarine Force (ComSubPac), instituted a test program in early 1944 that involved firing torpedoes at an underwater cliff in Maui, then recovering and examining them. Faced with the incontrovertible evidence of the faulty exploder, a crash program finally resolved the problem.

More submarines, with more aggressive commanders, and reliable weapons finally allowed the submarines to come into their own. In the end, the submarines had performed the most successful undersea campaign of the war, and were responsible for sinking 80 percent of Japanese merchant shipping.

By 1945, the blockade of Japan was complete, save for the Sea of Japan, the body of water between Japan, Korea, and Siberia. Known to the American Navy as "Emperor Hirohito's private ocean," entry and exit from the body of water was nearly impossible, since access was only through the Straits of Tsushima between Kyushu and Korea or La Pérouse Strait in the north between the islands of Hokkaido and Sakhalin. Currents were difficult in both, and they were narrow and easily patrolled. The Japanese had also mined the straits to block them to shipping.

The result was that the Japanese could move supplies and troops from Korea and Manchuria to the Home Islands without the threat of submarine attack.

Admiral Lockwood had long wanted to cut Japan off from Manchuria in the Sea of Japan. The first attempts were made in 1943. That July, *Plunger* (SS-179), *Permit* (SS-178), and *Lapon* (SS-260) entered the sea through La Pérouse Strait and were able to chart the minefields. In August, *Plunger* and *Wahoo* (SS-238) made a combat patrol into the enclosed waters. Penetrating the shallow Sea of Okhotsk and transiting La Pérouse Strait, *Wahoo* found a dozen targets within four days and attacked nine, with no results. Ten of the dreadful Mark 14 torpedoes broached, ran erratically, or hit their targets without exploding!

Wahoo's captain, Commander Dudley W. "Mush" Morton, who was the leading candidate for "most aggressive American submarine commander of the war," volunteered to return with better weapons. The new Mark 18 electric torpedo, based on captured German G7e torpedoes, had just been placed in production. Carrying a full load of Mark 18s, *Wahoo* left Pearl Harbor for her seventh patrol on September 9, accompanied by *Sawfish* (SS-276). Both boats topped off their fuel tanks at Midway.

The two arrived in the Sea of Japan via La Pérouse Strait on September 29. The campaign began on October 2, and over the next seven days the Japanese lost four ships. With success demonstrated, Admiral Lockwood ordered *Wahoo* home. Morton headed toward La Pérouse Strait, but was spotted running on the surface by a Japanese antisubmarine air patrol on October 11. Following the attack, the submarine was seen either to dive or sink below the surface. *Sawfish* successfully transited the strait on October 13 and when she returned to Pearl Harbor reported poor performance from her electric torpedoes.

On November 6, 1943, *Wahoo* was declared overdue/presumed sunk.

In 2004, a search for *Wahoo* on the western side of the strait using side-looking radar discovered an object shaped like a Gato-class submarine in 213 feet of water. In 2006, Boris Postovalov and Andrei Doroshenko led a Russian team that found *Wahoo*. The Japanese report of a hit with a single bomb was confirmed when the wreck was examined and the hole was found.

In early 1945, Admiral Lockwood was informed of a new FM sonar device that could detect minefields at close range. This was immediately seen as the tool that would allow submarines to penetrate the Sea of Japan. Commander W. B. "Barney" Sieglaff was put in charge of developing an operational capability in the form of a group of submarines able to use the new FM sonar technology to get into the Sea of Japan.

Nine submarines were chosen and fitted out with the new sonar in April and May. During the last week of May, the submarines were sent to Guam for final preparations. They were equipped with external and internal equipment to make the perilous trip through the treacherous minefields. Many days were spent testing and learning to operate the gear, which became known to the crews as "Hell's Bells" from the distinctive bell-like sound made when the sonar detected a mine.

The attack was named Operation *Barney*, in honor of the man who planned it. The plan had the submarines enter the Sea of Japan submerged, via Tsushima Strait. This allowed them to take advantage of the swift-flowing Kuroshio Current, an underwater river that started in the East China Sea and passed through Tsushima Strait into the Sea of Japan. The boats would exit via La Pérouse Strait using the Kuroshio Current to give them added speed.

While Admiral Lockwood claimed this attack would lower Japanese morale and confidence in the nation's leaders, most of the staffers and captains involved were certain Lockwood's primary motivation was to avenge Mush Morton's loss, since he had been the admiral's favorite skipper. During their time in the Sea of Japan, the crew of *Crevalle* (SS-291) celebrated the second anniversary of the submarine's commissioning with a huge cake bearing the inscription, "Was this trip necessary?"

Plans were changed when *Seahorse* (SS-304), one of the original nine boats, was subjected to a 16-hour depth-charging in the East China Sea that left the periscope, radio, and radar gear badly damaged, while causing numerous leaks. The FM Sonar gear was transferred from *Seahorse* to *Sea Dog* (SS-401), commanded by Commander Earl T. Hydeman. *Sea Dog*'s executive officer, LCDR James P. Lynch, remembered how the boat became part of Operation *Barney*:

> The *Sea Dog* was refitting in Guam and the decision was made by Admiral Lockwood to transfer the FM Sonar Mine detection equipment to the *Sea Dog* and have her replace the *Seahorse*. This was accomplished on an emergency basis and *Sea Dog* commenced a frantic period of approximately one week learning to operate the FM Sonar, under the guidance of Commander Barney Siegloff. A practice minefield had been set up offshore, just west of Guam, to afford realistic conditions for our training in using the FM Sonar mine detecting equipment ... So, in the course of two weeks' time, the *Sea Dog* went from what was to be a normal refit, in preparation for a routine fourth war patrol, to the lead submarine in the war's most adventurous and daring submarine operation.

As the senior commander, Hydeman was the leader of what became known as "Hydeman's Hellcats." The nine submarines were further divided into three operational wolf packs. "Hydeman's Hepcats" included *Sea Dog, Crevalle* and *Spadefish*.

"Bob's Bobcats" was named for LCDR Robert D. "Bob" Risser, commander of *Flying Fish* (SS-229), with *Bowfin* (SS-287) and *Tinosa* (SS-283). "Pierce's Polecats" was led by LCDR George E. Pierce, commander of *Tunny* (SS-282), with *Skate* (SS-305) and *Bonefish* (SS-223). The officers who were aware of the full details of the mission called the force "The Mighty Mine Dodgers."

The submarines departed Guam on Monday May 28 at 0400 hours, bound for Tsushima Strait. En route, *Tinosa* picked up ten fliers from a downed B-29. When the airmen found out where the submarine was going, they were unanimous in their desire to be put back into their rubber life rafts and take their chances on the open sea. *Tinosa* was able to arrange a rendezvous with *Scabbardfish* (SS-397), which was returning to Guam, and transfer the rescued fliers.

The Hellcats arrived at the strait on the evening of June 3, and the wolf packs went through Tsushima Strait on three different nights. In the early morning of Monday June 4, Hydeman's Hep Cats entered the Nishi Suido (west channel) of Tsushima Strait. The minefields protecting the entry into the Sea of Japan were ahead of them. The plan was that each of the boats would enter the minefields at a minimum depth of 160 feet, which was hopefully deeper than the mines, with the submarine depending on the FM sonar to warn them of the mines.

When *Sea Dog* began her run through the minefields, Captain Hydeman suggested that all personnel not on watch stay in their bunks to prevent confusion as well as to conserve oxygen, as the submarine would be submerged for longer than usual. The submarine was rigged with diversion cables over the bow and stern planes to prevent them from snagging a mine and pulling it down to the submarine, where it would explode on contact. There was additional concern that, even if the cables worked properly, side currents could push the submarine over far enough that it could pull a mine down. The current was running through the strait between 3 to 4 knots.

Sea Dog's XO, LCDR Lynch, recalled:

The passage through the straits will always remain one of the most vivid of my wartime experiences. I knew from the intelligence reports that three Antisubmarine Warfare mine fields were present in the straits. We were depending on the FM Sonar to locate any mines so that *Sea Dog* could maneuver to avoid. During our submerged passage through the straits, the FM Sonar gear appeared to be functioning normally. The CO and I divided the time in transit, monitoring the FM Sonar and navigating the straits. At no time did the FM Sonar make a positive contact on a mine.

On one of my "off watch" periods, I was in my bunk when I heard what sounded like a cable scraping alongside the hull. I held my breath and prayed. I was never more relieved, than when we surfaced after completing the transit and opened the hatch to let in the sweet night air. We had compensated accurately for the current and were right on schedule. Our immediate task was to charge batteries and get on station.

The amazing postscript to the story of our passage through the straits was that all of the other eight boats that followed *Sea Dog* detected several mines on their FM Sonar. Had *Sea Dog* passed through gaps in the minefields or were we just lucky?

It was later learned that the submarine had indeed been fortunate, since the FM sonar was not operating correctly.

Pierce's Pole Cats entered the strait on June 5 and the next day Risser's Bob Cats made their voyage through the deadly minefields. All were successful.

Skate discovered a mine 400 yards ahead and maneuvered past, with the cable scraping her hard from bow to stern. *Tinosa* came upon a mine so close she couldn't maneuver to miss it. Her captain ordered the engines stopped in order that the motionless screws would not catch the cable. As the submarine slid past, the cable scraped slowly along the starboard side, past the stern planes and then the screws, and finally clear of the boat.

All had made it into the Sea of Japan by nightfall of June 6, under orders to avoid enemy contact until sundown on the 9th, thus allowing each to arrive at its assigned position. Just after sundown at 2000 hours, *Sea Dog* was preparing to surface ten miles northeast of Hime Sake light on Sado Island when the sonar picked up noise from enemy ships. Captain Hydeman raised the periscope and sighted a small freighter running with its lights on. He fired a torpedo 15 minutes later at a range of 1,200 yards. The fish hit 45 seconds later, sinking the ship in just over a minute. *Sea Dog* found two empty lifeboats after she surfaced at 2023 hours.

Moments later the radar operator reported "S-J contact, bearing 060 true at 10,000 yards. A saturation pip, Captain."

Hydeman ordered the helm to bring the boat to course 135, telling the radar operator to keep his range reports coming in and ordered the forward torpedo room to make ready all tubes. A few minutes later, the "saturation pip: was visually identified as a large, fully loaded 10,500-ton tanker. Hydeman ordered the first of four torpedoes fired at 2044 hours. The first hit the ship's stern 90 seconds later, while the others missed astern.

While fire and steam billowed from the target's stern, *Sea Dog* pulled off to see what would happen. The ship's crew extinguished the fire in a few minutes and got under way at 5 knots. *Sea Dog* moved in to finish the job. A fifth torpedo was fired at 2112 hours that veered off course 25 degrees right and missed. The sixth was fired at 2113 hours and hit forward of amidships with a big explosion that broke off the bow, which sank. The remaining half burned brightly before sinking.

Both attacks drew no reaction from defensive forces despite the fact they happened with Hime Saki light on Sado Island burning bright, while the glare of the lights from the city of Niigata were visible to the southeast.

When *Sea Dog* surfaced at 2010 hours on June 13 to charge batteries, word came from the after torpedo room that they had heard a loud noise that sounded like an explosion, and that the starboard shaft was vibrating with excessive noise. It was quickly determined that the starboard clearing wire had come loose from its attachment point forward of the stern plane and was now wrapped around the shaft. Captain Hydeman maneuvered *Sea Dog* for an hour at various speeds to determine the problem's extent. At slow speeds there was a loud thump and clanking noise; the reason was that the cable with its eyebolt was striking the hull with each shaft revolution. At higher speeds the thump wasn't heard, but the vibration became heavier.

Sea Dog pulled away from the coast and stopped at midnight. Though the water was close to freezing, engineering officer Lt(jg) William Duckworth and Chief of the Boat Andrew Dell, who were both experienced divers, volunteered to go in and try to remove the cable from the shaft. When they went underwater, the masks of their Momsen Lungs filled with water, and they were unable to use the cutting torch in the rolling swells. After an hour's effort, the captain ordered a halt, since it was too dangerous to risk a possible surprise attack with swimmers in the water. *Sea Dog* was forced to run on her port shaft only in order to reduce noise.

Tuesday June 19 was memorable. The submarine was patrolling between Benki Misaki and Koma Misaki on Hokkaido at periscope depth at dawn. Haze over the water cut visibility. Suddenly, the officer on the periscope watch spotted three cargo vessels through the haze. The crew went to battle stations-torpedo and readied the forward tubes. Nine minutes later, they fired two torpedoes at the first ship. As the next salvo was ready to fire at the second ship, the first target went up in a huge explosion. Just as the second salvo was fired, the captain of the second ship put her helm hard over; one hit was heard but not observed. As the third ship turned into shallow water, Captain Hydeman spotted an aircraft approaching over the sinking first freighter. *Sea Dog* had land to starboard, a sinking ship to port and needed to get out of the cove fast. As they turned to starboard, Hydeman ordered "Take her deep!" The soundman replied there were only three fathoms (18 feet) below the bow.

Sea Dog hit the bottom a minute later. LCDR Lynch remembered:

As navigator, I was conscious of our position inside of the 50-fathom curve and had been keeping track of the water depth. When the CO spotted the aircraft and ordered the diving officer to take her deep, I warned him we were in shallow water, but it was too late to prevent grounding. After grounding we took stock and realized we had little room for maneuvering. When we had taken the necessary damage-control measures and not getting any indication that the aircraft knew our location, we figured the best course was to back off from our position rather than go forward and risk a collision with the sinking ship while turning away from the coast.

The depth gauges read 116 feet. A leak was reported in the forward torpedo room and the forward watertight hatch was quickly slammed closed and dogged shut. Radioman 3/c Eddie Griffith remembered, "It was really frightening when we had a leak in the forward torpedo room and the watertight door was closed. After the door was closed we were not sure if we would be able to stop the water leak."

The leak was caused by the sound head on the forward keel shearing off when the boat had bottomed and the water was coming in through the packing around the head shaft. The packing gland was tightened and the leak stopped. Machinist's Mate 1/c George Gressman explained, "While the boat was stuck in the mud, the mud was exerting pressure on the shaft, that made it impossible to tighten the packing glands properly. After we backed off the bottom, pressure was relieved and the sound head shaft was allowed to go back into proper position and the inflow of water stopped."

Sea Dog was in a very serious situation. The sinking cargo vessel was 400 yards north of her, while a point of land extended into the cove from the south; the water was too shallow for her to maneuver and the bow was soundly stuck in the mud while the stern was only some 50 feet underwater.

Hydeman ordered the electric motors into reverse, but this succeeded only in making enough disturbance in the water that the second ship could correct its fire on them. The officers conferred and determined they could abandon ship if they were unable to pull free of the mud by having the crew go out of the after torpedo room deck hatch and use inflatable life rafts to get ashore. If that succeeded, there was the unwelcome prospect of surrender to the Japanese.

The problem was finally solved by blowing the bow ballast, lightening the bow sufficiently that the motors could pull her free. Bow and stern planesmen traded positions and *Sea Dog* backed out of the cove at five knots. It had been a tense hour. Just as she cleared the cove and turned to head out to sea, several patrol craft and a destroyer escort showed up. With the enemy pinging to spot her, *Sea Dog* silently crept out into the Sea of Japan. Over the next five days she looked for more targets, but they had suddenly become scarce after the appearance of the submarines in the closed sea.

Lynch later remembered, "When the newspapers in Hawaii got word of this incident, they credited the *Sea Dog* with being the first US warship to make a landing and invade the soil of the Japanese empire in World War II."

Among the "Hepcats," *Spadefish* (SS-411) spent only a year in the Pacific, but she scored a record 88,091 tons and 21 ships in that time. The Sea of Japan operation was her fifth war patrol. On June 10, outside the breakwater of Tarukawa Wharf, she intercepted *Daigen Maru No. 2* and blew the ship apart with two hits. By the end of the day she had also sunk *Unkai Maru No. 8* and *Jintsu Maru*. On June 12, she sank three trawlers by surface gunfire. The next day she accidentally sank the Soviet merchant ship *Transbalt*. On June 14, *Seizan Maru* was sunk before *Spadefish* scored her final victory on June 17 when she sank the minelayer *Eijo Maru*.

Crevalle sank a freighter a day on June 9, 10 and 11, and on June 22 she inflicted heavy damage on an escort ship.

Bonefish sank *Oshikayama Maru*, a 6,892-ton cargo ship, on June 16. Two days later, she conducted a daylight submerged patrol of Toyama Bay on the Honshu coast. Japanese records revealed after the war that the 5,488-ton cargo ship *Konzan Maru* was torpedoed and sunk in Toyama Bay on June 19. The Japanese escorts *Okinawa*, *CD-63, CD-75, CD-158* and *CD-207*, counterattacked and debris and a major oil slick came to the water's surface. *Bonefish* was the next-to-last US submarine lost, with *Bullhead* (SS-332) being the last on August 9, 1945.

Tunny wasn't so successful. On June 9, she attacked a cargo ship with a dud torpedo. Three days later, she entered the harbor of Etomo Ko shortly before 2400 hours, but failed to find a target. An hour later she approached within 5,000 yards of the mouth of the harbor at Uppuri Wan, but retreated when she was located and illuminated by searchlights. On June 16, she sighted rafts filled with the survivors of a successful attack by *Bonefish* and took prisoner a chief petty officer, who had escaped the sinking ship. The following night, *Tunny* and *Bonefish* closed a target, but *Tunny* was suddenly taken under fire by a destroyer. She attempted to attack a 4,000-ton cargo ship on June 19, but was foiled by shallow coastal water.

Skate caught a Japanese submarine on the surface the morning of June 10, which she sank with two torpedoes. On the night of June 12, while off the Nanto Peninsula, she spotted an enemy convoy of three cargo ships with a single escort. Making a night surface attack, she evaded gunfire and an attack by the escort to sink all three merchant ships.

Operation *Barney* was *Flying Fish*'s 12th war patrol. The leader of "Bob's Bobcats" took her station off the east coast of Korea. She sank the 2,220-ton *Taga Maru* on June 10 and the 3,095-ton *Meisei Maru* the next day. On June 16 she sank ten fishing boats with gunfire and sent two of them onto the beach.

The Sea of Japan operation was *Bowfin*'s 9th war patrol. While she found few targets, she made the most of her two opportunities, sinking the 1,898-ton transport *Shinyo Maru* with four torpedoes on June 11 and the 887-ton freighter *Akiura Maru* with two hits on June 13. One of the few World War II fleet submarines to retain her original wartime configuration throughout her service, *Bowfin* has been a memorial at Pearl Harbor since 1971.

Operating off Honshu, *Tinosa* was able to make six torpedo attacks in which she sank three cargo ships. On June 12 she engaged in a surface gunnery fight with the *Keito Maru*, a Japanese sea truck. Overall she sank four Japanese ships and damaged a fifth during the operation.

The night of Sunday, June 24 was cold, dark, and creepy, with wisps of fog and mist slowly floating by when the submarines rendezvoused at 2400 hours west of La Pérouse Strait. *Bonefish*, which failed to arrive, had not been heard from for several days since requesting permission to move to a new area.

The submarines headed into the strait at flank speed, hoping the minefields were set deep to catch submerged submarines. Each had demolition bombs in place and all deck guns were fully manned. When *Sea Dog's* radar failed, *Crevalle* took the lead. CDR Hydeman recalled, "You have never seen such a straight line of boats, traveling in formation, in your life. I could see the formation they were traveling by the phosphorescence illumination as they passed in the water. If the boat in front of you made it then we should make it also, 'if' you passed exactly where he did."

LCDR Lynch, who was on the bridge, explained, "I'll always remember the feeling I had standing on the bridge as we cranked up flank speed and headed out through La Pérouse Strait. We were ready to fight our way out if necessary. Thank God, it wasn't and it was with great relief and thanksgiving that we cleared the straits and entered the Pacific Ocean."

When the little fleet was halfway through the straits, they came across a large ship headed into the Sea of Japan with all running lights on. Lynch remembered, "As we passed alongside the ship, they turned on their spotlight and moved it up and down on the eight submarines going past at full speed. If there were any enemy gun boats in the area, we were sunk or would have had a very hard time of it. The weather was cold. This was a hair-raising and chilling experience."

The ship was a Russian cargo vessel, which was there on purpose as the result of a special request by the American government, assigned to distract the enemy from detecting and firing on the submarines as they fled through the strait. Additionally, on June 24 two other submarines shelled buildings at Tsushima Strait to create a diversion.

At 0235 hours on June 25, 1945, the submarines cleared La Pérouse Strait and moved into the Sea of Okhotsk. *Tunny's* captain, LCDR George E. Pierce, requested permission to remain behind and see if *Bonefish* appeared. *Tunny* remained on station as the other seven boats headed out of the Sea of Okhotsk and into the Pacific. Three days later, Pierce was forced to concede that *Bonefish* was indeed missing and followed the others.

That submarines had been able to evade the minefields and escape from the Sea of Japan through La Pérouse Strait was considered one of the most difficult and dangerous submarine operations of the war by former submariner Admiral Nimitz. He said of Operation *Barney*, "It was one of the best planned and successful blows against the Japanese Empire. The objective of this operation was to cut Japan off from the Asiatic mainland whence came her absolutely essential raw materials, petroleum, food and other supplies that she was receiving from China and Korea."

The nine submarines that took part in Operation *Barney* sank a total of 31 ships and 16 small craft in the Sea of Japan for a total of 108,230 tons. The Hellcats arrived at Midway on Saturday, June 30, and headed on to Pearl Harbor the next day, where they tied up at the submarine base on July 5.

While the carriers of Task Force 38 bore the brunt of operations once the Third Fleet returned to Japanese home waters on July 5, the fleet's heavy surface forces also participated in the attacks, bombarding coastal targets in northern Japan that had previously been out of range of attack by B-29s from the Marianas. Most of these bombardment missions involved the new fast battleships of Task Force 34. While the attacks caused heavy damage to many of the targeted factories and other facilities, damage was also inflicted on nearby civilian areas, with the result that industrial absenteeism skyrocketed, while the people were given further demonstrations of the government's inability to defend them from attack. A major goal of the attacks was to provoke commitment of at least some of the reserve force of *kamikaze* aircraft into battle, where they could be hacked down before the invasion. The defenders did not rise to the bait and none of the warships involved suffered any damage.

An additional reason for turning the surface ships loose was the weather. The monsoon occurs between May and November, with increased rainfall and storms nearly every day in some parts of northern Asia. Thus, there were many days when flight operations were either canceled or severely constricted owing to weather conditions. The heavy surface forces were not so adversely affected by the weather as was the fleet's aerial component. Following Task Force 38's opening strikes against Tokyo on July 10, Task Force 38 sailed north to commence strikes against northern Honshu and Hokkaido on July 14. These regions were beyond B-29 range and by this point had not yet come under attack.

During several days of strikes, American aircraft met little opposition while sinking 11 warships and 20 merchant ships and damaging a further eight warships and 21 merchant ships. The carrier flyers claimed 25 Japanese aircraft shot down.

On July 14, the first naval bombardment of Japan occurred. Task Unit 34.8.1, led by Rear Admiral John F. Shafroth, attacked the ironworks of the Nippon Steel Company at Kamaishi in northern Honshu. The ironworks were among the largest in Japan, but a shortage of coking coal and other raw materials had forced them to run at less than half capacity. The battleships *South Dakota* (BB-57), *Indiana* (BB-58) and *Massachusetts* (BB-59), accompanied by heavy cruisers *Quincy* (CA-71) and *Chicago* (CA-136), escorted by nine destroyers made the attack. Unfortunately, US intelligence had not discovered that Allied prisoners of war were working in the factory and were housed in two nearby camps in Kamaishi.

The fleet opened fire at 1210 hours, firing initially from a range of 29,000 yards before moving close to the 100-fathom line. They did not cross owing to the danger of mines. Over two hours, the ships made six passes across the mouth of the harbor as they fired a total of 802 16-inch shells, 728 8-inch shells and 825 5-inch shells. While the majority hit within the ironworks, the explosions started kitchen fires across Kamaishi owing to the concussion from the hits. Shipboard aircraft were prevented by smoke from spotting fire for the warships, which were thus forced to fire on predetermined targets. There was no defensive response. When the shipboard aircraft photographed the target following the attack, the damage was underestimated by photo interpreters, who gave too much weight to the fact that no buildings were destroyed. After the war, the Navy discovered that in fact the ironworks had been extensively damaged; four weeks' production of pig iron and six weeks' of coke were lost. Five POWs who had been forced to work in the ironworks were killed.

At dawn on July 15, Rear Admiral C. Badger's Task Unit 34.8.2, which was composed of the newest and biggest battleships in the fleet, *Iowa* (BB-61), *Missouri* (BB-63) and *Wisconsin* (BB-64), accompanied by the light cruisers *Atlanta* (CL-104) and *Dayton* (CL-105), and eight destroyers, shelled the Wanishi Iron Works and the Japan Steel Company in the town of Muroran on Hokkaido's southeast coast. Third Fleet commander Admiral Halsey, with his flag on *Missouri*, was also present. Four other cruisers and six destroyers sought Japanese shipping along the east coast of Honshu, but failed to locate anything while this attack was under way.

Firing from 28,000–32,000 yards, the three battleships fired 860 16-inch shells over a period of six hours. Hazy conditions hampered aerial observation and only 170 shells hit the targets. All the same, the two facilities were badly damaged, losing 10 weeks of coke production and nine weeks of pig iron production; the city was also extensively damaged. Photo interpreters again underestimated the damage. During the attack, the ships were very vulnerable to air attack since they were visible from the shore. Halsey later recalled these hours as the longest of his life; the lack of response convinced him the Japanese were preserving aircraft for use against the invasion.

While the bombardment went on, Task Force 38's aircraft struck shipping ports on Hokkaido and northern Honshu, which devastated the fleet of ships carrying coal between the islands.

Third Fleet withdrew to sea to refuel following these attacks. On July 16, the Americans rendezvoused with the British Pacific Fleet, which had returned from its refit in Australia. On July 17, British and American carriers of Task Forces 37 and 38 attacked targets north of Tokyo. HMS *Formidable* sent a "Ramrod" of eight Corsairs of 1842 Squadron, and eight of HMS *Implacable*'s 1771 Squadron Fireflies hit airfields at Sendai, Masuda and Matsushima. The target was 250 miles north of Tokyo and the Corsairs and Fireflies were the first British aircraft to fly over the Japanese Home Islands. Later, an eight-Corsair Ramrod from *Victorious'* 1834 Squadron crossed Honshu and attacked targets on the Sea of Japan. While Seafires from *Implacable* flew CAP over the fleet, the cloudy weather prevented any enemy attacks.

That night, *Iowa, Missouri* and *Wisconsin,* along with *North Carolina* and *Alabama* and eight American destroyers, accompanied by *HMS King George V* and two British destroyers, attacked Hitachi, 80 miles northeast of Tokyo. Target location was difficult owing to rain and fog that also prevented the use of spotting aircraft. At 2310 hours, the six mighty battleships opened fire at a range of 23,000–35,000 yards, directing fire by use of radar and the LORAN electronic navigation system against nine industrial facilities. When the shelling ceased at 0110 hours on July 18, the Americans had fired 1,238 16-inch shells, while *King George V* fired 267 14-inch shells. Additionally, *Atlanta* and *Dayton* fired 292 5-inch shells at radar installations south of the city. Only three of the nine targets were hit, and overall damage to the industrial area was assessed as "slight."

Nonetheless, the bombardment had inflicted considerable damage to essential services and the civilian urban area; the following night a B-29 fire raid destroyed or damaged 79 percent of the urban area. Many Japanese later told American interviewers they considered the battleship bombardment more terrifying than the fire raid.

On July 18, the British and American carriers flew more air strikes in the Tokyo area. The main objective was to sink the battleship *Nagato,* moored at Yokosuka Naval Base. That night, Rear Admiral J. Cary Jones' Cruiser Division 17, composed of the light cruisers *Astoria* (CL-90), *Pasadena* (CL-65), *Springfield* (CL-66) and *Wilkes-Barre* (CL-103) and six destroyers attacked a radar station on Cape Nojima, firing 240 6-inch shells in five minutes, but scored no hits.

The Allied fleet withdrew to the east following these attacks and conducted replenishment from July 21–23. The fleet then moved to a point east of Shikoku island, from where strikes against the Japanese naval base at Kure and shipping in the Inland Sea were flown between July 24–28. Cruiser Division 17 entered the Kii Channel on the night of July 24 and bombarded the naval seaplane base at Kushimoto, an airfield near Cape Shionomisaki and a radio station in a 4-minute attack that caused only light damage.

The attack on Kure was the last large-scale American attack against the Imperial Navy of the war. Critics have wondered why it was that Admiral Halsey sent his fliers into such a heavily defended base as Kure, since the ships there were unable to sortie because of a lack of fuel and the fact that many of the ships had yet to be repaired from previous damage going back to the battles of Leyte Gulf the previous year. They were in use primarily as immobile antiaircraft batteries. Task Force 38 commander Admiral McCain and his staff strongly opposed the attack on the grounds the ships posed little threat. Halsey justified it on the grounds that he believed the attack would boost morale back home and be a retaliation for Pearl Harbor, that it would ensure no disruption of the Soviet invasion of Hokkaido planned for the fall, that destruction of the fleet would prevent Japan from using its fleet to secure better peace terms, and finally that Admiral Nimitz had ordered the attack. Despite the fact it was operating as a task group of the Third Fleet, Halsey directed that the British Pacific Fleet was to be excluded from attacking Kure in order that the British would not be able to claim any part of having destroyed the Imperial Navy and ordered that the British carriers attack the port of Osaka on the Inland Sea.

Kure was a sitting duck. The city and the naval base had been subjected to earlier aerial attacks by B-29s, which had successfully destroyed the Hiro Naval Aircraft Factory on May 5. Aerial mines had been dropped in the port's approaches on March 30 and May 5, which prevented any movement of the ships out of the harbor since the mines were of mixed versions that prevented successful minesweeping. On July 1, 40 percent of the city had been razed in a major fire raid. However, as the fliers would discover, the defenses were still sharp and dangerous.

On the first day of attacks, Task Force 38 aircraft flew 1,747 sorties, sinking the carrier *Amagi* and the Combined Fleet's flagship, the cruiser *Oyodo*. The battleships *Haruna*, *Hyuga*, and *Ise*, heavy cruiser *Tone*, and the old training cruisers *Iwate* and *Izumo* were all heavily damaged and settled to the bottom in the shallow water of the port. The heavy cruiser *Aoba*, badly damaged when she was attacked, was beached by her captain. The antiaircraft guns in the area were attacked with variable time-fused bombs to go after the crews.

The British attack on Osaka resulted in damaging the escort carrier *Kaiyo* and the sinking of *Escort Ships No. 4* and *No. 30*, while four aircraft were shot down by the heavy flak. The Seafires of *Implacable's* 880 Squadron participated in a strafing attack on the seaplane base at Tokushima at the northern entrance of the Inland Sea. Squadron commander LCDR Mike Crosley later described the mission:

> Our target was easy to find on the coast since it was in a clear patch of weather. None of us stayed around long enough to find out how we had got on. On the way back, we dived at Konatsushima. Here, the flak was very easy to see. They had obviously had warning from our attack further up the coast, so the gunners were ready for us. There were several twin-float seaplanes (Jakes) drawn up on the slipways, and we hit many of them. It was rewarding to see our cannon shells exploding in bright flashes in the dawn light as they hit the concrete slipways around the target. Once again, the attack was over in ten seconds and none of us were hit by flak.

Crosley had damaged a Mavis at Tokushima and a Pete at Konatsushima.

That afternoon, Crosley led another attack. "Our target was Takamatsu Airfield, supposedly crammed with 50 aircraft. We were briefed it was defended by 120 guns and there might be fighters. The weather was much better than we had expected and we once again did a quick in and out and hardly saw any flak."

Weather prevented further heavy attacks until July 28, though on July 25 VF-31's Hellcats engaged in what turned out to be the last major fight with fighters of the Japanese Army Air Force.

Fighting-31 on *Belleau Wood* was on its second Western Pacific deployment, having first entered combat aboard *Cabot* when it participated in the invasion of Kwajalein 19 months earlier. The squadron had been on the front line for the fast carrier offensive across the central Pacific, participating in the Marianas Turkey Shoot and Admiral Halsey's rampage through the Philippines, Okinawa and Formosa before returning home just before the Battle of Leyte Gulf.

The squadron went aboard *Belleau Wood* at Leyte in June and re-entered combat on July 10 with an attack on Kumagaya Airfield outside Tokyo. Now commanded by newly-promoted Commander Bruce S. Weber, a veteran of the Rabaul campaign, the pilots considered themselves lucky to be members of the top-scoring light carrier fighter squadron of the war and fourth-ranked of all carrier fighter squadrons (the fleet carrier squadrons had three times as many pilots in their units) with the highest victory ratio per pilot of any Navy fighter squadron ever. Lieutenant Cornelius N. Nooy, now the Senior Division Leader, had scored 15 victories during their first tour.

VF-31's Hellcats were assigned to attack Yokaichi Airfield, where unknown to them two *Chutais* of the elite 244th *Sentai* were based. The unit's 18 Kawasaki Ki-100 Goshiki-sen Type 5 fighters, modified Ki.61-II-Kai Tonys with a more reliable Mitsubishi Ha-112-II 14-cylinder radial engine, were so new they were unknown to the Americans. Warned of the approaching attack, they took off under the lead of the *Sentai* commander, the legendary 24-year-old Major Teruhiko Kobayashi, the youngest *Sentai* commander in the JAAF, as the Hellcats arrived overhead shortly after dawn.

A swirling dogfight quickly ensued at low altitude over the hangars on the field. The cloudy conditions restricted visibility, and Captain Tsutae Obara collided with the F6F-5 flown by Ensign Ed White, with both pilots killed. A Hellcat then shot down Warrant Officer Shin Ikuta, while Ensign Herbert Law was shot down by another Ki-100. Ikuta died in the crash of his Goshiki-sen, while Ensign Law successfully baled out of his stricken Hellcat, surviving to return to his comrades from a POW camp a month later. While the Japanese claimed 12 Hellcats shot down and the Americans claimed eight shot down and three probables, each side lost only two each. Lieutenant Connie Nooy claimed four, though he was the likely victor of the two actually lost, which confirmed his status as the top-scoring light carrier ace of the war.

Kobayashi had been under orders to keep his unit on the ground and await an incoming bomber raid. Newspapers quickly published details of the fight, since the 244th *Sentai* was very popular with the press, and Kobayashi's superiors decided to court-martial the young commander. He was rescued from this fate when news of the event reached the emperor, who let it be known he approved of Kobayashi's actions and the court martial was dropped.

Also on that night of July 25, as the British were withdrawing to refuel, a group of bogeys appeared on radar. Four "dusk patrol" Hellcat IIs from *Formidable's* 1844 night-fighting squadron detachment were on CAP. They were vectored onto four Aichi B7A "Grace" torpedo bombers, a new type, flying at 20,000 feet and headed for the fleet. Canadian Sub-Lieutenant Bill Atkinson and his New Zealander wingman, Sub-Lieutenant Mackie, suddenly found themselves alone when Sub-Lieutenant Foster suffered engine failure and returned to the carrier with his wingman Sub-Lieutenant Taylor. The Japanese torpedo bombers were spotted under the full moon, and Atkinson led Mackie into the attack. Atkinson shot down two while Mackie shot down a third, and they both took care of the fourth in a quick battle. Mackie lost his electrical system and radios in the fight and became disoriented in the dark and unable to find the carrier. Fortunately, he spotted the flash of light when Atkinson was cleared to land and made his way back to the ship. With these two victories, Bill Atkinson became the last Commonwealth pilot to become an ace in World War II.

On July 28, Task Force 38 returned to Kure. The fliers again hit the battleships *Ise* and *Haruna* and the heavy cruiser *Aoba*. The aircraft carrier *Katsuragi*, which had escaped attack in the earlier raid, and the light aircraft carrier *Ryuho*, which had been near-missed during the Mission Beyond Darkness the year before, were attacked. *Katsuragi* was heavily damaged.

Seventy-nine B-24 Liberators of the Fifth Air Force based on Okinawa raided Kure shortly after the Navy fliers departed. The B-24s scored four hits on the beached *Aoba*, which damaged the cruiser and caused her stern to break off. The heavy flak resulted in the loss of two B-24s shot down, while 14 others suffered varying damage.

During the two days of strikes, the fast carriers lost 133 aircraft and 102 aircrew in combat or accidents. These were the highest losses suffered by the Third Fleet in any of its operations. Other than the two VF-31 Hellcats lost in air combat on July 25, all the other losses were the result of the heavy antiaircraft defenses at the base. The only Japanese capital ship to escape destruction was *Nagato* at Yokosuka. With the Kure raid, the Imperial Navy was destroyed. The attacks allowed the Soviet Pacific Fleet to operate without fear of interdiction in the Sea of Japan following the Soviet declaration of war on August 9.

While the final day of strikes was flown against Kure, HMS *Formidable* launched a Ramrod of eight Corsair IVs from 1841 Squadron led by another Canadian pilot, Lieutenant Robert Hampton "Hammy" Gray, senior pilot of the squadron, in an attack against the naval base at Maisuru on northern Honshu. Gray led the Corsairs as they sank four ships and downed three defending aircraft. Gray's aggressive leadership of the mission resulted in his being awarded the Distinguished Service Cross.

The night of July 29, *South Dakota*, *Indiana* and *Massachusetts*, accompanied by the heavy cruisers *Quincy* and *Chicago*, attacked the city of Hamamatsu, between Nagoya and Tokyo. HMS *King George V* joined the task group, escorted by the destroyers HMS *Ulysses*, HMS *Undine* and HMS *Urania*.

At 2319 hours, *King George V* opened fire on the Japan Musical Instrument Company Plant No. 2, which was currently used to manufacture aircraft propellers, from a range of 20,075 yards. With aircraft spotting her fire, the battleship fired 265 14-inch rounds in 27 minutes but inflicted little damage. It marked the last time in history that a British battleship ever fired its guns in anger.

Massachusetts fired at Plant No. 1, scoring only a few hits. *South Dakota* and *Indiana* shelled the Imperial Government Railway locomotive works, as well as three other industrial facilities. Despite the lack of physical damage, the attack increased labor absenteeism and disrupted vital services, which resulted in the Hammatsu factories ceasing production while the locomotive works was out of operation for the next 90 days. Two bridges on the Tokaido Main Line were fired on though not hit, but the damage to railroad infrastructure closed the line for 66 hours. Japanese defenses offered no response.

During the night of July 30/31, Destroyer Squadron 25, under the command of Captain J. W. Ludewig aboard *John Rodgers* (DD-574), entered the Suruga Gulf in an unsuccessful search for Japanese shipping. At 0200 hours, the destroyers sailed deep into the gulf and fired 1,100 rounds of 5-inch shells over seven minutes, targeting a rail yard and aluminum plant in Shimizu.

At the end of July, the Allied fleet pulled away from the coast to replenish fuel and ammunition. A typhoon was detected southeast of Okinawa on August 2 during this operation, but fortunately it was tracked accurately and information was provided to the fleet in time for the ships to take evasive action.

With the replenishment operation completed by August 7, the Third Fleet sailed north to attack Japanese airfields in northern Honshu over August 9–10.

1841 Squadron's Lieutenant "Hammy" Gray led a mission from *Formidable* to strike Matsushima Airfield with eight Corsairs on August 9. The mission was changed to seek out targets of opportunity at the last minute, since the airfield had been heavily damaged in earlier attacks; ships in Onagawa Bay were chosen as the target. Intelligence was unaware that all these were heavily armed and prepared for an air attack. The antiaircraft positions in the surrounding hills created a killing zone over the bay.

Gray dived to attack the ocean escort vessel *Amakusa*. As he leveled out of his dive, one 500lb bomb was shot away by a hail of cannon and machine-gun fire from *Amakusa*, *Minesweeper 33*, *Ohama* and *Sub Chaser 42* that set his Corsair IV afire. Gray bored in and scored a direct hit on *Amakusa* that penetrated the engine room and triggered a massive explosion in the after ammunition magazine, sinking the ship in minutes.

The other pilots of the flight reported that Gray's Corsair, enveloped in smoke and flame, flying at an altitude of 50 feet, rolled to the right into the sea in an explosion of debris and water. They continued the attack, sinking several other ships.

On November 13, 1945, Lieutenant Robert Hampton Gray became one of 16 Canadians awarded the British Victoria Cross during World War II. It was the only VC awarded to a member of the Royal Canadian Navy, and the last awarded to a Canadian, since the Canadian government had recently created its own version of the Victoria Cross.

While the fliers claimed destruction of 720 Japanese aircraft in this operation, a major tragedy occurred on August 9 when *South Dakota*, *Indiana* and *Massachusetts*, accompanied by *Boston* (CA-69) and *St Paul* (CA-73), and the Commonwealth light cruisers HMS *Newfoundland* and HMNZS *Gambia*, escorted by the destroyers HMS *Terpsichore*, *Termagant* and *Tenacious*, attacked Kamaishi a second time in the mistaken belief that the ironworks had not been badly damaged. In what would turn out to be the final surface bombardment of the war, the task group opened fire at 1254 hours and made four passes across the harbor over the next two hours, while firing 803 16-inch shells, 1,383 8-inch shells and 733 6-inch shells from an average range of 14,000 yards. The bombardment resulted in more damage than the July attack, and the sounds of the bombardment were broadcast live on radio in the United States through a radio relay on *Iowa*. Unfortunately, one of the two POW camps was destroyed and 27 Allied POWs were killed.

On August 13, a final bombardment planned to be carried out by *King George V* and three Commonwealth light cruisers was canceled owing to the battleship's mechanical problems and the atomic bombings of Hiroshima and Nagasaki.

While the naval bombardments did not get the reaction hoped for from the Japanese air forces, they resulted in the disruption of what was left of the Japanese steel industry. Postwar assessment found the damage caused to industrial buildings even by 16-inch naval shells was less than the result of a hit by a 1,000–2,000lb general-purpose bomb, which supported Admiral McCain's view that the aircraft protecting the attacking ships could have caused more damage. The postwar United States Strategic Bombing Survey judged that the naval bombardments also affected Japanese morale, resulting in a significant loss of production from absenteeism. Additionally, the fact that Allied warships could operate off the coast with impunity convinced many civilians the war had been lost.

On August 5, the Wildcat, which had served in the front line of naval aviation since the first day of the war, fought its final battles of the war.

Task Group 95.9, a unit of the Carrier Support Force, the CVEs that had provided close air support for the Okinawa invasion and were now attacking Japanese targets on Kyushu, were in the East China Sea that morning. A division of four FM-2 Wildcats of VC-41 aboard *Makin Island* (CVE-93) was overhead on CAP at 1453 hours when radar detected an inbound bogey at 7,000 feet and the four stubby fighters were vectored to investigate.

Nearing the bogey, division leader Lieutenant H. L. Hokanson identified two Frances bombers and ordered the division to drop their wing tanks. Only Ensign Frank Yates was able to drop both tanks, which allowed him to pull ahead of the others as they pursued the speedy Japanese bombers. When one of the enemy nosed down and headed for the ocean's surface, Yates followed. That Frances escaped, but the second, which had followed its leader, was near enough that he was able to close to within 1,000 feet of the raider. His first burst from the four .50-caliber machine guns in the Wildcat's wings lit the port engine aflame. A second burst chopped pieces from the fuselage, while the next two bursts wrecked the starboard engine. As the Frances steepened its dive, Yates fired into the cockpit, shattering the canopy. It hit the ocean and exploded 40 miles from the ships.

Three hours later, at 1710 hours, task force radar plotted a single bogey bearing 070 degrees, headed southwest at 180 knots. Four Wildcats of VC-98 from *Lunga Point* (CVE-94) led by Lieutenant E. R. Beckwith closed in and identified it as another Frances. The enemy pilot put his throttle to maximum as all four FM-2s managed to drop their tanks and chase the bomber more than 100 miles until they were able to catch up to it, at which point the number four wingman tried to saw off the rudder with his prop. Lieutenant Beckwith opened up with his machine guns and set the Frances on fire; it crashed into the sea 55 miles from the task force to become the Wildcat's final victory.

The last 60 FM-2 Wildcats of 5,280 produced over the preceding two years had come off General Motors' Eastern Aircraft production line in New Jersey in May. British FAA fighter pilot and later world-famed test pilot Eric "Winkle" Brown said of Grumman's first fighter to enter combat, "I would assess the Wildcat as the outstanding naval fighter of the early years of World War II. I can vouch as a matter of personal experience, this Grumman fighter was one of the finest shipboard aeroplanes ever created."

Despite all the efforts of the Navy, when what would turn out to be the final carrier attacks of the war were over, it appeared on August 10 that a surrender by the Japanese was no closer than it had been when Task Force 38 commenced their attacks against the Home Islands 30 days earlier.

CHAPTER THIRTEEN

GYOKUSEN

The B-29 fire raids against Japanese cities and the naval blockade of the country on all sides brought increasing misery to the people of Japan, but failed to dissuade the "Big Six" and the armed forces that surrender was now the only viable option. Even the dropping of the atomic bomb on Hiroshima on August 6, 1945 did not bring the militarists on the War Council to step back from the cliff of national suicide and accept the Potsdam Conference call for unconditional surrender.

One more act was required.

Prior to the arrival in Japan of Portuguese explorers in 1543, Nagasaki, which was originally a small fishing village in a secluded harbor in southern Kyushu, had been of no significance in Japanese history. Fearing too much involvement with the Westerners, the Japanese government restricted them to Nagasaki as their port of entry. Trade expanded when the Portuguese were followed by the Spanish, and the fishing village began to grow.

The samurai warrior ruling class had little interest in the western goods brought by the Portuguese and Spanish until they discovered the power of firearms. Japan at the time was in the throes of civil warfare between warring clans, and the *daimyos* who equipped their samurai with muskets were soon ascendant.

Jesuit missionary St Francis Xavier arrived in Kagoshima, South Kyushu in 1549 and began to evangelize throughout Japan. He was successful in attracting several of the southern *daimyo* on Kyushu to convert to Christianity and bring their people with them before he departed to evangelize in China, where he found martyrdom in 1551. Most important of the converted *daimyo* was Sumitada Omura, who controlled the majority of Kyushu. His grant of a permit to develop a port at Nagasaki in 1569 led to the full flowering of the city when it was completed in 1571. The work was supervised by the Jesuit missionary Gaspar Vilela and Portuguese Captain-Major Tristão Vaz de Veiga, personally assisted by Lord Omura.

Nagasaki quickly grew to become a diverse and cosmopolitan port city. Western cultural influence expanded as the use of Portuguese products such as tobacco, bread, textiles and a Portuguese sponge cake called *castellas* became widespread and were assimilated into popular culture. (Tempura was derived from a Portuguese recipe originally known as *peixinho-da-horta*; the Japanese name comes from the Portuguese "*tempero*.")

Politically, what is known as the Sengoku Period saw widespread instability in Japan. Before his death, Lord Omura passed administrative control of Nagasaki to Jesuit Alexandro Valignano and the Society of Jesus, rather than see what was now a Catholic city dominated by a non-Catholic *daimyo*. In 1580, Nagasaki became a Jesuit colony and place of refuge for Japanese Christian refugees who experienced discrimination and maltreatment in other regions.

The campaign of national unification led by Hideyoshi Toyotomi arrived in Kyushu in 1587. The Jesuits were expelled, and he placed the city under his direct control. The expulsion order was largely unenforced, since Toyotomi soon left to continue his military conquest, and the majority of the city's population remained open Catholics.

Following the wreck of the Spanish galleon *San Felipe* off Shikoku in 1596, Toyotomi discovered the Spanish Franciscans planned to land in Japan and contest the Jesuits for followers. On February 5, 1596, Toyotomi ordered the crucifixion of 26 Catholics in Nagasaki, who became the "Twenty-six Martyrs of Japan." He allowed Portuguese traders to remain since they provided the muskets and cannon he needed. Nagasaki continued to thrive and Augustinian missionaries arrived in 1602.

Toyotomi was defeated the following year by Ieyasu Tokugawa, who became the founder of what would be known as the Tokugawa Shogunate. Since Tokugawa's victory would have been impossible without the support of the Catholic *daimyos* who had allied with him at the Battle of Sekigahara, he could not move against them until Osaka Castle was captured and the murder of Toyotomi's children assured his dominance. Since Dutch and English traders who had no interest in bringing their religions with them had arrived in Japan, Tokugawa could move against the Christian forces without fear of losing access to Western trade.

Shogun Tokugawa officially banned Catholicism and ordered all missionaries to leave in 1614. Faced with the shogunate's military power, a majority of the Catholic *daimyo* abandoned Christianity, forcing their subjects to follow their example. Those who refused were forced to leave the country, moving to the Portuguese colony at Macau or the Spanish colony of Luzon, where they founded "Japantowns" that spread throughout European-dominated areas of Southeast Asia. The shogunate's brutal campaign of persecution in Kyushu and the neighboring regions of Shikoku resulted in thousands of Christians being killed, tortured, or forced to renounce their religion.

The Christian Shimabara Rebellion of 1637 was the last major military action in Japan before the Meiji Restoration in 1880. Defeat saw the death of several hundred thousand Catholics on Kyushu and the religion was banned throughout the country. With this final victory, the shogunate closed Japan to the outside world. The only contact with the West was a single Dutch ship that was allowed to come to Nagasaki once a year. All Portuguese were expelled and the Dutch traders were ejected from their base at Hirado and forced to live in the specially constructed island-prison of Dejima in Nagasaki Harbor.

The shogunate lifted the ban on Dutch books in 1720. Following this, hundreds of scholars moved to Nagasaki to study European arts and sciences and the city became the center of *rangaku*, or "Dutch Learning." Throughout the 200 years of the Edo Period, Nagasaki was able to maintain western traditions and an outward focus, unlike the rest of Japan.

Throughout these two centuries, Catholicism continued underground, though the form of worship changed without Western priests; followers were known as *Kakure Kirishitan*. In the rest of Japan, Nagasaki was known in contemporary art and literature as a cosmopolitan port filled with the exotic products of the West. The city was also the center of underground resistance and opposition to the shogunate throughout the period, a tradition of opposition to imperial power that continued following the opening of Japan to the West in 1854.

In 1859 Nagasaki became a free port, with modernization starting in earnest in 1868. The Meiji Restoration in 1880 saw Japan open once again to diplomatic relations with other nations and foreign trade. Christianity was legalized and Nagasaki returned to its earlier role as a major center of Roman Catholicism in Japan. The city was proud of the fact that a visit to Nagasaki by Puccini, which led to a prolonged residence, resulted in the renowned opera *Madame Butterfly*. Throughout the period between the Meiji Restoration and the outbreak of the war, however, the city and its citizens, with their Westernized cultural beliefs, were viewed with suspicion by Japanese nationalists.

The forced modernization of Japan following the overthrow of the shogunate saw Nagasaki become a center of heavy industry, with shipbuilding the main activity. Mitsubishi Heavy Industries constructed the dockyards and became a prime contractor to the new Imperial Japanese Navy. Nagasaki Harbor was placed under control of the nearby Sasebo Naval District. Nagasaki became home to the Mitsubishi Steel and Arms Works, the Akunoura Mitsubishi Arms Plant, Mitsubishi Electric Shipyards, Mitsubishi Steel and Arms Works, and Mitsubishi-Urakami Ordnance Works. Ninety percent of the labor force worked in these companies.

In August 1944, southern Japan came within range of the B-29s operating from western China. Between August and November, five small air attacks by 136 aircraft dropped 270 tons of high explosive, 53 tons of incendiaries and 20 tons of fragmentation bombs on Nagasaki. The raid on August 1 saw bombs hit the shipyards and dock areas and the Mitsubishi Steel and Arms Works.

Skies were cloudy over most of mainland Japan on August 9, 1945, the result of the typhoon that had passed several days before, as well as the monsoonal weather.

At 0347 hours local time, just before dawn, a B-29 Superfortress of the 393rd Bombardment Squadron (Heavy), 509th Composite Wing, named "Bockscar," commanded by Major Charles Sweeney, took off from Tinian's North Field. Seriously overloaded, the Superfortress used nearly every inch of the 8,300-foot runway to get airborne.

Almost immediately, "Bockscar" flew into heavy weather. The 509th's first mission three days earlier had been easy. This would be the opposite in every way.

On August 6, Sweeney and his crew had flown "The Great Artiste" carrying instrumentation to record the mission of the B-29 "Enola Gay" on the Hiroshima mission. This mission was originally scheduled for August 11, but forecasted bad weather pushed the schedule forward. "Bockscar," usually flown by Captain Frederick C. Bock, had been substituted because there had been no time to remove the instrumentation from "The Great Artiste." During the preflight inspection, Sweeney had discovered a fuel tank would not feed, but he felt he had no alternative but to proceed. Sweeney's decision would be crucial in the coming events.

While "Enola Gay" had carried an atomic bomb called "Little Boy" that used Uranium-238 for the explosive, "Bockscar" carried a far more powerful bomb using Plutonium-239, named "Fat Man." It was the same type as the "gadget" that had been tested in New Mexico on July 16, 1945, and was far more powerful than "Little Boy." "Bockscar's" target was the industrial city of Kokura, home of the largest munitions plants in Japan.

The B-29 struggled through monsoon winds, rain, and lightning for eight hours. St Elmo's fire played along the wings and spinning propellers. Sweeney discovered their climb to a higher altitude in the face of the horrid weather had increased fuel consumption. The inability to access those 600 gallons in the defective tank was now a major threat to their success.

At 0700 hours they were halfway to Japan. The crew experienced a moment of terror when the bomb began arming itself as a red light on the weapon control panel blinked with increasing rapidity. If they lost altitude, it was possible it would explode. Weaponeer Navy Commander Frederick L. Ashworth grabbed the blueprints and crawled into the bomb bay, accompanied by his assistant weaponeer Lieutenant Philip M. Barnes. They removed the bomb casing and scrutinized the switches. It took ten tense minutes for Ashworth to discover the problem: two switches had been reversed by mistake during the arming process. Barnes flipped the two tiny switches to their correct positions and the red light stopped blinking.

Sweeney and his crew arrived off the Japanese coast at 30,000 feet at 0900 hours Tinian time. They were supposed to meet the escorting photo B-29 "Big Stink," flown by Major James I. Hopkins, and "The Great Artiste" over the island of Yakushima off the southern tip of Japan, but the continuing bad weather intervened. "Bockscar" arrived at the rendezvous with "The Great Artiste" at 0910 hours, but "Big Stink" was nowhere to be seen since Major Hopkins was orbiting 9,000 feet higher in clear air, searching for the others. Valuable time and – more importantly – valuable gasoline was lost as Sweeney circled for 15, then 30, then 45 fuel-burning minutes. Unable to make contact, the two bombers finally headed toward the target.

Hopkins, frantic over the failed rendezvous, broke radio silence and radioed Tinian, asking (in code) "Is Bockscar down?" The first word was dropped. On Tinian, they heard: "Bockscar down." Despair settled over the 509th that they had lost the weapon that would finally end the war.

"Bockscar" arrived over Kokura at 0944 hours local time (1044 hours Tinian time). Visibility was obscured by clouds and the smoke rising from nearby Yawata, which had been firebombed the night before. The orders for deployment of the bomb were specific: it was only to be dropped visually. Sweeney made three runs over the city but bombardier Captain Kermit Beahan couldn't get a visual drop. When they finally pulled away they were surrounded by flak bursts – Kokura was one of the most heavily defended cities in Japan.

The gas gauges were tipping toward half full at 1030 local when Ashworth convinced Sweeney they should proceed to Nagasaki, the secondary target.

They arrived over Nagasaki 20 minutes later to find the city obscured by clouds. "Bockscar" was now desperately short of fuel. They flew across the city on two fruitless runs. It was soon apparent there was no hope of returning direct to Tinian; they would have to make an emergency landing on Okinawa to refuel. With the fuel situation now critical, Sweeney turned back for the third run. It was now or never. They could now only make it to Okinawa without the bomb aboard. If they couldn't drop visually, their only choice would be jettisoning it over the ocean. Charles Sweeney would not be the man who returned to inform his superiors he had left the most important, most expensive, most valuable weapon of war ever created lying unused on the seabed off Japan.

Ashworth, convinced that if they did not drop the bomb no one would survive, conferred with Beahan, telling him he would take responsibility and that Beahan should drop by whatever means he had. Beahan saw the unmistakable shape of the Mitsubishi Steel Plant in Urakami Valley as it came into view on the radar screen and opened the bomb doors. Ashworth told him, "Use the radar."

At the last moment, Beahan shouted there was a hole in the clouds and he could bomb visually. Sweeney replied, "Okay, you own the plane." The bombardier had 45 seconds to set up the bombsight, kill the drift, and kill the rate of closure. "Bombs away!"

At 1201:40 hours Tinian time, "Fat Man" dropped away from "Bockscar." Twenty seconds later at 1202 hours, it exploded with a force of 22,000 tons of TNT, 1,840 feet above the city.

The men were thrown around by several shock waves. Radar Countermeasures Officer 2nd Lieutenant Jacob Beser thought the bomber would be torn apart as he was pinned to the floor.

Navigator 2nd Lieutenant Fred Olivi never forgot the sight of the mushroom cloud he saw out of his window:

> It was bright bluish color. It took about 45 or 50 seconds to get up to our altitude and then continued on up. I could see the bottom of the mushroom stem. It was a boiling cauldron. Salmon pink was the predominant color. I couldn't see anything down below because it was smoke and fire all over the area where the city was. I remember the mushroom cloud was on our left. Somebody hollered in the back: 'The mushroom cloud is coming toward us.' This is where Sweeney took the aircraft and dove it down to the right, full throttle, and I remember looking at the damn thing on our left, and I couldn't tell for a while whether it was gaining on us or we were gaining on it.

Sweeney pushed over into a second dive just in time to avoid flying through the cloud of atomic ash and smoke that continued to climb into the upper atmosphere.

"Bockscar" and "The Great Artiste" now turned south toward Okinawa in radio silence. Sweeney was so low on fuel he expected they would crash at sea and ordered everyone to check their Mae Wests. Their comrades back on Tinian still believed the mission had failed.

Having climbed to 30,000 feet, Sweeney descended in a semi-glide with minimum fuel consumption. Arriving over Okinawa, they found heavy traffic moving to and from the runways. With all fuel gauges on empty, Sweeney received no response to his emergency calls and told Olivi to fire flares. Olivi later remembered: "I took out the flare gun, stuck it out of the porthole at the top of the fuselage and fired all the flares we had, one after another. There were about eight or ten of them. Each color indicated a specific condition onboard the aircraft." The shower of different colored flares indicated every possible crisis: "Bockscar" was out of fuel, on fire, had wounded men, and every other possible crisis.

At 1351 hours local, "Bockscar" touched down on Yontan North Airfield just as the number two inboard engine died of fuel starvation. The Superfortress touched down at 140mph, 30mph too fast, and bounced 25 feet into the air before settling onto the runway. Pilot and co-pilot stood hard on the brakes as Sweeney engaged the special reverse propeller pitch as he desperately tried to slow. "Bockscar" sped past rows of fully-fueled B-24 Liberators loaded with incendiary bombs. Rolling now on fumes, Sweeney managed a full 180-degree turn at the end of the runway and headed the bomber toward a paved parking area.

As fire trucks, ambulances and other vehicles surrounded the plane, Sweeney ordered his crew to stay silent about the mission. Ashworth and Sweeney were quickly taken to headquarters. There newly arrived Eighth Air Force commander Lt General James H. "Jimmy" Doolittle asked Ashworth, "Who the hell are you?," to which Ashworth replied "What the hell is wrong with your control tower? We are the 509, Bockscar. We dropped an atomic bomb on Nagasaki."

Doolittle replied in amazement, "Bockscar? You're not lost? Thank God you didn't hit those B-24s. Just missed one hell of an explosion. Guess you already had one hell of an explosion. We heard you were down."

Afterwards, Doolittle told a friend the landing was "the scariest thing I ever saw."

Three hours later, "Big Stink" finally landed at Yontan. They had managed to photograph the results, despite the fact no one could operate the official camera, using an unofficial camera that physicist Harold Agnew had brought aboard. At 1730 hours, the three bombers departed Okinawa for Tinian, arriving at 2245 hours.

While fanfare and praise had greeted "Enola Gay" on her return, the Air Force did not publicize the story of the Nagasaki bomb or decorate the crew. There were some in favor of court-martialing Sweeney for disobedience to orders, but it was decided there was no reason to publicize a near-catastrophe.

Whether Fred Beaman was really able to bomb visually at the last minute, or followed Ashworth's suggestion to use the radar, will never be known for certain. For the rest of his life, the bombardier maintained he had followed instructions to the letter.

What is known is that what was seen on the radar screen was not the Mitsubishi munitions factory. It was the Urakami Catholic Church, the largest Christian church in all of Asia, built in the decades following the legalization of Christianity 60 years earlier through the donations of the parishioners who were the descendants of the shogun-hating *Kakure Kirishitan*. The downward force of the explosion flattened every part of the church other than the bell tower, which was directly beneath the center of the blast and immediately became the only structure still standing at what would come to be known as Ground Zero.

Less than a second after the detonation, the northern part of Nagasaki was destroyed and 35,000 people were incinerated, including 6,200 out of the 7,500 employees of the Mitsubishi Munitions plant, and 24,000 others employed in other war plants and factories nearby, as well as 150 Japanese soldiers, one of whom had his skull melted into the top of his helmet as his final remains. A total 96,000 people had died from the bombing and radiation as of a year later.

Still, it was not the bomb that forced the hand of the militarists. The night before, at 2300 hours Trans-Baikal time, Soviet Foreign Minister Vyacheslav Molotov had called Japanese ambassador Naotake Sato to his offices and told him the Soviet Union had declared war on the Empire of Japan, with effect from one minute past midnight, Trans-Baikal time on August 9.

At exactly that time, Marshal of the Soviet Union Aleksandr Vasilevsky began the invasion of the Japanese puppet state of Manchuoko. It was exactly 90 days following the surrender of Germany, as Stalin had promised at Yalta. News of the attack flashed to Tokyo at 0400 hours, Tokyo time.

The Soviet offensive commenced simultaneously on three fronts to the east, west and north of Manchuria. Japanese forces, weakened by the transfer of units to Kyushu to oppose the expected American invasion, fell back at all points. By August 14, the 1,000 tanks and self-propelled guns of the 6th Guards Tank Army that composed the Red Army's spearhead had captured objectives 700 miles inside Manchuria. Units were advancing so fast they were outrunning their supply lines.

The southern half of Sakhalin Island was invaded by the 16th Army at the same time the advance into Manchuria began. The 100,000 troops had orders to eliminate Japanese resistance and be prepared to invade Hokkaido, Japan's northernmost home islands, by August 24.

Emperor Hirohito had lost all confidence in the chances that Japan might achieve a military victory following the defeat on Okinawa in June. With the Soviet invasion, he saw the weakness of the Kwantung Army in Manchuria, of the navy, and of the army defending the Home Islands. Hirohito later wrote, "I was told that the iron from bomb fragments dropped by the enemy was being used to make shovels. This confirmed my opinion that we were no longer in a position to continue the war."

On June 9, Hirohito's confidante, Marquis Koichi Kido, had presented the "Draft Plan for Controlling the Crisis Situation," in which he had stated his belief that the ability of Japan to conduct modern war would be destroyed by the end of 1945 and that it would be unlikely the government could control civil unrest. "We cannot be sure we will not share the fate of Germany and be reduced to adverse circumstances under which we will not attain even our supreme object of safeguarding the Imperial Household and preserving the national polity."

Kido's plan proposed the emperor take direct action and offer the Allies an opportunity to end the war on "very generous terms," under which Japan would voluntarily withdraw from the former European colonies in southeast Asia, on the condition the colonial powers granted independence, would disarm so long as it did not happen under Allied supervision, and would be "content with minimum defense." Finally, there would be no Allied occupation, prosecution of war criminals, or change in the Imperial role. There was little likelihood the Allies would accept this offer.

Foreign Minister Togo was very supportive of the plan; Prime Minister Suzuki and Navy Minister Admiral Mitsumasa Yonai were cautiously supportive; Army Minister General Korechika Anami refused to support the plan, insisting that diplomacy must wait until "after the United States has sustained heavy losses" in Operation *Ketsugo*, the defense of Kyushu. Nevertheless, the emperor authorized Kido to make the offer.

The official military position was summed up in the War Journal of the Imperial Headquarters: "We can no longer direct the war with any hope of success. The only course left is for Japan's one hundred million people to sacrifice their lives by charging the enemy to make them lose the will to fight."

When Ambassador Sato presented the Kido proposal to the Soviets, it was made clear to him the terms were unacceptable. While the Soviets had reassured Japan in April when they gave the required one-year notice of non-renewal of the Nonaggression Pact that there would be no change in status during that year, Foreign Minister Togo now took the Soviet response to mean that Stalin had made an agreement with the Western Allies to join the Pacific War at some date in the near future. Suzuki, Yonai and Anami argued against this position.

On July 26, 1945, the Potsdam Declaration was issued. It called for the elimination "for all time [of] the authority and influence of those who have deceived and misled the people of Japan into embarking on world conquest;" the occupation of "points in Japanese territory to be designated by the Allies;" that "Japanese sovereignty shall be limited to the islands of Honshu, Hokkaido, Kyushu, Shikoku and such minor islands as we determine;" that "the Japanese military forces, after being completely disarmed, shall be permitted to return to their homes with the opportunity to lead peaceful and productive lives;" that "we do not intend that the Japanese shall be enslaved as a race or destroyed as a nation, but stern justice shall be meted out to all war criminals, including those who have visited cruelties upon our prisoners." The declaration then called for unconditional surrender: "We call upon the government of Japan to proclaim now the unconditional surrender of all Japanese armed forces, and to provide proper and adequate assurances of their good faith in such action. The alternative for Japan is prompt and utter destruction." It ended with the warning, "We will not deviate from them. There are no alternatives. We shall brook no delay."

The Potsdam Declaration also put forth the goal that "The Japanese Government shall remove all obstacles to the revival and strengthening of democratic tendencies among the Japanese people. Freedom of speech, of religion, and of thought, as well as respect for the fundamental human rights, shall be established."

Most importantly so far as the Japanese were concerned was the fact the Declaration made no mention of the emperor, which left the question of what Allied intentions were regarding the one issue of utmost importance to the Japanese. Would the emperor be considered one of those who had "misled the people of Japan," even a war criminal? Would he be allowed to be part of a "peacefully inclined and responsible government"? In order to have any response, the Japanese needed these crucial questions answered.

The text of the Potsdam Declaration had been officially broadcast and printed on leaflets that were dropped over Japan. On July 28 newspapers throughout the country reported that the Declaration had been rejected. In a rare press meeting, Prime Minister Suzuki stated:

> I consider the Joint Proclamation a rehash of the Declaration at the Cairo Conference. As for the Government, it does not attach any important value to it at all. The only thing to do is just kill it with silence. We will do nothing but press on to the bitter end to bring about a successful completion of the war.

On the afternoon of August 9, it was clear to anyone in the upper reaches of the Japanese government that the policy of "prompt and utter destruction" had been implemented by the Allies. Japanese physicists involved in the Japanese atom bomb project had visited

Hiroshima and reported that the destruction there was indeed the result of an atomic explosion. The initial response, as stated by Admiral Toyoda on receipt of this report, had been that the Americans could not have created more than one bomb. The bombing of Nagasaki demonstrated that Hiroshima was not a one-time event, and that further atomic attacks must be expected. The Soviet invasion of Manchuria posed the threat of an invasion from the north against minimal defenses, while Japanese forces were massed to oppose the expected American invasion in the south. Any Soviet occupation of Japan carried with it the definite knowledge that it would mean the absolute end of the imperial system.

Suzuki and Togo were both profoundly affected by the news of the bombing of Nagasaki and the Soviet invasion of Manchuria. Both now agreed the war must be ended at once if they were to prevent a Soviet invasion they knew was unstoppable. Minister of War Anami and the senior leadership of the Japanese Army, who underestimated the scale of the Soviet attack, opposed the prime minister and foreign minister.

When the Supreme Council met at 1030 hours on August 9, there was only the Soviet invasion to be discussed. Prime Minister Suzuki, who had just met with the emperor and understood his position on further hostilities, stated that continuing the war was impossible. Foreign Minister Togo gave his opinion that if the Allies would guarantee the position of the emperor, the terms of the Potsdam Declaration should be accepted. Navy Minister Yonai stated his position, which was that a diplomatic proposal must be made since it was impossible to wait for better circumstances. Army Minister Anami announced the Army would impose martial law to stop any attempt to make peace.

At about 1110 hours, the Council received news that Nagasaki had been hit by a second atomic bomb. Even with this, the Big Six were still split on the issue of seeking peace by the time a vote of 3–3 ended the meeting. Togo's one condition to accepting Potsdam had the support of Prime Minister Suzuki, Foreign Minister Togo, and Navy Minister Admiral Yonai. But Army

Minister General Anami, Army Chief of Staff General Umezu, and Combined Fleet Commander Admiral Toyoda continued to insist that three further terms be part of the Japanese proposal: that Japan handle her own disarmament; that Japanese war criminals be dealt with by the government; and there would be no occupation.

While the crew of "Bockscar" prayed they had enough gas left in the tanks to make it to Okinawa rather than crash land in the open ocean, and during their later flight back to Tinian, momentous events were taking place in Tokyo.

There was only one topic when the full cabinet met at 1430 hours: surrender. As with the Big Six that morning, neither Togo's nor Anami's proposal won a majority. In the midst of all, Anami revealed that a captured P-51 pilot had under torture confessed that there were 100 atom bombs in the American arsenal. Tokyo and Kyoto would be hit "in the next few days".

First Lieutenant Marcus McDilda, a pilot in the 46th Fighter Squadron of the 21st Fighter Group based on Iwo Jima, had baled out of his P-51D 44-63901, named "The Gator," 500 feet over the ocean and just off the coast of Honshu after having been hit by flak while attacking coastal shipping. In truth, he knew as much about the Manhattan Project and the atomic bomb as every other American in the Pacific – that two days earlier one had apparently been dropped on Hiroshima, as President Truman had announced. In an attempt to stop the excruciating torture he was undergoing, he lied to his interrogators and gave them the number of atomic weapons as 100, since it appeared that was what they wanted to hear. With the lie accepted, he was immediately classified a high-profile prisoner, which probably saved him from a planned beheading. The truth was that there were three bomb shells on Tinian, awaiting delivery of their nuclear cores. The first of these would be ready for use by August 19, and would likely have been used against Tokyo. A second shell would be operational by September. It was hoped as many as three more might be ready if needed by D-Day of Operation *Olympic* in November.

While the rest of the cabinet believed Anami's report, it still was not enough to change minds. The meeting adjourned at 1730 hours, having failed to find consensus. A second meeting called at 1800 hours lasted four hours; it also ended without consensus.

Suzuki and Togo met with Hirohito at 2300 hours. The emperor accepted Suzuki's proposal for an ad hoc imperial conference. The cabinet gathered in the presence of the emperor just before midnight. Suzuki presented Anami's four conditions as the consensus position of the Supreme War Council. Other Supreme Council members spoke. Privy Councilor Kiichiro Hiranuma, president of the Privy Council, spoke to the fact the nation was completely unable to defend itself and proceeded to list domestic problems, starting with the nationwide food shortage. There was more debate that resolved nothing.

Finally, at approximately 0200 hours on August 10, Prime Minister Suzuki asked the emperor to decide between the two positions. Togo later recalled that Hirohito stated:

> I have given serious thought to the situation prevailing at home and abroad and have concluded that continuing the war can only mean destruction for the nation and prolongation of bloodshed and cruelty in the world. I cannot bear to see my innocent people suffer any longer.
>
> I was told by those advocating a continuation of hostilities that by June new divisions would be in place in fortified positions ready for the invader when he sought to land. It is now August and the fortifications still have not been completed.
>
> There are those who say the key to national survival lies in a decisive battle in the homeland. The experiences of the past, however, show that there has always been a discrepancy between plans and performance. I do not believe that the discrepancy can be rectified. Since this is also the shape of things, how can we repel the invaders?

He then specifically referenced the increased destructiveness of the atomic bomb:

It goes without saying that it is unbearable for me to see the brave and loyal fighting men of Japan disarmed. It is equally unbearable that others who have rendered me devoted service should now be punished as instigators of the war. Nevertheless, the time has come to bear the unbearable.

I swallow my tears and give my sanction to the proposal to accept the Allied proclamation on the basis outlined by the Foreign Minister.

According to General Sumihisa Ikeda and Admiral Zenshiro Hoshina, Privy Counsellor Hiranuma then turned to the Emperor and asked: "Your majesty, you also bear responsibility for this defeat. What apology are you going to make to the heroic spirits of the imperial founder of your house and your other imperial ancestors?" The emperor then left the conference and Suzuki pushed for acceptance of the emperor's will, which was given.

Within a matter of hours, the Foreign Ministry contacted the Allies through the Swiss government and announced Japan would accept the Potsdam Declaration, but would not accept any conditions that would "prejudice the prerogatives" of the emperor. This meant no change in the form of government, since the emperor would remain in a position of real power.

American Secretary of State James F. Byrnes wrote the Allied response, which was approved by the British, Chinese, and Soviet governments, on August 12. On the status of the Emperor it said:

From the moment of surrender, the authority of the Emperor and the Japanese government to rule the state shall be subject to the Supreme Commander of the Allied powers who will take such steps as he deems proper to effectuate the surrender terms. The ultimate form of government of Japan shall, in accordance with the Potsdam Declaration, be established by the freely expressed will of the Japanese people.

The logjam had been broken.

President Truman ordered operations to continue pending reception of official word of Japanese surrender. He changed his position after news correspondents incorrectly interpreted General Carl Spaatz's statement there would be no B-29 missions on August 11 (which was due to bad weather) as confirming a ceasefire. Since the president did not want the Japanese to get the impression the Allies had abandoned peace negotiations and resumed bombing, he halted further missions.

Suzuki argued for rejection of Secretary Byrnes' response without an explicit guarantee of the imperial system and Anami maintained his opposition to occupation. Foreign Minister Togo told Suzuki there was no hope of better terms and Kido informed them it was the emperor's will that Japan surrender. When he met later with the emperor, Admiral Yonai stated, "I think the term is inappropriate, but the atomic bombs and the Soviet entry into the war are, in a sense, divine gifts. This way we don't have to say that we have quit the war because of domestic circumstances."

The reply to the Allied response was debated on August 13, with the cabinet again deadlocked. Doubt now began to grow among the Allies as they waited, having told the Japanese they could transmit an unqualified acceptance by radio. Intercepted military and diplomatic traffic seemed evidence of a pending "all-out *banzai* attack."

In order "to impress Japanese officials that we mean business and are serious in getting them to accept our peace proposals without delay," President Truman ordered that maximum intensity attacks resume. Coastal targets were shelled by the fleet's battleships while the largest bombing raid of the Pacific War saw over 400 B-29s attack that day, followed by 300 more that night.

The 315 Bombardment Wing (Heavy) flew the longest bombing mission of the war: 3,800 miles to hit the Nippon Oil Company refinery, the last refinery still operating in the Home Islands at Tsuchizaki on the northern tip of Honshu.

The day bombers dropped leaflets across the country, informing the people of the Japanese government's offer of surrender and the Allied response. Meeting at dawn on August 14 before he met with the most senior military officers, Hirohito, Suzuki, and Kido realized the day would end either with acceptance of the Allied terms or a military coup. In the later meeting, Field Marshal Shunroku Hata, who led the Second General Army defending southern Japan, stated he had no confidence he could defeat the invasion and did not dispute the imperial decision.

When Hirohito then conferred with the cabinet, Anami, Toyoda, and Umezu repeated their desire to continue. Hirohito then said:

"I have listened carefully to each of the arguments presented in opposition to the view that Japan should accept the Allied reply as it stands and without further clarification or modification, but my own thoughts have not undergone any change." He asked that they prepare an imperial rescript that he could broadcast to the nation. This was met by unanimous ratification of the imperial desire. The Foreign Ministry immediately ordered the embassies in Switzerland and Sweden to accept the Allied terms. Washington received word of the order at 0249 hours on August 14.

The news of surrender was delivered to Japanese commanders personally by the three princes of the imperial family who held military commissions, with Prince Tsuneyoshi Takeda going to Korea and Manchuria while Prince Yasuhiko Asaka went to the China Fleet and China Expeditionary Army; Prince Kan'in Haruhito traveled to Shanghai, South China, Indochina and Singapore.

The imperial rescript was finalized at 1900 hours on August 14 and presented to the cabinet to be signed. With the help of an NHK recording crew, Hirohito made a gramophone recording at 2300 hours that court chamberlain Yoshihiro Tokugawa hid in a locker in the empress's secretary's office.

The threat of a military coup was serious. Junior Japanese officers had assassinated political leaders who opposed militarism since the 1920s. Major Kenji Hatanaka, accompanied by lieutenant colonels Masataka Ida, Masahiko Takeshita, and Inaba Masao, joined by Chief of the Military Affairs Section Colonel Okitsugu Arao, met General Anami on August 12 to ask him to prevent any acceptance of the Potsdam Declaration. Anami refused to commit himself.

On their own, Hatanaka and the others decided to attempt a *coup d'état*; they gathered allies and sought support from senior officers in the Army Ministry on August 13.

A group of senior army officers met with Anami following the imperial conference that night. General Torashiro Kawabe proposed that all present sign an agreement that "The Army will act in accordance with the Imperial Decision to the last." All signed, sealing the fate of the junior officers' attempted *coup d'état* in Tokyo.

The planned coup was set in motion at 2130 hours on August 14. The Second Regiment of the First Imperial Guards had been ordered to the palace grounds, which doubled the defenses. Hatanaka, with Lt Col Jiro Shiizaki, convinced the unit's commander, Colonel Toyojiro Haga, to join them, falsely telling him Anami and Umezu and the commanders of the Eastern District Army and Imperial Guards Divisions had all agreed to the attempt. Hatanaka visited Shizuichi Tanaka, commander of the eastern region of the army, to persuade him to join. Tanaka refused and ordered Hatanaka to go home.

Hatanaka's hope was that occupation of the palace would demonstrate the beginnings of rebellion and the rest of the Army would rise against the surrender. The Second Regiment would occupy the palace at 0200 hours on August 15. While Hatanaka tried to convince his superiors to join the coup, General Anami committed ritual *seppuku*, leaving the message that, "I, with my death, humbly apologize to the emperor for the great crime."

Hatanaka and his men surrounded the palace just after 0100 hours. They went to the office of Lt General Takeshi Mori, commander of the 1st Imperial Guards Division, and asked him to join them. When he refused, Hatanaka killed him, while Uehara killed Mori's brother, Shiraishi, who was present. Hatanaka used General Mori's official stamp to authorize Strategic Order No. 584, a false set of orders increasing the forces occupying the Imperial Palace and Imperial Household Ministry, to "protect" the emperor. The conspirators disarmed the palace police and blocked the entrances. After detaining 18 people, including the NHK workers who had recorded the surrender speech, they searched for the recording.

The "bank vault," a large chamber beneath the Imperial Palace, became the hiding place of Lord Privy Seal Kido and Imperial House Minister Ishiwatari. When Chamberlain Tokugawa was found by the rebels, he lied, saying he had no knowledge of the location of the two men or the recording in the face of Hatanaka's threat of disembowelment. Communication was cut off between the palace and the outside world after the rebels cut the telephone wires.

Assassins led by Captain Takeo Sasaki went to Prime Minister Suzuki's office, but he was warned and escaped minutes before their arrival. They set fire to his home and went to assassinate Kiichiro Hiranuma, who also escaped. Suzuki spent the rest of the month sleeping in a different bed each night under police protection.

At 0300 hours, Hatanaka was told the Eastern District Army was headed to the palace and he should give up. He pleaded for 10 minutes on the radio, to explain what he was trying to accomplish and why, but was refused. When Colonel Haga learned the Army was opposed to the coup, he ordered Hatanaka to leave the palace grounds.

At 0500 hours, Hatanaka appeared at the NHK studio, brandishing a pistol as he desperately tried to get airtime. General Tanaka went to the palace at dawn, where he confronted the rebels and convinced them to return to their barracks. At 0600 hours, Hatanaka left the NHK studios. The rebellion was over by 0800 hours. Hatanaka shot himself an hour before the scheduled broadcast; Shiizaki stabbed himself, then shot himself. Authorities found Hatanaka's death poem in his pocket: "I have nothing to regret now that the dark clouds have disappeared from the reign of the emperor."

At noon on August 15 1945, the people of Japan heard their emperor's voice for the first time as he read the Imperial Rescript on the Termination of the War. His address was given in traditional Japanese, which many found hard to understand:

After pondering deeply the general trends of the world and the actual conditions obtaining in Our Empire today, We have decided to effect a settlement of the present situation by resorting to an extraordinary measure.

We have ordered Our Government to communicate to the Governments of the United States, Great Britain, China and the Soviet Union that Our Empire accepts the provisions of their Joint Declaration.

To strive for the common prosperity and happiness of all nations as well as the security and well-being of Our subjects is the solemn obligation which has been handed down by Our Imperial Ancestors and which lies close to Our heart.

"Indeed, We declared war on America and Britain out of Our sincere desire to ensure Japan's self-preservation and the stabilization of East Asia, it being far from Our thought either to infringe upon the sovereignty of other nations or to embark upon territorial aggrandizement.

But now the war has lasted for nearly four years. Despite the best that has been done by everyone – the gallant fighting of the military and naval forces, the diligence and assiduity of Our servants of the State, and the devoted service of Our one hundred million people – the war situation has developed not necessarily to Japan's advantage, while the general trends of the world have all turned against her interest.

Moreover, the enemy has begun to employ a new and most cruel bomb, the power of which to do damage is, indeed, incalculable, taking the toll of many innocent lives. Should we continue to fight, not only would it result in an ultimate collapse and obliteration of the Japanese nation, but also it would lead to the total extinction of human civilization.

Such being the case, how are We to save the millions of Our subjects, or to atone Ourselves before the hallowed spirits of Our Imperial Ancestors? This is the reason why We have ordered the acceptance of the provisions of the Joint Declaration of the Powers.

The hardships and sufferings to which Our nation is to be subjected hereafter will be certainly great. We are keenly aware of the inmost feelings of all of you, Our subjects. However, it is according to the dictates of time and fate that We have resolved to pave the way for a grand peace for all the generations to come by enduring the unendurable and suffering what is unsufferable.

To this day, the official Japanese history of the Pacific War, taught in the nation's schools, echoes the unreality of the Imperial Rescript.

The next day, Admiral Takejiro Ohnishi, who had begun the *kamikaze* campaign in the Philippines back in October 1944, committed *seppuku* in his quarters. In his suicide note, he apologized to the nearly 4,000 pilots he had sent to their deaths, and urged all young civilians to work towards rebuilding Japan and peace among nations, stating additionally that he offered his death as penance to the pilots and their families. Thus, he did not use a *kaishakunin* (second knife). It took 15 hours for him to die. Only a week earlier, Ohnishi had pushed for continuing the war, stating that the sacrifice of 20 million more Japanese lives would make the country victorious. The admiral was one of many senior military officers who chose a similar end.

The emperor's uncle, Prince Higashikuni, replaced Suzuki as prime minister on August 17, while Mamoru Shigemitsu replaced Foreign Minister Togo.

The last aerial combat took place on August 18. Two Consolidated B-32 "Dominator" bombers left Yontan Airfield on Okinawa on a photo-recon mission to record compliance with the surrender terms.

One B-32, "Hobo Queen II" was flying at 20,000 feet while the other was at 10,000 feet when the bombers encountered a formation of 14 A6M5 Zekes and three N1K2-J George fighters from the IJNAF airbase at Atsugi. The formation was led by leading surviving Japanese ace Saburo Sakai, who had fought from the first day of the Pacific War and been promoted to Lt(jg) the previous May. Before initiating the attack, Sakai initially misidentified the planes as B-29s as he attacked "Hobo Queen II." Her gunners claimed two Zekes shot down and a probable George, though no Japanese aircraft were lost.

The second B-32 was heavily damaged, with one of the dorsal gunners wounded in the first pass, while the second pass seriously wounded Photographer Staff Sergeant Joseph Lacharite in his legs and fatally wounded his assistant, Sergeant Anthony Marchione, who died during the return to Okinawa, the last American air combat death in World War II. Sakai and the others returned to Atsugi to discover their action had resulted in a new requirement that the propellers of all Japanese aircraft be removed as a condition of the surrender.

The dawn sky over Kyushu was clear the next morning when the B-25J flown by Major Jack McClure of the 498th "Falcons" Bomb Squadron and Major Wendell Decker's "Betty's Dream" of the 499th "Bats Outta Hell" Bomb Squadron orbited off the coast.

While the Pacific War had officially ended four days before, their crews were on alert for Japanese who did not heed the emperor's decision to surrender. This was perhaps the most important rendezvous of the Pacific War. Decker's turret gunner soon spotted distant shapes that resolved themselves as two G4M1 Betty bombers, with four Zekes as escort. All were painted white over their green-gray camouflage, with rising sun insignias replaced by green crosses. The Bettys carried the official Japanese surrender delegation.

The B-25s swung in to escort the bombers as the Zeros banked away. The honor of escorting the surrender delegation was an acknowledgment of the contribution to victory made by the 345th "Air Apaches" Bomb Group, which had fought from New Guinea to Okinawa in the previous two years. The four aircraft headed south to Okinawa.

At the airfield on Ie Shima island just northwest of Okinawa, every American who could arrange to get there waited for their arrival. The two Bettys made a low pass over the runway as though putting on a show before landing. They were quickly surrounded by American military police and the Japanese representatives were escorted to a waiting C-54 transport that took them to the meeting with General Douglas MacArthur and the other representatives of the victorious Allies in Manila to finalize concrete details for the surrender of the Empire of Japan.

Once the C-54 departed, the MPs allowed the men to surround the bombers, who seemed overwhelmed by the friendly response they received from those they had been told would eat them in an invasion of the Home Islands.

Twenty-five-year-old Major Vic Tatelman, pilot of the famed B-25 gunship "Dirty Dora II," the only member of the Air Apaches to have flown two tours, remembered, "It was certainly the biggest celebration I had ever attended."

The next day the C-54 returned with two complete sets of original surrender documents to be conveyed back to Tokyo in the Bettys. It had been discovered at Ie Shima that there was no fuel of low enough octane available for the Japanese aircraft to refuel with. The idea that higher-octane American fuel be mixed with the low-octane fuel remaining in the aircraft was rejected.

The first Betty took off to return to Tokyo, again escorted by two Air Apaches. Instead of landing on Kyushu to refuel, the Betty flew on for Tokyo. Over the Inland Sea, the Betty ran out of fuel. When the pilot attempted an emergency landing ashore, he crashed in the water and the plane broke up on impact.

There was now only one set of surrender documents in existence. The successful return of the second Betty to Japan was now crucially important.

The second Japanese crew now agreed to have American 100-octane fuel mixed with their 87-octane fuel. "Betty's Dream" was again the lead escort. Major Tatelman, the top-ranked pilot in the group in terms of operational accomplishment, got himself assigned as co-pilot for his friend Wendell Decker. "After everything I had gone through in the Pacific, there was no way I was going to miss this."

The three aircraft droned toward the Home Islands. Decker and Tatelman had decided that, once they were over the Home Islands, they would not allow the Betty to fly over water until they reached Tokyo; if anything mechanical went wrong, they would force the bomber down at the first airfield they came across to guarantee successful delivery of the precious cargo.

The Betty had enough fuel to return to Atsugi airbase. Saburo Sakai was among the Japanese on the ground who watched as the Americans stayed with the Betty until it touched down. Once it was down, the two Mitchells applied full power and roared the length of the runway before climbing back to altitude for the journey home.

For the men of the 345th Bomb Group, as well as everyone else, World War II in the Pacific was finally over.

Several days later, 2nd Lieutenant Lamar Gillet, an Army Air Forces pilot who had flown in the defense of the Philippines after Pearl Harbor and had managed to become the only P-35 pilot ever to shoot down a Zeke during the desperate fighting before he became a survivor of the Bataan Death March and nearly three years as a slave laborer in Japan, was awakened in his POW camp on a hill overlooking the Sea of Japan in western Honshu by the roar of engines. B-29s had flown over the camp many times before, but never this low. The men poured out of their barracks and hobbled or ran into the open field. Gillet, who now weighed 95 pounds, down from the 145 he had weighed when he first arrived at Clark Field in the summer of 1941 to join the 17th Pursuit Group, looked up as the first bomber opened its bomb bay doors. Objects fell from the bomber, quickly slowed in their fall by parachutes. The other bombers followed, and the sky was now full of parachutes.

"They got closer, and we could see they were crates. All of a sudden we were running away to dodge them as they fell into the field where we were. They came down hard, and several of them burst open on impact." Most of the crates were full of C-rations, while others were full of clothing and boots and other items. "I ran to one and grabbed a box of the C-rations, then ran to another and found a pair of GI boots that looked like they might fit." Gillet retreated from the scramble and pulled on his boots. "They were a bit big for me, but I didn't care. I had boots!" He then tore open the box of C-rations. "One of the cans was labeled 'peaches.' I hadn't seen a peach since the day before the Japanese had bombed Clark Field the first day of the war." There were no eating utensils in the box, but there was a can opener. "I opened that can, and I started scooping out those peaches and eating them with my fingers. I looked up at the bombers as they flew away, standing there in my boots and dripping peach juice down my chin, and I was in hog heaven."

On September 1, 1st Lieutenant William E. Barber, Jr., who had become commander of Easy Company, 2nd Battalion, 26th Marine Regiment, of the 5th Marine Division on Iwo Jima when the position became his on the fourth day of the battle owing to the deaths of all company senior officers, accompanied other officers of the division to the Kyushu beach they had been scheduled to land on in Operation *Olympic* after they had recently arrived in Sasebo to take up occupation duty. "We walked the beach and studied the defenses that were there. We were able to question a senior Japanese officer, and learn what defensive force would have opposed us. At the end, it was the considered opinion of everyone from the division commander down to me, the most junior company commander, that we would not have gotten off the beach, and it would have been impossible to evacuate the survivors under fire."

On the morning of September 2, the Allied fleet was at anchor in Tokyo Bay, ready for the arrival of the Japanese representatives and the formal surrender ceremony. Ten thousand feet overhead, 23-year-old Captain Paul Williams, a P-38 pilot in the 7th Fighter Squadron of the famed 49th Fighter Group, orbited over the fleet on combat air patrol. The "Forty Niners" were the first American fighter group to arrive in Australia after Pearl Harbor, and had participated in every battle from the defense of Darwin in the spring and summer of 1942, through all the fighting in New Guinea and the Philippines, up to Okinawa and the final missions over Japan. Captain Williams, however, had arrived "late to the party," as he described it. "I finally got a combat assignment in March 1945, but by the time I got to Clark Field and joined the group, there wasn't any fighting left in the Philippines." The group moved up to Okinawa in early June, and Williams flew missions to the coast of China and over Kyushu. Following the surrender, the Forty-Niners were the first USAAF fighter group to arrive in Japan a week earlier, taking up residence at the old Imperial Navy airbase at Atsugi.

As the sun rose over the western Pacific and the ships became silhouettes on the water below, Williams recognized the battleship *Missouri*, which was to be the site of the coming surrender ceremony. "I decided I wanted to have at least a minute of excitement to put in my memories of this war, so I radioed the ship and asked for permission to make a low pass over her. The radio shack said OK, so down I went."

On the way down to sea level, Williams decided he would make that minute not only memorable but spectacular. Rather than a low pass down the side of the ship, he decided to fly over it, between the massive stacks. "I figured I couldn't do it wings level, so when I was about a thousand feet out, I put the left wing high and went between the stacks wings-vertical at maximum speed, maybe 300 miles an hour. There was a moment when I thought I'd misjudged things and was going to become a dead bug on the after stack, but I went right through between them!"

Williams lowered his wing as he pulled back on the yoke and the big fighter soared into the dawn sky. It was time to return to Atsugi.

"I had the first inkling I was in some big trouble when two MP jeeps pulled out and followed me to where I stopped and shut down. I climbed out and this big MP lieutenant came up and put me under arrest." Williams was taken to the group headquarters and shown into a room. He snapped to a very rigid attention when he recognized the man behind the desk: Major General Paul D. "Squeeze" Wurtsmith, the general commanding Thirteenth Air Force. Wurtsmith had led the Forty-Niners to Australia in 1942, and was legendary throughout the Southwest Pacific as someone not to cross.

I had visions of spending Christmas in the stockade when he started an epic chewing-out about what the hell did I think I was doing, buzzing the flagship of the fleet. Didn't I know there were rules against that? I suddenly remembered I'd called the ship and gotten permission. I blurted that out, and the general stopped. Then he picked up the phone and it didn't take any time at all for him to be connected to the ship, and then to the radio shack. I was sure hoping those sailors might have written something down about my call. I was sucking attention like a first week ground school cadet while I listened to his side of the conversation. It seemed to take forever, but finally he hung up.

Williams was given the order to stand at ease. Wurtsmith glared at him for what seemed an hour before he finally said, "You're a lucky man, Captain. You get to walk out of here a Captain and not a Private. They did clear you to make that pass. Dismissed."

Williams turned to leave, but Wurtsmith stopped him. "They said to tell you that was one helluva buzz job, Captain." Fifty years later, Williams remembered he had difficulty getting through the door to leave the office, and it felt like he floated down the hallway. "I got to go home a Captain and not a Private, and I did have one memorable experience in the war."

The bloodiest, most terrible war in history was over. While Japan lay in ruin, the heart of the nation survived. Within a matter of years, the world would see that the jewel had not been smashed.

BIBLIOGRAPHY

Blair, Clay, *Silent Victory: The US Submarine War Against Japan* (Naval Institute Press, 2001)

Frank, Richard B., *Downfall: The End of the Imperial Japanese Empire* (Penguin Books, 1999)

Giangreco, D. M., *Hell to Pay: Operation* Downfall *and the Invasion of Japan, 1945–47* (Naval Institute Press, 2009)

Hastings, Max, *Retribution – The Battle for Japan, 1944–45* (Alfred A. Knopf, 2007)

Hobbs, David, *The British Pacific Fleet: The Royal Navy's Most Powerful Strike Force* (Naval Institute Press, 2011)

Morison, Samuel Eliot, *Victory in the Pacific: History of United States Naval Operations in World War II*, vol. 14 (University of Illinois Press, 1960)

Noble, Willie Z., "Saga of the Sea Dog: The Mighty Mine Dodgers," SubmarineSailor.com (August 1998)

Potter, E. B., *Bull Halsey* (Naval Institute Press, 1985)

Roscoe, Theodore, *United States Submarine Operations in World War II* (Naval Institute Press, 1949)

Sakaida, Henry, *Japanese Army Air Force Aces 1937–45* (Osprey Publishing, 1997)

Sakaida, Henry, *Imperial Japanese Navy Aces 1937–45* (Osprey Publishing, 1998)

Sears, David, *At War with the Wind: The Epic Struggle with Japan's World War II Suicide Bombers* (Citadel Press, 2008)

Sherrod, Robert, *History of United States Marine Corps Aviation in World War II* (Presidio Press, 1980)

Sloan, Bill, *The Ultimate Battle: Okinawa 1945–The Last Epic Struggle of World War II* (Simon & Schuster, 2007)

Thomas, Andrew, *Royal Navy Aces of World War 2* (Osprey Publishing, 2007)

Tillman, Barrett, *Corsair: The F4U in World War II and Korea* (Naval Institute Press, 1979)

Tillman, Barrett, *Hellcat: The F6F in World War II* (Naval Institute Press, 1979)

Tillman, Barrett, *Wildcat: The F4F in World War II* (Naval Institute Press, 1983)

Tillman, Barrett, *Hellcat Aces of World War 2* (Osprey Publishing, 1996)

Tillman, Barrett, *Corsair Aces of World War 2* (Osprey Publishing, 1994)

INDEX

Aaron Ward, USS 207–209
Abe, Capt Toshio 78–80
Abner Read, USS 51
Acheson, Dean 244
Admiralty Islands 15–16, 115
aircraft, British 119–25; Avengers 24;
   Fireflies 24; Seafire 17–18, 22–23,
   27, 125–26
aircraft, Japanese 32, 34; A6M5c
   Zero-sen ("Zeke") 20, 21, 22–23,
   35–36; D4Y3 *Suisun* ("Judy") 28, 57;
   J2M3 *Raiden* ("Jack") 19, 20; Ki.43
   "Oscar" 45–46, 62–63, 140–41;
   Ki.44 Tojo 128–29; Ki.84 *Hayate*
   ("Frank") 25, 26–27, 143; N1K2-J
   Shiden ("George") 25, 26, 156–57,
   159–60
aircraft, US 15, 52–53; B-25 Mitchell
   60; B-29 Superfortress 20, 116, 171,
   229–33; B-29 "Big Stink" 291, 294;
   B-29 "Bockscar" 15, 290–94; B-29
   "Enola Gay" 290, 294; B-32
   "Dominator" 308–309; F4U Corsair
   91–92, 93–94; F4F Wildcat 284–85;
   F6F Hellcat 24, 25, 92–93, 95, 98,
   100, 137–38, 139–40, 220–21; P-38
   "Lightning" 45–47; P-61 "Black
   Widow" 72; VF-101 Corsair 53;
   VMF(N) "Bat Eyes" 72–73
Akamatsu, ENS Sadaaki "Temei" 20, 21
Akishimo (ship) 60
Alabama, USS 276
Alaska, USS 133, 186
Altamaha, USS 86
Alward, Maj Everett V. 133, 142
Amend, Maj Jack R, Jr. 133, 135
Ammen, USS 51
Anami, Gen Korechika 234, 237; and
   surrender 297, 299–300, 301, 303,
   304–305
Anderson, 1Lt Donald R. 96, 105
Anderson, Lt R. H. 75
Andrea, LCDR James 90
Anthony, USS 225
Anzio, USS 86
Arao, Col Okitsugu 304–305
Archerfish (submarine) 78–79
Arnold, Gen "Hap" 228, 229
Asashimo (ship) 60, 185–86, 189
Ashworth, Cmdr Frederick L. 291, 292,
   294
Astoria, USS 133
Atkinson, Sub-Lt Bill 204, 280
Atlanta, USS 275, 276
atomic bombs 148, 240, 300, 301–302;
   see also Hiroshima; Nagasaki
Australia 115
Avery, ENS John 61
Aylwin, USS 89–90
Badger, Rear Adm C. 275
Bagley, USS 40

Bak, 1C Michael, Jr. 175
Baker, Lt(jg) Douglas 76
Baltimore, USS 89, 255, 256
banzai attacks 17
Barber, Col William E. 12–13, 312
Barfleur, HMS 16
Barnes, Lt Philip M. 291
Barnitz, Lt Barney 62
Batten, Lt(jg) Hugh N. 182–83
Beahan, Capt Kermit 292
Beckwith, Lt E. R. 285
Bedford, Capt William J. 106
Beebe, LCDR Marshall U. 158
Bell, Capt Tom 231, 233
Belleau Wood, USS 17, 24, 26, 40, 42,
   51; and Japan strikes 279; and
   Okinawa 183; and typhoon 255,
   256
Benham, USS 89–90
Bennett, USS 189
Bennington, USS 133, 134, 188, 194,
   256, 257, 258
Beser, 2Lt Jacob 293
Biloxi, USS 171
Bismarck Sea, USS 147
Blackwell, Lt 103–104, 105
Blandy, Rear Adm William H. P. 173
Block Island, USS 260–61
Bogan, Rear Adm Gerald 66
Bon Homme Richard, USS 15
Bonefish, USS 265, 270–71, 272–73
Bong, Maj Richard I. "Dick" 46
Boston, USS 133
Bowers, USS 200–201
Bowfin, USS 265, 271
Braine, USS 225
Brice, Lt(jg) Bob 62
Bridgers, John 57, 64
Bringle, Bush 205
Brocato, Lt(jg) Sam J. 182–83
Bryant, USS 199
Buchanan, USS 89–90
Buckner, Lt Gen Simon Bolivar, Jr. 226
Bunker Hill, USS 59, 92, 132, 133, 134;
   and Okinawa 159, 185, 194, 211,
   214–17
Burma 113
Burwell, Lt Walter B. 36–37
Bush, USS 175–79, 180–81, 182
Bushido code 42–44
Butehorn, Sgt Joseph L. 260
Byrnes, James F. 302, 303
Cabot, USS 66, 86
Cagle, Lt Malcolm W. 16–17
Cain, Lt Jim 176, 177–79
Callaghan, Capt William 192
Calling All Destroyers (handout) 206–207
Canada 115
Cantrel, Capt William A. 160
Cape Esperance, USS 86
Carmichael, Cmdr Joseph 216

Caroline Islands 54
Cascade, USS 90
Cassin Young, USS 182
Cebu 55
Ceylon 112, 113
Charles Carroll, USS 174
Chicago, USS 274, 281
China 43, 106–107, 229, 235; *see also*
   Manchuria
Chitose (ship) 30, 65
Choshi 17
Christianity 287–89, 295
Churchill, Winston 113, 228
Clark, Rear Adm J. J. "Jocko" 53, 99,
   183, 202; and typhoon 253, 254–55,
   258–59, 260
Clarke, LCDR W. E. 195, 196
Claxton, USS 51
Cleaver, PO L. Thomas 12
Coats, Lt Robert C. 158
Colhoun, USS 177, 179, 180–82
Collins, Lt C. B. 148–49
Coneff, 2Lt John J. 21
Coolidge, Lt Col Joseph B. 201
Cormier, Lt Richard L. "Zeke" 75–76,
   138
Cosford, Lt Robert H. "Bob" 56–57
Cotton, USS 97
Cowpens, USS 15, 86, 133, 139
Craig, Lt Charles M. 108
Cregut, Ed 175–76
Crescent City, USS 210
Crevalle, USS 265, 270, 272
Crommelin, LCDR Charles 16, 17
Crosley, LCDR Mike 278
Curtis, Tom 39
Cushing, USS 216
Dahm, ENS Kenneth J. 183
daimyos 286–87, 288
Davison, Rear Adm Ralph 163
Dayton, USS 275, 276
Decker, Maj Wendell 309–10
Deen, 2/c Loyce 56–57
Delewski, 1/c Lawrence "Ski" 198
Dennis, USS 31
Denniston, LCDR Radcliffe 64
Denzell, RM 3/c Digby 56–57
Dewey, USS 89
Dohi, ENS Saburo 192–93
Domke, Maj Fay V. 153
Donahue, Maj Archie 133, 214, 215
Donaldson, USS 90
Dooley, Maj George E. 133
Doolittle, Lt Gen James H. "Jimmy" 294
Dorosh, RM 2/c Sam 64
Doyle, Capt Austin K. 254, 255, 256
Duncan, LCDR George 56, 58–59
Duncan, Sub-Lt Don 23
Durgin, Rear Adm Calvin 146
Durno, Sub-Lt Leslie 118, 127
Dusenbury, Capt Julian D. 225, 226

Dutch traders 288–89
Dyson, USS 89–90
Eaker, Lt Gen Ira 238
East China Sea, battle of the (1945) 184
Eaton, Sgt James F. 12
Eckard, Lt Bert 217, 218
Ellis, Maj Henry A., Jr. 132
Emmons, USS 179–80
Enright, Cmdr Joseph 79
Enterprise, USS 40, 97–98, 114, 108–109; and Iwo Jima 146, 148, 149–52; and Okinawa 159, 190–92, 214, 221–23; and Tokyo 131–32, 133–34, 139–40
Essex, USS 50, 51, 57–58, 59–60, 67–68, 94; and Formosa 95–96, 103–104; and French Indochina 99–100; and Okinawa 153, 154, 158–59, 211; and Tokyo 133, 141, 142–43
Fanshaw Bay, USS 35, 174
Farrell, Lt William 225
Finn, Capt Howard J. 98
firebombing 229–33
Flatley, Jimmy 222
Fleming, Lt Patrick D. 76, 138, 142
Flying Fish, USS 265, 271
Foltz, Lt(jg) Ralph 62
Foote, Lt(jg) John 61
Ford, Lt Gerald R. 84–86
Formidable, HMS 204–205, 211–12; and Japan strikes 276, 280, 281, 282–83
Formosa 49, 94–96, 98–99, 103–105, 107–109, 170, 204
Forrestal, James 238, 259
Foster, ENS Carl G. 183
Foster, Sub-Lt Bill 204, 205
France 145–46
Francis Xavier, St 287
Franger, Lt Marvin 217, 218
Franklin, USS 40–42, 51, 154, 162–68
Franks, USS 174–75
Fraser, Adm Sir Bruce 116–17
French, Lt James B. 136, 139
French Indochina 99–102
Fritz, Capt Harold C. 166
Fuso (ship) 30
Gambia, HMS 16
Gandy, Lt(jg) D. W. 144–45
Garvin, Ted 19, 23
Gary, Lt(jg) Donald A. 165, 166
Gaylor, LCDR Noel A. M. 135
Gehres, Capt Leslie E. 162, 163
Geiger, Maj Gen Roy 226
Genda, Capt Minoru 155
Germany 13, 113, 122, 228; and surrender 243, 247, 295
Gilbert Islands, USS 261
Gillespie, Lt R. F. 183
Gillet, 2Lt Lamar 311
Graham, RM 3/c Ted 51, 61, 64
Gray, Lt Robert Hampton "Hammy" 281, 282–83

Great Britain *see* Royal Navy
Grew, Joseph L. 243, 244, 245, 246
Gunning, SSgt Edward T. 260
Hacksaw Ridge 10
Hadley, Lt(jg) Robert B. 110
Haga, Col Toyojiro 305, 306
Hagakure 43
Hall, Lt(jg) David 61–62
Halsey, Adm William F., Jr. 16, 28, 67, 99, 110–11; and Formosa 107, 109; and Japan attacks 275, 277; and Kyushu 253–54, 258–60; and Okinawa 170, 249, 252; and the Philippines 51, 55; and typhoon 83–84, 87, 88–89, 90–91
Hamakaze (ship) 78, 80, 187, 189
Hamrick, Lt L. L. 100, 101
Hancock, USS 25, 66, 87, 137–38, 154, 189
Hansen, Maj Herman, Jr. 133, 134
Hansen, Lt(jg) Ted 17, 25, 26
Hanson, Maj "Hap" 193–94, 257
Hara, Capt Tameichi 186, 188
Hardy, Lt(jg) Willis "Bill" 181
Harrington, LCDR Tommy 203
Harris, Lt Cecil 67
Harris, Brig Gen Field 53
Harrison, Lt(jg) "Howdy" 17, 19, 25, 26
Harry F. Bauer, USS 250
Hartsock, Capt Edmond P. 96, 153
Hata, FM Shunroku 304
Hatanaka, Maj Kenji 304–305, 306
Hay, Maj T. Ronald 117, 118, 119, 128, 130, 204
Hayakawa, Rear Adm Mikio 63
Heath, ENS Horace W. 195, 196
Hedrick, LCDR Roger 132, 143
Heermann, USS 31
Heffer, Sub-Lt Ben 117–18
Henrico, USS 174
Henry, Lt(jg) Don 101–102
Henry, Lt William E. 106, 108
Hermes, HMS 112
Herrin, 2Lt Douglas M. 260
Herschel, Lt Paul 25
Hickox, USS 88
Higashikuni, Prince 308
Hinrichs, Lt(jg) Gordon 148–49
Hiranuma, Kiichiro 301, 302, 306
Hirohito, Emperor 13, 27–28, 29, 233, 237; and peace proposal 244–46, 247; and surrender 296, 297, 298, 301–302, 304, 306–308
Hiroshima 10, 11–12, 21, 286, 290, 298–99
Hobbs, ENS Wright 17, 25, 26
Hobson, USS 200
Hockley, Sub-Lt Fred 18, 19, 22, 28–29
Hokanson, Lt H. L. 284
Hong Kong 106–107, 113
Honma, Lt(jg) Tadahiko 27
Hopkins, Lt Col Donald S. "Hoppy" 95
Hopkins, Maj James I. 291
Hornet, USS 64, 114, 158, 258; and

typhoon 254, 255, 256
Hoshina, Adm Zenshiro 302
Howe, HMS 115, 117, 212
Hugh W. Hadley, USS 217
Hull, Cordell L. 245
Hull, USS 88, 89, 90
Hydeman, Cmdr Earl T. 264, 265, 267, 268, 269–70, 272
Ichikawa, Capt Chuichi 233
Ida, Lt Col Masataka 304
Ienaga, Saburo 9–10
Iida, Lt Fusata 32
Ikeda, Gen Sumihisa 302
Ikuta, WO Shin 279
Illustrious, HMS 115, 117
Imperial Japanese Army 48–49, 233–34, 305–306; Fourteenth 50; 1st Dvn 50; 26th Dvn 50; 30th Dvn 50; 102nd Dvn 50; 426th Infantry Rgt 28–29; 244th *Sentai* 232–33; *see also* Kwantung Army
Imperial Japanese Naval Air Force 19–20, 31; 343rd Air Group 155–56, 159–61
Imperial Japanese Navy 8, 9, 30–31, 48, 183–89, 233–34; First Air Fleet 32, 34; 252nd Kokutai 27; 302nd Kokutai 19, 20, 26; 343rd Kokutai 26–27; 201st Group 34–38; 306th Showa Special Attack Sqn 213–14
Implacable, HMS 276, 278
Indefatigable, HMS 16, 17–18, 26, 117, 125, 127, 203
Independence, USS 15
India 113
Indian Ocean 112–13
Indiana, USS 186, 255, 274, 281, 283
Indianapolis, USS 133, 172
Indomitable, HMS 117, 118–19, 127
Ingersoll, Capt Stuart 85–86
Ingraham, USS 210, 211
intelligence 235–36, 237–38, 239–40, 241
Intrepid, USS 39, 51, 66–67, 164, 195–96
Iowa, USS 89, 250, 251, 275, 276
Ishino, Setsuo 192
Isokaze (ship) 78, 80, 187, 189
Italy 243, 247
Ito, Vice Adm Seiichi 184–85, 186, 188–89
Iwo Jima 144–45, 146–52
J. William Ditter, USS 250
Japan 8–13, 31, 232, 234–35, 237, 286–89; and air strikes 274–85; and bombs 77–82; and Bushido 42–44; and peace proposal 243–47; and the Philippines 74–75; and Soviet Union 248, 295–96; and surrender 296–308, 310, 312–13; and USA 227–29; *see also* Hiroshima; Nagasaki; Tokyo; V-J Day
Japanese Army *see* Imperial Japanese Army

Japanese Navy *see* Imperial Japanese Navy
Jewell, Lt(jg) Joe 148–49
Jicarilla, USS 90
John C. Butler, USS 31
Kaelin, ENS John 218
Kalinin Bay, USS 37
kamikazes 8, 18, 31–32, 34–44, 48,
　206–207, 234; and Formosa 108;
　and Iwo Jima 147, 148, 149; and
　Kyushu 237–38, 257–58; and
　Mindoro 75–77; and Okinawa
　155–56, 170–71, 174, 176, 180–81,
　189–94, 195–99, 202–203, 207–20,
　221–26, 249–52; and the Philippines
　51–52, 57–58, 60; and Royal Navy
　130
Kamitake, Isamu 66
Kan'in Haruhito, Prince 304
Kanno, Lt Naoshi 160
Kashii Maru (ship) 60
Kasumi (ship) 60, 189
Kato, Maj Hitoyuki 130
Katsumata, PO Tomisaku 36
Kawabe, Gen Torashiro 305
Kay, Sub-Lt Randall 21–22, 23, 211
Kelly, Walt 62–63
Kenney, Gen George 55, 72
Kenyon, Lt John 219
Kernagan, Sub-Lt J. H. 204
Kido, Marquis Koichi 296, 297, 303,
　304, 306
Kikusui (mass attack) 179–80, 190, 207,
　213–14, 224, 250
Kimberly, USS 171
Kimura, 2Lt Sadamitsu 233
King, Adm Ernest J. 54, 113, 114–15,
　228, 229; and Kyushu 235, 238, 239,
　240, 243
King George V, HMS 16, 203, 276,
　281–82, 283–84
Kippen, Lt Russell F. 98, 108–109
Kirkwood, Lt(jg) Phil 195–96
Kitkun Bay, USS 35, 37
Klingman, Lt Robert 212–13
Klinsmann, Cmdr George Otto 103,
　104–105
Knapp, USS 89
Kobayashi, Maj Teruhikuo 279, 280
Kobe 10–11, 143, 159, 161–62, 231
Koiso, Kuniaki 234
Kokura 291–92
Komura, Rear Adm Keiso 188
Konoe, Fumimaro 234
Konoe, Prince 246
Korean War (1950–53) 17
Kosco, Cmdr George F. 83, 84, 90
Krum, 1Lt George A. 195
Kure 78, 80, 159, 161–62, 277–78,
　280–81
Kurita, Adm 30
Kusaka, Vice Adm Ryunosuke 184–85
Kwajalein, USS 86–87
Kwantung Army 21, 59–60, 228, 236
Kyushu 12–13, 21, 155, 175, 252–54,
　257–58; and airfields 218–19; and

invasion 157–61; and planned
　invasion 235–43; and samurais
　286–87
Lacharite, SSgt Joseph 308–309
Laffey, USS 195, 196, 197–200
Laird, Lt D. E. "Diz" 141
Lambert, LCDR V.G. 63
Lambrecht, Lt Col Peter D. 72
Langley, USS 51, 62, 86
Lapon, USS 262
Latrobe, Lt(jg) Charles 219
Law, ENS Herbert 279–80
Lawton, Lt(jg) Ernie 148–49
LCS-14; 208–209
LCS-25; 208, 209
LCS-51; 199
LCS-64; 179, 180–81, 182
LCS-83; 208–209
LCS-87; 182
LCS-122; 252
Leahy, Adm William 235, 238, 239
LeMay, Gen Curtis 171, 229, 232
Lemieux, Roger 63
Leonard, LCDR William "Bill" 249–50
Lerch, ENS Alfred 195, 196
Levitt, Lt Dennis 129
Lexington, USS 28, 39–40, 136–37
Leyte Gulf 14, 30–31, 45–50, 59–63,
　74–75
Lindenberger, Lt William 164
Little, USS 207, 208
Livesay, ENS Mel 61
Lockwood, Adm Charles 261–62, 263,
　264
Lowden, Sub-Lt Victor 18, 22–23, 26
Luce, USS 209
Lunga Point, USS 285
Luzon 48–49, 65, 74, 94–95, 96–98
Lynch, LCDR James P. 264, 266,
　268–69, 270, 272
Lynch, 2Lt Joseph O. 100–101
MacArthur, Gen Douglas 47–48, 49, 72,
　235, 236, 309
McCain, Vice Adm John S., Sr. 51, 52,
　53, 90, 110, 249; and Kyushu 253,
　254, 260
McCampbell, Cmdr David 51–52,
　55–56, 57, 59, 60–61, 63–64
McCloy, John J. 238, 240, 245
McClure, Maj Jack 309–10
McCullough, LCDR R. J. 98
McDilda, 1Lt Marcus 300
McGregor, Cmdr L. D. 81
McGuire, Maj Thomas E., Jr. 46
Mackie, Sub-Lt 280
MacLeish, Archibald 244
McLennan, Sub-Lt Keith 130
Macomb, USS 209
McWhorter, Lt Hamilton 137, 157, 219
Maddox, USS 88
Mahan, USS 71
Makin Island, USS 284
Malaya 113
Manchuria 13, 21, 32, 295–96
Mandenberg, ENS Gene 17, 25, 26

Mannert L. Abele, USS 192–93
Manus 115
Marchione, Sgt Anthony 309
Marcus Island, USS 173–74, 205, 224
Marks, LCDR James A. 90
Marshall, Maj David E. 93
Marshall, Gen George C. 228, 238–39,
　240–41, 243, 244–45
Marshall Islands 54
Martin, Cmdr William I. 97, 98,
　108–109
Maryland, USS 173, 189
Masao, Lt Col Inaba 304–305
Massachusetts, USS 186, 274, 281, 282,
　283
Maxwell, Cmdr Porter W. 220–21
Mayes, Wendell 57, 58
Maze, Maj Robert C. 261
Meiji Restoration (1880) 288, 289
Melvin R. Nawman, USS 90
Miami, USS 89
Mikasa (ship) 9
Mikes, Capt Edward 21
Miller, 1Lt Fletcher 73
Miller, ENS Johnnie G. 183
Millington, Lt Col William A. 93, 94,
　96, 97, 99, 111; and Formosa
　105–106, 107, 109–10; and Iwo Jima
　145; and Tokyo 142–43
Mindoro 75–77
mines 171, 262, 263, 265–67
Mini, Cmdr Jim 61, 63
Mississippi, USS 226
Missouri, USS 8, 186, 192, 275, 276,
　312–13
Mitchell, Lt Harris E. 136, 138–39, 208
Mitchell, Maj Gen Ralph J. 72
Mitscher, Adm Marc 53, 111, 133, 143;
　and Okinawa 154–55, 159, 186,
　217, 223
Miyaki, ENS Tooru 21
Mobley, Maj Tom 159, 160
Molotov, Vyacheslav 295
Monaghan, USS 88, 89, 90
monsoon 55, 273–74
Monterey, USS 84–86
Montgomery, 2Lt Rod 72
Moore, David 88
Moore, ENS Clarence 28
Moranville, Lt(jg) Blake 102
Morgan, Lt(jg) H. G. "Crash" 181
Mori, Lt Gen Takeshi 305
Morimoto, ENS Muneaki 21
Morioka, Lt Yukio 20–21, 26
Morrison, USS 210–11
Morton, Cmdr Dudley W. "Mush" 262,
　264
Mullaney, LCDR Baron 217
Mullins, 1Lt Robert W. "Moon" 96
Murphy, Sub-Lt Gerry "Spud" 22,
　23–24, 25
Murray, Vice Adm George D. 53
Musashi (ship) 30, 65
Nachi (ship) 56–57, 65
Naganami (ship) 60

Nagasaki 10, 11–12, 13, 21, 286, 287–95, 299
Nagato (ship) 276–77, 281
Nagoya 231
Nagumo, Adm 113
Nantahala, USS 90
Napier, HMAS 16
Nash, ENS Edwin G. 106
Negishi, Sgt Nobushi 232–33
Nehenta Bay, USS 86
Nevada, USS 171
New Jersey, USS 67, 133, 175, 186
New Mexico, USS 219–20
New Zealand 115
Newell, Lt(jg) Harold P. 38
Newfoundland, HMS 16
night-fighting 72–73, 202, 229–33
Nimitz, Adm Chester 31, 54, 72, 170, 225, 273
  and Halsey 259, 260
  and Kyushu 235, 236, 239–40, 243
  and typhoon 90, 91
Nishizawa, Hiroyoshi 35–36, 38
Nizam, HMAS 16
North Carolina, USS 276
Noyes, Lt Roger 63–64
O'Brien, USS 171
O'Callahan, LCDR Joseph T. 164–66
Ogawa, ENS Kiyoshi 213–14, 215, 216–17
Ohnishi, Adm Takejiro 308
Ohta, ENS Mitsuo 77
Oi, Capt Atsushi 184
oil 115–16, 127–30
Okinawa 10, 12–13, 49, 153–55
  and battle (1945) 16, 169–203, 207–26, 249–52
Okinawa Maru (ship) 60
Olivi, 2Lt Fred 293
Olszewski, Lt(jg) Edward 145–46
Omura, Sumitada 287
Onayama, Lt Hideyaki 128
O'Neill, USS 224
Ōnishi, Vice Adm Takejiro 34
operations: *Banquet* (1945) 118; *Barney* (1945) 261–73; *Cockpit* (1945) 115–16; *Coronet* (1946) 240; *Crimson* (1945) 117; *Crossroads* (1946) 148; *Dragoon* (1944) 145–46; *Gratitude* (1945) 99–102; *Lentil* (1945) 127; *Light-B* (1945) 118; *Magic Carpet* (1945) 148; *Mascot* (1944) 125; *Meetinghouse* (1945) 230–31; *Meridian One* (1945) 112–13, 128–30; *Ten-Go* (1945) 183–89; *Transom* (1945) 116; *Tungsten* (1945) 122, 124
Ormoc Bay 50, 59–61, 68–71
Orth, ENS John 209
Osaka 231, 233, 278
Ota, Adm Minoru 226
Ota, Toshio 35
Outerbridge, William W. 71
Pasadena, USS 133
Pearl Harbor 8, 70–71

Penza, RM 2/c Lou 62
Permit, USS 262
Petrof Bay, USS 36
Philippines, the 34–42, 55–59, 63–71, 72–74; map **33**; *see also* Leyte Gulf; Luzon; Mindoro
Pierce, LCDR George E. 272–73
Pittsburgh, USS 255, 256
Plage, LCDR Henry Lee 89
Plunger, USS 262
Portugal 286–87, 288
Potsdam Conference (1945) 240, 245, 247; and Declaration 244, 297–98, 302
Pringle, USS 68, 200
prisoners of war (POWs) 311
Proctor, Lt(jg) Maury 17, 25–26
Pyle, Ernie 201–202
Quebec Conference (1944) 228
Queen Elizabeth, HMS 115
Quiel, ENS Norwald 195–96
Quincy, USS 274, 281
Rabaul 71
radar 52, 134
Radford, Rear Adm Arthur W. 15
Randolph, USS 155, 223, 257–58
Rawlings, Vice Adm Sir Bernard 117, 171
Raymond, USS 31
Red Army 247, 248, 296
Redfish, USS 80–81
Reno, USS 55
Renown, HMS 115
Renshaw, USS 68
Reusser, Capt Kenneth 212–13
Reynolds, Sub-Lt Richard 203, 211
Rigg, LCDR Jim 55, 61
Risser, LCDR Robert D. "Bob" 265
Ritchie, Lt Blyth 122
Roberts, Maj Edwin S., Jr. 132
Robinson, ENS David 145
Robley D. Evans, USS 217
Rodman, USS 180
Roosevelt, Eleanor 202
Roosevelt, Franklin D. 59, 234, 228, 250, 251; and Britain 114, 115; and death 194–95, 235
Roquemore, Lt Joseph 136
Rowell, Maj Gen Ross 54
Royal Air Force (RAF): 47 Fighter Wing 117, 118–19
Royal Marines 117
Royal Navy 119–26; British Pacific Fleet 15–16, 93, 112–16, 127–30, 171, 275–76, 278; East Indies Fleet 116–17; TF 57; 202–205, 211–12; 894 Sqn 18
Rushing, Lt(jg) Roy 56
Russo-Japan War (1904–05) 43
Sahloff, ENS Joe 17, 25, 26
Saigon 99–102
St Lo, USS 31, 36
St Louis, USS 69–70
Saipan 49
Sakai, Saburo 35, 155, 308–309

Sakhalin Island 13
Sakishima Islands 260–61
Salisbury, 1Lt Vernon 135
samurais 42–43, 286
San Jacinto, USS 17, 24, 40, 86, 139, 176
Sandor, LCDR John H. 145
Santa Fe, USS 166
Santee, USS 36, 37
Saratoga, USS 114, 115, 133–34, 146–47, 148
Sasaki, Capt Takeo 306
Sato, Naotake 245, 246, 247, 295, 297
Saufley, USS 68
Sawfish, USS 263
Schmidt, RM 2/c Norm 61
Sea Dog, USS 264, 265–66, 267–70
Sea of Japan 262–73
Seeba, 2/c Henry 200–201
Seitz, Capt Gene A. 215
Seki, Lt Yukio 34
seppuku see suicide
Shafroth, Rear Adm John F. 274
Shangri-La, USS 15, 17, 25, 211
Shasta, USS 90
Shea, USS 209–10
Sheehan, RM 1/c Paul 63–64
Shelton, ENS Doniphan B. "Don" 69–70
Sheppard, Sub-Lt D. J. 127, 128
Sherman, Rear Adm Frederic C. 50–51, 64
Sherrod, Robert 100
Shigemitsu, Mamoru 234, 308
Shiizaki, Lt Col Jiro 305
Shimabara Rebellion (1637) 288
Shinano (ship) 78–80
Shirai, Capt Nagao 232
Shock, Robert 216–17
Shuri Castle 224, 225–26
Sieglaff, Cmdr W. B. "Barney" 263
Singapore 112
Sitkoh Bay, USS 190
Skate, USS 266, 271
Smith, Lt Clinton L. 136, 139
Smith, Lt John M. 214
Smith, Capt Robert 68
Smoth, Lt K. D. 219
Solomon Islands 71–72, 114
Soryu (ship) 32
South China Sea 75, 99
South Dakota, USS 133, 186, 274, 281, 282, 283
Southerland, Cmdr J. J., II 182
Soviet-Japanese Neutrality Pact (1941) 234, 235
Soviet Union 13, 21, 32, 228, 247–48; and Japan 245, 246–47, 295–96, 297, 299
Spaatz, Gen Carl 303
Spadefish, USS 265, 270
special attack units *see* kamikazes
Spectacle, USS 224
Spence, USS 87–88, 89, 90

Spruance, Adm Raymond 110–11, 170, 172, 186, 202, 225, 236; and *New Mexico*, USS 219, 220
Stalin, Joseph 13, 228, 246–47, 248, 296, 297
Stanly, USS 193
Steinkemeyer, RM 2/c Neal 62
Stewart, Lt Jim 24, 25
Stilwell, Gen Joseph "Vinegar Joe" 226
Stimson, Henry 238, 239, 243, 244, 245
Stormes, USS 224
Stott, Sub-Lt Phil 129, 204
Strauss, Capt Elliott B. 174
Strimbeck, 1Lt George R. 106–107
submarine warfare 261–73
suicide 226, 241, 305, 308; see also *kamikazes*
Suluan Island 32
Sumatra 112, 115–16, 117–19, 127–30
Sumi, WO Tadao 233
Sunday, Lt "Billy" 95
Suwanee, USS 36–37, 38
Suzuki, Kantaro 234, 306; and surrender 297, 298, 299, 301, 303, 304, 308
Swanson, Cmdr Chandler 187–88
Swearer, USS 89
Sweeney, Maj Charles 290, 291, 292, 293, 294
Swett, Capt James 133
Swihart, RM 2/c Chuck 61
Tabberer, USS 89
Taclobar 45–47, 55
Takacu Maru (ship) 60
Takagi, Adm Sokichi 246–47
Takeshita, Lt Col Masahiko 304–305
Tamai, Cmdr Asaiki 34
Tanaka, Gen Shizuichi 305, 306
Tarantula, HMS 117
Tatelman, Maj Vic 310
Taylor, Sub-Lt Edward 129
Taylor, Cmdr Joe 163
Teazer, HMS 16
Tenacious, HMS 16
Tennessee, USS 171, 173, 193
Terauchi, FM Hisaichi 49, 50
Termagant, HMS 16
Thach, Cmdr John S., Jr. 44, 51–52, 53
Thomas, Capt Gus 93, 97
Thomsen, Capt Dave 73
Thomson, Lt Bill 204
Ticonderoga, USS 51, 62, 108, 220
Tinosa, USS 266–67, 271–72
Tirpitz (ship) 122, 124, 125
Toaspern, Lt(jg) Edward "Smiley" 24, 25
Togo, Shigenori 9, 234–35, 245, 246; and surrender 297, 299, 300, 301, 303, 308
Tojo, Gen Hideki 233
Tokugawa, Ieyasu 288
Tokugawa, Yoshihiro 304
Tokurozama 17, 25–26
Tokyo 11, 131–35, 137–40, 229–33, 276–77
Tomiyasu, Lt(jg) Shunsuke 221–22, 223

Tomlinson, Capt W. G. 183
Torrey, Cmdr Phil 139
Towers, Adm John 54
Toyoda, Adm Soemu 38, 49, 183–84, 234, 300, 304
Toyotomi, Hideyoshi 287–88
Trombina, RM 3/c Pete 62
Truax, ENS Myron M. 211
Truman, Harry 195, 202, 244, 300, 303; and Kyushu 235, 238, 239, 240–41
Tsuneyoshi Takeda, Prince 304
Tsuruta, ENS Mitsuo 21
Tsuruta, Yoshiko 8, 9, 10
Tunny, USS 265, 271, 272–73
Turner, Lt(jg) Raymond L. 64
Turner, Vice Adm Richmond K. 172
Twelve, Lt Wendell 56
typhoons 47, 59, 107; "Cobra" 83–91; "Connie" 252–56, 259–60
Ugaki, Vice Adm Matome 155, 190, 207
Ulithi 51, 90
Ulster Queen, HMS 203
Umezu, Gen Yoshijiro 234, 237, 300, 304
unconditional surrender 243, 245, 246, 247, 297–98
United Nations 114
United States of America 227–29, 240, 243–46, 247, 248
Unryu (ship) 80–81
Upham, Cmdr Fred K. 111, 153
US Air Force: Fifth 47–48, 49; 20th Bomber Command 116, 229–33; 49th Fighter Group 312–13; 315 Bombardment Wing 303
US Army: 77th Infantry Dvn 201–202
US Marines 53–54, 71–73, 149, 257, 260–61; Tactical Air Force 225–26; 6th Dvn 12–13; 26th Rgt 312; VMF-124; 93–97, 111; VMF-213; 93, 94–97, 111; and Okinawa 154, 193–94, 197
US Navy 30, 135–36, 169–70; Third Fleet 48, 49, 65, 68, 75, 83–91, 99–110, 249, 252; Fifth Fleet 111, 131–32, 157–58, 218–19; Air Group 4; 67–68, 143; Air Group 12; 257–58; Air Group 15; 50–51, 63–65; Air Group 17; 92; Air Group 84; 132–33, 141–42, 154; TF 34; 274–75; TF 38; 14–15, 16–17, 18–19, 50–53, 55–66, 94–96, 218, 252–57; TF 52; 173; TF 58; 133–35, 214–17; TF 95; 284–85; TF "Taffy-3" 31; VF-9; 136–39, 208–11; VF-10; 195–99; VF-12; 92; VF-83; 182–83; VMF-312; 212–13; VOC-1; 145–46, 173–74, 224; VOC-2; 174; 431st "Possum" Fighter Sqn 46–47
V-J Day (1945) 14–16, 17–29
Valencia, Lt Gene 135–36, 138, 208, 217–18

Valentine, Capt Herbert J. 225
Valiant, HMS 115
Valignano, Alexandro 287
Valle, Maj Gen Pedro del 225
Vandegrift, Gen Alexander A. 54
Vasilevsky, Aleksandr 295
Vian, Vice Adm Sir Philip 117
Victorious, HMS 114, 117–18, 127, 204, 212
Vietnam War (1955–75) 17
Vorse, LCDR Alexander O. 137–38
Vraciu, Lt Alex 76
Wahoo, USS 262–63
Wake Island, USS 146, 173
Wakeful, HMS 16
Waller, USS 68
war crimes 29
Ward, USS 70–71
Wasp, USS 15, 17, 87, 134–35, 163
Waterman, USS 90
weaponry, Japanese: Ohka bomb 77–82, 192–93
weaponry, US 261–63
Weber, Cmdr Bruce S. 279
West Virginia, USS 173, 175
Westvedt, 2Lt John H. 106–107
White Plains, USS 35
Wilkes-Barre, USS 133, 216
Wilkinson, Lt(jg) Charles B. 222
William D. Porter, USS 250–52
Williams, Capt Paul 312–14
Williams, Sub-Lt W.J. "Taffy" 22
Willicutts, Cmdr Morton D. 219, 220
Willoughby, Maj Gen Charles 236, 241–42
Wilson, Sub-Lt Edward 119, 203, 204
Wilson, Cmdr G. R. 179
Wisconsin, USS 186, 275, 276
Woedkerling, Brig Gen John 245–46
Wood, ENS Alfred R. 145
Wouk, Herman 87
Wrangler, HMS 16
Wright, Lt(jg) Robert F. 106
Wurtsmith, Maj Gen Paul D. "Squeeze" 313–14
Yahagi (ship) 185–86, 187, 188–89
Yalta Conference (1945) 228
Yamashiro (ship) 30, 142
Yamashita, Gen Tomoyuki 49–50
Yamato (ship) 30, 184, 185–86, 187–88, 189
Yasuhiko Asaka, Prince 304
Yasunori, Lt(jg) Seizo 213, 214–15
Yates, ENS Frank 284–85
Yentzer, ENS Richard V. 146
Yonai, Adm Mitsumasa 31, 234, 246, 297, 299
Yorktown, USS 15, 16, 26, 159
Yoshida, ENS Mitsuru 189
Yoshida, Capt Yoshio 233
Young, Lt Owen 218–19
Zuiho (ship) 30
Zuikako (ship) 30, 65